Handbook of Biometric Template Protection

Vedrana Krivokuća Hahn • Marta Gomez-Barrero •
Arun Ross • Sébastien Marcel
Editors

Handbook of Biometric Template Protection

Motivation, Methods and Metrics

Springer

Editors
Vedrana Krivokuća Hahn
Biometrics Security and Privacy Group
Idiap Research Institute
Martigny, Valais, Switzerland

Marta Gomez-Barrero
RI CODE
Universität der Bundeswehr München
Munich, Bayern, Germany

Arun Ross
Department of Computer Science and Engineering
Michigan State University
East Lansing, MI, USA

Sébastien Marcel
Biometrics Security and Privacy Group
Idiap Research Institute
Martigny, Valais, Switzerland

ISBN 978-981-95-0994-2 ISBN 978-981-95-0995-9 (eBook)
https://doi.org/10.1007/978-981-95-0995-9

This Springer imprint is published by the registered company Springer Nature Singapore Pte Ltd.
The registered company address is: 152 Beach Road, #21-01/04 Gateway East, Singapore 189721, Singapore

Preface

Biometric technology automates the recognition of individuals based on their biological traits, such as fingerprints, face, and iris. Since biometric systems store sensitive information about an individual's biological trait, it is important to consider the protection of the employed biometric "templates" (features representing the underlying biometric characteristics). To address this need, the Biometric Template Protection (BTP) research field has developed steadily for over two decades, with many innovative solutions proposed in this time. Despite the relatively high level of sophistication attained in the literature, the topic has remained largely within limited academic circles, with little to no evidence of practical adoption. The latter may be due to many factors, among which, we postulate, there are three main reasons:

1. A lack of awareness among biometric system deployers of the importance of protecting biometric data, or no incentive for doing so due either to the limited capabilities to enforce existing data protection regulations such as the EU GDPR or, in some cases, the absence of appropriate regulations
2. A preference for relying solely on traditional (established) data protection mechanisms, such as encryption, in favor of exploring newer methods stemming from BTP research (perhaps despite known limitations of the former)
3. Uncertainty about how the robustness of BTP techniques should be properly evaluated in practice, and, thus, reluctance to adopt such methods without being able to guarantee that they satisfy the necessary security and privacy requirements

Fortunately, as a result of rising concerns around the privacy and security of our biometric data (which is being increasingly demanded for identity management in practical applications), there appears to be renewed interest in BTP research. This may be attributed to emerging privacy regulations, which are pressuring practitioners to ensure that their biometric systems are legally compliant. There is thus a clear opportunity and an imperative need to explore the BTP research field further, to investigate its practical relevance, and to gauge the potential of BTP solutions for achieving more secure and privacy-preserving biometrics-based identity management. The *Handbook of Biometric Template Protection: Motivation,*

Methods and Metrics aims to facilitate this exploration, by paving the way towards a comprehensive understanding of the field and providing the reader with insights into various open challenges.

The remainder of this handbook is structured in three main parts, which collectively explain the current state of BTP research:

- **Part I:** Motivation—*Why is BTP research important?*
- **Part II:** Methods—*What types of BTP methods have been proposed?*
- **Part III:** Metrics—*How to evaluate BTP methods?*

Part I opens the discussion by explaining the motivation behind BTP research. This part of the book consists of three chapters. Chapter 1 focuses on the need to protect biometric templates to defend against various attacks that can be launched against biometric systems and which threaten both the privacy of the subjects (system users) and the security of the systems themselves. This chapter also presents a brief introduction on how to approach the evaluation of BTP methods from the point of view of existing technical standards. Chapter 2 builds upon the motivation for BTP research, by explaining why methods that are used for generic data protection (including traditional techniques like hashing, conventional encryption, distributed databases, and smart cards, and the more recent Trusted Execution Environments) are usually unsuitable for protecting biometric templates. This is due, in large part, to factors such as the intrinsic noisiness of biometric measurements versus the exactness requirements of mechanisms like cryptographic hashing and encryption. Finally, Chap. 3 explores the motivation for BTP research from a legal perspective, by examining the need for BTP in the context of recent privacy frameworks that regulate the processing of biometric data. An important insight gained from this chapter is that the coming into force of these (and future) privacy regulations should be a catalyst for investigating whether BTP techniques ensure the compliancy of biometric systems.

Part II ventures into more technical territory, describing in detail the various types of BTP methods that have been proposed as potential solutions. The first three chapters discuss *handcrafted* techniques, which are BTP algorithms designed by humans, and the last chapter explores BTP methods that are *learned* using neural networks. More specifically, Chaps. 4 and 5 focus on the two most traditional handcrafted BTP categories: Feature Transformations and Biometric Cryptosystems. The concepts behind these approaches are explained, examples of BTP methods that fall into these specific categories are provided, and advantages and disadvantages of the various techniques are discussed. Chapter 6 then explains how BTP could be achieved with the help of Homomorphic Encryption, which does not traditionally fall into the BTP domain, but which has been an important focus for BTP-oriented research in recent years. Finally, following the Handcrafted BTP approaches discussed in the first three chapters of Part II, the last chapter explores BTP methods learned by neural networks. In particular, Chap. 7 tracks the development of Learned BTP methods over the past few years: from the earliest approaches that trained a neural network to learn the mapping between a biometric template and a predefined code, to the most recent approaches that train a neural network to learn its own representation of a (renewable) protected template. Overall, therefore, Part II of this handbook presents a comprehensive overview of the types of BTP methods that have been proposed so far.

Part III complements the discussion on BTP methods from Part II, by delving into the techniques that have been used to evaluate BTP methods in the literature. This part of the handbook consists of three chapters, which correspond to the three main criteria that a BTP method is commonly expected to satisfy, in alignment with the ISO/IEC 24745 standard on biometric information protection and the ISO/IEC 30136 standard on performance testing of BTP schemes. Chapter 8 focuses on the methodologies and metrics that are used to evaluate the "recognition accuracy" criterion, including a discussion of additional factors that should be considered when evaluating a biometric system with a BTP component versus a biometric system without a BTP component. Chapter 9 is dedicated to the "irreversibility" criterion, presenting a detailed discussion on the different types of theoretical and empirical techniques that have been used to evaluate the irreversibility of BTP methods in the literature, including an analysis of the limitations of each approach. Finally, Chap. 10 explores the methods that have been proposed to evaluate the "unlinkability" criterion (related to the "renewability" criterion), with a particular focus on the two most recent empirical metrics based on likelihood ratios and maximal information leakage.

As a whole, therefore, the *Handbook of Biometric Template Protection: Motivation, Methods and Metrics* aims to tell a complete story of the BTP field, presenting a clear picture of the progress made thus far and challenges that remain to be tackled. To solidify the reader's understanding of the presented concepts, each chapter is supplemented with a set of study questions, which encourage reflection on what has been learned and inspire deeper thoughts on the underlying subjects. In this way, this book strives to serve as an introductory textbook on BTP, a go-to reference suitable for both academics interested in contributing to this burgeoning field of research and practitioners wishing to understand the opportunities and challenges around applying BTP to real-world biometrics-based applications. It is our hope, therefore, that the *Handbook of Biometric Template Protection: Motivation, Methods and Metrics*—the first book dedicated to exploring the important field of BTP research—will be instrumental in comprehensively disseminating this timely topic across diverse stakeholders.

Martigny, Switzerland
Munich, Germany
East Lansing, MI, USA
Martigny, Switzerland
Lausanne, Switzerland

Vedrana Krivokuća Hahn
Marta Gomez-Barrero
Arun Ross
Sébastien Marcel

Acknowledgments The editors wish to acknowledge the following sources of funding for the work performed in compiling this book: Swiss Center for Biometrics Research and Testing, NSF Center for Identification Technology Research (CITeR), DHS Center of Excellence in Criminal Investigations and Network Analysis (CINA), and Research Institute CODE.

Contents

Part I Motivation

Contributors

Marina Blanton Department of Computer Science and Engineering, University at Buffalo, Buffalo, NY, USA

Vishnu Naresh Boddeti Department of Computer Science and Engineering, Michigan State University, East Lansing, MI, USA

Christoph Busch ATHENE, Hochschule Darmstadt, Darmstadt, Germany

Xingbo Dong School of Artificial Intelligence, Anhui University, Hefei, China

Valentina Fohr Department of Computer Science, Hochschule Darmstadt, Darmstadt, Germany

Javier Galbally Capability Building Sector, EU Agency eu-LISA, Tallinn, Estonia

Marta Gomez-Barrero RI CODE, Universität der Bundeswehr München, Munich, Germany

Catherine Jasserand STeP, Faculty of Law, University of Groningen, Groningen, The Netherlands

CiTiP, Faculty of Law and Criminology, KU Leuven, Leuven, Belgium

Els J. Kindt eLaw, Universiteit Leiden, Leiden, The Netherlands

CiTiP, Faculty of Law and Criminology, KU Leuven, Leuven, Belgium

Vedrana Krivokuća Hahn Biometrics Security & Privacy Group, Idiap Research Institute, Martigny, Switzerland

Sébastien Marcel Biometrics Security & Privacy Group, Idiap Research Institute, Martigny, Switzerland

School of Criminal Justice, Université de Lausanne (UNIL), Lausanne, Switzerland

Nasser Nasrabadi Lane Department of CSEE, West Virginia University, Morgantown, WV, USA

Tiong-Sik Ng School of Electrical and Electronic Engineering, Yonsei University, Seoul, Republic of Korea

Hatef Otroshi Shahreza Biometrics Security & Privacy Group, Idiap Research Institute, Martigny, Switzerland

School of Engineering, École Polytechnique Fédérale de Lausanne (EPFL), Lausanne, Switzerland

Shantanu Rane Computer Science Laboratory, SRI, Menlo Park, CA, USA

Christian Rathgeb Department of Computer Science, Hochschule Darmstadt, Darmstadt, Germany

Homeland Security Division, Secunet Security Networks, Essen, Germany

Veeru Talreja Lane Department of CSEE, West Virginia University, Morgantown, WV, USA

Benjamin Tams Homeland Security Division, Secunet Security Networks, Essen, Germany

Andrew Beng Jin Teoh School of Electrical and Electronic Engineering, Yonsei University, Seoul, Republic of Korea

Matthew Valenti Lane Department of CSEE, West Virginia University, Morgantown, WV, USA

List of Abbreviations

AD: Auxiliary Data, 16
AES: Advanced Encryption Standard, 6
AFIS: Automated Fingerprint Identification System, 28
AI: Artificial Intelligence, 16
API: Application Programming Interface, 153
ARM: Attack on Record Multiplicity, 210
BC: Biometric Cryptosystem, 15
BCH: Bose-Chaudhuri-Hocquenghem (code), 154
BF: Bloom-Filter, 17
BFS: Brute Force Security, 94
BGV: Brakerski-Gentry-Vaikuntanathan (HE scheme), 113
BIPA: Biometric Information Privacy Act, 25
BTP: Biometric Template Protection, 15
CA: Certification Authority, 8
CAE: Convolutional Autoencoder, 161
CB: Cancellable Biometrics, 50
CCPA: California Consumer Privacy Act, 23
CKKS: Cheon-Kim-Kim-Song (HE scheme), 113
CMC: Cumulative Match Characteristic (plot), 179
CMR: Cross Match Rate, 227
CNN: Convolutional Neural Network, 142
CPA: Chosen Plaintext Attack, 5
CPRA: California Privacy Rights Act, 23
CPU: Central Processing Unit, 127
CRT: Chinese Remainder Theorem, 118
DBH: Deep Biometric Hashing, 146
DET: Detection Error Trade-off (plot), 177
DFT: Discrete Fourier Transform, 60
DIR: Detection and Identification Rate (plot), 179
DLL: Distance Logistic Loss, 147
DNN: Deep Neural Network, 143

DNNDBS: Deep Neural Network Decoding for Biometric Security, 147
DPA: Data Protection Authority, 30
DPIA: Data Protection Impact Assessment, 22
ECC: Error Correcting Code, 143
ECJ: European Court of Justice, 32
EDPB: European Data Protection Board, 24
EER: Equal Error Rate, 155
EU: European Union, 17
FAR: False Accept Rate, 155
FAS: False Accept Security, 93
FCMR: False Cross Match Rate, 227
FHE: Fully Homomorphic Encryption, 108
FMR: False Match Rate, 90
FNIR: False-Negative Identification Rate, 23
FNMR: False Non-Match Rate, 143
FPIR: False Positive Identification Rate, 179
FRR: False Reject Rate, 143
FRT: Face Recognition Technology, 24
FT: Feature Transformation, 15
FTA: Failure To Acquire (rate), 90
FTE: Failure To Enrol (rate), 95
FV: Fan-Vercauteren (HE scheme), 116
GAR: Genuine Accept Rate, 155
GDPR: General Data Protection Regulation, 9
GMR: Genuine Match Rate, 93
GPU: Graphics Processing Unit, 127
HE: Homomorphic Encryption, 18
IoM: Index-of-Max (hashing), 53
IP: Internet Protocol (address), 65
JL: Johnson-Lindenstrauss (lemma), 55
LED: Law Enforcement Directive, 19
LF: Linkage Function, 220
LHE: Leveled Homomorphic Encryption, 108
LR: Likelihood Ratio, 229
LSH: Locality Sensitive Hashing, 58
LT: Learned Transformation, 15
LWE: Learning With Errors, 201
MC: Maximum Curvature (feature extractor), 60
MEB: Maximum Entropy Binary (code), 142
ML: Maximum Likelihood, 151
MSE: Mean Square Error, 161
NECD: Neural Error-Correcting Decoder, 147
NIST: National Institute of Standards and Technology, 235
NTT: Number Theoretic Transform, 117
PAD: Presentation Attack Detection, 235

PAI: Presentation Attack Instrument, 14
PBT: Protected Biometric Template, 16
PHE: Partially Homomorphic Encryption, 107
PI: Pseudonymous Identifier, 18
PIC: Pseudonymous Identifier Comparator, 19
PIE: Pseudonymous Identifier Encoder, 18
PIR: Pseudonymous Identifier Re-coder, 18
QIM: Quantization Index Modulation, 225
R&D: Research and Development, 235
RBI: Remote Biometric Identification, 26
RBR: Renewable Biometric Reference, 15
RCW: Revised Code of Washington, 25
RNN: Recurrent Neural Network, 158
ROC: Receiver Operating Characteristic (plot), 227
RS: Reed-Solomon (code), 86
RTL: Repeated Line Tracking (feature extractor), 60
RTMR: Renewable Template Matching Rate, 227
SHA: Secure Hash Algorithm, 3
SHE: Somewhat Homomorphic Encryption, 108
SIMD: Single Instruction Multiple Data, 117
STL: Secure Triplet Loss, 159
SVP: Shortest Vector Problem, 201
TEE: Trusted Execution Environment, 2
TI: Template Inversion, 11
TMR: True Match Rate, 93
TPIR: True Positive Identification Rate, 179
UBM: Universal Background Model, 227
WLD: Wide Line Detector (feature extractor), 60
XOR: Exclusive Or, 193

Part I
Motivation

Chapter 1
Biometric Template Protection: Why and How

Christoph Busch, Marta Gomez-Barrero, and Hatef Otroshi Shahreza

Abstract This chapter examines the balanced relationship between the advantages of biometric systems and the disadvantage of immutable biometric characteristics. Potential attack points in biometric systems are discussed, and examples of real-life incidents in operational systems are provided, motivating the use of Biometric Template Protection (BTP) for the protection of biometric references. This chapter derives from risks in operational systems the design goals for template protection algorithms, namely non-invertibility and diversification among others. Such goals have been instrumental in the development of template protection mechanisms over the last 20 years. The chapter also reviews standardized evaluation methodologies for BTP methods and reflects on the threat models, which are applicable in evaluations of BTP mechanisms.

1 Introduction

Biometric applications have the primary purpose of providing access control with a non-delegable authentication factor. These applications are more convenient for users of an IT system and increase the security of access control. Biometric recognition, which is understood as the automated recognition of individuals based

---

C. Busch (✉)
ATHENE, Hochschule Darmstadt, Darmstadt, Germany
e-mail: christoph.busch@h-da.de

M. Gomez-Barrero
RI CODE, Universität der Bundeswehr München, Munich, Germany
e-mail: marta.gomez-barrero@unibw.de

H. Otroshi Shahreza
Biometrics Security & Privacy Group, Idiap Research Institute, Martigny, Switzerland

School of Engineering, École Polytechnique Fédérale de Lausanne (EPFL), Lausanne, Switzerland
e-mail: hatef.otroshi@idiap.ch

V. Krivokuća Hahn et al. (eds.), *Handbook of Biometric Template Protection*,
https://doi.org/10.1007/978-981-95-0995-9_1

on their behavioural and biological characteristics [32],[1] exploits the rich set of anatomical characteristics related to the structure of the body (fingerprint pattern, iris pattern, etc.). A biometric recognition process requires that an individual (i.e., the natural person) is known by the system in advance (*enrolment*) to create the necessary reference data. Biometric systems can either be designed as verification systems or as identification systems. In a verification system, the user specifies an identifier (i.e., an "identity") to which—they claim—exists a reference in the system. If biometric systems are combined with an authentication document (e.g., some sort of identity card), the biometric reference (e.g., a passport photo) may be stored on this document. From a privacy protection point of view, such a system is considerably more in favour of the individual, as they could essentially terminate the enrolment by destruction of the ID document. The verification system will serve the authentication request by comparing a biometric probe with exactly this one reference image (*1:1 comparison*). On the other hand, in the case of an identification system, the captured probe image is compared with many images that have been enrolled, and the most similar reference record is determined from this set (*1:n comparison*). However, the similarity between two images must reach a pre-defined threshold, so that a reliable assignment of the identity associated with the most similar reference image can be made. Identification systems tend to be used for some applications where there is no alternative, for example, when they are used to detect a duplicate enrolment, which must be avoided in a system that controls benefits for staff members of a company or for citizens of a state.

Biometric identification and verification systems must be secure and trustworthy. This requires that capture devices cannot be fooled by artefacts (e.g., gummy fingers) and that attacks on the enrolment process are reliably detected. This is important to prevent impersonation attacks targeted at misusing a victim's credentials. This will be discussed in detail in Sect. 2.3. In addition, biometric identification systems are potentially exposed to attacks that leak reference data in central storage or even replace biometric reference data, such that impersonation attacks are supported. Preventing such security risks is fundamental (see Sect. 2).

Biometric systems can only be successful if they are well adopted by the target population. At the beginning of this century, society was rather reluctant with regard to biometrics applications, as they were primarily associated with forensic investigations, which indeed constituted the major deployment area for more than 100 years. Moreover, the storage of biometric data in central databases has caused concerns [42]. Over the last decade, public perception of biometrics has improved a lot, as smartphones with fingerprint or face recognition have demonstrated the increase in usability and security, while at the same time keeping the storage of reference data under the full control of the data subject. However, a remaining challenge is to ensure that biometric algorithms treat different demographic groups

[1] The definition can be found in ISO/IEC 2382-37 and reads "*automated recognition of individuals based on their biological and behavioural characteristics*". See https://www.iso.org/obp/ui/#iso:std:iso-iec:2382:-37:ed-3:v1:en:term:37.01.03.

in a fair manner, meaning with the same recognition accuracy. Addressing this issue is fundamental in order to reach wide acceptability of biometrics in society, and we reflect on it more in Sect. 4.2.

Biometric data as an (additional) authentication factor is most attractive when it is important for the operator that the authentication factor cannot be delegated in violation of the security policy of the system. This unfortunately occurs frequently for knowledge- and token-based authentication factors, for instance, in financial transaction systems. Thus the inclusion of biometrics, as introduced with the payment service directive [14], promoted a factor that cannot be forgotten and cannot be delegated—two strong advantages of biometric characteristics.[2]

In spite of all the aforementioned advantages of biometric systems, acceptance by the operator *and* the target population can only be reached when the trade-offs between pros and cons are frankly discussed. An important aspect to consider is the immutable property of a biometric characteristic. The permanence is given for many different biometric modalities: It is known, for instance, that there is a strong persistence for fingerprint and iris patterns. For facial traits we anticipate the ageing process, which requires an update of our identity cards every 10 years. Thus, we can identify the major advantage and disadvantage as follows:

- **Advantage of Biometrics**: Biometric characteristics are *immutable* and cannot be delegated or forgotten.
- **Disadvantage of Biometrics**: Biometric characteristics are *immutable* and cannot be updated once they are "stolen".

The term *stolen* is strongly misleading and may confuse the reader. When a data subject enrols, for example, in a biometric fingerprint recognition system and for this purpose presents their biometric characteristic (e.g., a fingertip) to a capture device, a biometric reference is stored in the system's reference database. That biometric reference, regardless of whether it is a fingerprint image, a template containing a set of minutiae (i.e., features extracted from the image), or a protected biometric pseudo identity, is *derived* from the biometric sample and as such represents the biometric characteristic. This representation is an *image* of the biometric characteristic. Assuming that the reference database is attacked and the reference records are leaked, the biometric characteristic itself is **not** stolen. In this example situation the data subject still has the fingerprint pattern on their fingertips as before, meaning the usage of the terms *lost* or *stolen* is not appropriate. So, since this attack scenario and its motivation to conduct an impersonation attack is fundamental for this chapter and this handbook, we will use the term *leaking* instead.

While the balancing of the major advantage and disadvantage of biometrics may, at first, read like a dilemma, it is not. On the contrary, it is the motivation

[2] The definition for a **biometric characteristic** can be found in ISO/IEC 2382-37 and reads "*biological and behavioural characteristic of an individual from which distinguishing, repeatable biometric features can be extracted for the purpose of biometric recognition*". See https://www.iso.org/obp/ui/#iso:std:iso-iec:2382:-37:ed-3:v1:en:term:37.01.02.

for the research and work presented in this handbook, in order to disentangle the relationship between the biometric characteristic (i.e., the observed part of the physical body of the enrolled data subject) and the biometric enrolment data record[3] in the system. The methods described in this handbook will illustrate this disentanglement process by transformation of a biometric sample (e.g., a fingerprint image) or a biometric feature vector derived from that sample into a pseudonymous identity, which is still representing that very same sample. In the event that the pseudonymous identity is leaked from the reference database, a new pseudonymous identity can be generated with new seed values for the transformation process. The process of generating these pseudonymous identities falls under the umbrella of the Biometric Template Protection (BTP) research field, which is the topic of this handbook.

2 Attack Vectors and Incidents

Before we discuss template protection mechanisms, it is important to identify potential attack vectors that relate to the enrolment data records that are contained in biometric reference databases[4] and to discuss the motivation for an attack.

As illustrated with (1) in Fig. 1.1, the attacker might want to modify the enrolment data record in order to replace the biometric sample of the enrolled subject with their own sample. They could then successfully run verification attempts with probes from their own biometric characteristic and pretend to be the data subject they have impersonated. The victim would no longer be able to use the access control system, and it is likely that the attack would soon be spotted for this reason. It should be noted that a precondition for the attack is that the data storage subsystem is not properly integrity-protected, meaning that such manipulation is not detected (e.g., with hash value-based integrity analysis). In order to avoid being spotted by the victim, the attacker would need to act with a smarter type of manipulation that allows both themselves and the victim to be verified in a biometric comparison attempt against the new manipulated reference. For example, in a face recognition system, the attacker could morph their own facial image with the victim's image [56]. Implementations of morphing methods are freely available and can be used to create a *morph* from the parent face images of two subjects (e.g., the attacker and

[3] The definition for a **biometric enrolment data record** can be found in ISO/IEC 2382-37 and reads "*data record attributed to a biometric data subject, containing non-biometric data and associated with biometric reference identifier(s)*". See https://www.iso.org/obp/ui/#iso:std:iso-iec:2382:-37:ed-3:v1:en:term:37.01.03.

[4] While the standardized architecture of a general biometric system in ISO/IEC SC37 SD11 [29] uses the term **data storage subsystem**, the term in ISO/IEC 2382-37 is **biometric reference database**, and its definition reads "*database of biometric reference data records*". The two terms are synonyms. See https://www.iso.org/obp/ui/#iso:std:iso-iec:2382:-37:ed-3:v1:en:term:37.03.17.

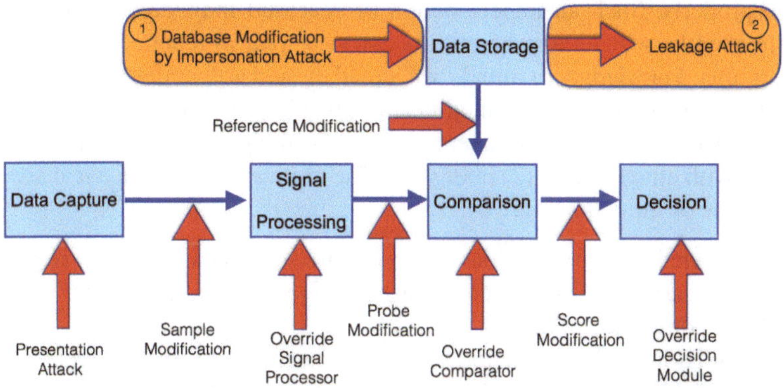

Fig. 1.1 Attack vectors against a data storage subsystem as a component in a generic biometric system. Specifically the impersonation attack (1) and the leakage attack (2) address the data storage (following [33])

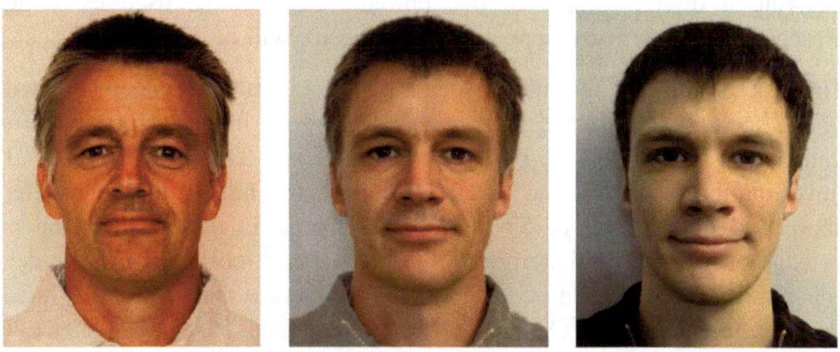

Fig. 1.2 Face images of the two parent subjects (left and right), as well as a morphed face image (middle), which could be stored in a passport

the victim). The result of this morphing process is shown in Fig. 1.2. The morph face image (in the centre) looks equally similar to the left and right parent images. It should be noted that morphed face images can fool face recognition systems and human examiners [19, 46]. In order to constitute a high morphing attack potential [16], parent images are selected from individuals that have the same gender, similar age, and corresponding skin tones. In other words, the attacker will employ social engineering to find the most suitable victim in the enrolment database.

If we now assume that the attacker is not capable of running a morphing attack, under which condition could they avoid being spotted with their modification of the victim's database record? Very simple: if for instance the impersonated victim is a deceased or missing person and the system administrator has failed to update their system properly. Such an impersonation of deceased individuals seems to occur quite frequently, with almost 2.5 million cases per year as reported on Fraud.net.[5]

With this knowledge in mind, we could assume that the database storage subsystem is well protected and modifications would be immediately spotted. In that case we must still consider the "silent" attack of leaking the biometric references, as indicated with attack vector (2) in Fig. 1.1. The motivation for such a leakage attack could be one of the following:

- Drawing statistical conclusions on the entire enrolment database (e.g., distribution of various demographic groups like age, gender, and alike), which will further be discussed in Sect. 4.1.
- Deriving additional information such as the health status of one specific person of interest with relevance to the public or to the economical wealth of the entity (e.g., the CEO or other leading manager) that is operating the identification system. In Sect. 2.1 we will discuss when and how unprotected biometric samples can reveal medical information about the data subject.
- Deriving a digital sample of one enrollee that can be used to produce a presentation attack instrument. This attack vector will be discussed in Sect. 2.3.

The risk of the leakage attack vector (2) should not be underestimated and has been specifically illustrated in recent years with incidents that occurred in operational systems. The U.S. Department of Defense (DoD) reported in 2015 on the investigations related to the breach of their central fingerprint image reference database and the leakage of 5.6 million fingerprint images.[6] Given the public knowledge on generating fingerprint artefacts that can fool many capture devices, one cannot really understand why the DoD assessment is that "*the ability to misuse fingerprint data is limited*". On the other hand, the impact of said data breach would have been marginal if a template protection mechanism had been in place in the operational identification system.

Another more recent incident was widely reported in the media as it had severe consequences for the enrolled data subjects. In this case, data had not leaked out, but the controller of the data storage subsystem was replaced by new operators with different policies. When the NATO troops left Afghanistan in Summer 2021, the unexpectedly fast exit resulted in biometric data (iris, face, and fingerprint images) being left behind and coming under control of the Taliban,[7] a situation that must be considered as severe function creep. The fear is that these databases and the

---

[5] Nearly 2.5 million dead people are victims of identity theft every year. Fraudsters intentionally use the identities of deceased individuals at the rate of more than 2,000 per day. See https://fraud.net/d/iod-impersonation-of-the-deceased-fraud/.

[6] Statement by the Office of Personnel Management and the Department of Defense on Background Investigations Incident (September 2015). See https://www.opm.gov/news/releases/2015/09/cyber-statement-923/.

[7] MIT technology review on the Afghan biometric databases (August 2021). See https://www.technologyreview.com/2021/08/30/1033941/afghanistan-biometric-databases-us-military-40-data-points/.

corresponding capture devices will eventually reveal which Afghan citizens had been serving for the NATO coalition forces. It is possible that the Taliban actors exploited this biometric database even before the power take-over in 2021: In a 2016 attack in Kunduz they were able to access the database and used it to identify security force members or supporters of the coalition forces. During the period of presence of the NATO troops, data was collected in various national identification systems, for instance, the Afghan Personnel and Pay System (APPS), which was operated by the Afghan ministry of interior with the intent to minimize the illegal collection of salary or state benefits. The same agency also operated the Afghan Automatic Biometric Identification System (AABIS) that was used to identify criminals and also targets for drone attacks. For the latter, data was collected for more than 10 years, reaching an enrolment database size of close to ten million Afghan citizens.

While the motivation to establish the aforementioned identification systems is understandable, the decision to store biometric data in unprotected form cannot be justified. This is especially crucial considering the consequences for female data subjects who were serving for the ministry of interior under the previous pre-Taliban government.[8] Reflecting on the impact that these incidents had for the enrolled data subjects should be strong motivation for the use of biometric template protection (BTP) mechanisms in any operational identification or verification system, especially one with central data storage (although BTP is recommended for any type of storage).

2.1 Medical Information

The General Data Protection Regulation (GDPR) [15], adopted in 2016, is important for the operation of large-scale biometric identification systems such as the ones described in the previous section. Following the spirit of the regulation, biometric data in whatever form (captured biometric sample, template or probe feature vector, and protected biometric reference) is considered as *personal data*, as it represents the unique biometric characteristic of the data subjects and serves the purpose of identifying a natural person. Moreover, Article 9 defines that "*processing of personal data revealing racial or ethnic origin, ..., biometric data for the purpose of uniquely identifying a natural person, data concerning health ... shall be prohibited*" as such data is considered *sensitive*. Besides the biometric data itself, additional information can be derived from biometric samples: ethnic origin from facial images, and as we will illustrate in this section, health related information is contained in various biometric samples.

[8] Human Rights Watch: New Evidence that Biometric Data Systems Imperil Afghans (March 2022). See https://www.hrw.org/news/2022/03/30/new-evidence-biometric-data-systems-imperil-afghans/.

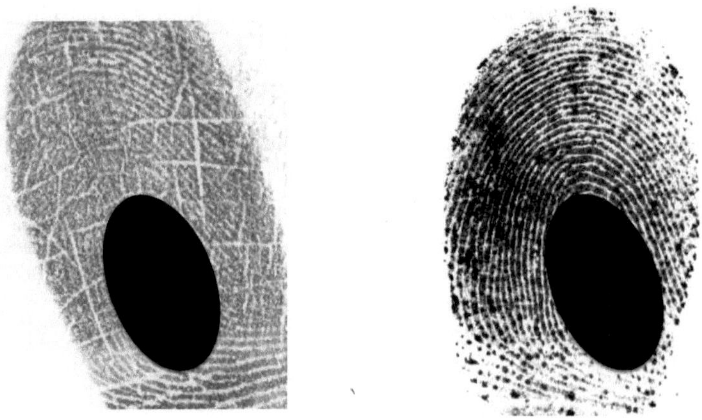

Fig. 1.3 Fingerprint images from the same finger with bad skin condition due to a temporary health issue (left) and good skin condition (right)

Fingerprint recognition with contact-based capture devices specifically releases information about dermatological problems that a data subject might have. It is estimated that in Western cultures, approximately 10% of the population suffers from skin diseases such as neurodermatitis (i.e., atopic eczema), hyper keratotic hand eczema, or thromboangiitis obliterans. The skin character (i.e., the properties of the skin) might be permanently or only temporarily distorted and will become obvious in fingerprint samples, as Fig. 1.3 illustrates. The finger captured on the right shows good skin condition; the image on the left shows a temporary health problem for the same finger instance. Capturing the fingerprint with contact-less capture devices [48] might reduce the impact, but it would still reveal the health condition.

Even more problematic might be the capturing of palmprints, as they reveal not only the skin condition but also potential genetic defects. In particular, the shape and orientation of palm creases reveal genetic defects. Figure 1.4 illustrates palmar flexion creases, which can be observed in a palmprint. The pattern on the left is called *Simian line* [49] and is a biometric trait present for data subjects that have Down's syndrome, a congenital malformation.

The health status of a capture subject can also be very transparent in iris samples. For example, the progression of iris melanoma can be directly observed by analysis of the decreasing size of the iris area that fulfils the quality criteria of sharpness and high contrast. The ophthalmologic literature[9] shows an extensive number of examples for the interested reader. Similarly, face images can reveal skin

[9] University of Iowa provides examples of iris melanoma and its progression over time (2019). See https://eyerounds.org/atlas/pages/iris-melanoma.html.

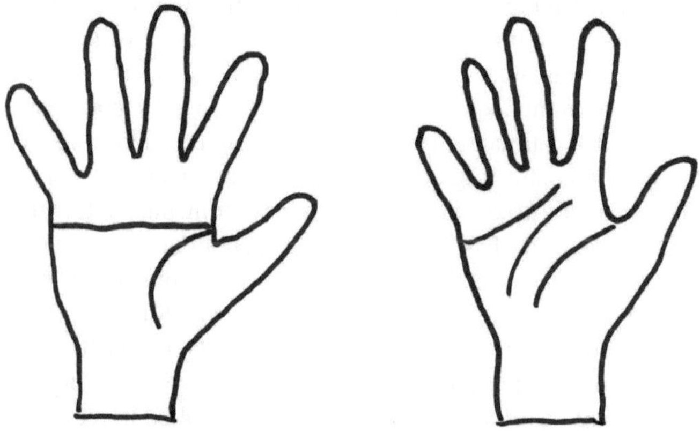

Fig. 1.4 Down's syndrome causing the Simian line (left) and normal healthy palmar flexion creases (right)

cancer[10] conditions and its progress over time. In addition, face images also disclose emotions observable by facial expressions and even the psychological state of a capture subject.

Biometric template protection, as described in this handbook, constitutes an effective "*safeguard mechanism for the fundamental rights and the interests of the data subject*" GDPR §9.2 [15], which can justify an exception from the prohibition of processing in GDPR §9.1 and thus has motivated many researchers to work in this field. For a detailed discussion on the impact of the GDPR on biometric systems, see Part I Chap. 3 of this book.

2.2 *Template Inversion*

In a Template Inversion (TI) attack, also referred to as template reconstruction attack or inverse biometrics [24], an adversary gains access to the templates stored in the database of the biometric system and tries to invert them to reconstruct the corresponding (i.e., underlying) biometric samples. Then, the adversary may use these reconstructed samples to impersonate a subject (see Sect. 2.3 for more details), thereby posing a severe security threat. In the particular case of face recognition, in addition to the aforementioned security threats, the reconstructed face images can also reveal privacy-sensitive information (such as age, gender, or

[10] Cases of face skin cancer and surgery reconstruction. See https://www.hdft.nhs.uk/services/maxillofacial-surgery/outcomes-after-surgery/.

ethnicity) of the underlying subject and can furthermore provide the adversary with an approximation of face images that may be recognizable by the human eye.

Initial studies in this area showed that fingerprint samples can be successfully reconstructed from minutiae-based templates [5, 55]. In both cases, minutiae information is used to estimate orientation fields, and a rendering step is undertaken to generate more realistic fingerprint images. More recently, [37] showed that an adversary can reconstruct finger vein images from binary templates (such as WLD [26], MC [44], or RLT [43]) to attack a finger vein recognition system.

Other inverse biometrics methods require knowledge of similarity scores instead of the reference templates to reconstruct faces [2, 17, 20], iris [18, 52], or hand shapes [21]. In addition to methodologies specifically designed to reconstruct a particular type of biometric sample, as is the case in [5, 55] for fingerprint images, general hill climbing-based approaches can also be applied to reconstruct different biometrics samples [1, 2, 17, 18, 20, 21, 45, 52]. In these cases, the attacker needs to have access to the comparison scores between the samples they generate and the reference stored in the database. In some cases, the feature extraction algorithm is also assumed to be known by the adversary. In the following, we will focus on methods requiring access to the stored reference templates. More details on other kinds of inverse biometrics methods can be found in [24].

Several methods have been proposed in the literature to reconstruct face images from facial templates [7, 9, 40, 58, 59, 61–63, 65, 68]. These methods can be categorized into *white-box* and *black-box* methods, based on the available knowledge about the face feature extractor model. In the *white-box* methods, such as [63, 65], the internal functioning and all the parameters of the face feature extractor model are known, and therefore the feature extractor model is used during training of the face reconstruction network or in gradient-based optimization to reconstruct face images. In contrast, in *black-box* methods [40, 68], the internal functioning of the face feature extractor model is unknown. Therefore, the feature extractor model cannot be used in the training process of the face reconstruction network but can be used in non-gradient-based optimizations. Since in the *white-box* methods more knowledge about the feature extractor model is available, better reconstruction performance can be achieved [59]. While most methods are proposed only for *white-box* or *black-box* scenarios, a few methods can be applied for both *white-box* and *black-box* template inversion [7, 58, 59].

Template inversion methods for face recognition systems can be categorized by their output based on the resolution and the quality of the reconstructed images. Methods based on convolutional neural networks (CNNs), such as [40, 63], often generate images that suffer from blurriness or other artefacts. In contrast, most GAN-based methods, such as [9, 59, 62, 68], generate high-quality and realistic images. In [58, 60], a geometry-aware face generator model was used to reconstruct a 3D face representation from facial templates. Figure 1.5 depicts 3D reconstructed face images in template inversion attacks against a face recognition system based on templates derived with ArcFace [8]. As can be observed, the reconstructed face images are very similar to the original images, and their templates also have a high similarity to the templates of the original images.

Fig. 1.5 Sample face images from the FFHQ dataset [36] (first row) and their corresponding frontal 2D (second row) and 3D (third row) reconstructions from facial templates in the white-box template inversion attack on ArcFace [8] templates, based on the template inversion method in [58, 60]. Numerical values show the cosine similarity between the templates of the original and frontal reconstructed face images

2.3 Attacks Exploiting Reconstructed Biometric Samples

The reconstruction of a biometric sample with an inversion attack makes sense only if there is an objective for doing so. The motivation of an attacker may be twofold: (i) They could be interested in retrieving additional information from the sample, as discussed in Sect. 2.1, or (ii) they may want to launch an impersonation attack with the intention of achieving a positive verification with the biometric reference of the victim from whom the attacker has reconstructed the biometric sample. Such impersonation attacks can be executed by an injection attack, which would require penetrating the system with a bypass of the capture device and feeding the sample directly to the signal processing subsystem. This is only possible if the integrity of subsystems in a biometric system is not protected by hash values. Otherwise, such modifications can easily be detected. These types of injection attacks have recently been discussed, and a European Standard is under development by CEN/TC 224/WG 18 [6].

Figure 1.6 illustrates the potential targets in a generic biometric system [29] that could be attacked by an adversary in possession of a digital copy of a biometric sample. The injection attack conducts a signal modification prior to the signal processing subsystem [6].

A more realistic approach may be for the attacker to convert the reconstructed digital sample to an analogue replica of the biometric characteristic of the victim (i.e., a presentation attack instrument (PAI)) and present this PAI to the data capture subsystem (i.e., the sensors in the capture device) [33] as illustrated in Fig. 1.6. As

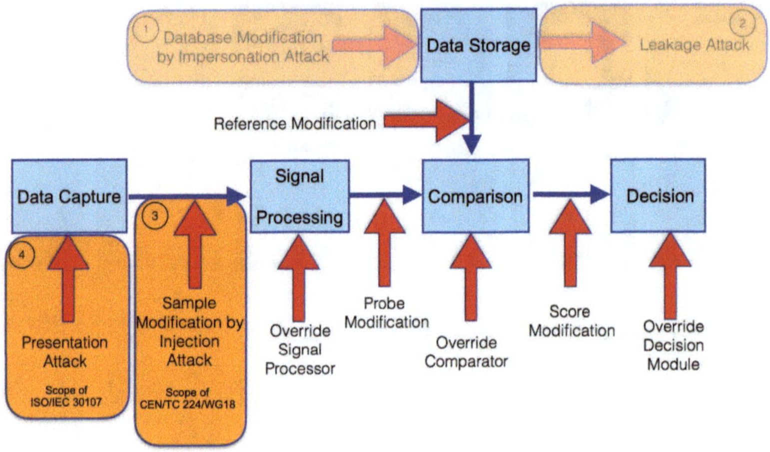

Fig. 1.6 Injection attack (3) and presentation attack (4) with an inverted biometric sample

is portrayed in many science fiction films, biometric capture devices (i.e., sensors) in operational access control applications can be fooled by presenting a photo to the camera or rendering a video of an authorized person on a laptop. In experiments, even the low image quality offered by a smartphone was sufficient to present the fake "*face biometric characteristic*" to a face capture device [41, 51, 67]. There are still too few systems that include liveness detection to prevent the faking of an identity using an inanimate object (e.g., a flat representation on a display).

More than 20 years ago presentation attacks were documented in the literature in the context of fingerprint capturing [57, 70]. Such attacks became a major concern when operational systems developed towards unsupervised enrolment or verification procedures. A presentation attack (PA) can be performed by any outsider that interacts with a biometric capture device. As a consequence, the need to develop a harmonized perspective for presentation attacks became obvious. The biometric community has developed a multipart standard ISO/IEC 30107 *biometric presentation attack detection* [33, 34] with the goal of providing a harmonized definition of terms and a taxonomy of attack techniques. Beyond that, this standard defines a testing methodology that can evaluate PAD mechanisms. While the international standardization in ISO/IEC had developed a Harmonized Biometric Vocabulary (HBV) ISO/IEC 2382-37 [32], the taxonomy was augmented with an additional standard formulating specific types of attack [33]: The *Active Impostor Presentation Attack* attempts to subvert the correct and intended policy of the biometric capture subsystem. Here, the attacker aims to be recognized as a specific data subject known to the system (i.e., an impersonation attack).

The potential of the attack (to succeed) will depend on the attacker's knowledge, the window of opportunity, and other factors, to create the object (i.e., PAI) used in the attack. The object that is employed in the attack can be manifold in nature: from sophisticated *silicone masks* over simple printouts of the reconstructed digital sample to a rubber stamp of a fingerprint pattern. An overview of presentation attack detection for face capturing is given in [50], while for fingerprint capturing the interested reader is referred to [66].

3 Protection Methods and Goals

In order to mitigate the risks posed by the attack vectors described in Sect. 2, Biometric Template Protection (BTP) mechanisms are needed [4]. BTP schemes transform a biometric template[11] or a biometric sample[12] directly into a renewable biometric reference[13] (RBR), also known as a *protected template*. Template protection mechanisms can be categorized either as Feature Transformations (FTs),[14] which transform the biometric sample or the extracted feature vector in a reproducible manner, in order to obtain the RBR through an intentional distortion that is potentially controlled by a key [53], or alternatively as Biometric Cryptosystems (BCs),[15] which bind a cryptographic key to a biometric reference or (re)generate such a key from said reference [53]. The approaches that exploit modern cryptographic algorithms yielding the option for computations (e.g., computations of similarity scores) in the encrypted domain are known as Homomorphic Encryption (HE)[16] [10, 38]. More recently Learned Methods (also referred to as Learned Transforms (LTs)[17] in this chapter) were proposed [39], which employ neural networks to generate an RBR. An overview of BTP mechanisms is illustrated in Fig. 1.7.

BCs are also known as helper data schemes and must compensate for the fuzziness or intra-class variance inherent to biometric feature vectors derived from the same biometric instance of the same subject. FTs apply a transformation to the biometric reference, where parameters of the transformation are controlled by

[11] The definition for a **biometric template** can be found in ISO/IEC 2382-37 and reads "*set of stored biometric features comparable directly to a biometric probe*". See https://www.iso.org/obp/ui/#iso:std:iso-iec:2382:-37:ed-3:v1:en:term:37.03.21.

[12] The definition for a **biometric sample** can be found in ISO/IEC 2382-37 and reads "*analogue or digital representation of biometric characteristics prior to biometric feature extraction*". See https://www.iso.org/obp/ui/#iso:std:iso-iec:2382:-37:ed-3:v1:en:term:37.03.21.

[13] The definition for a **renewable biometric reference** can be found in ISO/IEC 24745 and reads "*renewable identifier that represents an individual or data subject within a domain by means of a protected binary identity (re)constructed from the captured biometric sample, and fulfilling irreversibility requirements*". See https://www.iso.org/obp/ui/en/#iso:std:iso-iec:24745:ed-2:v1:en.

[14] More information on Feature Transformations can be found in Part II Chap. 4 of this book.

[15] More information on Biometric Cryptosystems can be found in Part II Chap. 5 of this book.

[16] More information on Homomorphic Encryption can be found in Part II Chap. 6 of this book.

[17] More information on Learned Methods can be found in Part II Chap. 7 of this book.

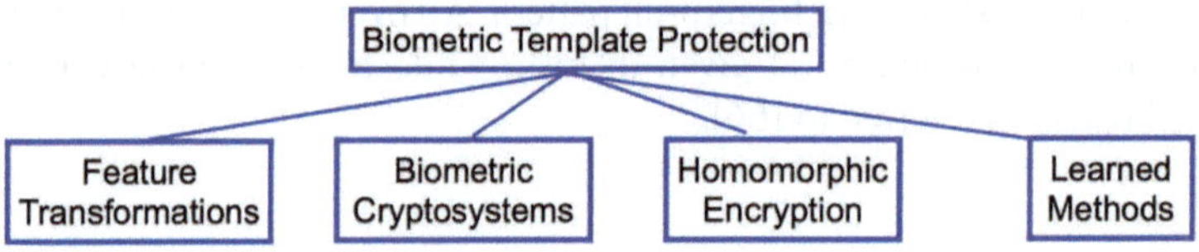

Fig. 1.7 Approaches for biometric template protection (following [27])

auxiliary data (AD),[18] and as the same transformation is applied to both reference and probe feature vectors, the comparison subsystem can operate in the protected domain.

The goals for BTP schemes have been formulated by Breebart et al. [4] as (i) protection against reconstruction of the original biometric sample, which would reveal sensitive information such as health data and alike, (ii) impossibility to link subjects across databases, and (iii) diversification capability. These goals were later adopted by the International Standard ISO/IEC 24745 *Biometric information protection* [27], which will be described in more detail in Sect. 3.1. Moreover the standard demands a list of criteria that a BTP mechanism must satisfy:

- **Recognition accuracy**,[19] such that the well-designed BTP mechanism should not lead to a degradation of recognition accuracy in terms of biometric performance [31].
- **Irreversibility**,[20] such that no biometric sample can be reconstructed from the stored RBR, meaning that neither presentation attack nor injection attack can be executed and that no statistical information on demographic attributes can be collected.
- **Confidentiality** such that there is no leakage of additional information related to the capture subject, to ensure that information on demographic attributes (e.g., skin tone) contained in the original sample does not leak. In addition, the RBR shall not indicate information about the health status of the data subject. Moreover confidentiality also relates to secrecy, meaning that the comparison can be executed in the protected domain. This requirement leads to both transaction time minimization and the expectation to keep the reference always secure.

[18] The definition for **Auxiliary Data** can be found in ISO/IEC 24745 and reads "*subject-dependent data that are part of a renewable biometric reference and may be required to reconstruct pseudonymous identifiers during verification, or for verification in general*".

[19] More information on recognition accuracy can be found in Part III Chap. 8 of this book.

[20] More information on irreversibility can be found in Part III Chap. 9 of this book.

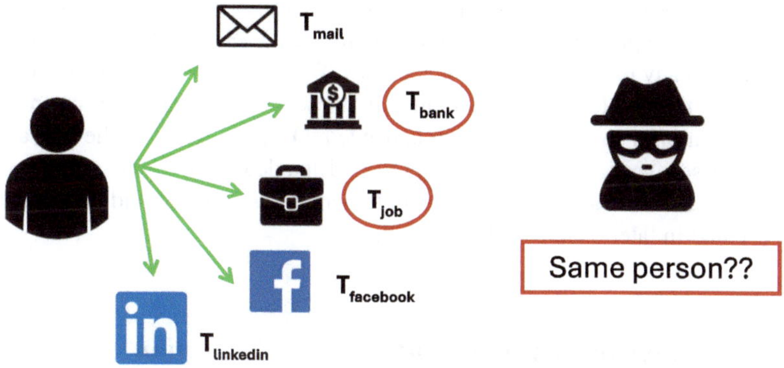

Fig. 1.8 Diversification in space across two different applications, such that biometric references T_{bank} and T_{job} cannot be correlated

- **Diversification**[21] capability of references in space (*unlinkability*) and in time (*renewability*).[22] The diversification in space relates to different applications/services, in which the data subject might enrol with a single biometric instance (e.g., their only face). This is illustrated in Fig. 1.8, which shows that an attacker should not be able to conclude from the two renewable biometric references T_{bank} and T_{job} that both were derived from the same data subject. Eliminating the cross-correlating of references across different systems and applications helps to avoid the profiling of data subjects, and this is the intention of said requirement. Whether the unlinkability of references in a cross-correlation attack is achieved [23] can be tested according to [30] as described in Sect. 4. The diversification in time relates to a potential breach of the data storage subsystem, as described in Sect. 2, such that the protected templates can be renewed if need be after the data breach. The most relevant property of the diversification in time is that it enables revocability[23] of the biometric reference.

The first of the aforementioned properties requires that the BTP algorithm does not cause a decrease in the biometric performance (i.e., FMR and FNMR). This is to ensure that the adoption of the protection mechanism does not prevent the correct functioning of the biometric system. As an example, one biometric template protection method that—depending on the design decisions—can maintain or even improve recognition accuracy is the Bloom-Filter (BF) approach [22, 54]. The more

[21] More information on renewability/unlinkability can be found in Part III Chap. 10 of this book.

[22] The definition for **diversification** can be found in ISO/IEC 24745 and reads "*deliberate creation of multiple, unlinkable, transformed biometric references from one or more biometric samples obtained from one subject for the purposes of security and privacy enhancement*".

[23] The definition for **revocability** can be found in ISO/IEC 24745 and reads "*ability to prevent future successful verification of a specific biometric reference and the corresponding identity reference*".

recent approaches using Homomorphic Encryption (HE), which allow mathematical operations to take place in the encrypted domain [3, 10, 38, 64, 69], also theoretically do not lead to any loss in recognition accuracy. Whether or not that can be achieved depends on the implementation details. In these systems, no decryption of the sensitive data prior to the comparison is needed. Only the result of the operation—the comparison score—may be decrypted and handed over to the access control system. More details about particular implementations of these and other schemes are presented in later chapters of this book.

3.1 Taxonomy on Biometric Information Protection

The international standard ISO/IEC 24745 *Biometric information protection* [27] established a BTP framework mapping the functional components of the various BTP mechanisms (i.e., FT, BC, HE and LT) to unified building blocks, which can then be identified with standardized terms. This framework is helpful for understanding the BTP concepts and the essential definitions and components. It also serves as the basis for evaluating and benchmarking competing technological solutions (see the discussion in Sect. 4).

An overview of this framework is given in Fig. 1.9, which illustrates all subsystems and data elements that are involved in BTP. During enrolment, the biometric sample captured by the sensor(s) is processed by a conventional feature extractor (e.g., minutia extractor) and the resulting feature vector is forwarded to a Pseudonymous Identifier Encoder (PIE).[24] The PIE then transforms the feature vector into a renewable reference, which consists of a pseudonymous identifier (PI)[25] and auxiliary data (AD). Once that transformation has been performed, the feature vector can be shredded or submitted to a secure fallback vault.[26]

For identity verification a new probe sample is captured and submitted to the equivalent feature extraction subsystem. The extracted feature vector is subsequently forwarded to a Pseudonymous Identifier Re-coder (PIR).[27] In addition

---

[24] The definition for a **Pseudonymous Identifier Encoder** can be found in ISO/IEC 24745 and reads "*system, process or algorithm that generates a renewable biometric reference consisting of pseudonymous identifier and possibly auxiliary data based on a biometric reference*".

[25] The definition for a **Pseudonymous Identifier** can be found in ISO/IEC 24745 and reads "*part of a renewable biometric reference that represents an individual or data subject within a domain by means of a protected identity that can be verified by means of a captured biometric sample and the auxiliary data (if any)*".

[26] Such a fallback vault would be needed if the data storage becomes compromised and the biometric references need to be renewed without a new capture process—for instance, if the database is quite large.

[27] The definition for a **Pseudonymous Identifier Re-coder** can be found in ISO/IEC 24745 and reads "*system, process or algorithm that reconstructs a pseudonymous identifier based on the provided auxiliary data and the extracted features*".

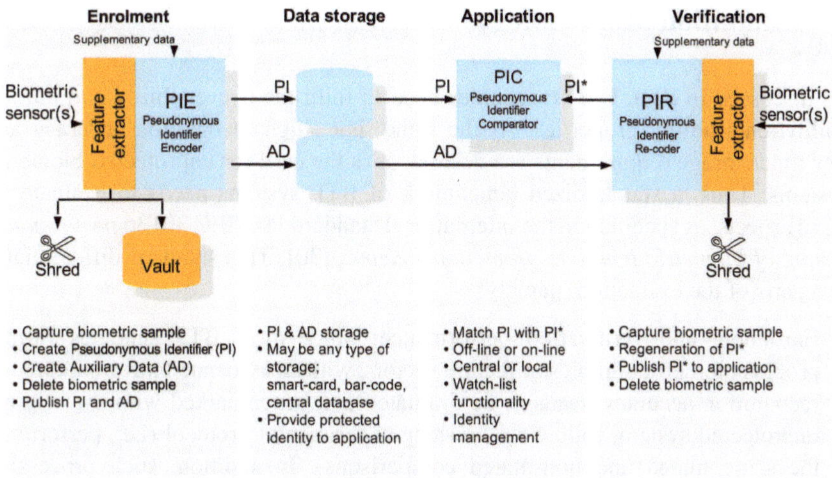

Fig. 1.9 Framework for biometric template protection (following [4, 27])

to the probe feature vector, the PIR needs access to the AD associated with the biometric claim. The output of the PIR is again a Pseudonymous Identifier (PI*). The Pseudonymous Identifier Comparator (PIC)[28] will compare PI and PI* and provide a similarity score between the two back to the application for it to make a *match* or *non-match* decision.

The fact that the RBR contains two parts (i.e., PI and AD) is valuable for a potential de-enrolment, when the two parts are stored in different locations—a secret sharing approach. The system could, for instance, store the PI in a central database of the system operator and the AD in a bar-code or smartcard that is under the control of the data subject. Such distribution enables equal power for both parties, the system operator and the enrolled data subject, when they want to initiate the de-enrolment: If the data subject does not trust the system operator any longer, he/she could destroy the physical copy of the AD, which is, for instance, the bar-code with the printed AD data. If the service operator does not trust the data subject any longer (e.g., as payments for consumed services were not made), the operator can simply delete the PI record from its central database. This is a pragmatic form of balanced bilateral security.

[28] The definition for a **Pseudonymous Identifier Comparator** can be found in ISO/IEC 24745 and reads "*system, process or algorithm that compares the pseudonymous identifier generated during enrolment by the pseudonymous identifier encoder and the pseudonymous identifier reconstructed during verification by the pseudonymous identifier re-coder and returns a similarity score representing the similarity between the two*".

4 Evaluation Methodology

As discussed in Sect. 3, BTP schemes need to fulfil the irreversibility and unlinkability/renewability properties. At the same time, high recognition accuracy and low time/storage requirements are desired, as is the case for unprotected biometric systems. Thus, a standardized benchmark of BTP systems needs to evaluate all these aspects, as specified in the international standard ISO/IEC 30136 *performance testing of biometric template protection schemes* [30]. This standard differentiates two parts of the evaluation, namely:

- Enrolment and verification performance: Since most BTP schemes further process biometric samples or feature vectors, with an associated information loss, recognition accuracy needs to be evaluated and benchmarked with the original unprotected system, following the same experimental protocol (i.e., performing the same mated and non-mated comparisons). In addition, such processing usually entails additional data to be stored and processed by the system—thus, the storage requirements and computational overhead need to be equally assessed. As mentioned above, the AD and PI databases may not both reside at the same place. Therefore, the number of bits needed for the AD database and the PI database shall be reported separately.
- Security and privacy protection: In this step, the irreversibility, unlinkability, and optionally the successful attack rates (SAR) of relevant attack vectors are evaluated. In other words, we need to estimate the adversary's success probability or advantage over a random guess when the adversary attempts to (i) retrieve biometric samples sufficiently similar to the original biometric samples (i.e., irreversibility property) or (ii) determine whether two given ADs and/or PIs are generated from the same subject's characteristic or from different subjects' characteristics (i.e., unlinkability property).

Such evaluations can be carried out in a theoretical or an empirical manner. Whereas a theoretical evaluation gives a higher mathematical assurance of the performance, mostly based on information-theoretical metrics, it should be noted that biometric data does not fulfil common assumptions such as data uniformity or conformance to a given data distribution. On the contrary, biometric data is in general difficult to model, and correlations are omnipresent. Thus, many evaluations resort to empirical approaches, more suitable for the noisy nature of biometric data. These empirical assessments therefore need metrics beyond traditional cryptographic or information-theoretical analysis. Relevant recognition accuracy and fairness metrics are presented in Sect. 4.2, and more information about the particular metrics used in the recognition accuracy, irreversibility, and renewability/unlinkability evaluation are included in Part III of this book.

Last but not least, as in any IT-security evaluation addressing specific attacks, we need to clearly describe the knowledge that is required by the adversary in order to carry out such an attack. Thus, specifying a threat model is a prerequisite for quantifying the security and privacy properties of BTP methods, and all metrics should be estimated with respect to each applicable threat model. An overview of the main threat models for the evaluation of BTP schemes is provided in Sect. 4.1.

4.1 Threat Models

To examine the threat that is imposed by the attack vectors described in Sect. 2, a classification of the attacker's capabilities and skills is needed. The international standard ISO/IEC 30136 [30] has introduced the following threat models:

- **Naive model:** The attacker has no information on the BTP algorithm, nor do they have access to a large biometric database. The attacker only has access to the protected RBRs, and the attacks must operate in a black-box analysis mode.
- **Collision model:** The attacker has access to a large amount of biometric data, which can be used, with a BTP mechanism of the attacker's choice, to generate a PI that is similar to the data in the enrolment database. This would help the attacker gain insight into the transformation function or learned mapping used as BTP.
- **General model:** The attacker has, according to Kerckhoffs's principle, full knowledge of the BTP mechanisms that are used and also knows statistical properties of the enrolled biometric data and has access to the protected data. The protection then depends on a secret key, which is known to the enrolled subject (*Standard model*) [30]. If the attacker is also capable of executing the protected BTP sub-systems, then the threat corresponds to a chosen-plaintext attack and chosen-ciphertext attack in cryptography (*Advanced model*) [30]. Eventually the attacker may also get access to the secret keys, which can be used in their attack (*full disclosure model*) [30].

Identification systems, especially, are exposed to attacks as they are, by nature, continuously online, meaning that the window of opportunity is unlimited. If RBRs from the central data storage are leaked, they support collision model or general model attacks. Preventing such security risks is fundamental. Following Kerckhoffs's principle, the advanced model at least, and full disclosure model ideally, should be applied.

4.2 Recognition Accuracy and Fairness

A fundamental requirement for template protection mechanisms is to maintain the recognition accuracy. The recognition accuracy of biometric algorithms should be determined following the International Standard ISO/IEC 19795-1 [31]. Test procedures for evaluating recognition accuracy are well known since the biometric performance testing standard ISO/IEC 19795-1 was established in 2006 [28] and then revised in 2021 [31]. To measure the performance, a corpus of biometric samples of diverse sample quality is needed, from which insight into the performance of the feature extractor, the template protection mechanisms, and eventually the biometric comparison subsystem can be obtained. When computing the measures, independent trials should be considered. This is relevant when, for example, multiple instances of a biometric characteristic type are captured (e.g., ten fingerprints or two eyes per data subject). The evaluator should respect that within-individual comparisons are not equivalent to between-individual comparisons and shall thus not be included in the set of non-mated comparison trials. For non-mated (i.e., impostor) comparisons, a False-Match constitutes the undesired case that a probe matches a non-mated biometric reference, which has been created for a different identity. The definition for the corresponding **False-Match-Rate (FMR)** can be found in ISO/IEC 19795-1 [31] and reads:

False-Match-Rate: *proportion of the completed biometric non-mated comparison trials that result in a false match*

$$\text{FMR}(t) = \int_t^1 \phi_{nm}(s)ds \tag{1.1}$$

Together with the **False-Non-Match-Rate (FNMR)**, the FMR is the key metric to be used in biometric technology testing and is understood to characterize a security property of a biometric system. Note that some literature uses the term False-Accept-Rate in the meaning of FMR. For mated (i.e., genuine) comparison trials a False-Non-Match constitutes the undesired case that a probe does not match a mated biometric reference, which has been created for the same subject from the same source (e.g., the same index finger). The definition for the corresponding **False-Non-Match-Rate** (FNMR) can be found in ISO/IEC 19795-1 [31] and reads:

False-Non-Match-Rate: *proportion of the completed biometric mated comparison trials that result in a false non-match.*

$$\text{FNMR}(t) = \int_0^t \phi_m(s)ds \tag{1.2}$$

Together with the False-Match-Rate (FMR) the FNMR is the key metric to be used in biometric technology testing and is understood to characterize a convenience property of a biometric system.[29] The biometric performance for a verification system is either reported in terms of the FNMR at a specific FMR that corresponds to the defined security level[30] or in a visual representation that illustrates the outcome of a benchmark. A benchmark of various algorithms (biometric comparison subsystems) with and without biometric template protection is illustrated for various

[29] Note that some literature uses the term False-Reject-Rate in the meaning of FNMR.

[30] For instance, at FMR = 0.001 or 0.1%, which has been recommended by FRONTEX for operational border control systems.

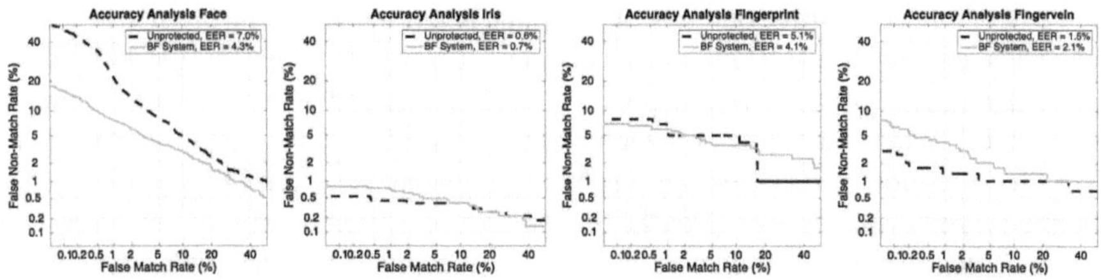

Fig. 1.10 Detection Error Trade-Off (DET) Curve for biometric algorithm with and without BTP (in this case, the Bloom-Filter method has been applied)

biometric modalities in Fig. 1.10, where we plot the FNMR over the FMR for a range of working points (i.e., thresholds that can be configured in the system). We can see that the best-performing system corresponds to the lowest area under the curve. We can also see that for the Bloom-Filter-based BTP, in some cases the BTP-based system even has better recognition accuracy compared to the unprotected system. This is due to the fact that the transformation function not only protects the raw features but moreover also singles out the relevant stable feature elements. An improvement in recognition accuracy is a common phenomenon of several BTP methods, due to factors such as the use of user-specific transformation parameters.

For identification systems, which have the strongest need for biometric template protection as they hold the biometric references in a central database, the first-order estimation of the false-positive and false-negative identification rates for open-set systems can be derived from FMR and FNMR. However, such estimates cannot take into account any correlations in the comparisons involving the same data subject and consequently can be quite inaccurate [31]. The definition for the corresponding **False-Positive Identification Rate** (FPIR) can be found in ISO/IEC 19795-1 [31] and reads:

False-Positive Identification Rate: *proportion of identification transactions by capture subjects not enrolled in the system for which a reference identifier is returned.*

The approximation for the FPIR can be given by

$$\mathrm{FPIR} = N * \mathrm{FMR} \tag{1.3}$$

which indicates that the false-positive error scales with the size of the reference database. The definition for the corresponding **False-Negative Identification Rate** (FNIR) can be found in ISO/IEC 19795-1 [31] and reads:

False-Negative Identification Rate: *proportion of a specified set of identification transactions by capture subjects enrolled in the system for which the subject's correct reference identifier is not among those returned.*

Performance analysis of large-scale identification systems reveals the need for indexing algorithms that can reduce the workload (i.e., low transaction times) and the risk of a false-positive outcome. Firstly, the performance of the biometric system in terms of low transaction times becomes specifically relevant for large-scale identification systems, where a probe will be compared to billions of biometric references. Workload reduction techniques are essential for such systems [11]. Workload reduction methods are a subject of current research [47]. Secondly, the biometric performance addresses the recognition accuracy in terms of low error rates for false-positive or false-negative errors [31]. Acceptability of a template protection mechanism also requires that data subjects have confidence that they are treated in a fair manner by the biometric algorithm and by the BTP algorithm. With the artificial intelligence (AI) evolution and the intensive use of AI algorithms in biometric systems, recently there has been much focus on whether the incorporated artificial neural networks are treating different demographic groups in the same manner. The NISTIR 8280 investigated the extent to which the biometric performance shows a differential performance,[31] meaning a difference in the mated and non-mated comparison score distributions. Such an investigation is specifically of interest for categorical demographic variables[32] such as the gender categories *male*, *female*, or *neutral*. It is important to validate prior to deployment that a biometric (e.g., face) recognition system is not biased towards a specific demographic group. An overview of the effect of algorithmic bias in biometric systems and a survey on the recent literature is given in [12]. The reasons for bias are manifold and range from unbalanced training datasets to systematic effects in the training procedures [13, 25]. On the path to reaching fair biometric systems, a testing methodology is needed. Recent proposals for fairness measures [25] are now under consideration to become the testing methodology in the International Standard ISO/IEC 19795-10 [35].

However the challenge remains open, specifically in the BTP field where bias of template protection methods has not yet been investigated. Moreover, bias mitigation techniques that can ensure a fair biometric system are still in their infancy. The immediate approach, to reach a balanced size of demographic subsets in the training [35], does not fully solve the problem due to the complexity of training procedures.

5 Conclusion

Operational biometric systems must demonstrate a balanced relationship between the advantages of biometric systems and the disadvantage of the more or less immutable property of the biometric characteristic. Therefore the attack vectors

[31] The International Standard ISO/IEC 19795-10 [35] defines **differential performance** as "*difference in biometric system metrics across different demographic groups*".

[32] The International Standard ISO/IEC 19795-10 [35] defines **categorical demographic variable** as "*demographic characteristic of an individual that is nominally or ordinally described*".

of the biometric reference database need to be well understood, and appropriate countermeasures, including template protection mechanisms in combination with presentation attack detection, must be in place. A BTP method should satisfy the criteria of recognition accuracy, irreversibility, confidentiality (e.g., non-leakage/secrecy), and diversification (i.e., renewability/unlinkability). The system operator should always anticipate that (protected) references may be leaked from the system at some point in time; therefore, BTP mechanisms should be considered a necessary part of any biometric system.

6 Summary

- **Motivation:** Some operational systems require central storage of biometric references.
- **Biometric characteristic:** Some immutable and non-delegable authentication factor.
- **Attack vectors:** Incidents illustrate that biometric data can leak from storage.
- **Medical information:** Biometric samples can contain sensitive data about a data subject's medical state.
- **Template inversion:** Biometric templates do NOT, on their own, protect the data.
- **Protection:** Protection methods include Feature Transformations, Biometric Cryptosystems, Homomorphic Encryption, and Learned Methods.
- **Standard:** Biometric template protection mechanisms should follow the ISO/IEC 24745 standard.
- **Evaluation:** BTP methods should be evaluated according to the evaluation criteria: recognition accuracy, irreversibility, confidentiality, and diversification.
- **Benchmarking:** Benchmarks evaluate whether the criteria recognition accuracy, irreversibility, confidentiality, and diversification are fulfilled.
- **Threat models:** These models describe the potential of an attacker.

7 Study Questions

1. What is the motivation to work on the protection of biometric reference data and what legal regulations support this?
2. Why is an intrinsic advantage of biometrics also considered as a disadvantage? What does immutable characteristic mean?
3. Which incidents illustrate the need for template protection?
4. Which biometric modality generates samples that contain information on one's medical state?
5. Why does a biometric template not protect the sensitive biometric data from which it was generated?
6. What are the types of protection methods included under BTP?

7. Which standard should BTP mechanisms follow?
8. Which criteria are relevant in a BTP evaluation?
9. What is the role of fairness in BTP methods?
10. What is described by threat models?

Acknowledgments This research work has been funded by the German Federal Ministry of Education and Research and the Hessian Ministry of Higher Education, Research, Science, and the Arts within their joint support of the National Research Center for Applied Cybersecurity ATHENE. This research is also based upon work supported by the H2020 TReSPAsS-ETN Marie Skłodowska-Curie early training network (grant agreement 860813).

References

1. Adler, A.: Sample images can be independently restored from face recognition templates. In: Proceedings of the Canadian Conference on Electrical and Computer Engineering (CCECE), pp. 1163–1166 (2003)
2. Adler, A.: Images can be regenerated from quantized biometric match score data. In: Proceedings of the Canadian Conference on Electrical and Computer Engineering (CCECE), pp. 469–472 (2004)
3. Bauspieß, P., Grimmer, M., Fougner, C., Vasseur, D., Thaulow, T., Rathgeb, C., Kolberg, J., Costache, A., Busch, C.: HEBI: Homomorphically encrypted biometric indexing. In: Proceedings of International Joint Conference on Biometrics (IJCB), pp. 1–10. IEEE (2023)
4. Breebaart, J., Busch, C., Grave, J., Kindt, E.: A reference architecture for biometric template protection based on pseudo identities. In: BIOSIG 2008, Proceedings of the Special Interest Group on Biometrics and Electronic Signatures, pp. 25–37. Gesellschaft für Informatik (2008)
5. Cappelli, R., Maio, D., Lumini, A., Maltoni, D.: Fingerprint image reconstruction from standard templates. IEEE Trans. Pattern Analy. Mach. Intell. **29**(9), 1489–1503 (2007)
6. CEN/TC 224/WG 18: CEN NP TS Biometric data injection attack detection. European Committee for Standardization (2021)
7. Cole, F., Belanger, D., Krishnan, D., Sarna, A., Mosseri, I., Freeman, W.T.: Synthesizing normalized faces from facial identity features. In: Proceedings of the IEEE Conference on Computer Vision and Pattern Recognition, pp. 3703–3712 (2017)
8. Deng, J., Guo, J., Xue, N., Zafeiriou, S.: ArcFace: Additive angular margin loss for deep face recognition. In: Conferemce on Computer Vision and Pattern Recognition (CVPR), pp. 4685–4694 (2019)
9. Dong, X., Miao, Z., Ma, L., Shen, J., Jin, Z., Guo, Z., Teoh, A.B.J.: Reconstruct face from features based on genetic algorithm using GAN generator as a distribution constraint. Comput. Secur. **125**, 103026 (2023)
10. Drozdowski, P., Buchmann, N., Rathgeb, C., Margraf, M., Busch, C.: On the application of homomorphic encryption to face identification. In: Proceedings of the IEEE International Conference of the Biometrics Special Interest Group (BIOSIG), pp. 1–5 (2019)
11. Drozdowski, P., Rathgeb, C., Busch, C.: Computational workload in biometric identification systems: an overview. IET Biom. **8**(6), 351–368 (2019)
12. Drozdowski, P., Rathgeb, C., Dantcheva, A., Damer, N., Busch, C.: Demographic bias in biometrics: A survey on an emerging challenge. IEEE Trans. Technol. Soc. **1**(2), 89–103 (2020)
13. Drozdowski, P., Rathgeb, C., Busch, C.: The watchlist imbalance effect in biometric face identification: Comparing theoretical estimates and empiric measurements. In: International Conference on Computer Vision Workshops (ICCVW), pp. 1–9. IEEE/CVF (2021)

14. European Banking Authority: Regulatory technical standards on strong customer authentication and common and secure communication under PSD2 (directive 2015/2366) (2016)
15. European Council: Regulation of the European parliament and of the council on the protection of individuals with regard to the processing of personal data and on the free movement of such data (general data protection regulation) (2016)
16. Ferrara, M., Franco, A., Maltoni, D., Busch, C.: Morphing attack potential. In: 10th International Workshop on Biometrics and Forensics (IWBF) (2022)
17. Galbally, J., McCool, C., Fierrez, J., Marcel, S.: On the vulnerability of face verification systems to hill-climbing attacks. Pattern Recogn. **43**, 1027–1038 (2010)
18. Galbally, J., Ross, A., Gomez-Barrero, M., Fierrez, J., Ortega-Garcia, J.: Iris image reconstruction from binary templates: An efficient probabilistic approach based on genetic algorithms. Comput. Vision Image Understand. **117**(10), 1512–1525 (2013)
19. Godage, S., Løvasdal, F., Venkatesh, S., Raja, K., Raghavendra, R., Busch, C.: Analyzing human observer ability in morphing attack detection - where do we stand? IEEE Trans. Technol. Soc. **4**(2), 125–145 (2023)
20. Gomez-Barrero, M., Galbally, J., Fierrez, J., Ortega-Garcia, J.: Face verification put to test: a hill-climbing attack based on the uphill-simplex algorithm. In: Proceedings of the International Conference. on Biometrics (ICB), pp. 40–45 (2012)
21. Gomez-Barrero, M., Galbally, J., Morales, A., Ferrer, M.A., Fierrez, J., Ortega-Garcia, J.: A novel hand reconstruction approach and its application to vulnerability assessment. Inf. Sci. **268**, 103–121 (2014)
22. Gomez-Barrero, M., Rathgeb, C., Galbally, J., Fierrez, J., Busch, C.: Protected facial biometric templates based on local Gabor patterns and adaptive Bloom filters. In: 2014 22nd International Conference on Pattern Recognition (ICPR), pp. 4483–4488 (2014)
23. Gomez-Barrero, M., Galbally, J., Rathgeb, C., Busch, C.: General framework to evaluate unlinkability in biometric template protection systems. IEEE Trans. Inf. Forensics Secur. **13**(6), 1406–1420 (2017)
24. Gomez-Barrero, M., Galbally, J.: Reversing the irreversible: a survey on inverse biometrics. Comput. Secur. **90**, 101700 (2020)
25. Howard, J., Laird, E., Rubin, R., Siroting, Y., Tipton, J., Vemury, A.: Evaluating proposed fairness models for face recognition algorithms. In: Proceedings of the International Conference on Pattern Recognition (2022)
26. Huang, B., Dai, Y., Li, R., Tang, D., Li, W.: Finger-vein authentication based on wide line detector and pattern normalization. In: 2010 20th international conference on pattern recognition, pp. 1269–1272. IEEE (2010)
27. ISO/IEC JTC1 SC27 Security Techniques: ISO/IEC 24745:2022. Information Technology - Security Techniques - Biometric Information Protection. International Organization for Standardization (2022)
28. ISO/IEC JTC1 SC37 Biometrics: ISO/IEC 19795-1:2006. Information Technology – Biometric Performance Testing and Reporting – Part 1: Principles and Framework. International Organization for Standardization (2006)
29. ISO/IEC JTC1 SC37 Biometrics: ISO/IEC SC37 SD11 General Biometric System. International Organization for Standardization (2010)
30. ISO/IEC JTC1 SC37 Biometrics: ISO/IEC 30136:2018. Information technology – Performance testing of biometric template protection. International Organization for Standardization (2018)
31. ISO/IEC JTC1 SC37 Biometrics: ISO/IEC 19795-1:2021. Information Technology – Biometric Performance Testing and Reporting – Part 1: Principles and Framework. International Organization for Standardization and International Electrotechnical Committee (2021)
32. ISO/IEC JTC1 SC37 Biometrics: ISO/IEC 2382-37:2022 Information Technology - Vocabulary - Part 37: Biometrics. International Organization for Standardization (2022)
33. ISO/IEC JTC1 SC37 Biometrics: ISO/IEC 30107-1:2022. Information Technology - Biometric Presentation Attack Detection - Part 1: Framework. International Organization for Standardization (2023)

34. ISO/IEC JTC1 SC37 Biometrics: ISO/IEC 30107-3. Information Technology - Biometric presentation attack detection - Part 3: Testing and Reporting. International Organization for Standardization (2023)
35. ISO/IEC JTC1 SC37 Biometrics: ISO/IEC 19795-10. Information Technology – Biometric Performance Testing and Reporting – Part 10: Quantifying biometric system performance variation across demographic groups. International Organization for Standardization (2024)
36. Karras, T., Laine, S., Aila, T.: A style-based generator architecture for generative adversarial networks. In: Proceedings of the IEEE/CVF Conference on Computer Vision and Pattern Recognition, pp. 4401–4410 (2019)
37. Kauba, C., Kirchgasser, S., Mirjalili, V., Uhl, A., Ross, A.: Inverse biometrics: Generating vascular images from binary templates. IEEE Trans. Biom. Behav. Identity Sci. **3**(4), 464–478 (2021)
38. Kolberg, J., Drozdowski, P., Gomez-Barrero, M., Rathgeb, C., Busch, C.: Efficiency analysis of post-quantum-secure face template protection schemes based on homomorphic encryption. In: International Conference of the Biometrics Special Interest Group (BIOSIG) (2020)
39. Krivokuća Hahn, V., Marcel, S.: Biometric template protection for neural-network-based face recognition systems: A survey of methods and evaluation techniques. IEEE Trans. Inf. Forensics Secur. **18**, 639–666 (2023). https://doi.org/10.1109/TIFS.2022.3228494
40. Mai, G., Cao, K., Yuen, P.C., Jain, A.K.: On the reconstruction of face images from deep face templates. IEEE Trans. Pattern Analy. Mach. Intell. **41**(5), 1188–1202 (2018)
41. Mandalapu, H., Reddy, P.N.A., Raghavendra, R., Rao, K.S., Mitra, P., Prasanna, S.R.M., Busch, C.: Multilingual audio-visual smartphone dataset and evaluation. IEEE Access **9**, 153240–153257 (2021). https://doi.org/10.1109/ACCESS.2021.3125485
42. Meints, M., Biermann, H., Bromba, M., Busch, C., Hornung, G., Quiring-Kock, G.: Biometric systems and data protection legislation in Germany. In: IEEE Intelligent Information Hiding and Multimedia Signal Processing (IIHMSP09), pp. 1088–1093. IEEE Press (2008)
43. Miura, N., Nagasaka, A., Miyatake, T.: Feature extraction of finger-vein patterns based on repeated line tracking and its application to personal identification. Mach. Vision Appl. **15**, 194–203 (2004)
44. Miura, N., Nagasaka, A., Miyatake, T.: Extraction of finger-vein patterns using maximum curvature points in image profiles. IEICE Trans. Inf. Syst. **90**(8), 1185–1194 (2007)
45. Mohanty, P., Sarkar, S., Kasturi, R.: From scores to face templates: a model-based approach. IEEE Trans. Pattern Analy. Mach. Intell. **29**, 2065–2078 (2007)
46. Nichols, R., Rathgeb, C., Drozdowski, P., Busch, C.: Psychophysical evaluation of human performance in detecting digital face image manipulations. IEEE Access **10**, 31359–31376 (2022)
47. Osorio-Roig, D., Rathgeb, C., Shahreza, H., Busch, C., Marcel, S.: Indexing protected deep face templates by frequent binary patterns. In: 2022 IEEE International Joint Conference on Biometrics (IJCB). IEEE (2022)
48. Priesnitz, J., Rathgeb, C., Buchmann, N., Busch, C.: An overview of touchless 2D fingerprint recognition. EURASIP J. Image Video Process. **2021**, 8 (2021)
49. Purvis-Smith, S.: The Sydney line: a significant sign in Downs syndrome. Aust. Paediatr. J. **8**, 198–200 (1972)
50. Raghavendra, R., Busch, C.: Presentation attack detection methods for face recognition systems: a comprehensive survey. ACM Comput. Surv. **50**(1), 1–37 (2017)
51. Ramoly, N., Komaty, A., Krivokuća Hahn, V., Younes, L., Awal, A.M., Marcel, S.: A novel and responsible dataset for face presentation attack detection on mobile devices. In: The IEEE International Joint Conference on Biometrics, p. 8 (2024)
52. Rathgeb, C., Uhl, A.: Attacking iris recognition: An efficient hill-climbing technique. In: Proceedings of the International Conference on Pattern Recognition (ICPR), pp. 1217–1220 (2010)
53. Rathgeb, C., Uhl, A.: A survey on biometric cryptosystems and cancelable biometrics. EURASIP J. Inf. Secur. **2011**, 1–25 (2011)

54. Rathgeb, C., Breitinger, F., Busch, C.: Alignment-free cancelable iris biometric templates based on adaptive bloom filters. In: 2013 International Conference on Biometrics (ICB), pp. 1–8. IEEE (2013)
55. Ross, A., Shah, J., Jain, A.K.: From template to image: reconstructing fingerprints from minutiae points. IEEE Trans. Pattern Analy. Mach. Intell. **29**, 544–560 (2007)
56. Scherhag, U., Rathgeb, C., Merkle, J., Breithaupt, R., Busch, C.: Face recognition systems under morphing attacks: a survey. IEEE Access **7**, 23012–23026 (2019)
57. Schuckers, S., Hornak, L., Norman, T., Derakhshani, R., Parthasaradhi, S.: Issues for liveness detection in biometrics. In: Proceedings of the Biometric Consortium Conference (2002)
58. Shahreza, H.O., Marcel, S.: Comprehensive vulnerability evaluation of face recognition systems to template inversion attacks via 3d face reconstruction. IEEE Trans. Pattern Analy. Mach. Intell. **45**, 14248–14265 (2023)
59. Shahreza, H.O., Marcel, S.: Face reconstruction from facial templates by learning latent space of a generator network. In: Thirty-Seventh Conference on Neural Information Processing Systems (2023)
60. Shahreza, H.O., Marcel, S.: Template inversion attack against face recognition systems using 3d face reconstruction. In: Proceedings of the IEEE/CVF International Conference on Computer Vision, pp. 19662–19672 (2023)
61. Shahreza, H.O., Marcel, S.: Face reconstruction from partially leaked facial embeddings. In: Proceedings of the IEEE International Conference on Acoustics, Speech and Signal Processing (ICASSP). IEEE (2024)
62. Shahreza, H.O., Marcel, S.: Template inversion attack using synthetic face images against real face recognition systems. IEEE Trans. Biom. Behav. Identity Sci. **6**, 374–384 (2024)
63. Shahreza, H.O., Krivokuća Hahn, V., Marcel, S.: Face reconstruction from deep facial embeddings using a convolutional neural network. In: Proceedings of the IEEE International Conference on Image Processing (ICIP), pp. 1211–1215. IEEE (2022)
64. Shahreza, H.O., Rathgeb, C., Osorio-Roig, D., Krivokuća Hahn, V., Marcel, S., Busch, C.: Hybrid protection of biometric templates by combining homomorphic encryption and cancelable biometrics. In: 2022 IEEE International Joint Conference on Biometrics (IJCB), pp. 1–10. IEEE (2022)
65. Shahreza, H.O., Krivokuća Hahn, V., Marcel, S.: Vulnerability of state-of-the-art face recognition models to template inversion attack. IEEE Trans. Inf. Forensics Secur. **19**, 4585–4600 (2024)
66. Sousedik, C., Busch, C.: Presentation attack detection methods for fingerprint recognition systems: a survey. Biom. IET **3**(1), 1–15 (2014)
67. Stokkenes, M., Raghavendra, R., Mohammadi, A., Venkatesh, S., Raja, K., Wasnik, P., Poiret, E., Marcel, S., Busch, C.: Smartphone Multi-modal Biometric Presentation Attack Detection, pp. 521–544. Springer Nature Singapore, Singapore (2023). https://doi.org/10.1007/978-981-19-5288-3_19
68. Vendrow, E., Vendrow, J.: Realistic face reconstruction from deep embeddings. In: Proceedings of the NeurIPS 2021 Workshop Privacy in Machine Learning (2021)
69. Yang, W., Wang, S., Cui, H., Tang, Z., Li, Y.: A review of homomorphic encryption for privacy-preserving biometrics. Sensors **23**(7), 1–23 (2023)
70. Zwiesele, A., Munde, A., Busch, C., Daum, H.: BioIS study - comparative study of biometric identification systems. In: 34th Annual 2000 IEEE International Carnahan Conference on Security Technology (CCST), pp. 60–63 (2000)

Chapter 2
Traditional and Emerging Data Protection Methods

Marina Blanton

Abstract This chapter treats data protection mechanisms not covered in other parts of the book and examines whether they can be used to protect biometric templates in verification and identification applications. The considered mechanisms include cryptographic, non-cryptographic, and hardware-based solutions, which are divided into traditional and emerging mechanism categories. The chapter demonstrates that many of these protection mechanisms are not suitable as solutions for Biometric Template Protection (BTP). For example, cryptographic constructions such as encryption schemes and hash functions possess strong security properties; however, the strong obfuscation they achieve by erasing all patterns from the input is the reason they are not suitable for working with noisy biometric data. We also discuss potential solutions that rely on distributed databases, smart cards, and trusted execution environments (TEEs) and only consider TEE as conceptually suitable for achieving the necessary security guarantees for protecting biometric templates in verification and identification applications.

1 Introduction

The second part of this book describes techniques and solutions that can be used to protect biometric templates in various applications. The goal of this chapter is to outline several data protection mechanisms not covered in other chapters. In particular, many conventional tools used for data protection, e.g., hash functions or encryption schemes, can be thought of as potential solutions for protecting biometric templates. However, while these tools can be used for achieving strong security properties in other contexts, e.g., for protecting data at rest, they fall short of achieving the necessary security guarantees when used for biometric-based verification or identification.

M. Blanton (✉)
Department of Computer Science and Engineering, University at Buffalo, Buffalo, NY, USA
e-mail: mblanton@buffalo.edu

V. Krivokuća Hahn et al. (eds.), *Handbook of Biometric Template Protection*,
https://doi.org/10.1007/978-981-95-0995-9_2

In this chapter, we discuss traditional data protection mechanisms, including the use of hashing, conventional encryption, distributed databases, and smart cards. Section 2 describes these techniques, as well as why they are, on their own, unable to achieve the desired security properties. We also discuss the use of an emerging technology, Trusted Execution Environment (TEE), as a potential solution to protecting biometric templates. This material is covered in Sect. 3. We afterward conclude and provide questions for further study.

2 Traditional Data Protection Mechanisms

This section discusses traditional data protection mechanisms. We begin with definitions of the relevant methods and then proceed to show why they fall short of achieving the desired security properties for biometric-based verification or identification. We start with cryptographic solutions that use hash-based techniques and conventional encryption, and this is followed by a discussion on distributed databases and smart cards.

2.1 Hashing

A cryptographic hash function is an algorithm that, given a string of arbitrary size, produces a digest that must satisfy certain security properties. More formally, let $h : \{0,1\}^* \rightarrow \{0,1\}^k$ be a hash function that takes an input of arbitrary size and produces a k-bit output. A cryptographic hash function must meet the following security properties:

1. *Preimage resistance:* Let y be the output of h on some input. Given h and y, it is infeasible to find any x such that $h(x) = y$.
2. *Second preimage resistance:* Given h and x, it is infeasible to find x' such that $x' \neq x$ and $h(x') = h(x)$.
3. *Collision resistance:* Given h, it is infeasible to find x and x' such that $x' \neq x$ and $h(x') = h(x)$.

When we say that it is infeasible to find x or x' to violate one of the security properties above, we refer to this term's formulation in a rigorous cryptographic sense. That is, given a security parameter λ, we consider an adversary who can perform arbitrary computation and employ any strategy of their choice in breaking the security. The important assumption is that the adversary is computationally limited and is constrained to run in polynomial time in the security parameter λ.

Definition 1 A function is said to be *negligible* in security parameter λ, denoted by $\mathrm{negl}(\lambda)$, if it diminishes faster than the inverse of any polynomial function in λ.

More precisely, a function $f(\cdot)$ is negligible if for every polynomial $p(\cdot)$ there exists a constant c such that for all $\lambda > c$ it holds that $f(\lambda) < \frac{1}{p(\lambda)}$.

A simple example of a negligible function is $\frac{1}{2^\lambda}$, while more generally any function of the form $\frac{1}{g(\lambda)}$ for a super-polynomial $g(\cdot)$ is negligible. This means that, having control over the security parameter λ, it is always possible to reduce $\mathrm{negl}(\lambda)$ to any sufficiently small value. Going back to the formulation of the security properties of a hash function, "infeasible" means that, given a security parameter λ, any probabilistic polynomial-time adversary has at most negligible probability in violating the property.

In practice, the choice of security parameter λ is driven by our computational abilities and the best known algorithms for breaking the security property in question. For example, performing work on the order of 2^{128} in a reasonable amount of time is considered today to be out of reach. In the context of hash functions, generic attacks on preimage resistance and second preimage resistance require work on the order of 2^k hash function evaluations when the hash function output is k bits long. However, achieving at least 50% probability of success for violating the collision resistance property requires time on the order of $2^{k/2}$ hash function evaluations. This dictates the choice of the hash output length k, which plays the role of the security parameter. That is, achieving 128-bit security while satisfying all three security properties dictates the use of $k = 256$ or longer for constructions without algorithm-specific weaknesses. Hash functions without algorithm-specific weaknesses are those for which there are no faster ways to violate one or more of the security properties than generic attacks, while having an algorithm-specific weakness removes a candidate hash function from consideration as having a design flaw.

Common hash function algorithms used today are SHA-256 and SHA-3 [3, 4]. SHA stands for Secure Hash Algorithms, which are a family of cryptographic hash functions published by the US National Institute of Standards and Technology (NIST). SHA-0 and its revised version SHA-1 were designed by the US government, produce 160-bit output, and are no longer in use due to both short output size and discovered weaknesses. SHA-2 is based on a similar design and supports different block sizes as specified in the names of the hash functions; for example, SHA-256 produces 256-bit hashes, while SHA-512 has a 512-bit output. SHA-3 was adopted most recently after an open public competition process. It has a significantly different design structure from those of the rest of the SHA hash functions and also supports different hash sizes.

Cryptographic hash functions find their uses in a large number of applications. One representative and relevant application is for protecting the storage of passwords. In particular, to prevent recovery of passwords of all users stored in a system in the event of a computer compromise or privilege abuse, passwords are not stored in the clear and are instead hashed. In its simplest form, a user record could look like this:

$$\mathsf{userid},\ h(\mathsf{pwd})$$

This prevents immediate password disclosure and instead requires one to search through the password space to determine a matching password. That is, because a hash function's preimage resistance property guarantees that the hash function is one way, recovering pwd can only be achieved by applying the hash function, h, to different password guesses. For example, to enumerate all eight-character passwords consisting only of English alphabet lowercase letters, one needs to try 26^8 hash function evaluations. A more intelligent attack that tries dictionary words with common substitutions would need to go through all passwords in the dictionary file to determine if pwd is one of them. Verification of a legitimate password, on the other hand, is simple and proceeds by hashing a user-supplied password and comparing it to the stored hash.

Now suppose that we would like to use a similar mechanism for protecting biometric templates. A fundamental challenge arises when we consider that biometric samples (and therefore templates) are noisy and thus do not result in an exact match. This is problematic because cryptographic tools, including hash functions, are designed to amplify input differences in order to produce outputs which are difficult to distinguish from random strings. This means that related biometric templates will produce hashed values with no similarities. For example, consider this 5-byte sequence (listed in binary notation) and another, related, sequence with two bits flipped (marked in bold):

10001**1**0100101001010101**1**11010101110010011

10001**0**0100101001010101**0**11010101110010011

The corresponding SHA-256 hashes (in hexadecimal) are

978959aca040da961eba72299cd04d39bf7dadf1eeea6e9aeacfa4b8371cf974
8aa4b2c0a9a6ded735627c5da8bc54d4b5768bccccd3a360497e2d4a3c76b8fd

Therefore, since even small differences between a reference and probe biometric template would result in completely different hashes, cryptographic hashing does not work as a protection mechanism for biometric data.

Now consider that we would like to apply a hash function in a different way. Because a biometric template (after feature extraction) is represented by a number of elements, we could apply the hash function to each element of the template separately instead of to the template as a whole. That is, given a biometric template $B = (b_1, b_2, \ldots, b_n)$, we would have the server store

$$h(b_1), h(b_2), \ldots, h(b_n)$$

Then two biometric representations would be considered a match if the number of the elements equal to each other is above a predefined threshold.

With this solution, if the individual elements are sufficiently fine-grained, we are looking for exact equality, and the use of a hash function would not interfere with matching. However, this approach does not lead to adequate protection of the stored templates. That is, because each element comes from a small space, it is possible for someone with access to the database to hash all possible values for individual elements b_i of the biometric template and consequently recover the templates stored at the server.

2.2 Conventional Encryption

General-purpose encryption provides strong data confidentiality protection against anyone without access to the decryption key. An encryption scheme is defined by three algorithms: key generation KeyGen that takes a security parameter and produces a fresh key, encryption Enc that takes a message and a key and produces a ciphertext, and decryption Dec that takes a ciphertext and a key and produces a decrypted message or outputs failure.

Encryption can be *symmetric*, which may also be called secret key, or asymmetric, which is widely known as *public key*. Symmetric encryption uses the same key for encryption and decryption, and thus the key must remain private. That is, given a key k generated according to the corresponding key generation algorithm, we encrypt a message m to obtain a ciphertext c as $c = \mathsf{Enc}(k, m)$, and we decrypt a ciphertext c to obtain the corresponding plaintext m as $m = \mathsf{Dec}(k, c)$.

With public-key encryption, on the other hand, key generation produces a key pair $(\mathsf{pk}, \mathsf{sk})$, where pk is a public key, which is widely disseminated, and sk is the corresponding private (secret) key. Anyone with access to the public key can encrypt a plaintext message m as $c = \mathsf{Enc}(pk, m)$, while only the key owner with access to the private key sk will be able to decrypt the ciphertext c as $m = \mathsf{Dec}(sk, c)$.

Symmetric and public-key encryption schemes have fundamentally different designs, which reflects on their speed. Symmetric encryption is normally realized using a block cipher, while public-key encryption uses number-theoretic constructions. Symmetric encryption algorithms are significantly faster than public-key encryption, while public-key cryptography is more powerful and allows for additional functionalities which cannot be realized by means of symmetric key primitives alone.

Secure encryption of any kind must meet stringent security requirements. There are different formulations of security based on the capabilities an adversary is assumed to have. However, for a general-purpose encryption algorithm to be of practical relevance, it must be secure at least against what is known as ciphertext *indistinguishability* under an *adaptive chosen plaintext attack* (CPA). The intuition is that a realistic adversary, who is allowed to receive multiple encrypted messages and influence what is being encrypted, should be unable to obtain any information about the content that a ciphertext encrypts besides the obvious observable information such as the ciphertext size. More formally, an adversary is allowed to request encryptions of messages of their choice and at some point produces two messages of the same size. One of those messages, the challenge, is encrypted, and the ciphertext is given to the adversary. The adversary's goal is to determine which message from those two was encrypted.

Similar to other cryptographic functionalities, security guarantees are tied to a security parameter specified at key generation time. As before, the adversary is bound to run in polynomial time in the security parameter, and now the adversary's success beyond a random guess in determining which message was chosen as the challenge is bound by a probability negligible in the security parameter. Once again, the security parameter is guided by the best known algorithms for breaking the security of a construction. Public-key encryption algorithms require larger key and message sizes than symmetric key encryption, and this is what contributes to the performance gap.

The formulation of secure encryption above requires that no information about encrypted messages can be deduced by analyzing ciphertexts. An important implication of the above is that an adversary is unable to tell whether two different ciphertexts encrypt the same message. This means that secure encryption is necessarily randomized: A single message encrypts to a large number of possible ciphertexts using randomness drawn at the time of encryption, and a ciphertext is longer than the original plaintext.

Now, let us return to the task of securely comparing two biometric templates. For concreteness, let us assume symmetric encryption with ciphertexts of the form $c = \mathsf{Enc}(k, m)$. This can be realized by using a strong block cipher such as AES [2] in a secure encryption mode. Then encrypting a biometric template and storing the ciphertext on a server will not allow the server to discover any information about the biometric if it does not possess the key.

Now, a challenge arises when we would like to compare two biometric templates in a protected form. Because encrypting the same message multiple times produces different ciphertexts, two ciphertexts cannot be meaningfully compared to determine if they encrypt the same message. Otherwise, the encryption discloses information about whether two ciphertexts have the same plaintext content, trivially violating the necessary security guarantees.

Suppose that we degrade security to use a deterministic encryption algorithm (which on the same key-message pair always produces the same output) such as a plain invocation of a block cipher, which does not qualify as secure encryption. Even in that case, comparing two biometric templates in an encrypted form is not feasible. This, once again, stems from the fact that biometric templates are approximate and differ with each capture of the biometric sample. Cryptographic tools, on the other hand, and encryption in particular, are designed to amplify any differences in the input. Specifically in the context of block ciphers, a 1-bit difference in a plaintext block impacts all of the bits of the corresponding ciphertext block, obfuscating all information about input similarities. This is an intentional design choice of block cipher algorithms to erase any patterns from a ciphertext.

Now consider the possibility that the server is granted access to the key at the time of biometric matching: It decrypts a stored encrypted template, performs the comparison, and securely erases the decrypted value. Unfortunately, this variant does not meet the expected security guarantees. Namely, the server gains cleartext (i.e., unprotected) access to sensitive biometric data, which is no longer protected. Then any abuse of the system in the form of insider access or system compromise can lead to large-scale disclosure of sensitive biometric information.

2.3 *Distributed Databases*

A distributed database corresponds to multiple interconnected databases distributed across different physical locations or computers. The design goals are to improve performance (e.g., throughput and latency of content delivery to users), availability, security (e.g., fault tolerance), and scalability. In the context of this chapter, we are interested in investigating whether the use of distributed databases could also aid in protecting the privacy of biometric templates.

A possible solution could be to distribute biometric data in such a way that the entire database of biometric templates is not available on a single computer or at a single location. For example, we could partition a biometric template so that a portion of it is stored at one location, another portion at a different location, etc. Unfortunately, this approach does not lead to adequate protection: Sensitive biometric data is still accessible to the servers, and they compare templates in the clear (which leads to opportunities for abuse).

2.4 *Smart Cards*

Another possible mechanism for protecting sensitive biometric templates is to store them on smart cards that will control how the biometric template is accessed. Because the goal is to protect biometric data from the server, a smart card will need to be able to determine the outcome (e.g., recognition decision) without sending a user's biometric data to the server. This means that each user's template would need to be stored on a separate smart card, which makes this approach unsuitable for identification. Thus, we can only attempt to realize verification in this distributed setting.

A smart card is a physical card with an embedded integrated circuit that has limited storage and limited computational capabilities. It is powered by a smart card reader and interacts with it. Smart cards are designed to be tamper-resistant and use encryption to protect their memory content. They find uses in various domains, often providing authentication and other functionalities.

If we would like to employ a solution that relies on a smart card for biometric verification, the card issuer would first take a biometric reading and load the corresponding biometric template on a card. Then at the time of verification, the user would take a fresh biometric reading, which would be processed and communicated to the smart card to perform approximate matching with the template it stores.

Conceptually, this accomplishes the goal of biometric-based verification but falls short of providing critical properties.

The most profound drawback is that biometric templates are not protected from the entity issuing smart cards. That is, for a user to register for the service and obtain a smart card, the service provider needs to receive the user's biometric template and load it onto the user's smart card. This means that the service provider still sees all biometric templates and is able to store them. Once again, this opens up opportunities for abuse of sensitive biometric data.

Besides privacy concerns, this solution also has significant usability drawbacks. First, a user's biometric template needs to be available at the physical location where smart cards are issued if we want to minimize the template's exposure. Second, using smart cards with biometric templates requires both a biometric reader and a smart card reader at the time of verification. This limits the applicability of this approach and does not make it suitable for mobile or desktop users.

3 Emerging Data Protection Mechanisms

Besides exploring conventional data protection mechanisms, we can also turn our attention to emerging technologies such as Trusted Execution Environments (TEEs). A TEE is an isolated area of a CPU that allows us to securely execute applications on private data. This includes confidentiality and integrity protection of data used in the computation and using only trusted software to work with the data.

Hardware isolation prevents other processes (including the operating system and other users) from observing the data placed inside the TEE. The TEE also comes with private keys embedded directly into the chip at manufacturing time. This private key material is likewise not accessible outside the TEE. Any software executed by the TEE must be certified using a key to which the TEE can build a chain of trust from a key loaded into it.

The notion of *chain of trust* is a common security concept that refers to a sequence of certificates from a public key that one trusts to a public key that needs to be verified. A *certificate* is a credential that permits one to verify the validity of the (public) key of an unfamiliar entity and use the key in security applications. In the simplest form, a certificate is a binding between the name of the entity and its public key, but often it contains additional data including the expiration date. The binding is achieved by means of a digital signature, which for an entity with name A and public key pk_A looks as follows:

$$\mathsf{data} = (A, \mathsf{pk}_A, \ldots), \sigma_{CA}(\mathsf{data}).$$

Here, let CA be a certification authority that we trust, and let $(\mathsf{pk}_{CA}, \mathsf{sk}_{CA})$ be the authority's public-private key pair. The trust is typically achieved by preloading CA's public key pk_{CA} into one's computer. $\sigma_{CA}(\mathsf{data})$ is a cryptographic signature on input data produced using the private portion sk_{CA} of CA's key. A *signature scheme* is a cryptographic tool that uses public-key cryptography for ensuring data integrity. It guarantees a strong security property called *existential unforgeability*. Informally, a signature scheme is existentially unforgeable when it is infeasible for someone without access to the private key to produce a signature on any new message that has not been previously signed using that key. A signature is verified using the corresponding public key. As before, "infeasible" means having at most negligible probability in the appropriate security parameter of succeeding in this task.

As a result, a certificate produced by an authority we trust provides validation of the data included in the certificate and extends the trust to another party. That is, if we believe that *CA* will not sign bogus data, we now have assurance that pk_A is the key associated with *A*, and we can trust it. For example, if *A* is an online retailer, we can use pk_A to securely communicate payment information to *A* over the insecure Internet.

In the context of the current discussion, the key that the TEE trusts is the signing key of a certification authority which was loaded into the TEE at manufacturing time. The key that needs to be verified is the key with which the software to be run by the TEE was signed. The path from the trusted key to the key we want to use can be longer than of length 1. In that case, we follow and verify a sequence of certificates. For example, if we trust key pk_{CA} and would like to verify key pk_A which *CA* did not sign, we need to find a sequence of certificates from *CA* to *A*, e.g., *CA* signed the key of *B* and *B* signed the key of *A*. This is why we refer to the concept as a chain of trust.

This process prevents TEEs from executing unauthorized software. In addition, any software that has been certified but subsequently altered will also fail verification and thus will fail to run. On the other hand, software that passes verification can be executed by the TEE and obtains access to the privileged information stored inside the TEE. Thus, this mechanism permits only trustworthy applications to access and handle data within the TEE.

When the application is not running, it can store private data outside the TEE in a protected form. The protection mechanism must guarantee both data confidentiality and integrity, which can be achieved by means of *authenticated encryption* designed to meet both security objectives at once.

We can imagine building an application that handles protected biometric templates for verification or identification purposes as follows:

1. When a biometric sample is captured (e.g., a fingerprint or face image), it will be processed and securely communicated to the TEE by trusted software run by the TEE.
2. The trusted software can use the key material embedded in the TEE to apply confidentiality and integrity protection to the biometric template and store it outside of the trusted environment.
3. Additional encrypted templates can be added to the protected storage over time when new individuals enroll.

4. When a new biometric sample is to be compared to one or more templates in the secure storage, the trusted software will load a protected reference template (from the secure storage) into the trusted environment, verify its integrity, decrypt it, and then compare the template from the new (probe) biometric sample to the stored (decrypted) template.

This conceptual realization of biometric verification or identification achieves proper protection of biometric templates. That is, both confidentiality and integrity of biometric templates are achieved when they are stored outside of the TEE. Furthermore, when biometric templates are processed, all operations on cleartext biometric data are performed securely in the isolated environment using key material inaccessible to the operating system and users of the system.

While conceptually attractive, realizations of TEE-based solutions in practice require additional considerations and have certain drawbacks. Potential areas of concern include:

1. The solution requires hardware support and cannot be realized on systems where the processor, the motherboard, or the operating system does not support TEE or on which the support is not enabled in the BIOS. Many computers are now capable of supporting a TEE.
2. The solution requires software attestation and certification. This is the most complex component of the process, because it requires proper management of various keys and ensuring that software being certified meets certain expectations (e.g., does not have vulnerabilities).
3. Most importantly, TEE is a relatively new technology and may not exhibit the level of maturity necessary for security applications. We can demonstrate that on the example of Intel SGX [1], which is a popular realization of the TEE architecture. A number of attacks and vulnerabilities on Intel SGX have been discovered that can lead to significant security violations (see, e.g., [6, 7]). One illustrative example is an attack on the chain of trust that allows for the recovery of a private key, which in turn enables execution of illegitimate software inside the SGX [5]. In the context of protecting biometric templates using TEE as described earlier, a successful attack of this kind would permit malicious software to obtain access to both stored biometric templates and incoming biometric samples and perform arbitrary actions with them.

Thus, additional work needs to be conducted before TEE-based constructions can become a reliable solution for biometric template protection.

4 Conclusions

In this chapter, we discussed a couple of traditional cryptographic tools that are often used as data protection mechanisms. They include hash functions and standard encryption. We showed that it is challenging to use these tools by themselves to achieve adequate biometric template protection for the purposes of verification or identification. The main challenge stems from the misalignment of the properties of cryptographic tools and biometric matching mechanisms: Cryptographic tools are designed to destroy any patterns in the data to which they are applied, while biometric data is inherently noisy and thus requires approximate matching. Other mechanisms that provide certain security properties, such as distributed databases and smart cards, are also not suitable for this purpose because they do not provide data confidentiality guarantees.

Trusted Execution Environments, an emerging technology, can be utilized to build a solution that supports secure storage of biometric templates and performs biometric matching by relying on hardware isolation. The main challenge here is that this is a relatively recent technology, which may not yet be widely adopted, may not have a desired level of maturity, and thus may be prone to attacks.

5 Summary

Traditional data protection mechanisms in the context of biometric template protection:

- **Hash functions** compute a fixed-length digest given an arbitrary-length input:
  - Hash functions have the one-way and collision resistance properties.
  - Hashes of two related biometric samples do not have any similarities.
  - Hashing individual elements of a biometric template does not achieve confidentiality.
- **Encryption** provides strong confidentiality guarantees as long as the decryption key is private:
  - Ciphertexts cannot be meaningfully compared for biometric matching purposes.
  - Downgrading security to deterministic obfuscation still does not permit comparison of noisy biometric samples or templates.
  - Access to the decryption key during biometric matching nullifies protection offered by encryption.
- **Distributed databases** and **smart cards** do not provide data confidentiality guarantees.

Emerging data protection mechanisms:

- **Trusted Execution Environments (TEEs)** rely on hardware isolation to achieve strong security properties:
  - Unprotected biometric templates reside only inside the TEE and are stored protected outside the TEE.

– Decryption keys are used during biometric matching and are not accessible outside the TEE.
– TEE realizations have been a subject of powerful attacks.

6 Study Questions

1. What purpose does a security parameter play in cryptographic constructions such as encryption schemes and hash functions?
2. Recall the simple mechanism for protecting stored user passwords described in Sect. 2.1. Now suppose that it is used for protecting the PIN number associated with a user's bank card. How many hash invocations would an attacker with access to the storage need to try to recover a user's four-digit PIN stored in this form?
3. Suppose that someone uses deterministic encryption and sends a sequence of ciphertexts, where each ciphertext encrypts a single letter of the message. What can an adversary observing the sequence of transmitted ciphertexts deduce about the (plaintext) message?
4. Section 2.2 mentioned that block ciphers are designed in such a way that a single-bit difference in the input block (plaintext) impacts all bits of the produced output block (ciphertext). This is achieved by relying on the fact that block ciphers operate in rounds, where the difference gets amplified from one round to another. That is, a 1-bit difference in the input to round 1 results in a 2-bit difference in the output from that round, a 2-bit difference in the input to round 2 results in a 4-bit difference in the output from round 2, etc. What is the minimum number of rounds that a block cipher with n-bit blocks needs to have to guarantee that a 1-bit difference in the input plaintext impacts all n bits of the output ciphertext?
5. By going through your web browser's settings, can you determine how many certification authorities your browser recognizes?
6. What is the reason that a malicious user with access to the computer, the TEE of which performs privacy-preserving biometric matching, is unable to recover stored biometric templates?

References

1. Intel Software Guard Extensions (SGX). https://www.intel.com/content/www/us/en/products/docs/accelerator-engines/software-guard-extensions.html
2. National Institute of Standards and Technology: Advanced Encryption Standard (AES). FIPS 197 (2001). https://doi.org/10.6028/NIST.FIPS.197-upd1
3. National Institute of Standards and Technology: Secure Hash Standards (2015). https://doi.org/10.6028/NIST.FIPS.180-4

4. National Institute of Standards and Technology: SHA-3 Standard: Permutation-Based Hash and Extendable-Output Functions. FIPS 202 (2015). https://doi.org/10.6028/NIST.FIPS.202
5. van Schaik, S., Kwong, A., Genkin, D., Yarom, Y.: SGAxe: How SGX fails in practice. https://sgaxe.com/ (2020)
6. Vulnerability CVE-2022-33196 (2023). https://cve.mitre.org/cgi-bin/cvename.cgi?name=CVE-2022-33196
7. Vulnerability CVE-2022-38090 (2023). https://cve.mitre.org/cgi-bin/cvename.cgi?name=CVE-2022-38090

Chapter 3
A Legal Obligation to Protect Biometric Information: A Brief Analysis

Els J. Kindt and Catherine Jasserand

Abstract Due to technical advancements, biometric information can easily be collected and used, possibly compromising the security of the data and allowing the reconstruction of the biometric features of individuals. In that context, Biometric Template Protection (BTP) techniques promise to ensure both the security and privacy of biometric templates. The purpose of this chapter is to address biometric template protection from a regulatory and data privacy perspective. We will first briefly present a summary of the uses of biometric information in various domains and the related risks to biometric data. We also remind the reader of the legal concept of biometric data and information. We point to different legal approaches, in particular in the European Union (the GDPR), in the Council of Europe (the Convention 108+), and in the USA (through various states' legislation and also omnibus data privacy acts such as in California). A brief analysis of the advantages offered by protected biometric templates will be made, followed by a presentation of the criteria to ascertain when data are personal data. There is an ongoing discussion about the qualification of protected biometric templates under data privacy rules, as to whether they still relate to an identified or identifiable individual (and are thus personal data) or whether they can be considered anonymous data.

E. J. Kindt (✉)
eLaw, Universiteit Leiden, Leiden, The Netherlands

CiTiP, Faculty of Law and Criminology, KU Leuven, Leuven, Belgium
e-mail: els.kindt@kuleuven.be

C. Jasserand
STeP, Faculty of Law, University of Groningen, Groningen, The Netherlands

CiTiP, Faculty of Law and Criminology, KU Leuven, Leuven, Belgium
e-mail: c.a.jasserand@rug.nl

V. Krivokuća Hahn et al. (eds.), *Handbook of Biometric Template Protection*,
https://doi.org/10.1007/978-981-95-0995-9_3

1 Introduction

This chapter addresses the protection of biometric templates from a data privacy and Artificial Intelligence (AI) perspective.[1] Due to technical advancements, traditional biometric templates are easy to attack, compromising the security of the personal data they relate to and allowing the reconstruction of the biometric features from which the templates were generated [18]. In that context, can Biometric Template Protection (BTP) techniques ensure both the security and privacy of biometric templates? From a data privacy perspective, using BTP techniques raises two interesting legal issues. The first one relates to BTP techniques as privacy-enhancing solutions. The second question concerns the status of protected biometric templates ("PBTs") under data privacy rules: Do PBTs still "relate" to an identified or identifiable individual (and are PBTs thus personal data), or can PBTs be considered anonymous data?

This chapter will first recapitulate in Sect. 2 how biometric technologies and the capture of biometric information have become part of our daily lives and are used by the private and public sectors. From these multitudes of uses of the technologies for various reasons, specific risks and concerns arise. Building on this analysis, Sect. 3 presents a summary of the regulatory approaches to biometric data processing, including a comparison between the different legal frameworks in Europe and outside Europe (mainly the USA). Section 4 then discusses PBTs from a data protection point of view and whether or not PBTs could be considered anonymous.

2 Biometric Technologies: Applications, Risks, and Concerns

In Sect. 2.1, we describe examples of some of the most common biometric applications, and in Sect. 2.2 we explain the risks and concerns resulting from the use of biometric technologies.

2.1 *Applications of Biometric Technologies in Daily Life*

Biometric technologies have become part of our daily lives. They are used by the public and private sectors in applications such as border control (e.g. for identity

[1] In this chapter, we use "data protection" and "data privacy protection" indifferently. In Europe, the term "data protection" is commonly used to refer to the protection of personal data as regulated by the GDPR and related legislation, whereas outside Europe (e.g. in the USA), the term commonly employed is "data privacy" and is linked with personally identifiable information. With "PBTs" we refer to the noun of protected biometric templates as such, while BTP refers to the verb of protecting biometric templates and its techniques. We further use and adhere to the biometric vocabulary as set forth in the international standard ISO/IEC 2382-37, 3rd edition, 2022-03.

checks), banking (e.g. for ID management and payment services), criminal investigations (e.g. for identification purposes), public transport (e.g. for surveillance purposes or smart ticketing), schools (e.g. for access control or payment purposes), and access to applications through smart devices (e.g. logging into a smartphone through a fingerprint or via facial recognition). We describe this further below.

Border Control

For the past two decades, biometric technologies have been increasingly used for border control, at the entrance and sometimes the exit of a country (such as the United States of America) or a common area (such as the Schengen Area in Europe). Different technologies are used: first for verification purposes (a comparison of a (live) image with the facial image contained in an ID or a passport document) and then for identification purposes (to see if an individual entering a country is known in given criminal databases or in large-scale EU information systems or to check whether the individual still fulfils the conditions of a temporary stay). Border controls were initially limited and often focused on identity verification. However, access to border management databases has repeatedly been expanded and extended to law enforcement authorities.[2] As a result, the biometric systems used at the borders perform both verification and identification processes. Fingerprint and facial recognition technologies are commonly used, but other biometric modalities, such as iris or palm prints, can be added [16].

Banking Sector

Biometric technologies are used in the banking sector for security (e.g. to secure access to a service) but also for convenience (for seamless access). Face recognition and voice recognition are usually used for verification (sometimes also commonly called authentication) purposes. Iris recognition and behavioural biometric recognition systems are also considered. According to Allied Market Research, the biometric banking market is expected to grow to 127.32 billion dollars by 2032.[3]

Law Enforcement

One of the initial uses of biometric data was in the context of criminal investigations, to identify a suspect by comparing fingerprints. This comparison was originally performed manually. The techniques have immensely improved, relying on pattern and computer image processing and vision techniques among others. Law enforcement authorities are using not only fingerprints, but also face, voice, gait, and other behavioural recognition technologies.

[2] See, for instance, the EURODAC (fingerprint) database for asylum seekers in the EU and its expansion in 2013 to law enforcement authorities' access by Regulation (EU) 603/2013.

[3] https://www.alliedmarketresearch.com/press-release/biometric-technology-market.html

Access to Services and Applications

Biometric technologies have multiple other uses, including controlling access to public transportation, schools, sports arenas, mobile devices, or online applications. Not all the uses are permitted. For instance, concerning the use of facial recognition to access sports arenas and schools, the French Data Protection Authority, called the CNIL, found no legal basis, justification or necessity to trial these systems on fans in football arenas[4] and on minors in schools.[5] Concerning the use of facial recognition technologies (FRTs) in schools, an administrative Court in France found it disproportionate and unnecessary.[6] In Sweden, a school was fined for deploying FRTs.[7]

2.2 *Risks and Concerns*

From these multiple uses of biometric technologies, specific risks and concerns arise. Those can be linked, among others, to data sharing (without consent or any other legal basis) or data reuse, including by parties that should not have access to the data in the first place, identity theft, impersonation for identity frauds that represent a serious threat with the growing use of malicious deepfakes relying on biometric information, as well as risks linked to the way models are trained with datasets that might embed biases and generate discrimination.

3 Regulatory Approaches to Biometric Data Processing and Technologies

Biometric technologies process biometric information from the capture of the biometric characteristics to their transformation into templates, the format of which allows their comparison with previously recorded templates. From a technical perspective, biometric information and biometric data can take different forms. But when is biometric data considered personal data and biometric personal data from a data privacy perspective?[8] As explained in this section, the General Data Protection

[4] CNIL, *Reconnaissance faciale et interdiction commercial de stade: la CNIL adresse un avertissement à un club sportif*, 18.02.2021; see analysis in Jasserand C. (2021), *Yellow Card to a French Football Club: No Facial Recognition System to Monitor their Supporters*, CiTiP blog.

[5] For the CNIL's position, see CNIL, *Expérimentation de la reconnaissance faciale dans deux lycées: la CNIL précise sa position*, 29.11.2019.

[6] Administrative Court of Marseille, 27 February 2020, available at https://www.laquadrature.net/wp-content/uploads/sites/8/2020/02/1090394890_1901249.pdf.

[7] See EDPB, *Facial recognition in school renders Sweden's first GDPR fine*, 22 August 2019.

[8] Biometric data fall into the category of biometric personal data if they meet the criteria applicable to biometric data (including the functionality criterion) as defined in the GDPR. If the data do not meet the criteria for biometric data, such data can still fall into the generic and broader category of personal data. The distinction is further explained in Sect. 3.1.1.

Regulation (GDPR) has introduced in the general EU data protection landscape the legal concept of biometric data, as is the case in Convention 108+ and foreign legislation outside the EU.

This section will describe the different data protection regimes and will provide some elements for comparison with several US state laws. Beyond the GDPR and data protection regulation, a few elements from the EU AI Act will also be discussed.

3.1 Data Protection Regulations

This subsection will provide a brief overview of data protection rules in Europe and in the United States, explaining, among others, the legal concept of biometric data, the notions of identification and identifiability from a legal perspective, and the ad hoc legislation in the United States.

3.1.1 Europe

Different Frameworks

In Europe, a distinction should be made between the European Union ("EU" or "Union") level, which consists of 27 Member States, and the level of the Council of Europe, which is a pan-European institution with 46 Members, including Turkey.

At the EU level, the most important instrument in terms of data protection legislation is the General Data Protection Regulation, known as the GDPR [14]. The GDPR provides rules applicable to the processing of personal data, obligations for the entities processing these data (controllers and processors) and rights for the data subjects, i.e. the individuals to whom the personal data relate.[9] The Law Enforcement Directive, or LED, complements the GDPR [13]. The LED provides the rules applicable to the processing of personal data in the field of law enforcement. Contrary to the GDPR, the LED is not directly applicable in the Member States but needs to be transposed into national laws by the Member States.

At the Council of Europe level, Convention 108+, the modernised version of Convention 108 adopted in 1981, provides rules applicable to the processing of personal data, including in the law enforcement domain. Its provisions are aligned with the GDPR's and LED's provisions but are not entirely similar as explained below [5].

[9] The GDPR replaces the previous Data Protection Directive, Directive 95/46/EC, which was not suitable for regulating issues arising from the new technological environment.

Legal Concept of Biometric Data

The GDPR and the LED have introduced a legal definition of biometric data in the realm of personal data. Under the previous regime of the 1995 Data Protection Directive, the European Data Protection Supervisor viewed biometric data as "sensitive", while no official definition existed.

A legal definition of biometric data was only introduced in 2016 in the general EU data protection landscape in the GDPR and LED. Previously, biometric data were not defined from a data protection perspective.

According to Article 4(14) GDPR and Article 3(13) LED, biometric data are:

> Personal data resulting from specific technical processing relating to the physical, physiological or behavioural characteristics of a natural person, which allow or confirm the unique identification of that natural person, such as facial images or dactyloscopic data.

Biometric data must, according to this definition, meet four criteria:

1. As a pre-requisite, the data shall meet the characteristics of personal data, as defined in Article 4(1) GDPR / Article 3(1) LED.
2. The data result from "specific technical processing".
3. The data relate to biometric characteristics, described as physical, physiological, or behavioural characteristics.
4. The data allow or confirm the unique identification of a natural person.

No further precision is made about the terminology used in that definition, except that in the context of the GDPR, photographs are not systematically considered biometric data. According to Recital 51 GDPR, photographs must undergo processing "through specific technical means", allowing "unique identification or authentication". So, facial images processed, i.e. transformed (such as, e.g. passed through a feature extractor to generate the representative templates), for biometric recognition would be considered biometric data, whereas photographs that might have sufficient quality to be used for facial recognition but are not processed or transformed for that purpose might not be considered biometric data from this perspective.

The definition of biometric data is tied to that of personal data. According to Article 4(1) GDPR / Article 3(1) LED, personal data are defined as:

> any information relating to an identified or identifiable natural person; an identifiable natural person is one who can be identified, directly or indirectly, in particular by reference to an identifier such as a name, an identification number, location data, an online identifier or to one or more factors specific to the physical, physiological, genetic, mental, economic, cultural or social identity of that natural person.

Identifiability, Identification, and Unique Identification

From a data protection perspective, the identification threshold in the GDPR is low as *individuals* to whom the personal data relate *do not need to be identified but only identifiable*. The identification can be direct or indirect, with a combination of elements. In that context, identification does not necessarily mean establishing someone's identity and also includes being able *to single someone out* or *to distinguish* someone from a group of individuals [10]. Concerning *unique identification*, the concept already existed under the previous data protection regime. Some authors considered it the "highest degree of identification" achieved through data that create a unique link to an individual. According to some scholars, such data include biometric or genetic data, e.g. [29]. Some authors have built on this interpretation to suggest that unique identification in the context of biometric data does not refer to a specific biometric recognition operation but to a threshold of identification from a regulatory perspective. While some types of personal data, such as a person's address, might not always be distinctive enough to single someone out, e.g. because several persons may live at the same address, biometric data, genetic data, and a unique identifier number (such as a social security number) are. Subsequently, these authors argue that both biometric recognition operations, i.e. biometric identification or verification, allow for the *singling out* of an individual and, thus, for the unique identification of a person with their biometric data [23]. This is also the approach favoured by the Information Commissioner's Office in the UK ("ICO") in their Biometric Data Guidance on Facial Recognition [21]. In their guidance, they consider that when biometric data are used for purposes other than biometric recognition (which covers both identification and verification operations), such as categorisation (i.e. classifying individuals only based on their gender or age, for instance), the data are not processed to uniquely identify someone. However, other scholars consider that *unique identification* is limited to biometric identification. Consequently, they exclude the processing of biometric data for verification purposes from the scope of forbidden (safe exceptions) "sensitive" biometric data processing as regulated in Article 9 GDPR [30].

Establishing the meaning of "unique identification" goes beyond a terminological discussion as the criterion is also used to determine when biometric data processing qualifies as "sensitive" biometric data processing in Article 9 GDPR. Sensitive data are specific categories of personal data subject to a higher level of protection due to their nature (some concern health, or reveal political views, religious beliefs, or sexual orientation) or to their processing purpose (like "unique identification" by biometric data).[10] Under the GDPR regime, the processing of "sensitive" data is *prohibited unless one of the ten exceptions applies.*[11] These exceptions include an individual's explicit consent, substantial public interest, public health, vital interests, and scientific or historical research purposes (under specific conditions).

Formats: From Samples to Templates

Besides the meaning of "unique identification", the definition of biometric data raises another issue concerning the meaning of "specific technical processing".

[10] Article 9(1) GDPR and Article 10 LED; both articles provide a limitative list of "sensitive data", the processing of which is, according to the GDPR, in principle forbidden save exceptions.

[11] Article 9(2) GDPR; the regime applicable to sensitive data processed for law enforcement purposes is different.

Which data formats are covered by the definition? Recital 51 GDPR explains that (pre-processed) photographs, i.e. untransformed, are excluded from the scope of biometric data, as mentioned above. By contrast, processed or transformed facial images to perform facial recognition are covered, as they are also cited as an example of biometric data in the definition. Logically, the definition should also cover templates resulting from a mathematical representation of the salient features used for biometric recognition. The nature of biometric templates as personal data has been the subject of doctrinal discussions. In the 1990s, for example, it was believed that information from which biometric templates had been generated could not be reconstructed. Consequently, some authors considered biometric templates anonymous data [19]. Since these initial beliefs, it has been demonstrated that this assumption is not correct, as templates can still be compared and because biometric templates are reversible in the sense that biometric samples can be reconstructed, e.g. [2].[12] We discuss this further in Sect. 4. We also explain that the *discussion on the nature of biometric templates has shifted to protected biometric templates*, in particular, whether they still have characteristics that can be considered personal data or even biometric data.

Obligations Linked to Biometric Data Processing

Different *obligations* are linked to the processing of biometric data. When biometric data are processed at a large scale or used to monitor publicly accessible areas systematically, their processing is subject to a Data Protection Impact Assessment (DPIA).[13] A DPIA is a mechanism, a tool, through which data controllers, i.e. those responsible for the processing operations, will assess the risks that a processing operation entails for individuals' rights and freedoms. They will identify the risks, the legal basis for the processing, and the corrective measures to address them.

Furthermore, data controllers must implement "Data Protection by Design and by Default" measures, which are inspired by the concept of Privacy by Design, to take into account data privacy issues at the design stage of a product, service, or system [3]. Data controllers must adopt technical and organisational measures to implement data protection principles, integrate safeguards to protect individuals' rights and freedoms, and respect the data minimisation requirement.[14] These "technical and organisational" measures are not defined. However, the GDPR and the LED give the example of pseudonymisation techniques as such measures. BTP could be considered, without a doubt, as a (mandatory) technique for data protection by design and default.

Beyond the EU, Convention 108+

Beyond the EU but still in Europe, Convention 108, the first binding instrument on data protection at the international level, was revised in 2018 to align its provisions

---

[12] See also the discussion on template inversion in Part I, Chap. 1 of this handbook.

[13] Article 35(1) GDPR and Article 27(1) LED.

[14] Article 25 GDPR and Article 20 LED.

with the EU data protection rules, which include the GDPR and the LED. The revised version of the Convention is called Convention 108+. That new version includes biometric data within the data protection landscape of the Convention. The Explanatory Report to Convention 108+ defines biometric data as:

> data resulting from a specific technical processing of data concerning the physical, biological or physiological characteristics of an individual which allows the unique identification or authentication of the individual.

The difference between the definition in the GDPR/LED and that in Convention 108+ lies in the description of the functionality of biometric data. The purpose of processing is described here as unique identification or authentication, the latter often understood as verification [11]. Yet, only biometric data used to uniquely identify an individual are considered sensitive.[15] From the wording, Convention 108+ excludes biometric data processed for verification purposes from the scope of sensitive biometric data. However, as mentioned in the analysis of the GDPR/LED, biometric data processed for other purposes that would reveal "sensitive" information are, and should still be considered, sensitive data [24, 28].

3.1.2 Beyond Europe: Example of the United States of America

Beyond Europe, different data privacy laws also refer to the protection of biometric data or biometric information. This is the case in Australia,[16] New Zealand,[17] and other countries, including the United States. This section focuses on the latter because the country has complex layers of legislation divided into federal, state, and local levels. Besides, the regulation of biometric information or data is split into regulation thereof in general data privacy legislation (such as in California) and *ad hoc* legislation on biometric information (such as in Illinois).

General Privacy Legislation

First, despite numerous attempts to introduce a federal privacy law, no general privacy law is applicable at the federal level in the United States. However, at the state level, 15 states have a comprehensive privacy law.[18] Since California was the first state to introduce general data protection legislation, this paragraph will focus on California laws. The California Consumer Privacy Act (CCPA) was adopted in 2019 and amended in 2020 by the California Privacy Rights Act (CPRA). The CCPA defines biometric information as covering biometric characteristics (i.e. physiological, biological, or behavioural characteristics), including DNA information. The purpose of use is to "establish individual identity". The definition refers to

[15] Para 58 of the Explanatory Report and Article 6 (Special categories of data) of Convention 108+.

[16] Privacy Act 1998.

[17] Privacy Act 2020.

[18] Most of them apply to consumers and the state's residents and do not include public authorities. See list https://pro.bloomberglaw.com/insights/privacy/state-privacy-legislation-tracker/.

different forms of biometric characteristics and information, such as fingerprint, face, hand, vein patterns, or voice recording, "from which an identifier template, such as a faceprint, a minutiae template, or a voiceprint can be extracted". Besides, the definition refers to behavioural information such as keystrokes, gait patterns, etc.[19] Biometric information falls into the category of "personal information"[20] and is considered sensitive personal information if processed "for the purpose of uniquely identifying a consumer".[21]

3.2 *Specific Legal Instruments on Biometric Technologies*

In addition to the general legislation covering data protection and biometric data, *specific legal instruments* regulating biometric practices, both in Europe and beyond, were adopted.

3.2.1 The Council of Europe's 2021 Guidelines on Facial Recognition Technologies and the EDPB's 2022 Guidelines

In January 2021, the Consultative Committee of Convention 108 of the Council of Europe published Guidelines on Facial Recognition Technologies [6]. Although non-binding, these guidelines suggest measures that legislators and policymakers, developers, manufacturers, service providers, and users are invited to adopt in order to ensure responsible use of the technologies. Different situations are covered, including the deployment of FRTs in public spaces. The guidelines identify certain practices that should be prohibited, such as using FRTs to determine protected attributes such as skin colour, ethnic origin, religious beliefs, and health, among others, or "extracting biometric templates" from available digital images such as on the Internet. There is not much discussion about the status of biometric samples or templates or about protected biometric templates. In 2022, the European Data Protection Board (EDPB), mainly composed of the data protection authorities in the Union, issued guidelines for the use of FRTs by law enforcement [7]. These guidelines remained the most important guiding document on FRTs in Europe until the adoption of the AI Act (see Sect. 3.3 for further details).

3.2.2 The USA: Ad Hoc Biometric Legislation

Besides the general data privacy state laws, several US states have adopted specific biometric privacy legislation. Illinois was the first state to adopt the Biometric Infor-

[19] As codified in Civil Code, Section 1798.140 (c) of the CCPA.

[20] Section 1798.140 (v)(1)(E) of the CCPA.

[21] Section 1798.140 (ae)(2)(A) of the CCPA.

mation Privacy Act or BIPA. It regulates the collection and use, including retention, disclosure, and destruction, of biometric identifiers and biometric information *by private entities*.[22]

Then, Texas adopted the Capture or Use of Biometric Identifier Act as part of personal identity information within the Business and Commerce Code.[23] In that new section of the Business and Commerce Code, biometric identifiers are defined as "a retina or iris scan, fingerprint, voiceprint, or record of hand or face geometry".[24] Only the collection or use of biometric identifiers *for commercial purposes* is regulated.[25]

The State of Washington has also introduced a specific chapter on biometric identifiers in the Revised Code of Washington.[26] Biometric identifiers are defined as "data generated by automatic measurements of an individual's biological characteristics, such as a fingerprint, voiceprint, eye retinas, irises, or other unique biological patterns or characteristics that is used to identify a specific individual".[27] Photographs, whether analogue or digital, are excluded from the scope of biometric identifiers. This additional chapter only regulates the enrolment, disclosure, and retention of biometric identifiers for *commercial purposes*.[28] Several other states have introduced bills to regulate the use of biometric information or data. Several of these bills are currently under discussion (in Colorado,[29] Massachusetts,[30] and New Jersey,[31] among others). In addition, several US states and cities have adopted rules on the use of facial recognition technologies by law enforcement authorities for investigation purposes [17, 25] or temporary bans on the deployment of FRTs in public spaces, including streets.[32] However, there are no harmonised and federal rules applicable to FRT use in the USA.

---

[22] 740 ILCS 14, Biometric Information Privacy Act.

[23] Section 503.001, Capture or Use of Biometric Identifier Act.

[24] Section 503.001 (a).

[25] Section 503.001 (b)(c).

[26] Chapter 19.375 RCW.

[27] RCW 19.375.10.

[28] RCW 19.375.10 and RCW 19.375.20.

[29] Privacy of Biometric Identifiers and Data, HB24-1130.

[30] An Act to Protect Personal Biometric Data, S.195.

[31] See Bill A1488, prohibiting the collection of biometric identifier information by public and private entities under certain circumstances.

[32] For example, in San Francisco, Oakland, and Boston, among others.

3.3 The European Union's Artificial Intelligence Act

In April 2021, the European Commission proposed a new regulation on the development, putting on the EU market, and use of certain AI systems.[33] In December 2023, the EU institutions politically agreed on the future Artificial Intelligence Act (AI Act) text.[34] The final text of the AI Act Regulation (EU) 2024/1689 was adopted and published in July 2024. It will enter into force in stages, with Article 5 on prohibited practices applicable from 2 February 2024 [15]. The AI Act introduces a classification of AI systems which might *pose risks to safety or fundamental rights. Depending on their classification* (unacceptable, high-risk, limited, or low/minimal), the systems are subject to different AI Act provisions. Only systems that pose low or minimal risks do not fall within the scope of the regulation. Concerning biometric technologies, the AI Act regulates Remote Biometric Identification systems (RBIs), which include FRTs and other biometric recognition systems that capture biometric data at a distance and without individuals' cooperation. RBIs are subject to a ban or prohibition only when they are used in public spaces, in real time, for law enforcement purposes.[35] Other uses of RBIs, such as retrospective use in public spaces for law enforcement purposes or both retrospective and real-time use of RBIs for non-law enforcement purposes (such as commercial purposes), are not banned but are subject to the rules of high-risk AI systems.[36] Besides, the ban provides for *three situations in which real-time RBIs can exceptionally be used in publicly accessible areas for law enforcement purposes*. These situations cover the search for victims of certain crimes and missing persons,[37] the prevention of imminent threats to life or of terrorist attacks,[38] and the identification and localisation of suspects of certain serious crimes as listed in an Annex to the AI Act.[39] These exceptions must be laid down in national legislation and are *subject to conditions and safeguards* (including, in principle, prior authorisation by an independent authority to deploy the biometric systems and fundamental rights impact assessments).[40] The AI Act also regulates *emotion recognition and biometric categorisation AI systems*. As these two types of systems do not capture biometric characteristics to identify individuals, but rather to profile or classify them based on shared characteristics (such as age, gender, etc.) or

[33] Commission's Proposal for a Regulation of the European Parliament and of the Council laying down harmonised rules on artificial intelligence (Artificial Intelligence Act) and amending certain union legislative acts, COM (2021) 206 final.

[34] https://www.europarl.europa.eu/news/en/press-room/20231206IPR15699/artificial-intelligence-act-deal-on-comprehensive-rules-for-trustworthy-ai

[35] Art. 5(1)(h) AI Act.

[36] Art. 6 AI Act.

[37] Art. 5(1)(h)(i) AI Act.

[38] Art. 5(1)(h)(ii) AI Act.

[39] Art. 5(1)(iii) AI Act; Annex III of the AI Act.

[40] Art. 5(2)-(7) AI Act.

expression of emotions, the AI Act adopted a definition of biometric data, which is specific for the AI Act and which is different from the definition of biometric data in the GDPR/LED as it does not refer to the "unique identification" functionality of the processing anymore.

Article 3(34) of the AI Act defines biometric data more precisely as:

> personal data resulting from specific technical processing relating to the physical, physiological or behavioural characteristics of a natural person, such as facial images or dactyloscopic data.

Further, the AI Act does not refer in the adopted text to "unique identification" but to "biometric identification", distinguishing biometric identification from "biometric verification". It also specifies that authentication is included in biometric verification, although the biometric community depreciates the use of the term "authentication" as a synonym for biometric verification or identification due to the confusion it may entail.[41] What is further puzzling is that the legislator specifies that the notion of biometric data in the AI Act should be interpreted *in light of* the notion of biometric data in the data protection framework.[42] Yet, "in light of" is not the same as "in compliance with" and provides room for interpretation. Hence, the AI Act is, in our opinion, likely to create additional questions and possibly legal uncertainty by introducing a proper notion of "biometric data", besides the definitions of the GDPR and the LED in the data protection framework, which remains unchanged. Overall, the (new) definitions in the AI Act do not seem to alter any conclusions reached under the GDPR and the LED frameworks as described above. After all, the GDPR regulation remains the yardstick for assessing whether data qualify as personal data or not.

4 The Need and Obligation to Protect Biometric Information

In this section, we delve into the obligation of privacy and data protection by design and default and the role of Protected Biometric Templates (PBTs) in this regard.

4.1 Templates, Standards and Biometric Information Protection

Regulatory authorities have long advocated for the use of biometric templates, instead of "raw" biometric information (i.e. biometric samples), in biometric

[41] See Term 37.08.01, "authentication", in ISO/IEC 2382-37:2022.

[42] Recital 14 AI Act.

systems. We hereunder explain in more detail what biometric templates are and why they need to be protected.

4.1.1 Biometric Templates

In general language, and also in information technology language, a "template" usually refers to (a) reduced information from a given information source and (b) a guide, pattern, or model for producing similar things, for arranging information, and/or for comparison.[43] For biometric systems, the use of biometric templates has been advocated because such templates contain less information than the biometric samples, which are an analogue or digital representation of biometric characteristics before the feature extraction (so-called raw biometric information or samples). The templates are typically based on, and are hence just a set of, particular features extracted from the samples (e.g. the ridge structure or set of minutiae of a fingerprint, the face topography or geometry distances of a facial image, the representative embedding learned by a deep neural network, etc.). Such templates are equally suitable for making a comparison[44] in a biometric system and are therefore often stored as representations of the biometric identities in biometric recognition systems. The precise definition of "Biometric Template" in the Biometric Vocabulary is as follows: "set of stored biometric features (…) comparable directly to a biometric probe (…)". An alternative term for Biometric Template[45] is "Reference Biometric Feature Set". For any fruitful debate on biometric recognition, it remains very important to use the internationally adopted biometric vocabulary and correct terminology [27] (pp. 42–63).

The use, and especially the storage, of templates rather than biometric samples has been preferred for a long time from privacy and data protection perspectives. This is because biometric templates contain reduced information about the data subject (as explained earlier), hence complying with the data minimisation principle [9] (p. 4 and pp. 7–9) [27] (p. 507 (position of the Belgian Data Protection Authority) and p. 855). On the other hand, many systems, in particular in the law enforcement domain, prefer to store the images rather than the templates (e.g. fingerprint images in the Automated Fingerprint Identification System ("AFIS")) for similar but reverse reasons, which is that images contain more information and hence are more fit to be used by different authorities for diverging purposes.[46]

---

[43] See Cambridge Dictionary, "Template", at https://dictionary.cambridge.org/dictionary/english/template (online).

[44] This is sometimes also referred to as "template matching", i.e. the attempt to find the similarity or dissimilarity between two or more given templates.

[45] See term 37.03.22, "Biometric template", in Biometric Vocabulary ISO/IEC 2382-37:2022.

[46] This includes, for example, the use for crime investigation. For fingerprints and the use of AFIS, see, e.g. K. Moses, "Chap. 6. Automated Fingerprint Identification Systems (AFIS)", p. 34, in *The Fingerprint Sourcebook*, available at https://www.ojp.gov/pdffiles1/nij/225326.pdf.

4.1.2 The Need and the Obligation to Protect Biometric Information

Because of the risks when biometric information is compromised, including biometric images, such as one's loss of identity and identity information, unauthorised access to secure systems, the risks of linkability of information in databases and "function creep",[47] biometric templates should be protected. This biometric template protection (BTP) aims *not to reveal information* about the original reference (e.g. the fingerprint or the facial image) ("irreversibility" [22] (term 3.26)), to *disable linking* between templates or with an individual ("unlinkability" [22] (term 3.38)) since biometric information is a great "identifier" (as explained earlier), and to *allow for revocation and renewability*. The latter is equally important to enable individuals to *enrol again* with their (unchanged) biometric information (e.g. facial image, fingerprint, or voice for a banking application) if the biometric information is compromised, just like enabling the issuance of a new password [26].

4.1.3 What Do Data Protection Authorities Say?

The Article 29 Data Protection Working Group (i.e. the group of representatives of the national data protection authorities of the Union, the Commission, and the European Data Protection Supervisor) not only *supports the use of templates* but also *advises on the protection* of the biometric information. In their Opinion 3/2012 on developments in biometric technologies, they stated that templates should be "specific to that biometric system" and "not used by other controllers of similar systems in order to make sure that a person can only be identified in those biometric systems that have a legal basis for this operation" [11] (p. 31). Furthermore, they stated that a system should allow for multiple and independent biometric templates to be extracted from the same source in order to be able to replace them in the case of a data breach or a technological evolution. Biometric systems should be designed to allow us to revoke the identity link, either to renew it or to permanently delete it, e.g. when the consent is withdrawn [11] (see p. 32).[48]

4.1.4 Research on Template Protection and Standards

The technical and legal aspects of the protection of biometric templates have been researched in several research projects over the years. One of the first interdisciplinary international EU funded projects was the Turbine project, which

---

[47] See, e.g. the Clearview AI case, where images posted on social networks are repurposed for law enforcement objectives.

[48] In this Opinion, reference was also made to the research and technology developed in the EU's 7th Research Framework Programme research project *Turbine* and the Opinion of the EDPS (see also Sect. 4.1.4).

developed the architecture for protecting biometric templates [1]. The concept was also submitted for advice to the European Data Protection Supervisor, who was very positive about its privacy-enhancing qualities [8].

BTP has also become a subject of international standards. We refer, in particular, to the standard adopted by the International Standardization Organization—International Electrotechnical Committee known as the ISO/IEC 24745:2022 standard [22] and the IEEE Standard for Biometric Privacy [20].

4.2 Protected Biometric Templates: Would They Escape the GDPR?

In Sect. 4.1, we explained that the protection scheme for biometric information aims to further reduce the information relating to biometric traits or features. The reason for this is to *prevent re-identification* of the individual/data subject, *cross-linking* of information where such is not allowed or desired, and *revocation.*

The question that still remains, however, is the following: To what extent does the usage of Protected Biometric Templates ("PBTs") solve all issues and obligations under the data protection regulation? Even before that, the first question to consider is whether PBTs even fall within the subject matter (scope *ratione materiae*) of data protection regulations at all. In other words, *does the reduction of information in PBTs render the remaining information anonymous or not?* To answer this question, we will first recall the relevant "handgrips" provided by the GDPR and the guidance by Data Protection Authorities (DPAs) in relation to anonymisation of personal data. We will then look at the particular assessments in relation to PBTs. We will attempt to adhere as closely as possible to defined terms, as there is a lot of confusion when misleading terms or reasonings are used.[49]

4.2.1 GDPR "Handgrips" and DPA's Guidance Relating to Anonymous and Pseudonymous Information

While the GDPR clarifies and defines many concepts, including personal data and pseudonymisation, it *does not provide a definition of anonymous data*; however, this is, in our view, not a major obstacle. Anonymous data are the antipode of personal data, which is defined in Article 4(1) GDPR as meaning "any information" "relating to an identified or identifiable natural person ("data subject")(. . .)". The concept has

[49] For example, some also refer to "anonymous" biometric information, pointing to biometric samples (e.g. a fingerprint) with no additional (identifying) information such as a name or a number. See also term 37.03.01 of the ISO Biometric Vocabulary. From a legal point of view, however, biometric data records, including samples, without additional identifying details with the sample, are generally accepted to be "pseudonymous" personal data because individuals can be identified with the biometric information.

been further analysed by data protection authorities. For example, the information can be of any type and format, including *information stored in a binary format* [10] (pp. 7–8). This is important because protected biometric templates will often be recorded as numerical vectors. Furthermore, the "relating to" should be understood in various ways and can *not only because of the content* (the "about" for a data subject) but *also because of the purpose* of the use or the *result* (the "impact" for the data subject) be personal data [10] (pp. 7–8).

Pseudonymisation is defined in the GDPR/LED as the processing of personal data in such a way that the personal data can *no longer be attributed* to a specific individual *without the use of additional information*, the latter being kept *separately* secured by technical and organisational measures.

One shall further note that the GDPR definition of personal data also states that an "identifiable natural person is one who can be identified, *directly or indirectly*, in particular by *reference to an identifier* such as a name, an identification number (...) or to *one or more factors specific to the physical, physiological* (...) *identity* of that person" (emphasis added). This definition, hence, explicitly mentions elements specific to the physical or physiological biometric identity of a person as elements that allow to identify that person. It is precisely such elements and characteristics that are used in biometric systems.

Anonymous data are, therefore, (i) data that do not relate to an identified or identifiable natural person or (ii) personal data that have been rendered anonymous so that the person is not, or is no longer, identifiable.[50] Such identifiability can be avoided not only by removing all directly identifying elements but also by removing any indirectly identifying elements. It is especially about the content, scope, and nature of these indirectly identifying elements that there has been a lot of discussion and debate, also in the context of biometric information protection.

To ascertain whether information is anonymous, one needs to assess whether the individual can still be identified. The Article 29 Working Party, which has become the European Data Protection Board in the GDPR, has shed more light on the effectiveness of various anonymisation techniques that are often used for rendering information "more anonymous", such as generalisation, randomisation, K-anonymity, ... At the same time, the Working Party also stated that "*removing directly identifying elements in itself is not enough to ensure that identification of the data subject is no longer possible. It will often be necessary to take additional measures to prevent identification*, once again *depending on the context and purposes* of the processing for which the anonymized data are intended" (emphasis added) [12]. In other words, *the context and the purpose* of the application or system shall always be taken into account and remain crucial. The context is also one of the major criteria used by the Working Party to assess the anonymisation techniques used.

[50] See also Recital 26 GDPR in fine. It requires also that so-called de-identification would be irreversible.

For assessing whether information *still relates to an individual who is identifiable*, the ultimate test, according to Recital 26 of the GDPR, is to ascertain

> (...) *all the means reasonably likely to be used, such as singling out*, either by the *controller* or by *another person* to identify the natural person directly or indirectly. To ascertain whether means are reasonably likely to be used to identify the natural person, account should be taken of *all objective factors*, such as the *costs* of and the amount of *time* required for identification, taking into consideration the available *technology* at the time of the processing and technological *developments*. (...) (emphasis added).

The European Court of Justice ("ECJ") has clarified that the "means reasonably likely to be used" should be an objective criterion and *not* a subjective or relative criterion, i.e. from the point of view of the controller or of the entity having the information at hand.[51] This is a confirmation of Recital 26 above, stating that one shall also look at the means *available to third parties*. The Court further added that "means" shall also be seen as to whether the law and "legal channels" would allow the efforts and means used to identify.[52] In other words, the ECJ seems to say that data could also be anonymous because identification is prohibited by law or practically impossible because of disproportionate efforts.[53] At the same time, if a party could obtain access to additional identifying information, for example, through legal proceedings, the data would be qualified as personal data. In more recent case law, the Court further may seem to indicate that, for some entities, the information may be personal data if they have at their disposal the means enabling them to link the information to an identified or identifiable natural person, while for others it may be anonymous, to be determined from case to case.[54] We remain, however, cautious as to this reasoning. The Court may seem to deploy here a relative approach under certain conditions that may not hold. Indeed, as we explained above and according to previous interpretations, including by the ECJ, one shall not take a

[51] ECJ, Breyer C-582/14, 19.10.2016, EU:C:2016:779, §43 and §46. This decision qualifies dynamic IP numbers collected from visitors by websites as personal data, even if the websites have no (direct) access to the additional identifying information allocated by the Internet service provider to the IP number users. The Court therein held that a means is not reasonably likely to be used to identify the data subject where the identification of that person *is prohibited by law or impossible in practice*, on account of the fact that it requires a disproportionate effort in terms of time, cost, and labour, so that the risk of identification appears in reality to be insignificant (see §46—emphasis added).

[52] *Ibid.* §47. For the present case, it means that one shall not only assess from the point of view of the entity having the PBT but also take into account the means of third parties, such as a law enforcement authority which may have particular data and/or the legal means to claim access to additional information or algorithms in the hands of a third party, controller, or otherwise. See also ECJ, *Inspektor v Inspektorata kam Visshia sadeben savet*, C-180/21, 8.12.2022, EU:C:2022:967, §70.

[53] See also the Opinion of the Advocate-General (§68) to which the Court of Justice refers in its decision.

[54] See, e.g. ECJ, *Gesamtverband Autoteile-Handel eV v Scania CV AB*, C-319/22, 9.11.2023, ECLI:EU:C:2023:837, §49. See also General Court, *SRB v EDPS*, T-557/20, 23.4.2023, the latter being appealed by the EDPS and the judgment set aside in the ECJ decision of 4 September 2025 while referring the case back to the General Court (Case C-413/23 P).

subjective approach, and an entity shall take into account *also the means available to others* (e.g. law enforcement and other persons or entities who could (legally) ask for access (e.g. for investigation of crime)) for assessing whether the information they hold is personal data.

4.2.2 DPA's Assessment and Qualification of Biometric Templates

On top of the general "handgrips" summarised above, the DPAs have—as mentioned already—also looked specifically into the *qualification of templates as personal data* or not. They did so also when assessing the privacy-enhancing qualities of biometric templates because of data reduction and minimisation, and the need for pseudonymisation and renewability, as mentioned above. We explain this in some more detail here.

The Article 29 WP stated in 2003 that "measures of biometric identification or their digital translation in a *template form in most cases* are personal data" [9] (p. 5). They explained that biometric data, *by its very nature*, provide information about a given person and therefore can always be considered as "information relating to a natural person" [9] (p. 5).[55] Moreover, they stated that "[i]n the context of biometrical identification, the person is generally identifiable, since the biometric data *are used for identification or authentication/verification* at least in the sense that the data subject is distinguished from any other". In a footnote with this last sentence, it was, however, added that this would further depend on the availability of other data.

There are three interesting aspects to this. Firstly, the Article 29 Working Party attaches quite some importance to the *function and use* of the data: If used in an identification or verification biometric system, the data are personal data. Their position seems not to have changed much in the meantime.

Secondly, the former statement indicated also that *the transformation by algorithms* of the biometric images or samples (e.g. a facial image or fingerprint sample) into (e.g. numerical) the templates does not prevent the data of the templates and the templates themselves from being considered personal data. We present an example of a biometric template in Fig. 3.1.

It should not come as a surprise that the DPAs qualify "normal" or "ordinary" biometric templates as personal data, as the extraction of the biometric features and the transformation by the algorithm into templates are not protected in the sense that re-identification would become more difficult or excluded.

Thirdly, in this statement, there was a footnote in which the Article 29 Working Party *left the possibility open that templates are not personal data.* In this footnote, it was stated that "[i]n cases where biometric data, like a template, are stored *in a*

[55] The Article 29 WP stated it as follows: "It appears that biometric data can always be considered as 'information relating to a natural person' as it concerns data, which provides, by its very nature, information about a given person".

4.10E-02	-9.48E-03	-8.16E-02	8.34E-02	1.18E-01	1.08E-01	-6.30E-03	1.03E-01
1.40E-01	1.14E-01	-6.18E-02	8.47E-02	6.56E-03	2.23E-02	-1.48E-01	-8.18E-02
-1.72E-01	1.08E-01	-2.25E-01	-6.59E-02	-1.14E-01	1.51E-02	-3.35E-02	7.34E-02
6.58E-02	1.08E-01	1.10E-01	5.90E-03	-5.67E-02	1.21E-01	-1.37E-01	9.47E-03
2.43E-02	5.13E-02	2.48E-02	-9.27E-02	-8.10E-02	-6.14E-02	6.41E-02	1.10E-01
-9.98E-02	-9.22E-02	-5.76E-02	-8.50E-02	1.79E-01	5.32E-02	-6.78E-02	-1.50E-01
-3.31E-02	5.47E-02	1.05E-01	-5.23E-04	-4.70E-02	6.37E-02	7.64E-03	-1.51E-02
2.62E-02	1.24E-01	-1.31E-01	1.17E-01	5.71E-02	-1.86E-02	-4.16E-02	-9.22E-02
2.73E-01	3.73E-02	-7.80E-03	-5.87E-02	-1.47E-02	1.65E-02	2.32E-02	2.22E-01
2.11E-01	7.90E-02	-1.84E-02	2.83E-02	6.78E-02	-8.90E-02	-4.58E-02	6.30E-02
-1.03E-01	5.55E-02	2.44E-02	-1.72E-02	-5.84E-02	-8.76E-02	3.74E-02	1.05E-01
2.32E-01	-2.32E-02	2.39E-02	8.53E-02	-1.07E-01	8.01E-03	5.64E-02	-8.08E-02
5.54E-02	2.24E-02	-6.60E-02	-8.31E-02	-1.09E-01	5.51E-02	1.31E-01	-3.58E-02
-4.81E-03	-6.01E-02	-2.29E-03	2.49E-03	3.73E-02	1.97E-01	-1.48E-02	-2.08E-02
5.46E-02	6.78E-02	-1.26E-02	4.22E-02	-1.35E-02	-5.09E-02	-1.63E-01	8.38E-02
-1.56E-02	-8.76E-02	4.79E-02	8.40E-02	-1.50E-02	1.43E-02	-6.41E-02	-2.12E-02

Fig. 3.1 Biometric numerical template of a facial image—neither name nor other additional identifiers are mentioned with the template (but could be stored separately): (pseudonymous) personal data: An individual is identifiable (upon comparison), or the template could be complemented with the separately stored additional identifying information. Courtesy and ©R. Veldhuis

way that *no reasonable means* can be used by the controller or by any other person to identify the data subject, those data should not be qualified as personal data" (emphasis added).[56]

To summarise, we could say that the functionality and the *use* of the template *in a given biometric system or application and its context* will always be important to consider,[57] while the transformation of the biometric information by the algorithm into a template is considered by the DPAs as less important. However, the question remains whether the use of more advanced algorithms and methods for making the templates irreversible, unlinkable, and renewable affects this qualification as (pseudonymous) personal data.

As to the further transformation of biometric templates into PBT and the legal qualification of PBT, there is less specific guidance by the DPAs. Therefore, we provide hereunder a first assessment.

[56] *Ibid.*, p. 5, footnote 11 of the document. In this phrase of the footnote, the WP 29 Working Party seems to refer to the *possibility* for the controller to use reasonable means ("(…) in a way that no reasonable means can be used (…)"). Some scholars have indeed argued that when templates are stored on personal cards, the information would no longer qualify as personal data or would fall outside the scope of application of data protection regulation. This was criticised: see Kindt, Biometric applications 2013, p. 561, nr. 517.

[57] See also the "functional approach" of the legislator when regulating the use of biometric data in the GDPR, where the focus is on the use for "uniquely identifying", rather than the storage of the biometric identifiers. See on this approach, criticised because the legislator does not regulate the storage and the potential of biometric data, E. Kindt, "Having Yes, Using No? About the new legal regime for biometric data", in *Computer Law and Security Report* 2018, 523–538.

4.2.3 Our Legal Understanding and Assessment of the Qualification of Protected Biometric Templates ("PBTs") as Personal Data Under the GDPR

From a legal perspective, it remains important to reiterate and first understand how PBTs are generated.[58] This may be complex as various techniques and methods are possible. Nevertheless, a general recapitulation and a summary of the methods to protect biometric templates are an important start for a legal analysis. Hereunder we attempt to provide a summary of the key elements.

Summary of Methods and Techniques to Protect Biometric Templates
Overall, one could say that a BTP algorithm creates and employs a *renewable biometric reference* ("RBR"), which is also defined in the ISO standard Biometric Information Protection as term 3.34 [22]. The RBR serves as an irreversible and renewable identifier in a given domain. By way of example, it could consist of (1) a *pseudonymous identifier* ("PI") and possibly also *auxiliary data* ("AD"). The AD [22] (term 3.2) is then specifically generated in a specific domain (e.g. banking application) for an individual during her or his enrolment into the specific biometric application and would be required for verification. For the AD, we could use a so-called embed function to combine the biometric features of the individual with a secret string [22] (p. 52). The *captured biometric sample (from which the features are extracted) does not need to be retained* or stored within the system but should be securely destroyed. The PI [22] (term 3.29) is created using, for example, a one-way function. A (newly) *captured biometric sample is then (only) required for the comparison with the* pseudonymous identifier in the application, for example, for (digital) access control, and the AD, if any. *By extracting the biometric features and combining them with the application of specific identifiers* and possibly *additional input*, such as a secret PIN or public information [22] (p. 53), this BTP process *allows for the unlinkability and renewability* of the PBT, while being irreversible.

The storage of several data elements and the comparison of these elements can be done in various ways, including on a server or on a "client" or token, either distributed or not. Separated databases can be used with separate control and usage, allowing to detect if content is compromised. In other words, the architecture of a BTP system is also of key importance. Moreover, multiple other methods and technologies exist for biometric information protection and deriving renewable biometric references.[59] Splitting of information is, for example, another protection mechanism.

The encoding of the PI and AD during enrolment and the verification using PI* and AD is illustrated in Fig. 3.2, as mentioned in Annex C to the ISO standard Biometric Information Protection ISO/IEC 24745:2022 [22] (p. 53).

[58] The generation of PBTs is also described and explained in Part II of this book.

[59] ISO standard Biometric Information Protection ISO/IEC 24745:2022, p. 52, Table C.1.

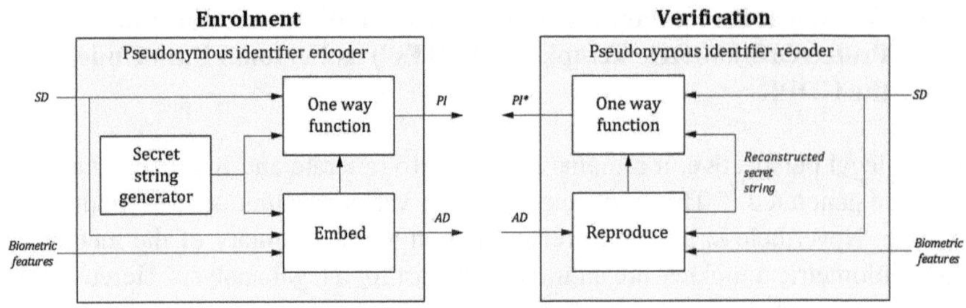

Fig. 3.2 Enrolment and verification using PI and AD for PBT (from ISO/IEC 24745:2022, p. 53)

As the architecture, the methods, and the technologies are not fixed, but rather allow for several possibilities and different amounts of security, each element of the BTP scheme will have to be reviewed and assessed for each particular scenario,[60] including whether such an element qualifies as personal data or not.

Both the PI and the AD used for BTP may contain biometric information, i.e. information from the features extracted from the biometric samples, depending on the BTP method used. At the same time, if the data elements are securely stored, protected, and controlled, e.g. by cryptographic means, distributed storage, information splitting, and/or the use of Trusted Third Parties, the question remains: *What means could reasonably likely be (considered to be) used to relate this information to an individual?* And does this need to be reviewed from the perspective of the various parties involved (relative approach) or in an objective way? If this could be solved, we could draw a conclusion on how to qualify these data elements and this information, whether individually or combined, as personal, pseudonymous, or anonymous data under data protection regulations. One should also keep in mind that *without* a "fresh"/new biometric sample (which is not stored), arguably belonging to a known or identified individual, and features extracted from such a sample, *one cannot recode* the pseudonymous identifier for comparison. A pseudonymous identifier could only be used in combination with any (new) biometric sample in the comparison.[61]

The question hence remains, in other words, whether such additional information, means, and/or methods—meant to protect biometric information—could be of the kind to make PBTs anonymous and hence could make PBTs escape the data protection obligations.

There is very limited guidance or criteria from the EU legislator and the data protection authorities as to any irreversibility of a "de-identification".[62] In its 2012

[60] See ISO standard Biometric Information Protection ISO/IEC 24745:2022, which explains 11 possibilities.

[61] In this case, such a pseudonymous identifier would be used to confirm a claim or could be attributed to and related to an identified or identifiable individual based upon a ("fresh"/new) biometric sample only.

[62] This is different compared to e.g. the USA, where there are, for example, standards for Privacy of Individually Identifiable Health Information in relation with the Health Insurance Portability and Accountability Act.

Opinion on developments in biometric technologies, the Article 29 WP merely referred to its 2003 Working document WP80 and repeated that "biometric data are in most cases personal data" and that therefore "they may only [be] processed if (...) the processing is adequate, relevant and not excessive in relation to the purposes for which they are collected and/or further processed" [11].

As to the ISO standard Biometric Information Protection ISO/IEC 24745:2022, the international standard does refer to security and privacy concerns without going into much detail.[63]

Other methods to protect biometric information include encryption and homomorphic encryption. In general, the encryption process cannot be inverted to recover the original data (plaintext) from the encrypted data (ciphertext), unless we have access to the decryption key (which should be securely stored). However, since encryption operations are designed to exaggerate differences in the input data[64] and biometric templates are by nature not 100% reproducible, encrypted biometric data would have to be decrypted during the comparison stage, which would expose the templates to attacks. Homomorphic encryption, on the other hand, allows for computations to be carried out on ciphertext, meaning that the data does not need to be decrypted into plaintext for the comparison,[65] offering higher security than mere encryption of the data at rest or during transfer. Autonomous or machine learning methods could create vectors that—according to some—cannot be used to re-compute the original input (however, there is currently insufficient evaluation to support this claim). This approach is described in IEEE Standard for Biometric Privacy [20]. At the same time, it is accepted by data protection authorities and legal scholars that, in general, encrypting personal data may render the data pseudonymous but does not render the data anonymous as such.[66]

Which are "all the means reasonably likely to be used" to be taken into account and how to interpret "by whom" in a highly complex, multi-disciplinary, and multi-stake environment as for BTP?

As pointed out in Sect. 4.2.1, the criterion for identifiability includes "(...) all the means reasonably likely to be used". This is mentioned in Recital 26 of the GDPR and, hence, not in a binding provision. This recital further refers to several factors that would allow for the identification or the mere singling out of the person. In addition, it is clearly stated that anyone may identify the natural person directly or

[63] The ISO standard Biometric Information Protection ISO/IEC 24745:2022 does mention that biometric data "when associated with linked subject identity information stored on a system" "can be used to identify the subject", and hence stored biometric data "are classified as personally identifiable information (PII)" (see p. 12).

[64] See Part I, Chap. 2 of this book for more details on encryption.

[65] See Part II, Chap. 6 of this book for more details on homomorphic encryption.

[66] See, e.g. the AEDP (the Spanish DPA) and the EDPS in their Guidance document *10 misunderstandings related to anonymisation*, p. 4; J. Schreurs, *Anonymisation, pseudonymisation & encryption in the Cloud*, CiTiP blog, 18.7.2017. Others also point to the need to assess the accessibility to the encryption keys to consider whether the data are personal data or not. See, e.g. J. Gresham, *Is encrypted data personal data under the GDPR?*, 2019.

indirectly and not only the controller. Finally, it states that all objective factors shall be included in the evaluation, in particular *costs, time, and available technology both now and in the future*.

The short high-level description of how PBTs are created above illustrates that the creation and the deployment of PBTs can be done in various ways and involves several variants, including many actors/stakeholders. This will be confirmed when reading the ISO standard Biometric Information Protection ISO/IEC 24745:2022 and the IEEE standard. So, there is not just one way to protect biometric information, and each method will have its own requirements, assumptions, and difficulties to "break".

Furthermore, PBTs are at the cross-roads of technology, standards and legislation.[67] The technology involves, as mentioned, many disciplines, including image and signal processing, encryption, and cryptography.[68] From these perspectives, the "objective factors" to be taken into account are multiple, and they will vary depending on the *methods* used and the *assumptions* made. Side-channel methods for identifying an individual may always remain.[69] Some main factors to be taken into account are likely to include, for example, the security and the secrecy of the encryption keys, whether for example the secret keys are shared[70] or not to avoid misuse, and various other assumptions which may matter. These could also relate to the storage, including of additional helper data, benefits and risks of using specific techniques,[71] and many other related vulnerabilities.[72] All these methods with trade-offs and related assumptions (such as in relation to risks of hacking) are quite *likely to have an effect on the extent to which it is reasonable to say that possible means* could be used by particular actors (including hackers and others), whether in collusion or not, to identify individuals or to single them out based on their biometric characteristics.

Connecting all these methods and procedures with the legal criteria for the assessment of when they make information personal data is *likely to end up with*

---

[67] See also Udo Mahlmeister, moderator of the EAB Workshop on the matter of 1 March 2023, which was covered by Ch. Burton in Biometric Update.com, see Ch. Burton, "EAB explores how to comply with GDPR mandate for biometric template protection", 2.3.2023, and Ch. Burt, "Biometrics Beyond Encryption; 'unlinkability' and pseudonymization under GDPR. EAB panel has advice but no easy answers" in *Biometric Update*, 6.3.2023 ("Burt, Biometrics Beyond Encryption").

[68] We explained above that the process for creating PBTs by PI and AD requires state-of-the-art encryption or other methods and procedures, with multiple variations, as demonstrated by the list of examples of available techniques in the ISO standard Biometric Information Protection ISO/IEC 24745:2022. Also the use of fully homomorphic encryption is possible through different means and methods, as explained in IEEE Standard for Biometric Privacy.

[69] See also F. Hahn of Twente University, speaker at the EAB Workshop of 1 March 2023 on the matter (see above).

[70] This is for example the approach to protect the centralised biometric databases in Israël.

[71] Such as the use of differential privacy and any other specific approaches, like the use of so-called Bloom filters or multi-party computation.

[72] See also Burt, Biometrics Beyond Encryption.

the question that needs to be answered, and the criterion defining "all the means reasonably likely to be used", which need to be taken into account to relate the information back to an individual. And by whom? By which means? And in what context?

Another question to be solved is whether there is any qualification of the person/entity who would be deemed to use the "means". Information processing operations have become increasingly complex in today's society, and this is not different for the protection of biometric information. As we explained, knowledge of many highly specialised disciplines is required, also for the possibility of finding the link between PBT and the individuals involved. How specialised should one be to be considered to have and to possibly deploy available means? A decision of the General Court has looked into this criterion for one of the first times—to our knowledge—in a rather interesting way. To assess whether, in the given case, personal data were involved, the General Court looked at "the average person", not the person able to use sophisticated means.[73] While this decision has been reversed, this nevertheless initiated the question of whether the bar should be lowered or not. It also puts our analysis in some perspective.

Purpose and Context: A Practical Key Guiding Principle?

A final and important aspect besides the factors above is the *context and the objective* of the system which uses the PBT, as we already mentioned in Sect. 4.2.1. Arguing that a biometric system processes no personal data while the system's objective is to recognise or to identify persons is, in our opinion, indeed not very plausible.[74] This will remain, therefore, a very practical key guiding principle in deciding whether personal (biometric) data are anonymous or not.

---

[73] See General Court, *OC v European Commission*, T-384/20, C-479/22 P, 4.05. 2022, ECLI:EU:T:2022:273. This decision was, however, appealed. The appellant stated that the court "erred in law when it held that only means which are trivial or insignificant, capable of demonstrating easily and quickly the identity of the person to whom the information relates, are covered by the concept of 'means reasonably likely to be used' to identify the person to whom the personal data relate" (§33). The ECJ reversed the decision and stated that the Court erred in law in its classification for legal purposes of the facts by holding that the identifiers at issue did not reasonably allow the appellant to be identified, either on the basis of a simple, objective reading of that press release or by means "reasonably likely to be used" by one of its readers (§64). See ECJ, *OC v. European Commission*, 7.3.2024, ECLI:EU:C:2024:215. In this case, which was mainly a liability case for reparation of harm caused by a press release of OLAF, the Court warned that in the case at hand, the question of whether information contained in a press release emanating from a Union institution or body is covered by the concept of "personal data" shall not be confused with the liability question and that this first question was erroneously made dependent on considerations relating to the imputability of an act to the European Union (§55).

[74] See also the position of the Article 29 Working Party about the "context" as mentioned above.

Preliminary conclusion: **PBT and/or its components are in most cases not anonymous, but personal data.**

Overall, we are of the opinion that the separate elements of a BTP scheme in a system are likely to allow identification of the individual involved, whether by the system or in the presence of this individual, allowing to compare the biometric information. After all, the objective of most of these systems is to compare. This would mean that PBT and/or its components are, in most cases, not anonymous data but personal data; however, a case-by-case reasoning and assessment will be needed.

4.3 A Legal Obligation for Data Minimisation, Privacy, and Data Protection by Design and by Default

As mentioned in Sect. 4.1.2, biometric templates are deployed and recommended because they *contain less information* about the data subject. This is in line with the GDPR obligation of Article 5.1.c GDPR to process data which is "adequate, relevant and limited to what is necessary in relation to the purposes for which they are processed ('data minimisation')". This principle is of general application, to any data processing operation. This would imply that the use of PBTs complies with this principle and is even mandatory.

The need to protect biometric information also follows from the GDPR obligation to provide data protection by design and by default, as mentioned explicitly in Article 25 GDPR (see also Sect. 3.1.1). Data controllers must implement "Data Protection by Design and by Default" measures, which are inspired by the concept of "Privacy by Design", to take into account data privacy issues at the design stage of a product, service, or system. This has been advocated—also specifically with regard to the protection of biometric information—by the former Information & Privacy Commissioner of Ontario in Canada for a long time [3, 4] and [27] (p. 855 et seq.), as well as by data protection authorities in general.[75] It also implies that data controllers must adopt technical and organisational measures to implement data protection principles and integrate safeguards to protect individuals' rights and freedoms, as well as to respect the data minimisation requirement.[76] These "technical and organisational" measures are not defined. However, the GDPR and the LED give the example of pseudonymisation techniques as such measures. BTP could, without a doubt, be considered a (mandatory) technique for data protection by design and default.

[75] See e.g. ICO, "How do we keep biometric data secure?" in UK GDPR guidance and resources, February 2024.

[76] Article 25 GDPR and Article 20 LED.

5 Conclusion

We have explained why the use of biometric information in various domains contains risks which need to be limited. Legislators have therefore attempted to regulate the use of biometric systems by adopting general definitions and prohibitions (e.g. the GDPR in the European Union and the Convention 108+ in the Council of Europe) or ad hoc regulation (e.g. the AI Act in the European Union and legislation in the United States). At the same time, the protection of biometric information is also of high importance for protecting the essence of the fundamental rights and freedoms of individuals, to respect the need for privacy and data protection. *Additional methods are, hence, needed to make biometric identifiers containing biometric information irreversible, unlinkable, and renewable.* This requires effort to develop suitable protection techniques, of which there is a large variety. In this chapter, we focused on whether these techniques for transforming biometric information into PBTs could render the identifiers anonymous, and hence whether PBTs would escape data protection regulation.

To answer this question, we explained the various legal criteria, in particular, "all means reasonably likely to be used" for re-identification. We mentioned that BTP is at the crossroads of technology, standards, and legislation. A relevant mapping of reasonable means and risks of re-identification for PBT is therefore needed but is not possible without the involvement, analysis, and collaboration between these disciplines.[77]

But what to do with the *possibility left open by some that (protected biometric) templates are not personal data because the various elements of a system are distributed or because they are stored in a way* that *no reasonable means* can be used by the controller or by any other person to identify the data subject as mentioned above? Because of the many factors and components, protection techniques, and involved parties, it may be necessary to take a closer look at each specific method and application to determine *how reasonably likely* it is that all or some of these means *could be (mis)used for identification*, and by whom, to come to a conclusion on the qualification of the PBTs as personal data or not. Such assessments are, therefore, likely to be a multidisciplinary effort and exercise. As for other data protection assessments, it may come as no surprise that we deem it essential to conduct a case-by-case assessment, which would likely be necessary, and that further involvement of the legislator may be necessary.

[77] In other words, this technology will require input from experts in signal and biometric processing, cryptographers, standards, applications, and legal experts. This also seems to be the point of view of the US National Institute of Standards and Technology's Patrick Grother, who is of the opinion that the specific application, threat model, and mechanisms used must be taken into account, together with data separation, see also Ch. Burt, "Biometrics Beyond Encryption; 'unlinkability' and pseudonymization under GDPR. EAB panel has advice but no easy answers" in *Biometric Update*, 6.3.2023.

At the same time, insofar as PBTs *are used* in identification or verification applications, where the *purpose of the system is precisely to identify* a person, it would be contradictory to hold the view that the PBTs (the PI and AD) would not be personal data. Moreover, they usually contain biometric information, which is precisely used to identify or single out individuals. Therefore, we believe that this and any other biometric information needs to be protected in a biometric system. The use of PBTs is a big step forward in applying data protection by design and by default, as PBTs offer enhanced privacy and data protection. This also aligns with the position and the previous statements of the group of DPAs as early as 2003. What remains is to acknowledge any remaining risks of PBTs, including, in particular, by making a DPIA, and to provide additional technical and organisational measures to protect the data.

6 Summary

- **Concept of personal data:** Personal data are a concept that has been defined for a long time in data protection regulation. It is information relating to an identified person but could also be information relating to a person not yet identified but identifiable, either in a direct way or in an indirect way, by one or more identifiers such as an identification number or by one or more factors specific to an individual's physical, physiological, mental, economic, cultural, or social identity (based on Article 4 GDPR).
- **Identifiability:** Identifiability from a legal perspective refers to enabling the identification of an individual by identifying elements, such as not only by a unique number but also by indirectly identifying elements, such as for example factors relating to the physical characteristics of a person.
- **Concept of biometric data:** The notion of biometric data is generally defined in (i) the EU general data protection legislation and (ii) the 2024 adopted EU AI Act. In both cases, the definitions mention the examples of facial images and dactyloscopic data. The two definitions, however, differ. While both state that it is "personal data resulting from specific technical processing relating to the physical, physiological or behavioural characteristics of a natural person", only the definition of the general data protection legislation (in particular the GDPR and the LED) states that biometric data "shall allow or confirm the unique identification of that person". The AI Act does not contain the latter wording and hence introduces a broader concept for purposes of the regulation of the AI systems within its scope, in particular emotion recognition and biometric categorisation.
- **Anonymised data:** Anonymous data are (i) data which do not relate to an identified or identifiable natural person or (ii) personal data which have been

rendered anonymous so that the person is not, or is no longer, identifiable. For assessing whether information still relates to an individual who is identifiable, one shall ascertain all the means reasonably likely to be used, such as singling out, either by the controller or by another person to identify the natural person directly or indirectly. One shall hereby take into account all objective factors, such as the costs of and the amount of time required for identification, in view of present and future technology.

- **Protected Biometric Templates:** Protected Biometric Templates will, in most cases, be considered personal biometric data, albeit pseudonymised if no directly identifying elements are present. The test as to whether the individual is still identifiable is to assess all the means reasonably likely to be used, either by the controller or by another person to identify the natural person directly or indirectly. One shall hereby take into account all objective factors, such as the costs of and the amount of time required for identification, in view of present and future technology. The functionality and use of a biometric template, including of a protected biometric template, in a given biometric system or application and its context will moreover always be important to consider whether the data are personal data.
- **Pseudonymised data:** Pseudonymised data are personal data that can no longer be attributed to a specific individual without the use of additional information, such as identity details of an individual whose protected biometric template is stored, provided such additional information is kept separately secured by technical and organisational measures.

7 Study Questions

1. What are the criteria to assess whether data are personal data under the General Data Protection Regulation (GDPR)?
2. What are the GDPR criteria to ascertain whether data are biometric personal data? Are these the same as in the AI Act?
3. What is the difference in the approach of the legislator in Europe, compared to that of the United States of America, when regulating the use of biometric information?
4. Explain the notion of identifiability in the data protection legislation and its importance.
5. What are anonymised data and are they protected?
6. Give an example of pseudonymised personal data.
7. What is, in your opinion, the main argument for or against the qualification of PBTs as personal data?

Acknowledgments The research and publication has been partially funded by the projects PRIMA, TreSPasS, and DATAFACE, funded by the European Union's Horizon 2020 research and innovation programme under the respective Marie Skłodowska-Curie grant agreements No. 86031, No. 860813, and No. 895978, the EU Union's Horizon 2020 research and innovation programme iMars under grant agreement No. 883356, by the Norwegian Research Council funded project SALT and by the Cybersecurity Initiative Flanders—Strategic Research Program (CIF). The article reflects only the authors' views and not of any of the aforementioned funding organisations which are not liable for any of the information contained herein.

References

1. Breebaart, J., Busch, C., Grave, J., Kindt, E.: A reference architecture for biometric template protection based on pseudo identities. In: BIOSIG 2008, Proceedings of the Special Interest Group on Biometrics and Electronic Signatures, pp. 25–37. Gesellschaft für Informatik (2008)
2. Cao, K., Jain, A.K.: Learning fingerprint reconstruction: from minutiae to image. IEEE Trans. Inf. Forensics Secur. **10**(1), 104–117 (2014)
3. Cavoukian, A.: Privacy by design: the 7 foundational principles. Inf. Privacy Commissioner Ontario **5**, 12 (2009)
4. Cavoukian, A., Stoianov, A., Carter, F.: Biometric encryption: Technology for strong authentication, security and privacy. In: Policies and Research in Identity Management: First IFIP WG11. 6 Working Conference on Policies and Research in Identity Management (IDMAN'07), RSM Erasmus University, Rotterdam, The Netherlands, October 11–12, 2007, pp. 57–77. Springer (2008)
5. Council of Europe: Convention 108+, Convention for the protection of individuals with regard to automatic processing of personal data. In: Council of Europe (2018)
6. Council of Europe: Consultative Committee of the Convention for the Protection of Individuals with regard to Automatic Processing of Personal Data (2021), Guidelines on Facial Recognition. In: Council of Europe (2021)
7. European Data Protection Board (EDPB): Guidelines 05/2022 on the use of facial recognition technology in the area of law enforcement. In: EDPB (2022)
8. European Data Protection Supervisor (EDPS): Opinion of the European data protection supervisor on a research project funded by the european union under the seventh framework programme (FP7) for research and technology development - Turbine (TrUsted Revocable Biometric IdeNtitiEs). In: EDPS (2011)
9. European Union: Article 29 Data Protection Working Party (2003), Working document on biometrics, WP 80 (2003)
10. European Union: Article 29 Data Protection Working Party, Opinion 4/2007 on the concept of personal data (WP 136) (2007)
11. European Union: Article 29 Data Protection Working Party, Opinion 3/2012 on developments in biometric technologies (WP 193) (2012)
12. European Union: Article 29 Data Protection Working Party(2014), Opinion 5/2014 on Anonymization techniques (WP216) (2014)
13. European Union: Directive (EU) 2016/680 of the European Parliament and of the Council of 27 April 2016 on the protection of natural persons with regard to the processing of personal data by competent authorities for the purposes of the prevention, investigation, detection or prosecution of criminal offences or the execution of criminal penalties, and on the free movement of such data, and repealing Council Framework Decision 2008/977/JHA. Offi. J. Eur. Union **119**, 89–131 (2016)

14. European Union: Regulation (EU) 2016/679 of the European Parliament and of the Council of 27 April 2016 on the protection of natural persons with regard to the processing of personal data and on the free movement of such data, and repealing Directive 95/46/EC (General Data Protection Regulation). Offi. J. Eur. Union **119**, 1–88 (2016)
15. European Union: Regulation (EU) 2024/1689 of the European Parliament and of the Council of 13 June 2024 laying down harmonised rules on artificial intelligence and amending Regulations (EC) No 300/2008, (EU) No 167/2013, (EU) No 168/2013, (EU) 2018/858, (EU) 2018/1139 and (EU) 2019/2144 and Directives 2014/90/EU, (EU) 2016/797 and (EU) 2020/1828 (Artificial Intelligence Act). Offi. J. Eur. Union **12.7.2024**, 1–444 (2024)
16. European Union Agency for Fundamental Rights (FRA): Under watchful eyes: biometrics, EU IT systems and fundamental rights. Publications Office of the European Union (2018)
17. Garvie, C.: A forensic without the science: face recognition in US criminal investigations. Center Privacy Technol. Georgetown Law **6** (2022)
18. Gomez-Barrero, M., Galbally, J.: Reversing the irreversible: a survey on inverse biometrics. Comput. Secur. **90**, 101700 (2020)
19. Grijpink, J.: Privacy law: biometrics and privacy. Comput. Law Secur. Rev. **17**(3), 154–160 (2001)
20. IEEE Standards Association: The International IEEE Standard for Biometric Privacy, IEEE Std 2410-2021. IEEE (2021)
21. Information Commissioner's Office (ICO): Biometric data guidance: Biometric recognition (2024)
22. ISO/IEC JTC1 SC27 Security Techniques: ISO/IEC 24745:2022. Information Technology - Security Techniques - Biometric Information Protection. International Organization for Standardization (2022)
23. Jasserand, C.: Reprocessing of Biometric Data for Law Enforcement Purposes: Individuals' Safeguards Caught at the Interface between the GDPR and the 'Police' Directive? (PhD Thesis) (2019)
24. Jasserand, C.: Chapter 15 - Biometric Data, Within and Beyond Data Protection. In: The Boundaries of Data. Amsterdam University Press, Amsterdam (2024)
25. Kak, A.: Regulating biometrics: Global approaches and urgent questions (2020). https://ainowinstitute.org/publication/regulating-biometrics-global-approaches-and-open-questions
26. Kindt, E.J.: The use of privacy enhancing technologies for biometric systems analysed from a legal perspective. In: IFIP PrimeLife International Summer School on Privacy and Identity Management for Life, pp. 134–145. Springer, Berlin (2009)
27. Kindt, E.J.: Privacy and data protection issues of biometric applications. A Comparative Legal Analysis, vol. 12. p. 42, Springer, Berlin (2013)
28. Kindt, E.J.: Chapter 18 - Biometric data processing: Is the legislator keeping up or just keeping up appearances? In: Research Handbook on Privacy and Data Protection Law, pp. 375–401. Edward Elgar Publishing, Cheltenham (2022)
29. Kotschy, W.: Article 2, Directive 95/46/EC. Concise European IT Law (2010)
30. Tosoni L. and Bygrave L.: Article 4(14), Biometric Data. The EU General Data Protection Regulation (GDPR): A Commentary (2020)

Part II
Methods

Chapter 4
Feature Transformation-Based Biometrics Template Protection

Xingbo Dong and Andrew Beng Jin Teoh

Abstract Biometric recognition systems have gained widespread adoption due to their effectiveness in providing secure and convenient authentication. However, unlike credit cards and passwords, which can be canceled and reissued when compromised, biometric data is permanently linked to the user. As a result, people are growing more worried that biometric technology may compromise their personal biometric information and, therefore, their privacy. For this reason, to prevent the leakage of biometric information, it is desirable to protect it through revocable and irreversible transformations to generate cancelable biometric templates. Feature transformation-based biometric template protection (FT-BTP) is a promising solution to address these challenges. It involves applying a mathematical transformation to the biometric template, which is typically non-invertible. Consequently, it becomes difficult or impossible to reconstruct the original biometric data from the transformed template. This chapter aims to thoroughly understand FT-BTP methods, offering a step-by-step guide for researchers, practitioners, and students interested in this field. This chapter is intended to be a self-contained tutorial, but the reader will be referred to recent reviews and papers for additional details. A set of study questions and links to some open-source implementations of FT-BTP methods are provided at the end of the chapter.

1 Introduction

A biometric template is a mathematical representation of an individual's unique physical or behavioral characteristics, such as features from fingerprints, facial images, iris patterns, and voice recordings. The enrollment process of a biometric

X. Dong
School of Artificial Intelligence, Anhui University, Hefei, China
e-mail: xingbo.dong@ahu.edu.cn

A. B. J. Teoh (✉)
School of Electrical and Electronic Engineering, Yonsei University, Seoul, Republic of Korea
e-mail: bjteoh@yonsei.ac.kr

V. Krivokuća Hahn et al. (eds.), *Handbook of Biometric Template Protection*,
https://doi.org/10.1007/978-981-95-0995-9_4

system involves capturing source data, converting it into this mathematical format, and securely storing it for future comparison. During the authentication process, new biometric data is collected, transformed into a template, and compared to the stored templates for verification or identification.

As discussed in Part I of this handbook, using biometric templates has prompted heightened scrutiny regarding security and privacy. There are two main issues to consider:

- Compromised biometric templates cannot be revoked or changed (since biometric system users cannot alter their biometric data), making it difficult to address security breaches. This leaves users vulnerable to identity theft and exploitation.
- Breached or shared biometric databases can compromise identities across various platforms. This heightens the potential for user tracking and surveillance, raising concerns about privacy and data protection.

One way to address the above issues is by using standard cryptographic encryption (e.g., DES) or cryptographic hashing (e.g., MD5) algorithms, as shown in Fig. 4.1. Cryptographic hashing can protect biometric data by computing a one-way digest, and these one-way functions are challenging to reverse: Even minor alterations in the input result in significantly different digests.[1] However, due to environmental conditions, biometric raw data that is acquired in practical applications will never be the same across multiple acquisitions. For instance, changes in illumination can significantly impact face and iris biometrics. As a result, these functions cannot be directly applied in practice since they only apply to precise data. Additionally, as shown in Fig. 4.1, encryption methods such as DES require decryption to match the data, which exposes the biometric data during the comparison stage and thus leads to high privacy leakage.

A better way to alleviate the issues above is to employ feature transformation-based biometric template protection (FT-BTP) (also known as Cancellable Biometrics (CB) [19]). FT-BTP is one of the main techniques used for Biometric Template Protection (BTP) in the literature, along with other categories of BTP approaches that are analyzed in depth in the subsequent chapters of this book.

FT-BTP schemes intentionally distort biometric data to create a protected template called a pseudonymous identifier (PI), with the help of auxiliary data (AD) such as user-specific transformation parameters. A diagram of a general FT-BTP scheme is shown in Fig. 4.2. The PI is an identifier that can be used to recognize an individual without revealing their actual identity. It can be generated from a captured biometric sample and the AD. The AD is typically user-specific information (e.g., serves to parameterize that user's transform) and may be required to render the PI during verification. The AD also should not reveal any personally identifiable information.

An FT-BTP scheme should meet the below requirements in terms of security and privacy according to the ISO/IEC 24745:2022 standard [9]:

[1] Refer to Chap. 2 in Part I of this handbook.

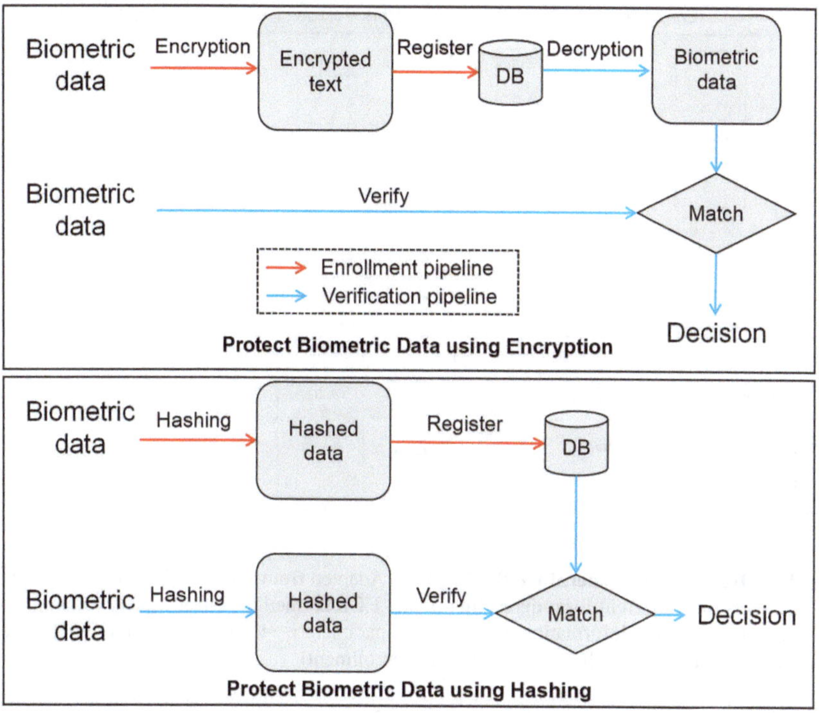

Fig. 4.1 Cryptographic solutions. Cryptographic methods like encryption and hashing pose challenges in biometric data security. Encryption requires decryption for comparison, exposing the data and increasing privacy risks. Hashing, which is sensitive to changes in the input, struggles with biometric data variability as biometric inputs fluctuate between acquisitions

- **Irreversibility**: It must be computationally challenging to reconstruct the original biometric reference from one or more PI instances, whether or not the AD is present.
- **Revocability**: Revoking or reissuing PI is crucial to ensuring security in the event of a compromise. This allows for the replacement of the compromised PI with a new PI.
- **Unlinkability**: Computational difficulty in distinguishing between two or more PIs derived from the same biometric reference is essential. Unlinkability safeguards privacy by preventing cross-matching across different applications, preserving an individual's anonymity.
- **Performance Preservation**: The performance of the biometric system, in terms of recognition accuracy, when the PI is used should be maintained compared to when the original, unaltered biometric templates are used.

It is worth noting that FT-BTP schemes can operate either directly on raw biometric signals or on biometric features extracted by a specific feature extractor. Works that apply FT-BTP on biometric images such as iris, fingerprint, face, and

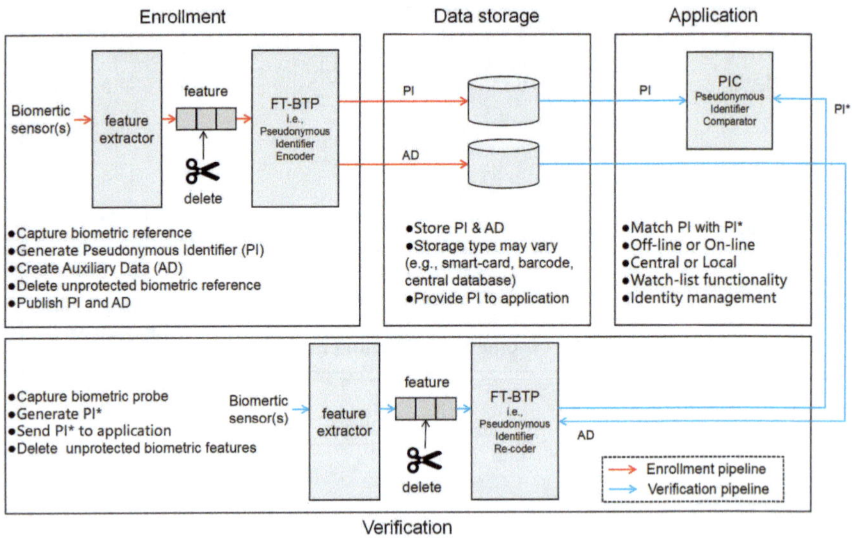

Fig. 4.2 Overview of a general FT-BTP system. Adapted from ISO/IEC 24745:2022. Note that the AD takes on a different form depending on the FT-BTP method, but it usually refers to some external (often random) information that is used to parameterize the transformation function (e.g., generated separately for each system user during enrollment)

vein images can be found in [1, 7, 13, 20]. On the other hand, feature-based transformation is a more widely adopted approach, characterized by a two-stage pipeline consisting of feature extraction and FT-BTP transformation (as shown in Fig. 4.2). This is the primary approach utilized in the BTP domain, providing a systematic procedure for altering biometric data while retaining crucial features essential for accurate recognition.

2 Taxonomy of Feature Transformation Techniques

Given the operational principles of FT-BTP techniques and the specific schemes' utilization of random supplementary information, namely the AD, the FT-BTP taxonomy comprises two primary categories, as illustrated in Fig. 4.3: (1) salting transform and (2) non-invertible transform. Non-invertible transform schemes support user-specific (i.e., different for each user that is enrolled in the biometric system) or system-specific (i.e., the same for all enrolled users) AD, while salting transforms mainly support user-specific AD because system-specific AD (typically referred to as "stolen-token scenario" in the literature) in salting schemes usually degrades accuracy.

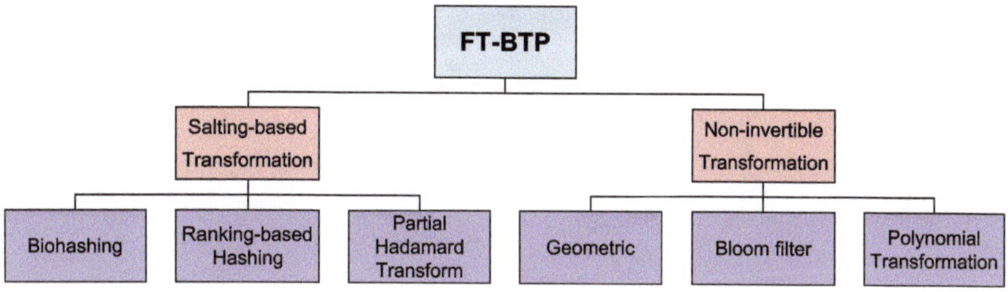

Fig. 4.3 Taxonomy of FT-BTP methods

2.1 Salting Transformation

The salting transformation secures biometric data by combining it with a random value (salt) to create unique templates. The upcoming sections cover how it works, case studies like Biohashing and IoM hashing, applications to various biometric modalities, and key management challenges for enhanced data protection.

2.1.1 How Does It Work?

The salting transformation is similar to the traditional salting algorithm in cryptography. As shown in Fig. 4.4a, a cryptographic salting algorithm concatenates a random salt r, which is a random value unrelated to the secret, with a secret k, and then stores the hash $H(r+k)$ and the salt r in the database, where $H(\cdot)$ is a hashing function. In the authentication stage, a new hash will be generated by the same process and compared to the stored hash to make the match/no match decision. As shown in Fig. 4.4b, a biometric salting transformation adheres to a similar principle, wherein a user-specific AD, such as a password or user-specific random numbers, is fused with biometric data and subsequently transformed by a specifically designed transform function to generate a protected biometric template PI. The PI and AD are stored in the database during the enrollment phase. During authentication, the system calculates the PI of the user to be authenticated in the same way. It then computes the distance between the probe PI (i.e., PI$'$) and the enrolled user's PI. The system completes the identity authentication by computing the distance or similarity between PI and PI$'$ and comparing it to a predefined threshold.

The primary benefit of a salting transformation lies in the significantly low or even zero correlation observed among the protected templates (PIs). This phenomenon is ascribed to the external parameter, the secret or the AD, which plays a crucial role in fulfilling the requirements of recognition accuracy, unlinkability, and revocability.

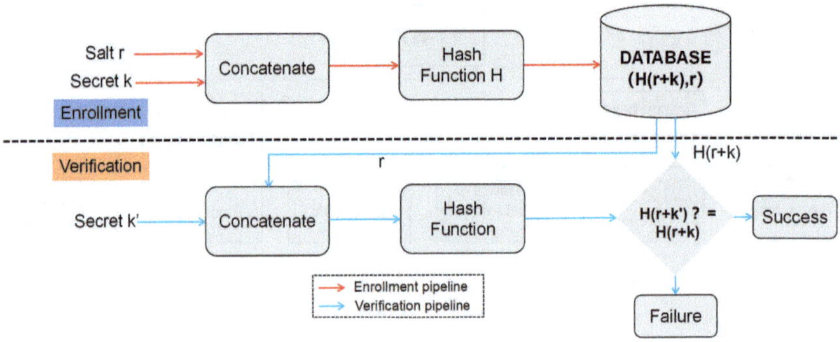

(a)

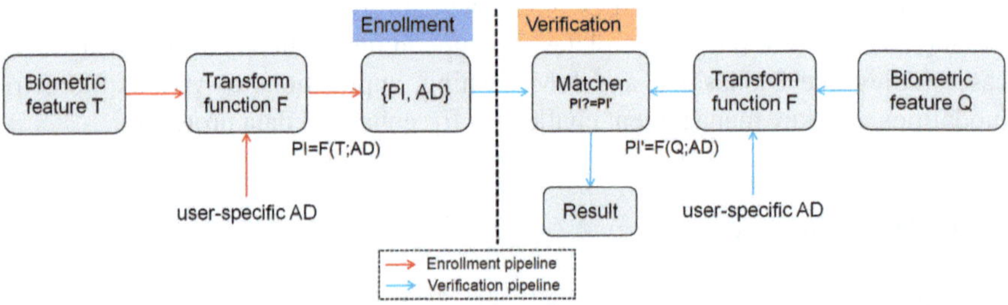

(b)

Fig. 4.4 Overview of salting-based feature transformation. (**a**) Traditional salting algorithm in cryptography. (**b**) Salting-based feature transform

2.1.2 Case Studies

This subsection highlights salting-based transformations like Biohashing, IoM hashing, and Partial Hadamard Transform, showing how these schemes secure biometric data for face, fingerprint, and iris modalities.

Biohashing

- **Input:** Features extracted from face, fingerprint, iris, etc. A user-specific token or password is used as the random seed (AD) to generate the projection matrix.
- **Output:** n-bit binary vector (PI)

Biohashing, introduced by Teoh et al. in [10], is a salting-based construct that utilizes a user-specific password or token. This approach has been successfully applied to face, iris, finger vein, and fingerprint biometrics. The algorithm converts a real-valued vector into a binary vector. The process involves the following steps:

1. Pseudorandom vectors v_i of length n are created (derived from a random, user-specific seed, which is the AD) and assembled into a pseudorandom matrix.
2. The Gram-Schmidt algorithm is applied to the m vectors v_i of the matrix to produce m orthonormal vectors $V_1, \ldots, V_m$.
3. For each $i = 1, \ldots, m$, scalar products $p_i =< F, V_i >$ are calculated using the feature vector F and the m orthonormal vectors V_i. Orthonormal vectors are adopted because they preserve the distance between pairs of corresponding points.
4. The m-bit binary vector (PI) $B = (B_0, \ldots, B_m)$ is obtained using a quantization process:

$$B_i = \begin{cases} 0 \text{ if } p_i < t \\ 1 \text{ if } p_i \geq t, \end{cases}$$

where t is a specified threshold, commonly set to 0 according to [10].

In the enrollment phase, the initial biometric feature vector is transformed using a user-specific key, resulting in a binary vector (i.e., BioHash). The original feature vector is discarded, and the reference binary vector and its associated user key (the random seed) are stored at the database and end user devices, respectively. During verification, a binary vector for the probe biometric feature vector (template) is generated using the same algorithm and the corresponding user's key (random seed). The verification outcome is determined by calculating the Hamming distance between the reference and probe binary vectors (BioHashes). Figure 4.5 illustrates the Biohashing process.

The Biohashing method employs the concept of random projection [2], which maps an n-dimensional feature vector to a lower dimensional space with dimension m. To meet the accuracy requirements discussed earlier, a biometric recognition system must preserve the relative distances between any two points in the output random space. Biohashing achieves this by employing the Gram-Schmidt algorithm, which transforms an arbitrary basis (essentially a random coordinate system) into an orthonormal basis. This transformation is crucial for meeting the performance requirements, as it ensures that the scalar products with the orthonormal vectors maintain the relative distances. This property is supported by the Johnson-Lindenstrauss (JL) lemma [12]:

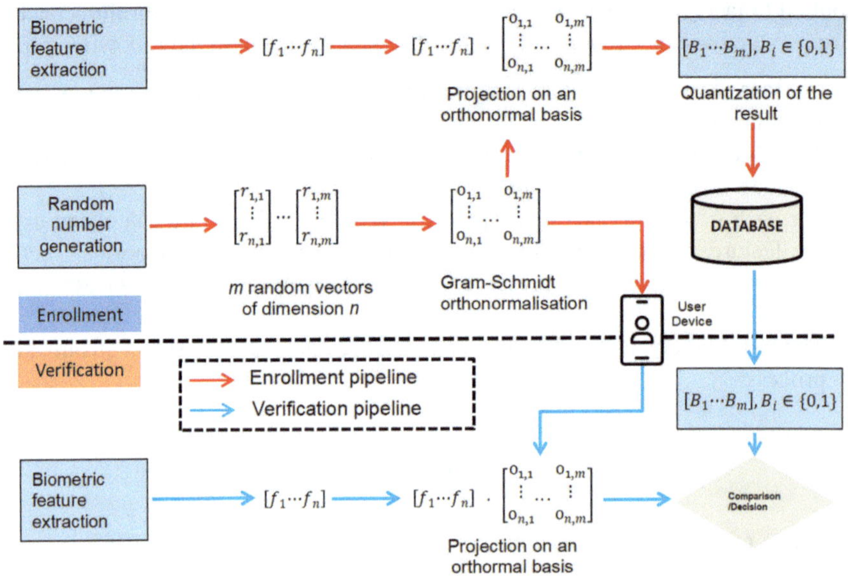

Fig. 4.5 Overview of Biohashing. Biohashing enhances security by combining biometric data with user-specific randomness, resulting in unique, non-invertible binary templates

Lemma 1 *Johnson-Lindenstrauss Lemma. Given N vectors $v_1, v_2, \cdots, v_N \in \mathbb{R}^m$ and $n > \frac{C \log N}{\varepsilon^2}$, where a random matrix $A \in \mathbb{R}^{n \times m}$ is independently sampled from a Gaussian distribution with mean 0 and variance $1/n$, and $\varepsilon \in (0, 1)$ and C is a given constant, then with probability at least $\frac{N-1}{N}$, for all $i \neq j$, it holds that*

$$(1-\varepsilon)\|v_i - v_j\|^2 \leq \|Av_i - Av_j\|^2 \leq (1+\varepsilon)\|v_i - v_j\|^2.$$

The lemma essentially states that a set of N points in $\mathbb{R}^m$ can be mapped into a lower dimensional space of approximately $O(\log N)$ dimensions such that their relative distances do not deviate by more than ε, regardless of the original dimensionality of those N points. This property is leveraged by Biohashing and other similar salting transformation schemes, which alter the original data structure while retaining its statistically significant features for recognition purposes. Here statistically significant features are unique and distinctive characteristics extracted from biological traits (like fingerprints, facial features, iris patterns, or voice) that are crucial for identifying or verifying individuals.

Biohashing is designed to be irreversible by transforming the biometric data into a fixed-size hash code using a specific transformation. This process is one way, meaning that it is not possible to retrieve the original biometric data from the generated hash code. However, when the user-specific seed is known to an attacker, the irreversibility will be potentially compromised. Biohashing achieves unlinkability by applying randomization techniques that obscure the relationship between the biometric data and the resulting hash. Each time a biometric sample is hashed, the transformation can incorporate different random elements (a different random matrix), producing distinct hash values for the same biometric trait. Thus, even if the same biometric input is hashed multiple times across different applications, the outputs are not necessarily the same, so unlinkability is theoretically possible.

Index-of-Max Hashing:

- **Input:** Features extracted from face, fingerprint, iris, etc. A user-specific token is a random seed to generate the projection matrices (AD).
- **Output:** IoM hash code (PI)

The Index-of-Max (IoM) hashing is a form of ranking-based hashing that projects biometric features onto the rank space. As shown in Fig. 4.6, the method to generate an IoM hash code can be condensed into a two-step procedure as follows:

1. Given a biometric vector $\mathbf{x} \in \mathbb{R}^d$, generate m random Gaussian projection matrices derived from AD, where each matrix consists of q random d-dimensional vectors, $\left\{\mathbf{w}_j^i \in \mathbb{R}^d \mid i = 1 \ldots, m, j = 1, \ldots, q\right\} \sim \mathcal{N}(0, I_d)$, and thus a random Gaussian projection matrix $\mathbf{W}^i = \left[\mathbf{w}_1^i, \ldots, \mathbf{w}_q^i\right]$ can be formed.
2. Record the m indices of the maximum values resulting from computing, for each of the m projection matrices, the dot product between the biometric vector and each of the matrix's q vectors

$$\phi\left(\mathbf{W}^i, \mathbf{x}\right) = \arg \max_{j=1\ldots q} \left\langle \mathbf{w}_j^i \mathbf{x} \right\rangle$$

as t_j. The IoM hash code (PI) is hence $T = \{t_i \in \mathcal{U} \mid i = 1, \ldots, m\}$. In other words, T is the collection of indices t_i obtained from the maximum values of each projection matrix, effectively encoding the most important features of the biometric vector into a compact hash code.

Let the reference and probe biometric vectors be denoted as $\mathbf{x}$ and $\mathbf{x}'$, respectively. Then the similarity function for IoM hashing is simply the total number of collisions (number of matched entries) between $\boldsymbol{T}$ and $\boldsymbol{T}'$. Therefore, the similarity function $S\left(\boldsymbol{T}, \boldsymbol{T}'\right)$ for IoM hashing is a variant of the Jaccard similarity coefficient.

IoM hashing preserves the recognition capability of the biometric system, as shown by the mathematical analysis in Section 4.2 from [32]. The rank representation nature of IoM hashed features ensures the strong concealment of biometric

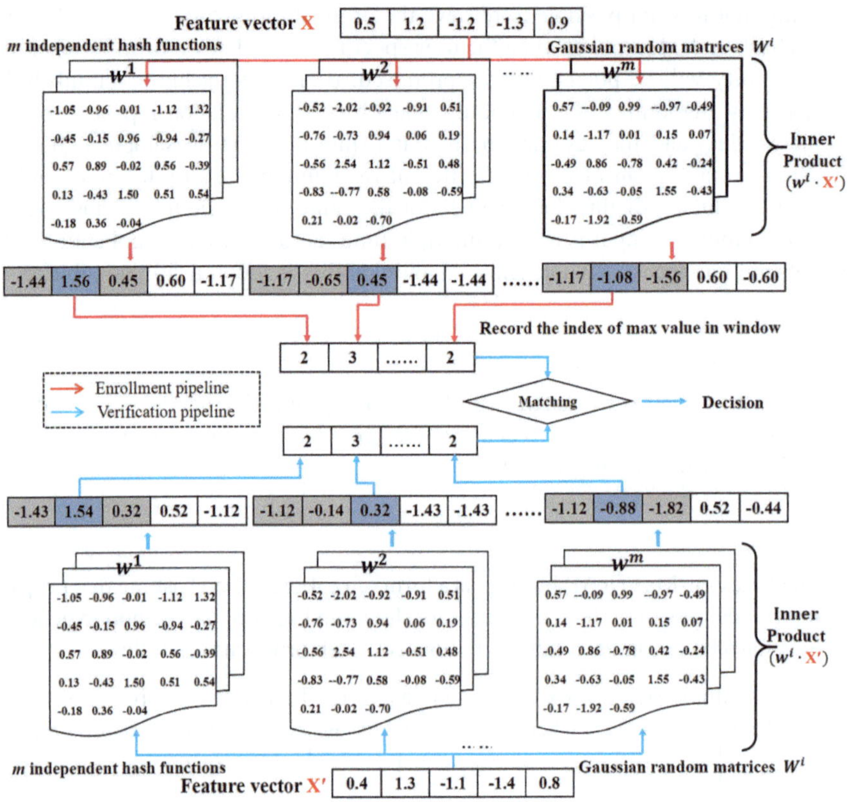

Fig. 4.6 Overview of IoM hashing [11]

features. As discussed in [11] the adversary has no viable method to deduce the real-valued biometric feature vector directly from the hashed code. Additionally, possessing the tokens (AD) does not help in recovering the feature vector, as there is no direct correlation between the tokens and the original features. Therefore, the only option for an adversary is to attempt to guess the real-valued features. The use of random projection matrices introduces randomness into the hashing process, ensuring that even if two biometric inputs belong to the same individual, their hashed representations will vary sufficiently. This variability contributes to the unlinkability of the hashes.

IoM hashing and Biohashing both use random projections to preserve global structures and distort locally and are grounded in Locality-Sensitive Hashing (LSH). They differ in several aspects. IoM hashing employs multiple independent Gaussian projection matrices, whereas Biohashing uses a single random orthonormal matrix. The output of IoM hashing consists of discrete index values, while Biohashing produces binary feature vectors. Lastly, the projection matrix in Biohashing must remain secret to ensure maximum security. In contrast, IoM hashing does not rely on private projection matrices, allowing the use of system-specific rather than user-specific matrices while still demonstrating good accuracy. This approach enhances security and flexibility.

Partial Hadamard Transform:

- **Input:** Binary features extracted from biometric template. A user-specific token is used as the random seed for the Hadamard Matrix (AD) row selection.
- **Output:** Complex vector (PI)

Another form of template projection, proposed for protecting fingerprints in [30], is based on the Partial Hadamard transform using Walsh functions. The Partial Hadamard transform method shows significant promise, particularly in security and accuracy in stolen-token scenarios, compared to Biohashing and IoM hashing. In the Partial Hadamard transform, a submatrix $\mathbf{H}_p$ is generated by randomly selecting m rows from the full-order Hadamard matrix $\mathbf{H}$ of size $n \times n$, where $m < n$. Unlike the full-order Hadamard matrix, which is orthogonal and symmetric, the submatrix $\mathbf{H}_p$ of size $m \times n$ has a deficient column rank, making it non-invertible. As a result, this projection is called the Partial Hadamard Transform and is defined mathematically as

$$\mathbf{y} = \left(\mathbf{H}_p\right)(\mathbf{x}).$$

Here, $\mathbf{y} \in \mathbb{R}^m$ represents the transformed template from the original biometric data $\mathbf{x}$. Figure 4.7 illustrates this process.

2.1.3 Other Biometric Modalities

Applying the salting transformation algorithms discussed above is straightforward for biometric modalities like face, signatures, palm prints, veins, speech, and multimodal biometrics, as long as the extracted features are in fixed-length form.

For example, Shahreza et al. [28] employ Biohashing to protect face feature vectors extracted from deep neural networks, while maintaining the corresponding

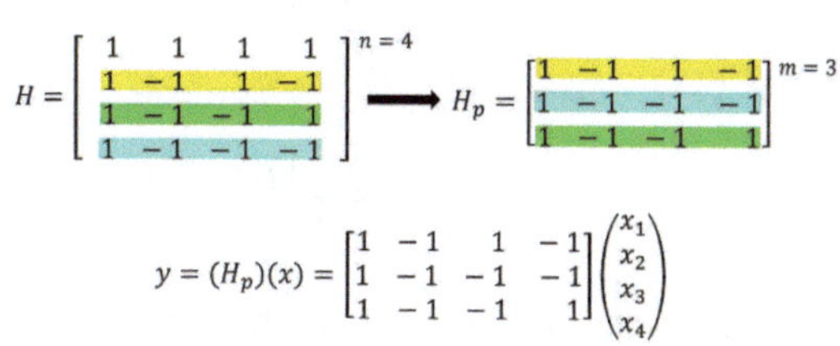

Fig. 4.7 Overview of partial Hadamard transform

recognition accuracy achieved by the unprotected system under the constraint of establishing the minimum BioHash vector length. Krivokuća et al. [15] leverage Biohasing to protect finger vein patterns extracted using the Wide Line Detector (WLD), the Repeated Line Tracking (RTL), and the Maximum Curvature (MC) feature extractors. Multi-biometric systems, which combine multiple biometric features, in general offer enhanced recognition accuracy and security compared to uni-biometric systems. Yang et al. [33] proposed a cancelable multi-biometric system based on fingerprints and finger veins to enhance biometric template security. This system fuses minutia-based fingerprint features with image-based finger vein features using a feature-level fusion strategy. An Enhanced Partial Discrete Fourier Transform (EP-DFT) is also applied to the extracted features. This transform projects the features using a unitary DFT matrix W, ensuring the matrix multiplication operation is invertible.

2.1.4 Supplementary Data Handling in Practice

One drawback of the salting schemes is their susceptibility to being inverted back to the original biometric data from the protected template (e.g., hash) if the AD (i.e., the user-specific key, such as the random seed that defines the projection matrix in Biohashing) is known to the adversary [17]. It is crucial to highlight that maintaining the security of the key is essential for preserving the non-invertibility of the salting scheme.

Inversion involves recovering the initial biometric template from the protected template. The invertibility of this process depends on computational complexity and the number of attempts required for recovery. Sometimes, it can be relatively simple to directly retrieve a close approximation of the original biometric template when the key is known. For the salting scheme, the original biometric features x can be obtained as a solution to a specific problem; for example, given the Biohashing face features b (extracted by Eigenface), the transformation matrix V, and the binarization threshold t [17], we aim to minimize the distance to a reference vector a, thus achieving the inversion from a to x:

$$\arg\min \|x - a\|_2,$$

subject to

$$\sum_{j=1}^{n} V_{ij} x_j < t, \text{ if } \quad b_i = 0,$$

$$\sum_{j=1}^{n} V_{ij} x_j \geq t, \text{ if } \quad b_i = 1,$$

where a is one of the unrelated biometric feature vectors from a database, V is the transformation matrix, b is the transformed feature, and t is the threshold. The researchers in [17] use the "lsqlin" function available in the MATLAB optimization toolbox to obtain a solution to this problem. A weighted combination of multiple solutions is the final estimate of x. The experimental results show that numerous distinctive features from the original face image are also evident in the reconstructed image, highlighting the efficacy of their inversion algorithm.

Therefore, storing the key securely is critical. Several solutions, such as [29], have been proposed to rectify this problem. In [29], a novel parameter management scheme for cancelable biometrics is introduced. It uses a server-side parameter management model to improve system usability and security. The model has a parameter management server for user-specific parameters, which is separated from the authentication server with transformed templates. To address the vulnerability of parameter exposure to clients in the server-side model, authentication protocols with one-time parameters and templates (valid for a single authentication session) are proposed. These protocols are based on certain mathematical properties like the semigroup and group properties and consider function composition commutativity for secure biometric data handling. The work [29] also discusses encrypting communication channels and the need for secure clients to enhance system security, making cancelable biometric systems more robust against threats.

2.2 *Non-invertible Transformation*

Non-invertible transformations secure biometric data by making it computationally difficult to reverse the transformation in order to invert the protected template to obtain the original one. The upcoming sections explain how these transforms work, highlighting their irreversibility. Case studies include techniques like geometric transformations, Bloom filters, and polynomial transforms applied to biometrics. Additional examples of non-invertible transforms show their use in protecting palm prints, voice, and other types of biometrics.

2.2.1 How Does It Work?

A non-invertible transform, such as a one-way function $F(x)$, is characterized by being computationally efficient in the forward direction, running in polynomial time where its execution time is bounded by a polynomial expression in the input size, $T(n) = O(n^k)$ for some positive constant k, but is challenging to reverse, making it a valuable tool for data protection. A secret key determines the transformation function's parameters. This secret key can be user-specific, meaning each user possesses a different key. Alternatively, it can consist of additional information that is shared among users, which is system-specific, indicating that it is common to all users within the system. The transformed biometric feature (v) is stored in the database during enrollment. During verification, the probe biometric features and the secret key are used to generate the transformed feature set v', which is then compared with the stored counterpart v to complete the verification process.

The primary characteristic of a non-invertible transform is the computational complexity involved in attempting to invert it. This complexity presents a challenge for adversaries trying to reconstruct the original biometric feature set, even if they know the secret key and the transformed feature set. In general, a non-invertible transform is irreversible due to the information loss in transforming the original template to the protected template. This information loss is the result of a many-to-one mapping in the forward direction, which translates to a one-to-many mapping in the inverse direction. The larger this information loss, the more difficult the transform becomes to invert, at least to the original template, because the pre-image space becomes larger, i.e., the number of possible solutions increases.

2.2.2 Case Studies

This section highlights non-invertible transformations like geometric transforms, Bloom filters, and polynomial transforms, applied to secure biometrics such as fingerprints, faces, and irises.

Geometric Transformations:

- **Input:** Fingerprint minutiae, face images, etc. Random keys as AD.
- **Output:** Transformed minutiae, transformed face images (PI)

An early realization of a non-invertible transform was proposed by Ratha et al. [23, 24], wherein fingerprint data is transformed by a sequence of three non-invertible transformation functions. These functions utilize Cartesian, polar, and surface folding transformations applied to the minutiae points, as shown in Fig. 4.8.

In the Cartesian transformation, the fingerprint minutiae space is divided into a rectangular grid aligned with the positions of singular points. Each cell, potentially containing minutiae, undergoes a non-invertible transformation that shifts it to a new position. Although the cell itself has been moved to a new location, distances or directional relationships between minutiae inside each cell are unchanged, preserving the local structure or layout during the transformation process. The polar transformation is similar to the Cartesian transformation, except that it tessellates the image into polar sectors. The size of these sectors may vary based on their location, and a translation vector generated from the random key controls the radial distance of the transformed sectors. In summary, the Cartesian and polar transforms employ non-injective mapping (which refers to a mapping in which at least two different inputs map to the same output), with the random vector defining the random translation.

The main limitation of the Cartesian and polar transforms is their sensitivity to intra-user variability, which refers to the changes in a user's fingerprint image due to factors like humidity, pressure of the finger on the fingerprint scanner, and

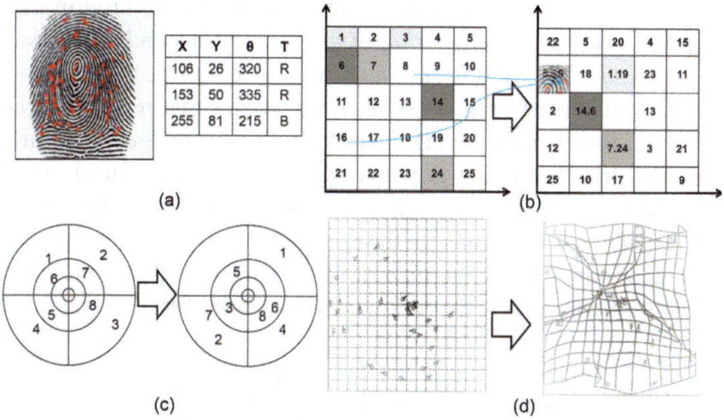

Fig. 4.8 Illustration of the methods proposed by Ratha et al. [23] to transform fingerprint minutiae (**a**) to protected feature templates, including three approaches: Cartesian transformation (**b**), polar transformation (**c**), and surface transformation (**d**)

angle. These transformations can cause significant shifts in the positions of feature points, affecting the accuracy of fingerprint matching. To overcome this challenge, a solution is proposed in [24] to employ a locally smooth but globally not smooth transformation called the functional or surface folding transformation. Ratha et al. [30] highlight the importance of imposing several constraints on the surface folding transformation:

1. The transformation must demonstrate local smoothness, ensuring that a small change in a minutia's position before transformation leads to a similarly small change in the minutia's position after transformation.
2. The transformation should avoid global smoothness. If the post-transformation minutiae positions strongly correlate with their pre-transformation counterparts, the transformation becomes vulnerable to easy inversion. Additionally, the transformation should be many-to-one (non-injective mapping), preventing unique inversion and the recovery of the original minutiae pattern.
3. Minutiae-based matchers tolerate a certain level of uncertainty in minutiae positions and orientations to accommodate feature extraction inaccuracies. Therefore, each minutia position must be pushed beyond the tolerance limit of the matcher after transformation. Thus, ensuring a minimum amount of translation during the transformation is essential.

In [24], functional transformation is achieved by applying the potential field function or two-dimensional Gaussian function to transform the minutiae points of the fingerprint. A definition of the potential field (vector-valued) function in the scheme is first given by

$$F(z) = \sum_{i=1}^{K} \frac{q_i (z - z_i)}{|(z - z_i)|^3}.$$

In this equation, $z = x + iy$ represents the position of a minutia in the complex plane. The positions z_i and strengths[2] q_i of the charges[3] depend on the random keys $z_1, z_2 \ldots, z_K, q_1, q_2, \ldots, q_K$ (AD), which introduces a level of randomness and security to the transformation process. K is an integer that represents the number of charges. Here, the charges are parameters used in the mathematical formulation of the functional transformation function, which is based on an electric potential field model. These charges, along with positions, are used to define the directions and magnitudes of the translations for the minutiae transformations. The modulus of this function determines the magnitude of the translation, $|F(z)|$, and the direction of translation is determined by the following translation direction (phase) function:

$$\Phi(x, y) = \frac{1}{2} \arg \left\{ \sum_{i=1}^{K} \frac{q_i (z - z_i)}{|(z - z_i)|^3} \right\}.$$

The two-dimensional Gaussian function is defined as

$$\sum_{i=1}^{K} \frac{\pi_i}{|2\pi \boldsymbol{\Lambda}_i|} \exp \left\{ -\frac{1}{2} (z - \mu_i)^{\mathrm{T}} \boldsymbol{\Lambda}_i^{-1} (z - \mu_i) \right\},$$

where $z = x + iy$ represents the position, and the random keys determine the weights π_i, covariance matrices $\boldsymbol{\Lambda}$, and centers of the kernels u_i. The magnitude of the translation is determined by the modulus $|F(z)|$ of this function, and the phase function determines the translation direction:

$$\Phi_F(z) = \frac{1}{2} \arg\{\nabla F\} + \Phi_{\mathrm{rand}},$$

where Φ_{rand} is a random phase offset.

To this end, the transformation of the fingerprint minutiae positions and directions can be represented as

$$\begin{aligned} X' &= x + K|G(x, y)| + K \cos(\Phi_F(x, y)), \\ Y' &= y + K|G(x, y)| + K \sin(\Phi_F(x, y)), \\ \Theta' &= \operatorname{mod}(\Theta + \Phi_G(x, y) + \Phi_{\mathrm{rand}}, 2\pi), \end{aligned}$$

where x, y, Θ represent the coordinates and orientation angle of a minutia point before transformation, and X', Y', Θ' represent the coordinates and orientation angle of the minutia after transformation (PI). Φ_G is the phase function of G (AD).

[2] In the analogy with electrostatics, the strength of an electric charge determines how strongly it influences the electric field around it.

[3] The concept of "charges" is borrowed from the analogy with electrostatics in physics.

In the surface folding transformation, the locally smooth nature of the employed transformations minimally impacts error rates compared to the previous two transforms. However, given that a slight alteration in the original fingerprint's minutiae positions can result in a substantial change post-transformation, especially when crossing a sharp boundary, it becomes essential to ensure proper pre-alignment with respect to the core point's position. This ensures consistent transformation of different instances of the same minutia template.

All three transformation functions facilitate many-to-one mapping, where multiple minutiae can be mapped to the same point in the transformed domain. For instance, in the Cartesian transformation, two or more cells can be mapped to a single cell. This design enhances security because even if an adversary obtains the key—and thus the transformation rules between cells—they still cannot determine the original cell associated with a particular minutia. In other words, a minutia could have come from one of several potential cells, which creates ambiguity in its original position. This irreversibility is crucial for privacy, as it prevents the adversary from determining the positions of the original minutiae and thus linking the original minutiae layout to a specific individual. Therefore, the approach guarantees some degree of irreversibility in the resulting template. Furthermore, since the transformations can be altered by changing the random keys, these BTP methods also have the potential to satisfy the renewability/unlinkability criterion, provided that the transformed templates are sufficiently different from each other.

Bloom Filter:

- **Input:** Features extracted from face, iris, etc. Hashing functions h_k (AD)
- **Output:** Binary Bloom filter vectors (PI)

Bloom filters [3] serve as compact probabilistic data structures for representing sets, enabling the addition of elements to a set and the efficient checking of whether an element is present in the set. They are commonly employed in network routing tables to swiftly ascertain if a destination IP address corresponds to any entry in the routing table.

As shown in Fig. 4.9, the components of a standard Bloom filter include a binary vector V of length m (initialized to all zeros) and k ($k \leq n$) independent hash functions $h_1, h_2, \ldots, h_k$, each of which can map an element of a set $A = \{a_1, a_2, \ldots, a_n\}$ to a bit in V. To add an element a to set A, the indices $h_1(a), h_2(a), \ldots, h_k(a)$ are calculated, and the value of the bit in vector V at position $h_i(a)$ ($i = 1, 2, \ldots, k$) is set to 1. To search for an element b in set A, the indices $h_1(b), h_2(b), \ldots, h_k(b)$ are calculated, and then the values of the bits in vector V at positions $h_i(b)$ ($i = 1, 2, \ldots, k$) are checked to see if they are all 1 (perform a bitwise "AND" operation on these bits; if the result is 1, then these bits are all 1). If these positions are all 1, then $b \in A$; otherwise, $b \notin A$ or a false positive error occurs.

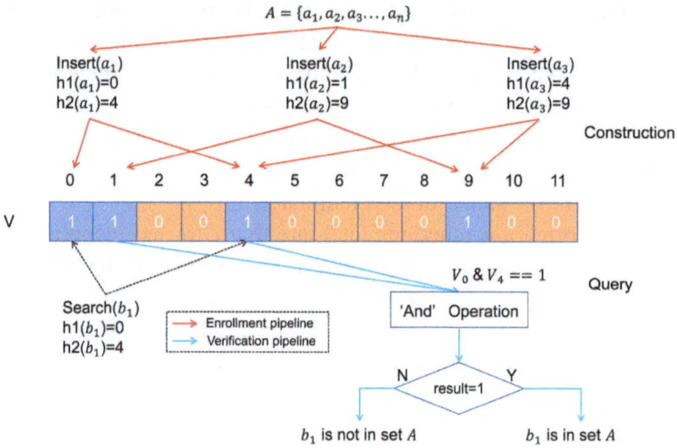

Fig. 4.9 Overview of the standard Bloom filter

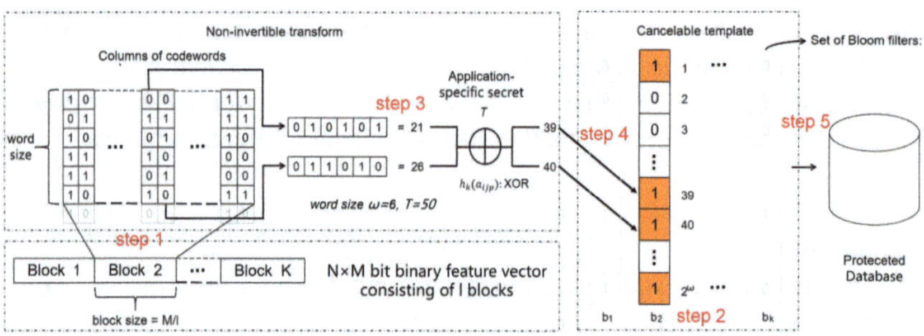

Fig. 4.10 Adaptive Bloom filter for iris recognition workflow [26]. Step 1: Divide matrix J into blocks. Step 2: Initialize Bloom filter vectors and select hash functions. Step 3: Convert subblock columns to decimal. Step 4: Compute hash values and set Bloom filter bits. Step 5: Store results as a template

In 2013, Rathgeb et al. proposed an FT-BTP method based on Bloom filters and applied it to the protection of iris templates [25–27]. Given the iris template as an $N \times M$ binary matrix J, the basic idea is to generate a Bloom filter vector during registration, with the essential steps illustrated in Fig. 4.10:

1. Divide matrix J into blocks, with l horizontal blocks (each block has a width of M/l columns) and N/ω vertical blocks (each block has a height of ω rows or word size of ω), so matrix J is divided into $l \times N/\omega$ blocks.
2. Initialize $l \times N/\omega$ binary Bloom filter vectors of length 2^ω, set all positions of these vectors to 0, and select hash functions $h_1, h_2, \ldots, h_k$.
3. Convert each column (code word) (a ω-bit binary number) of each subblock J_{ij} $(i = 1, 2, \ldots, l.\ j = 1, 2, \ldots, N/\omega)$ of J to a decimal number a_{ijp} $(p = 1, 2, \ldots, M/l)$.

4. Calculate $h_1(a_{ijp}), h_2(a_{ijp}), \ldots, h_k(a_{ijp})$, where $p = 1, 2, \ldots, M/l$, and set the values of the $h_1(a_{ijp}), h_2(a_{ijp}), \ldots, h_k(a_{ijp})$ bits of the Bloom filter corresponding to this subblock J_{ij} (the jth block) to 1, finally obtaining $l \times N/\omega$ Bloom filter vectors.
5. Store the above result as a template or concatenate them by column into a feature vector of length $2^{\omega} \times (l \times N/\omega)$ and store it as a template b (PI).

During authentication, a fresh template b' is generated in a similar way. Then, the Hamming distance between b' and b is calculated and compared to a set threshold to determine the success of the authentication.

Due to the use of hash operations, which may map multiple numbers to the same position in the Bloom filter, the above algorithm essentially constitutes an irreversible mapping. Rathgeb further extended this algorithm to protect templates in multimodal biometric systems [25], such as face and iris. Bloom filters can maintain recognition accuracy by carefully choosing the parameters (size of the bit array and number of hash functions), such that the false positive rate can be minimized to an acceptable level for many applications. However, the analysis in [8] revealed that neither of these two schemes [26, 27] possesses unlinkability as they rely on a single, simplistic hash function. Furthermore, [4] pointed out that the scheme in [26] assumes IrisCodes to be uniformly random for proving irreversibility, an assumption that overlooks the correlations between iriscodes, potentially leading to an overestimation of irreversibility. To overcome these problems, Gomez et al. [6] redesigned the original Bloom filter and proposed an additional step called "structure-preserving feature rearrangement." This process cleverly reorders the biometric feature vector, preserving the structural integrity of the original data while rendering it into a new, distinct, and irreversible representation, thereby ensuring the system's accuracy and robustness against unauthorized linkages.

Polynomial Transform:

- **Input:** Point-set biometric data, consisting of discrete points representing specific features, such as facial features extracted from neural networks and fingerprint minutiae. The coefficients and exponents (AD) of the polynomial
- **Output:** Projected point sets (PI)

This method involves applying random polynomial functions of order $m \in \mathbb{N}^+$ to transform biometric data, as initially conceptualized in [22]. For instance, individual high-order polynomial functions could be utilized to transform each biometric data element x, defined as

$$y = f(x) = \sum_{i=0}^{m} s_i x^i,$$

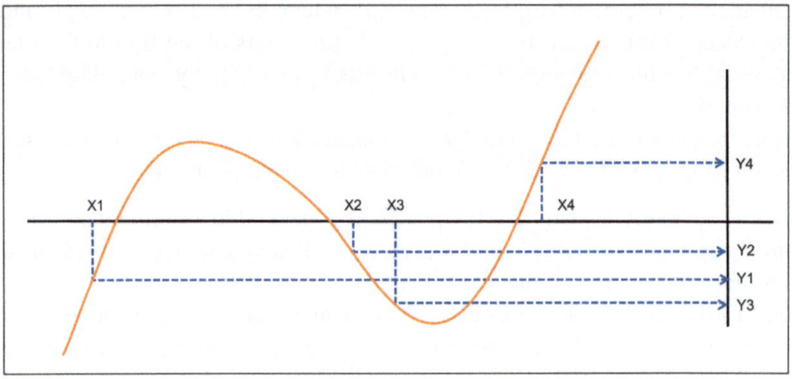

Fig. 4.11 Third-order polynomial transformation. This figure illustrates the non-injective mapping of biometric data using a third-order polynomial

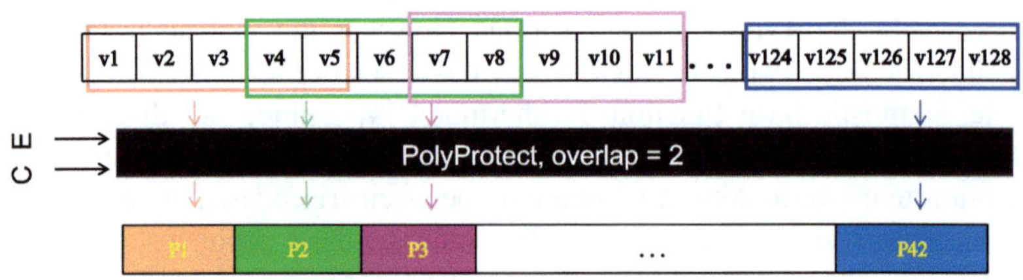

Fig. 4.12 Mapping 128-dimensional V to P via PolyProtect, using $C = [c_1, c_2, \ldots, c_5]$ and $E = [e_1, e_2, \ldots, e_5]$, for an overlap of 2 (Adapted from [16])

where $s_i \in \mathcal{N}(0, 1)$ is the coefficient of the polynomial for $i = 0, 1, 2, \ldots, m$. Figure 4.11 illustrates a third-order polynomial with a one-to-many (non-injective) mapping. For example, in Fig. 4.11, while x_1 maps uniquely to y_1, the inverse mapping from y_1 back to x is one-to-many, as indicated by the three intersection points between the horizontal line at y_1 and the polynomial curve. These intersections represent multiple possible x values that could correspond to the same y_1, illustrating why the function is non-invertible.

Krivokuća Hahn et al. [16] proposed a specific implementation of a polynomial transformation, namely PolyProtect, to protect face templates (when they take the form of embeddings extracted from a neural network-based feature extractor). Given a set of multivariate polynomials defined by m user-specific ordered, unique, nonzero integer coefficients $C = [c_1, c_2, \ldots, c_m]$, and exponents $E = [e_1, e_2, \ldots, e_m]$, an n-dimensional face embedding $V \in \mathbb{R}^n$ is transformed into a new k-dimensional vector $P \in \mathbb{R}^k$ (PI), where $k < n$. As shown in Fig. 4.12, the process can be broken down into the following steps:

1. **Mapping the first subset to p_1:** The first m consecutive elements of V, denoted as $v_1, v_2, \ldots, v_m$, are mapped to the first element in P, p_1, using the following equation:

$$p_1 = c_1 v_1^{e_1} + c_2 v_2^{e_2} + \cdots + c_m v_m^{e_m}.$$

2. **Mapping subsequent subsets to $p_2, p_3, \ldots, p_k$:**

   - The elements used to generate p_2 depend on the desired overlap between successive sets. If the overlap is 0, p_2 is generated using elements $v_{m+1}, v_{m+2}, \ldots, v_{m+m}$.

$$p_2 = c_1 v_{m+1}^{e_1} + c_2 v_{m+2}^{e_2} + \cdots + c_m v_{m+m}^{e_m}.$$

   - If the overlap is $m - 1$, then p_2 is generated using elements $v_2, v_3, \ldots, v_{m+1}$.

$$p_2 = c_1 v_2^{e_1} + c_2 v_3^{e_2} + \cdots + c_m v_{m+1}^{e_m}.$$

   This process continues similarly for $p_3, p_4, \ldots, p_k$ until all elements in V are used.
3. **Handling incomplete sets:** If the last set of elements from V is incomplete because the dimensionality of V is not divisible by the required number of element sets m and the amount of overlap, V is padded with sufficient zeros to complete the last set.

This method safeguards biometric templates by utilizing a non-injective mapping. As demonstrated in [16], irreversibility is influenced by the degree of overlap in the mapping: Greater overlap increases the likelihood of the protected template being invertible, while a smaller overlap enhances privacy in terms of guaranteeing a higher degree of irreversibility. Recognition accuracy is also affected by the amount of overlap, with increased overlap leading to improved accuracy. Unlinkability is achieved by varying user-specific polynomial parameters, including coefficients and exponents.

2.2.3 Other Biometric Modalities

Various non-invertible transformation template protection schemes have been proposed for other biometric modalities, such as signatures [18], palm prints [21], veins [13, 33], voice [5, 31], multimodal biometrics [14], and more.

In [21], an innovative palm print template protection scheme is introduced, which leverages the unique properties of chaotic theory and multidirectional Anisotropic Filters (AFs) to enhance both the security and privacy of palm print-based biometric systems. The proposed scheme is designed to address the fundamental challenge of creating a cancelable biometric template that can be regenerated if compromised, without sacrificing the accuracy of the recognition process. The scheme begins with the application of AFs to the raw palm print images to extract detailed orientation features. These features are then processed through a chaotic matrix, which introduces a degree of randomness and non-ergodicity, ensuring that the resulting template is irreversible and cancelable. The chaotic matrix operates on the principle of piecewise linear chaotic maps, which are characterized by their pseudo-randomness and unpredictability. In finger vein recognition, Piciucco et al. [13] suggest utilizing two classical transformations, namely block remapping and image warping, to establish cancellable biometrics from finger vein pattern images. The study delves explicitly into examining the impact of these distortions on recognition accuracy, along with exploring the effects stemming from the selection of their parameters. For speech template security, a cancellable transformation known as Random Binary Orthogonal Matrices Projection (RBOMP) hashing is introduced in [5]. This approach protects a widely used speech representation, specifically the i-vector. In summary, RBOMP hashing involves projecting the i-vector using random binary orthogonal matrices and capturing the resulting discrete value like IoM hashing. The nonlinearity of RBOMP ensures the resilience of the hashed code against template invertibility attacks. In [14], Kaur et al. introduce an innovative template transformation technique known as the Random Distance Method (RDM). This technique enhances biometric security and privacy by converting original biometric identities into pseudo-biometric identities. It functions by mapping biometric features as points in Cartesian space and calculating their distances from a user-specific random point. After processing these distances through median filtering to ensure non-invertibility, the resulting transformed template is both discriminative and privacy-preserving. RDM also significantly reduces the template size by 50% without compromising matching accuracy, making it suitable for various biometric modalities and robust against a multitude of security threats. This study applies to various biometric modalities, including face, palm print, palm vein, and finger vein.

3 Pros and Cons of Each Category of FT-BTP

Table 4.1 summarizes the pros and cons of the two fundamental FT-BTP categories: salting and non-invertible transforms.

Salting transformations offer the advantage of a user-specific key, which addresses intra-user variability and enhances security. Even for the same user whose input data might have some natural variations over time or in different instances, the specific key can account for and manage those differences. Moreover, it enhances security as the user-specific key makes it more difficult for unauthorized parties to access or manipulate the data. On the other hand, this approach is also relatively easy to implement. However, salting has its drawbacks. Additional storage is required for the salt value, which can increase system complexity and cost. Moreover, the security and privacy of salting are not only partially dependent on the quality and randomness of the salt generation process but also critically hinge on keeping the

Table 4.1 Pros and cons of each category of FT-BTP

Category	Example	Characteristic	Merits	Demerits
Salting	1. Biohashing	Mimics the traditional salting algorithm in cryptography	1. Addresses intra-user variability	1. Requires extra storage
	2. IoM hashing		2. Easy to implement	2. Security depends on the quality and safekeeping of the salt
	3. Partial Hadamard transform			
Non-invertible	1. Geometric transform	Non-invertible and computationally efficient (polynomial time) in the forward direction but challenging to reverse	1. Strong protection against inversion attacks	1. Complex design
	2. Bloom filter		2. Computationally efficient while maintaining security	2. May affect recognition accuracy
	3. Polynomial transform			

salt secret. If the salt is compromised, the security of the entire system can be at risk, as attackers may use it to reverse engineer the hash or create more effective brute-force attacks. Therefore, it is essential to implement robust measures to protect the salt, ensuring that it remains confidential and inaccessible to unauthorized parties.

The second main category of FT-BTP methods, non-invertible transformations, provides strong protection against template inversion attacks by ensuring that the transformation cannot be reversed to obtain the original template. These types of algorithms can be designed to be computationally efficient while maintaining a high level of security, offering a balance between efficiency and protection.

Nonetheless, implementing non-invertible transformations comes with challenges. One of the primary challenges is balancing irreversibility and recognition accuracy. The more non-invertible a transformation is, the more information is typically lost, which can degrade the system's ability to correctly match biometric templates. This trade-off must be carefully managed, especially in security-critical applications where both protection and performance are essential.

Another challenge is the complexity of designing the transformation. Ensuring that a transformation is truly non-invertible, while still preserving enough discriminative features for matching, requires careful consideration. The transformation must prevent attackers from reversing or approximating the original data, even if the transformation parameters are compromised, but it must also be efficient enough for practical use in real-time systems.

Scalability is another concern. Non-invertible transforms that work well for small datasets or limited biometric features may struggle to scale effectively when applied to larger datasets or more complex biometric modalities, such as multimodal biometrics or high-dimensional data. Ensuring that the transformation remains secure, while also being able to handle large-scale applications, requires further research and optimization.

Finally, compatibility with existing systems presents a challenge. Many commercial systems prioritize recognition accuracy and may not be designed to accommodate the added complexity of non-invertible transformations. Integrating these methods into existing infrastructure may require significant adjustments, in terms of both system architecture and user experience, without sacrificing usability or performance.

Understanding these pros and cons is crucial for selecting the most appropriate biometric template protection scheme for a given application. Each scheme has its trade-offs, and the choice depends on the specific requirements and constraints of the system.

4 Future Trends and Research Directions

This chapter focused on handcrafted FT-BTP schemes not optimized with other components, such as feature extractors. FT-BTP schemes may benefit from integration into learning-based algorithms. This integration could enhance performance by leveraging the capabilities of machine learning models to adapt and optimize the protection process, ultimately improving the trade-off between accuracy and security.

FT-BTP offers a promising approach to enhancing security and privacy. By minimizing intra-user variability and maximizing inter-user variability, FT-BTP effectively protects, and enables the revocability (cancellability) of, biometric information. Future advancements in FT-BTP may focus on integrating hardware components like secure enclaves, trusted platform modules (TPMs), or biometric sensors with built-in encryption to help protect against physical attacks, such as tampering or side-channel attacks. Hardware components provide a trusted execution environment, ensuring that sensitive operations (e.g., encryption, template generation, and matching) are isolated from potential software vulnerabilities or external tampering.

It is essential to develop more commercial biometric products incorporating BTP techniques. While many BTP techniques are developed in academia, commercial products often lag, with most existing products focusing on improving recognition accuracy rather than ensuring robust template protection. Addressing this gap requires considering factors such as computational cost and execution time, ensuring that BTP techniques can be effectively implemented in real-world applications.

Additionally, it is crucial to evaluate the potential degradation in recognition accuracy, ensuring that enhanced security does not come at the expense of performance. Another critical factor is the need for legislative measures, which could motivate commercial products to adopt stronger security standards. Regulatory compliance may drive innovation and encourage the integration of more robust BTP techniques in the commercial sector. Equally important is the development of a robust evaluation framework to assess BTP methods in practical applications. Such a framework would ensure that these techniques can be effectively tested and validated for real-world use, addressing both security and performance considerations.

A hybrid approach combining different BTP techniques could offer a more robust solution. A hybrid approach can provide a balanced trade-off between accuracy and security by leveraging the strengths of various techniques, such as transformation-based and encryption-based methods. Ultimately, satisfying and balancing the critical BTP criteria—recognition accuracy, irreversibility, renewability, and unlinkability—should remain a central focus in future research and development.

5 Summary

- FT-BTP schemes intentionally distort biometric data to create a protected template called a pseudonymous identifier (PI), with the help of auxiliary data (AD), such as user-specific transformation parameters.
- FT-BTP schemes can operate directly on biometric raw signals or features extracted by a specific feature extractor.
- FT-BTP schemes can be divided into salting and non-invertible transform categories.
- The main advantage of salting methods is the notable lack of correlation among protected templates, although they may become invertible when the AD is revealed.
- The main advantage of non-invertible transforms is the difficulty of reversing the transform to recover the original biometric template from the protected template (due to the nonexistence or computational complexity of the inverse transform). However, this may come with a trade-off, potentially impacting accuracy performance.

6 Study Questions

1. Describe the difference between salting and non-invertible transformations in FT-BTP.
2. What roles does AD play in FT-BTP schemes?
3. Which BTP criterion does the salting transform most effectively fulfill?

4. Why is a consideration of intra-class variance critical to designing a robust, non-invertible transform BTP scheme?
5. What is the role of pseudonymous identifiers (PIs) in FT-BTP? Discuss the significance of PIs and how they contribute to protecting biometric data.
6. Discuss the trade-offs between accuracy and irreversibility in FT-BTP schemes. How do different transformation methods impact the balance between maintaining biometric recognition accuracy and ensuring template security?
7. How do environmental factors influence the performance of biometric systems and their template protection mechanisms? Consider the impact of varying conditions, such as lighting, noise, and sensor quality, on the robustness of biometric template protection.
8. Compare and contrast Bloom filter-based and polynomial transform-based methods for biometric template protection. What are each method's advantages and disadvantages in terms of security and computational efficiency?
9. What are the future trends and research directions in FT-BTP? Discuss potential advancements and emerging technologies that could enhance the security and efficiency of FT-BTP methods.

7 Resources

1. Bloom filter source code: https://github.com/dasec/face-bf-btp
2. Index-of-Max hashing and Biohashing source code: https://github.com/xingbod/OnCBrisks/tree/master/btp/
3. PolyProtect source code: https://gitlab.idiap.ch/bob/bob.paper.polyprotect_2021

References

1. Ang, R., Safavi-Naini, R., McAven, L.: Cancelable key-based fingerprint templates. In: Australasian Conference on Information Security and Privacy, pp. 242–252. Springer (2005)
2. Bingham, E., Mannila, H.: Random projection in dimensionality reduction: applications to image and text data. In: Proceedings of the Seventh ACM SIGKDD International Conference on Knowledge Discovery and Data Mining, pp. 245–250 (2001)
3. Bloom, B.H.: Space/time trade-offs in hash coding with allowable errors. Commun. ACM **13**(7), 422–426 (1970)
4. Bringer, J., Morel, C., Rathgeb, C.: Security analysis of bloom filter-based iris biometric template protection. In: 2015 International Conference on Biometrics (ICB), pp. 527–534. IEEE (2015)
5. Chee, K.Y., Jin, Z., Cai, D., Li, M., Yap, W.S., Lai, Y.L., Goi, B.M.: Cancellable speech template via random binary orthogonal matrices projection hashing. Pattern Recogn. **76**, 273–287 (2018)
6. Gomez-Barrero, M., Rathgeb, C., Galbally, J., Busch, C., Fierrez, J.: Unlinkable and irreversible biometric template protection based on bloom filters. Inf. Sci. **370**, 18–32 (2016)

7. Hämmerle-Uhl, J., Pschernig, E., Uhl, A.: Cancelable iris biometrics using block re-mapping and image warping. In: International Conference on Information Security, pp. 135–142. Springer (2009)
8. Hermans, J., Mennink, B., Peeters, R.: When a bloom filter is a doom filter: security assessment of a novel iris biometric template protection system. In: 2014 International Conference of the Biometrics Special Interest Group (BIOSIG), pp. 1–6. IEEE (2014)
9. ISO/IEC 24745:2011 - Information technology – Security techniques – Biometric information protection. https://www.iso.org/standard/52946.html
10. Jin, A.T.B., Ling, D.N.C., Goh, A.: Biohashing: two factor authentication featuring fingerprint data and tokenised random number. Pattern Recogn. **37**(11), 2245–2255 (2004)
11. Jin, Z., Hwang, J.Y., Lai, Y.L., Kim, S., Teoh, A.B.J.: Ranking-based locality sensitive hashing-enabled cancelable biometrics: index-of-max hashing. IEEE Trans. Inf. Forensics Secur. **13**(2), 393–407 (2017)
12. Johnson, W., Lindenstrauss, J.: Extensions of Lipschitz mappings into a Hilbert space. Conf. Modern Analy. Probab. **26**, 189–206 (1982)
13. Kauba, C., Piciucco, E., Maiorana, E., Gomez-Barrero, M., Prommegger, B., Campisi, P., Uhl, A.: Towards practical cancelable biometrics for finger vein recognition. Inf. Sci. **585**, 395–417 (2022)
14. Kaur, H., Khanna, P.: Random distance method for generating unimodal and multimodal cancelable biometric features. IEEE Trans. Inf. Forensics Secur. **14**(3), 709–719 (2018)
15. Krivokuća, V., Marcel, S.: On the recognition performance of biohash-protected finger vein templates. In: Handbook of Vascular Biometrics, pp. 465–480. Springer, Cham (2020)
16. Krivokuća Hahn, V., Marcel, S.: Towards protecting face embeddings in mobile face verification scenarios. IEEE Trans. Biom. Behav. Identity Sci. **4**(1), 117–134 (2022). https://doi.org/10.1109/TBIOM.2022.3140472
17. Nagar, A., Nandakumar, K., Jain, A.K.: Biometric template transformation: a security analysis. In: Media Forensics and Security II, vol. 7541, pp. 237–251. SPIE, Bellingham (2010)
18. Pal, S., Pal, U., Blumenstein, M.: Signature-based biometric authentication. In: Computational Intelligence in Digital Forensics: Forensic Investigation and Applications, pp. 285–314. Springer, Cham (2014)
19. Patel, V.M., Ratha, N.K., Chellappa, R.: Cancelable Biometrics: a review. IEEE Signal Process. Mag. **32**(5), 54–65 (2015). https://doi.org/10.1109/MSP.2015.2434151
20. Piciucco, E., Maiorana, E., Kauba, C., Uhl, A., Campisi, P.: Cancelable biometrics for finger vein recognition. In: 2016 First International Workshop on Sensing, Processing and Learning for Intelligent Machines (SPLINE), pp. 1–5. IEEE (2016)
21. Qiu, J., Li, H., Zhao, C.: Cancelable palmprint templates based on random measurement and noise data for security and privacy-preserving authentication. Comput. Secur. **82**, 1–14 (2019)
22. Ratha, N.K., Connell, J.H., Bolle, R.M.: Enhancing security and privacy in biometrics-based authentication systems. IBM Syst. J. **40**(3), 614–634 (2001)
23. Ratha, N., Connell, J., Bolle, R.M., Chikkerur, S.: Cancelable biometrics: A case study in fingerprints. In: 18th International Conference on Pattern Recognition (ICPR'06), vol. 4, pp. 370–373. IEEE (2006)
24. Ratha, N.K., Chikkerur, S., Connell, J.H., Bolle, R.M.: Generating cancelable fingerprint templates. IEEE Trans. Pattern Analy. Mach. Intell. **29**(4), 561–572 (2007)
25. Rathgeb, C., Busch, C.: Cancelable multi-biometrics: mixing iris-codes based on adaptive bloom filters. Comput. Secur. **42**, 1–12 (2014)
26. Rathgeb, C., Breitinger, F., Busch, C.: Alignment-free cancelable iris biometric templates based on adaptive bloom filters. In: 2013 International Conference on Biometrics (ICB), pp. 1–8. IEEE (2013)
27. Rathgeb, C., Breitinger, F., Busch, C., Baier, H.: On application of bloom filters to iris biometrics. IET Biom. **3**(4), 207–218 (2014)
28. Shahreza, H.O., Krivokuća Hahn, V., Marcel, S.: On the recognition performance of biohashing on state-of-the-art face recognition models. In: Proceedings of the IEEE International Workshop on Information Forensics and Security (WIFS), pp. 1–6. IEEE (2021)

29. Takahashi, K., Hirata, S.: Parameter management schemes for cancelable biometrics. In: 2011 IEEE Workshop on Computational Intelligence in Biometrics and Identity Management (CIBIM), pp. 145–151. IEEE (2011)
30. Wang, S., Deng, G., Hu, J.: A partial Hadamard transform approach to the design of cancelable fingerprint templates containing binary biometric representations. Pattern Recogn. **61**, 447–458 (2017)
31. Xu, W., He, Q., Li, Y., Li, T.: Cancelable voiceprint templates based on knowledge signatures. In: 2008 International Symposium on Electronic Commerce and Security, pp. 412–415. IEEE (2008)
32. Yagnik, J., Strelow, D., Ross, D.A., Lin, R.s.: The power of comparative reasoning. In: 2011 International Conference on Computer Vision, pp. 2431–2438. IEEE (2011)
33. Yang, W., Wang, S., Hu, J., Zheng, G., Valli, C.: A fingerprint and finger-vein based cancelable multi-biometric system. Pattern Recogn. **78**, 242–251 (2018)

Chapter 5
Biometric Cryptosystems

Christian Rathgeb, Valentina Fohr, and Benjamin Tams

Abstract In deployments of biometrics, secure storage of biometric information is necessary in order to protect the users' privacy. Within this context, biometric template protection (BTP) mechanisms are designed to meet key requirements of biometric information protection, enabling privacy-preserving storage and comparison of biometric data. *Biometric cryptosystems*, a subset of biometric template protection methods, are explored in this chapter, which presents a general introduction to their principles and applications. Based on a categorisation of existing schemes, popular cryptographic primitives, i.e. the fuzzy commitment and fuzzy vault scheme, are described in detail along with relevant works applying them to different biometric characteristics. Error correction coding techniques that are frequently employed in biometric cryptosystems are explained. In addition, the concept of feature-type transformation in order to make biometric feature vectors compatible with biometric cryptosystems is discussed. Subsequently, implementations based on different types of biometric cryptosystems are presented and obtained results are reported. Finally, open challenges are discussed.

C. Rathgeb (✉)
Department of Computer Science, Hochschule Darmstadt, Darmstadt, Germany

Homeland Security Division, Secunet Security Networks, Essen, Germany
e-mail: christian.rathgeb@h-da.de

V. Fohr
Department of Computer Science, Hochschule Darmstadt, Darmstadt, Germany
e-mail: valentina.fohr@stud.h-da.de

B. Tams
Homeland Security Division, Secunet Security Networks, Essen, Germany
e-mail: benjamin.tams@secunet.com

V. Krivokuća Hahn et al. (eds.), *Handbook of Biometric Template Protection*,
https://doi.org/10.1007/978-981-95-0995-9_5

1 Introduction

The widespread deployment of biometric technologies has prompted various privacy concerns regarding the potential misuse of biometric data. To address this issue, contemporary privacy regulations include provisions governing the storage and utilization of biometric data. For instance, the General Data Protection Regulation (GDPR) [16] broadly categorises biometric data as sensitive information necessitating protection.[1] It is crucial to recognise that this classification encompasses both biometric samples and biometric templates. Although the latter may not be easily interpretable by humans, they can still be exploited for cross-matching attacks, and approximations of biometric samples can be derived from unprotected biometric templates [19].[2]

It is widely acknowledged that conventional cryptographic techniques are inadequate for safeguarding biometric data, primarily because of the inherent intraclass variance of biometric characteristics. Specifically, this variance renders symmetric ciphers and traditional hash functions impractical for handling biometric input data, as even minor alterations in the unprotected domain result in significant changes in the protected domain. Consequently, employing conventional cryptographic methods fails to ensure permanent protection.[3] For the use of symmetric ciphers, a decryption of protected biometric data prior to comparison becomes necessary.[4]

To address the aforementioned challenge, various biometric template protection methods have been proposed, as referenced in [3, 45, 59]. These methods utilise auxiliary data to generate pseudonymous identifiers from unprotected biometric data. Subsequently, biometric comparisons are conducted using these pseudonymous identifiers while discarding the original unprotected biometric data. These techniques are typically classified as *biometric cryptosystems*, cancellable biometrics,[5] and biometrics in the encrypted domain.

> *Biometric cryptosystems enable the retrieval of keys using biometric data through error-tolerant key-generation or key-binding processes that protect the original biometric data.*

This means that, in biometric cryptosystems, a biometric comparison is indirectly conducted by verifying the correctness of a retrieved key [69]. This enables the retrieval of digital keys from protected biometric templates. In contrast, cancellable biometrics apply specific transforms in the signal or feature domain, facilitating biometric comparison in the transformed (protected) domain [35, 49].[5] Alternatively,

[1] Chapter 3 in Part I of this book discusses the GDPR and other privacy frameworks.

[2] Chapter 1 in Part I of this book discusses template inversion attacks.

[3] Chapter 2 in Part I of this book discusses the unsuitability of traditional data protection mechanisms, like hashing and encryption, for biometric template protection.

[4] Storage and comparison of biometric data with tamper-resistant hardware, e.g. specialised chip cards, represents an alternative way of securely managing biometric data.

[5] Chapter 4 in Part II of this book discusses cancellable biometrics, also referred to as feature transformations.

Table 5.1 Properties of template protection categories

BTP category	Unlinkability	Irreversibility	Performance preservation	Efficient comparison
Biometric cryptosystems	(✓)	✓	(✓)	(✓)
Feature transformations	✓	✓	(✓)	✓
Homomorphic encryption	✓	✓	✓	(✓)

✓ fulfilled (✓) partially fulfilled

homomorphic encryption is frequently proposed for biometric template protection [1, 2].[6] Homomorphic encryption allows for computation of operations in the encrypted domain that are functionally equivalent to those in the plaintext domain, thereby enabling the estimation of certain distances between protected biometric templates.

The main requirements for biometric template protection schemes are outlined in ISO/IEC IS 24745 [26]:

- **Unlinkability**: Refers to the infeasibility of determining if two or more protected templates were derived from the same biometric trait. By fulfilling this property, cross-matching across different databases is prevented. In case unlinkability is fulfilled, the secondary requirement of renewability, i.e. the ability to revoke protected templates, is also achieved.
- **Irreversibility**: Denotes the infeasibility of reconstructing the original biometric data from a protected template and its corresponding auxiliary data. This property enhances privacy and strengthens system security against presentation and replay attacks.
- **Performance preservation**: Ensures that the biometric performance is not substantially diminished by the protection scheme.

Table 5.1 gives an overview of the mentioned types of biometric template protection and their properties with respect to the above criteria and efficient biometric comparison. In contrast to homomorphic encryption, the majority of works on biometric cryptosystems (as well as cancellable biometrics) report a performance gap between protected and original (unprotected) systems [45]. Regarding the comparison efficiency, biometric cryptosystems usually require computationally complex key retrieval methods, making them less suitable for biometric identification [14]. Unlinkability is not traditionally satisfied by biometric cryptosystems like the fuzzy commitment and fuzzy vault, as well as by typical key-generation methods. However, solutions to achieve unlinkability in biometric cryptosystems have been proposed, which will be further discussed in the following section. Irreversibility is generally achieved by biometric cryptosystems. In contrast to feature transformations and homomorphic encryption, biometric cryptosystems

[6] Chapter 6 in Part II of this book discusses homomorphic encryption for biometric template protection.

enable the retrieval of digital keys based on biometric data. This is particularly relevant for key management where the use of biometrics represents a suitable alternative to the common PIN- or password-based key release mechanism, since biometrics cannot be delegated, thus providing a strong user binding.

In the past two decades, numerous proposals for biometric cryptosystems have been published in the scientific literature. This chapter aims to provide an overview of the fundamentals of biometric cryptosystems along with a detailed description of representative applications to different biometric characteristics, i.e. face and fingerprint. Some experimental evaluations are presented and, finally, a summary and an outlook are provided.

This chapter is organised as follows: Sect. 2 introduces different categories of biometric cryptosystems and describes frequently used schemes in detail, along with relevant error correction codes and feature-type transformations. Subsequently, Sect. 3 provides a detailed description of the implementation of two different biometric cryptosystems, including employed datasets, software, preprocessing, evaluation metrics, and experimental results. Open challenges are discussed in Sect. 4. Finally, Sect. 5 summarises the chapter and points to future research directions.

2 Biometric Cryptosystems

This section introduces a well-established categorisation of biometric cryptosystems. Subsequently, two widely used biometric cryptosystems are described in detail. Finally, important building blocks of many biometric cryptosystems, i.e. error correction codes and feature-type transformations, are explained.

2.1 Categorisation

Biometric cryptosystems are commonly categorised as key-generation or key-binding schemes, see Fig. 5.1. Both types of methods aim at retrieving a stable key in an error-tolerant way during the presentation of biometric data:

- **Key-generation schemes**: An essential processing step of key-generation approaches is to extract stable biometric features. This can be achieved through quantisation. For instance, intervals can be defined for each feature element based on which feature values are encoded, i.e. interval boundaries represent the helper data [53]. Alternatively, compact representations can also be extracted by deep learning techniques. Deep hashing is used as an umbrella term for methods which aim at extracting compact and stable representations with deep learning techniques [6]. In the recent past, deep hashes have been extracted from different biometric characteristics in various ways, e.g. in [27, 64]. On the one hand,

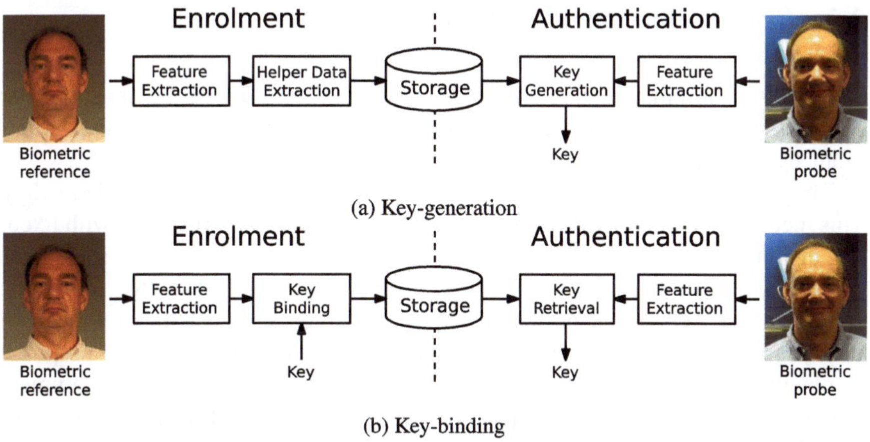

Fig. 5.1 Basic processing steps in key-generation and key-binding schemes

quantisation may result in a loss of biometric performance due to information loss [13]. On the other hand, it achieves a certain degree of irreversibility. In order to additionally guarantee unlinkability, the stable biometric identifiers have to be further obscured, e.g. through encryption methods that utilise an application-specific key.

- **Key-binding schemes**: In a key-binding scheme, a predefined key is combined, i.e. bound, with biometric data. This process is performed with the aim that neither the key nor the biometric data can be derived from the combined (protected) record. If this property is fulfilled, the requirement of irreversibility is met. In the retrieval process, it should be possible to reconstruct the key by presenting biometric data that is sufficiently close to the one used during the binding process (i.e. during enrolment). Error tolerance is usually controlled by the use of error correction codes, e.g. in a fuzzy commitment [30] or a fuzzy vault [29]. The type and capacity of the employed error correction codes needs to be adjusted to the representation of biometric feature vectors and expected error distributions. Unlinkability and renewability are not achieved by default in key-binding schemes (e.g. simply changing the key generally does not achieve unlinkability). However, unlinkability and renewability may be achieved by randomising the used keys as well as the biometric data, e.g. through feature permutations [31], which could be seen as a hybrid template protection scheme.

In summary, on the one hand, the majority of biometric cryptosystems published in the scientific literature are key-binding schemes, most of which build upon, or are variants of, the fuzzy commitment or fuzzy vault scheme. Section 2.2, therefore, presents these two key-binding methods in more detail. On the other hand, advanced methods, e.g. deep learning techniques, which allow for the extraction of stable identifiers from fuzzy data, could renew the interest in key-generation schemes.

2.2 Fuzzy Commitment and Fuzzy Vault

The fuzzy commitment and fuzzy vault schemes represent two of the most popular and well-explored cryptosystems that have been applied in different ways to various biometric characteristics.

The fuzzy commitment scheme was introduced by Juels and Wattenberg [30]. This method enables protection and error-tolerant biometric verification with fixed-length binary strings. Early works employed the fuzzy commitment scheme to protect binary iris feature vectors (iris code), e.g. in [5, 22]. For other biometric characteristics, for which the features are usually not represented as fixed-length binary codes, feature-type transformations (see Sect. 2.4) have been proposed to obtain binary feature vectors prior to the construction of fuzzy commitment schemes, e.g. for fingerprints [31] or voice [4]. More recently, deep neural networks have been used to extract feature vectors from faces, which are subsequently binarised to be protected in a fuzzy commitment [18].

In the fuzzy commitment scheme, during the key-binding stage (i.e. enrolment), a binary biometric feature vector of length n, $\mathbf{x} \in \{0, 1\}^n$ (referred to as a witness), is protected. In order to do so, a secret key κ is chosen and put through the encoder of an error-correcting code to obtain the binary codeword[7] of the same length as the witness, $enc(\kappa) = \mathbf{c}$ with $\mathbf{c} \in \{0, 1\}^n$. Subsequently, the function F maps the witness and the codeword to a so-called difference vector (also referred to as helper data) by applying the XOR operation,

$$F(\mathbf{x}, \mathbf{c}) = \mathbf{x} \oplus \mathbf{c} = \delta \tag{5.1}$$

with $\delta \in \{0, 1\}^n$. In other words, an XOR-based encryption (similar to a one-time pad) is applied to protect the biometric feature vector. Finally, a cryptographic hash $H(\kappa)$ is stored along with δ. That is, the pair $(F(\mathbf{x}, \mathbf{c}), H(\kappa))$ is stored as the commitment.

At the time of key retrieval (i.e. during the authentication stage), a probe binary vector $\mathbf{x}'$ is employed to retrieve κ. After XORing the difference vector δ with $\mathbf{x}'$, the decoder of the error-correcting code is applied. If $\mathbf{x}'$ is sufficiently close to $\mathbf{x}$, i.e. $|\mathbf{x} \oplus \mathbf{x}'|$ is smaller than or equal to the error correction capacity, it should be possible to reconstruct the key with $\boldsymbol{\kappa} = dec(\delta \oplus \mathbf{x}')$. Finally, the hash value $H(\kappa)$ can be used to verify the correctness of the retrieved κ. An overview of the processing steps within a fuzzy commitment scheme is provided in Fig. 5.2.

Security analyses have shown that statistical attacks can break the irreversibility of fuzzy commitments if offline attacks are feasible [55, 62]. Specifically, an attacker uses a relatively small dataset of biometric samples with which impostor authentications are performed. The number of appearances of each possible output codeword is counted, i.e. a histogram is generated. The bin corresponding to the

[7] Not necessarily a single codeword, but a sequence of concatenated codewords.

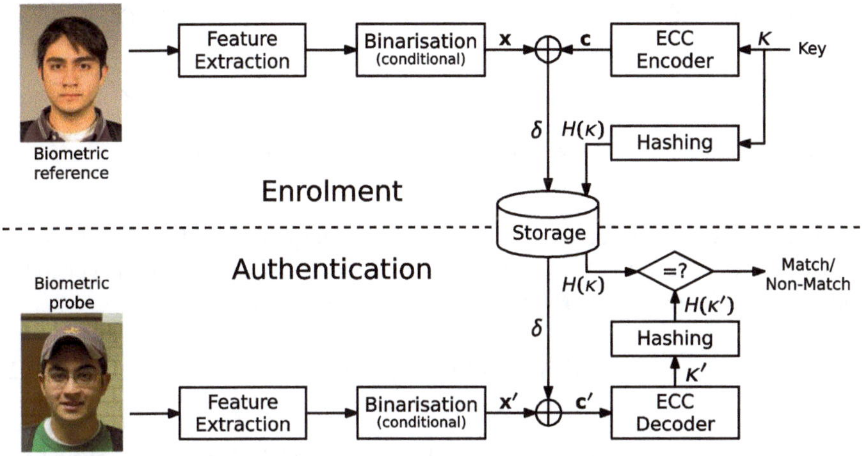

Fig. 5.2 Overview of processing steps in a fuzzy commitment scheme

histogram maximum is declared a winner, thus yielding a likely codeword. The attack works if the expected normalised Hamming distance for an impostor is below 0.5. Consequently, the correct codeword has a slightly higher probability of appearance, so that the attacker just needs enough statistics [62]. Moreover, specific linkage attacks can be launched against the original concept of the fuzzy commitment scheme [61], which violates the unlinkability requirement. It was shown that, if the offset between two difference vectors is decodable, the two difference vectors are most probably derived from the same subject. This holds for the use of linear codes, e.g. Hadamard codes. Consequently, different research efforts have been devoted to improving the fuzzy commitment scheme, e.g. in [31, 65].

The fuzzy vault scheme was introduced by Juels and Sudan [28, 29]. This method enables protection of, and error-tolerant verification with, (unordered) integer-based feature sets. The fuzzy vault scheme was suggested for the protection of fingerprint minutiae sets in [8]. Building upon this preliminary analysis, a series of implementations for minutiae-based fingerprint fuzzy vaults was proposed in [43, 46]. A useful guide for constructing a fuzzy vault scheme is provided in [34]. Until now, the fuzzy vault scheme has been applied to various physiological as well as behavioural biometric characteristics, e.g. iris [36] and online signatures [51]. Additionally, multi-biometric fuzzy vaults have been presented, e.g. in [56, 66]. Dodis et al. [11] presented an improved version of the fuzzy vault scheme, which is resistant to certain correlation attacks and generates much smaller records.

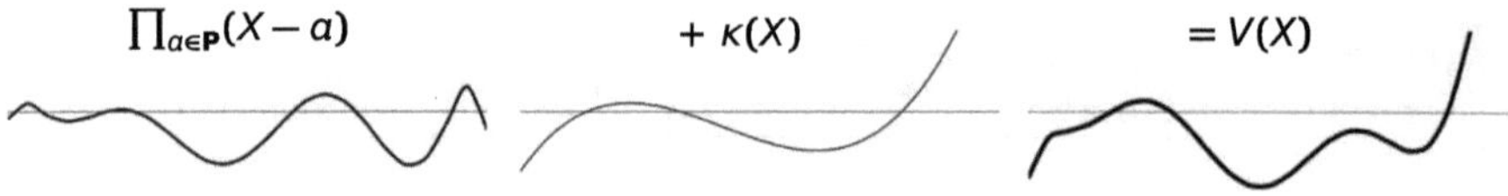

Fig. 5.3 Visualisation of the construction of an improved fuzzy vault instance

In the fuzzy vault scheme, an integer set **A** is interpreted as elements of a finite field,[8] $\mathbf{P} \subset \mathbf{F}$. A secret polynomial $\kappa \in \mathbf{F}[X]$ of degree smaller than k is generated and bound to the feature set **P** by computing the polynomial

$$V(X) = \kappa(X) + \prod_{a \in \mathbf{P}}(X - a) \tag{5.2}$$

as an instance of the improved fuzzy vault scheme [11]. This process is visualised in Fig. 5.3. As the final step of the enrolment, a cryptographic hash $H(\kappa)$ is stored along with $V(X)$, such that the pair $(V(X), H(\kappa))$ is considered as the vault record.

At key retrieval, $\mathbf{U} \subset \mathbf{F}$ is obtained from an integer set **B**. By evaluating the polynomial $V(X)$ on its elements, a set of pairs $\{(b, V(b)) | b \in \mathbf{U}\}$ is obtained. The set **U** contains $\omega = |\mathbf{P} \cap \mathbf{U}|$ genuine pairs lying on the function curve of the secret polynomial $\kappa(X)$. If the number ω of genuine points is at least k, i.e. $\omega \geq k$, it is possible to reconstruct the polynomial κ from **U**. The correctness of κ can be verified by using the hash value $H(\kappa)$. An overview of the processing steps within a fuzzy vault scheme is provided in Fig. 5.4.

Different security analyses have found that the original fuzzy vault scheme [29] (not described in this chapter) is vulnerable to a certain kind of linkage attack, which violates the requirements [32, 60]. This conflicts with the aforementioned requirement of unlinkability as well as irreversibility. Regarding the improved fuzzy vault [11], a linkage attack has been discovered that uses the extended Euclidean algorithm and can find the differences of feature sets of two records if they overlap substantially. The attack can be avoided by passing the feature sets through a public but random permutation process [40, 67]. Specifically, a public but random permutation may be applied to **A**, to avoid linkage attacks [67]. At the time of authentication, the same permutation is applied to **U**.

While correct keys are released by a biometric cryptosystem during authentication, incorrect keys result in a failure message. This prevents an attacker from potentially learning anything from (partially) erroneous keys.

[8] A finite field or Galois field is a mathematical construct containing a finite number of elements on which certain operations satisfy basic rules.

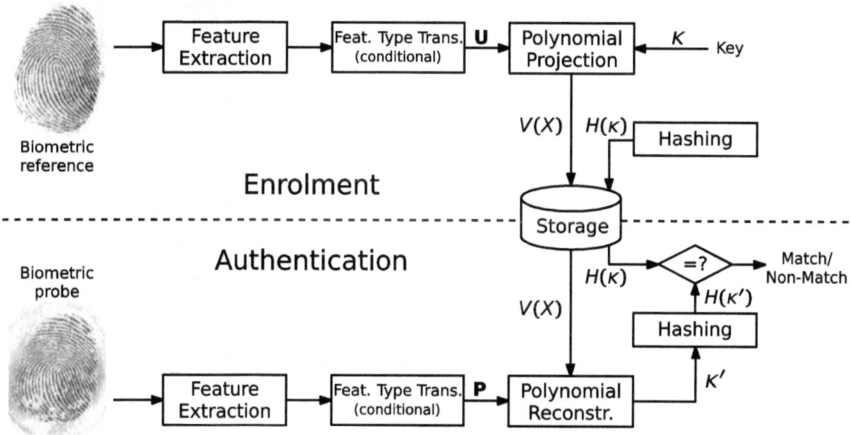

Fig. 5.4 Overview of processing steps in a fuzzy vault scheme

2.3 *Error Correction Codes*

Many biometric cryptosystems, e.g. the aforementioned fuzzy commitment and fuzzy vault, utilise error correction codes to overcome the intraclass variance of biometric data. This means that differences between the protected biometric template and the one presented during key retrieval are interpreted as errors. Depending on the number and type of expected errors, a suitable error correction configuration has to be chosen. More specifically, the used error correction should be capable of only correcting the errors occurring between genuine key-retrieval attempts, but not for impostors. This may hamper the achievement of desired performance rates, in contrast to unprotected biometric systems, in which this is usually done by adjusting decision thresholds.

Regarding the use of binary feature vectors, the use of bit-level error correction is recommended if single-bit flips are expected to occur. Here, some error correction codes have been proven to be optimal for bit blocks up to a certain size. Essentially, bit-level error correction codes encode a bit string into a corresponding codeword of larger size, where the entire set of possible codewords shares a minimum pair-wise distance. This distance allows for the correction of errors by translating a bit string to its closest codeword. The correction works if the number of errors is below a specific threshold. Otherwise, the correction may fail by mapping a bit string to a wrong codeword. Hadamard codes represent a prominent example of bit-level error correction. These are based on Hadamard matrices. A Hadamard matrix H is a square matrix of order 2^n. Based on the Sylvester construction, it can be recursively defined as $H_{2^n} = \begin{bmatrix} H_{2^{n-1}} & H_{2^{n-1}} \\ H_{2^{n-1}} & -H_{2^{n-1}}, \end{bmatrix}$ for $n \geq 2$ and $H_1 = 1$. The Hadamard code is then constructed by using the rows from H_{2^n} and $-H_{2^n}$ as codewords. The -1 entries are replaced by 0. This way 2^{n+1} codewords of length 2^n exhibiting a minimum pair-

$$H_1 = 1$$

$$H_2 = \begin{bmatrix} 1 & 1 \\ 1 & -1 \end{bmatrix}$$

$$H_4 = \begin{bmatrix} 1 & 1 & 1 & 1 \\ 1 & -1 & 1 & -1 \\ 1 & 1 & -1 & -1 \\ 1 & -1 & -1 & 1 \end{bmatrix}$$

Fig. 5.5 Examples of Hadamard matrices (left) and a Hadamard code based on the matrix H_{32} (right)

wise Hamming distance of 2^{n-1} can be formed.[9] For instance, a Hadamard code consisting of 64 codewords of length 32 bits is shown as part of Fig. 5.5. This code has a minimum Hamming distance of 16 between codewords, i.e. up to $32/4-1 = 7$ bit errors can be corrected.

The use of Hadamard codes has been suggested for fuzzy commitment schemes, e.g. in [22]. In order to retrieve keys of a sufficient length, it is recommended to split the entire feature vector into blocks and apply bit-level error correction block-wise (the relation between the number of blocks and the resulting key size will be detailed in the subsequent section). In cases where burst errors[10] are unavoidable, e.g. due to partial occlusions of a biometric characteristic, error correction codes operating on bit level fail with high probability. If this happens for a single block in a fuzzy commitment scheme, the reconstructed key is erroneous. To avoid this, the use of a second layer of error correction operating jointly on all blocks was recommended in [22], e.g. by applying a Reed-Solomon code.

Reed-Solomon codes represent polynomial codes over certain finite fields and are also used in the fuzzy vault scheme. By adding check symbols to the data, a Reed-Solomon code can correct a predefined number of erroneous symbols. The error-correcting capability of a Reed-Solomon code depends on two parameters: the length of the codeword n and the number of original data symbols k. The difference between these two, $n - k$, determines how many errors the code can correct. Specifically, the number of symbols that a Reed-Solomon code can correct is $(n - k)/2$. For example, an $RS(15, 9)$ Reed-Solomon code, consisting of a total number of 15 symbols and 9 original data symbols, can correct $(15 - 9)/2 = 3$ erroneous symbols.

[9] Between two binary vectors of equal length, the Hamming distance is the number of positions at which the corresponding bits are different. Their normalised Hamming distance is in the range [0,1], i.e. the closer the value is to 0, the more similar the two binary vectors are.

[10] A burst error is a localised bit interval in which many consecutive bit errors occur.

In the context of biometric cryptosystems, a chosen key is first divided into bit blocks, i.e. symbols, that are encoded with a Reed-Solomon encoder, resulting in an increased set of bit blocks. Then, each block is encoded further using a Hadamard code. Subsequently, key binding is performed in a fuzzy commitment scheme. At the time of key retrieval, a small number of flipped bits is corrected, followed by a correction of burst errors. To improve the error correction capability in a fuzzy commitment, the use of two-dimensional error correction codes has been suggested in [5]. This means that rows as well as columns represent codewords of an error correction code. Thereby, it is possible to perform an iterative row- and column-wise decoding.

For constructing a fuzzy vault-based cryptosystem, an error correction decoding strategy is needed, too. To this end, a Reed-Solomon decoder [17] has been proposed in the original fuzzy vault scheme [28, 29]. In [46], the repeated use of a Lagrange-based decoder has been suggested and adopted for other implementations [12, 43, 67]. An iterated Lagrange decoder chooses a subset of size k elements from the unlocking set $\mathbf{U}$ and estimates a unique polynomial interpolating them. This procedure is repeated until k genuine elements are chosen, which enable the reconstruction of the correct key. However, this strategy can become too costly and hence impractical depending on the size of the unlocking set and the key. A reasonable trade-off between decoding time and verification performance can be achieved by using a Guruswami-Sudan-based decoder [21], which is described in detail in Sect. 3.

2.4 *Feature-Type Transformations*

Common feature representations have been established for templates of different biometric characteristics, e.g. minutiae sets for fingerprints. However, biometric template protection schemes, in particular biometric cryptosystems, require templates in a specific type of feature representation, e.g. fixed-length binary strings for the fuzzy commitment scheme. In order to make biometric templates compatible with a biometric cryptosystem, a feature-type transformation may be necessary [38]. This is particularly the case for multi-biometric cryptosystems, where fusion should be performed at the feature level to achieve high security levels [41].

A common feature representation is a real-valued vector of fixed dimension. This is especially the case for deep-learning-based feature extractors, which are increasingly being used in the field of biometrics. Note that the extraction of fixed-length vectors is also possible for biometric characteristics where templates are usually of variable size, e.g. fingerprints. In [15], it was shown that deep networks

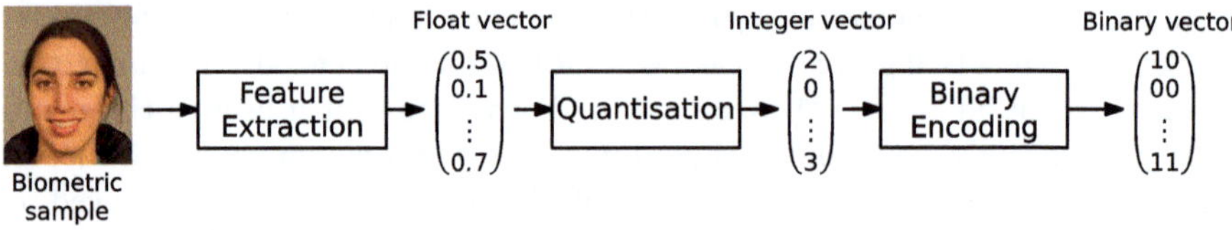

Fig. 5.6 Feature-type transformation: creating integer and binary vectors from float vectors

can learn to extract fixed-length fingerprint representations incorporating domain knowledge, such as alignment and keypoint (minutiae) detection.[11]

Fixed-length real-valued vectors can be mapped to other representations using common procedures [38]. Based on statistical information about feature distributions, the feature space of each feature element can be divided into (equally probable) integer-labelled intervals. Subsequently, a quantisation can be performed by mapping each feature element to the integer value representing its interval, resulting in an integer vector. To obtain a binary feature vector, each feature element can be mapped to a binary string. This process is illustrated in Fig. 5.6. Different binary encoding methods have been suggested in the scientific literature [38]. For instance, in a binary-reflected Gray code [20], the encoding is done so that the distance in the Hamming domain between codewords resulting from successive decimal values is always 1. In contrast, a linearly separable subcode [37] offers ideal separability, i.e. the distances between two values are the same in the decimal and Hamming domains. These feature-type transformation steps may result in a loss of biometric performance, due to information loss caused by coarse quantisation. However, if parameters are chosen appropriately, biometric performance may be maintained, e.g. in [13]. A binary vector can be transformed back to an integer vector by mapping consecutive chunks of bits to their decimal representations. Further, a binary vector can be transformed into an integer set of variable length. For instance, this feature set could consist of all indices of 1s in the binary vector. Such feature-type transformations have been successfully applied to established biometric feature extractors, e.g. in [44, 57].

3 Implementation

This section describes the implementation of a face-based fuzzy commitment and a multi-fingerprint fuzzy vault. Well-established feature extractors are employed in combination with feature-type transformations. Subsequently, the corresponding

[11] Note that a fixed-length fingerprint representation is different from a fixed-length minutiae (vicinity) representation, e.g. in [7], which usually results in a variable-length fingerprint representation.

biometric cryptosystems are constructed using appropriate error correction codes. Evaluation metrics are defined, and obtained results are reported and discussed.

3.1 Datasets

Regarding the fuzzy commitment scheme, a subset of the FRGCv2 dataset [50] containing facial images of 533 subjects is utilised. Face images are labelled as references (984 images) or probes (1,726 images). Example images are depicted in Fig. 5.7. Facial reference images exhibit greater constraints (neutral expression, homogeneous illumination, *etc.*), while probe images are generally less constrained. This mirrors scenarios encountered in real-world face recognition applications, e.g. automated border control, where enrolments are conducted in a more controlled environment. The availability of reference and probe images varies among different subjects, leading to 4,786 mated comparisons (references with probes of the same subject) and 141,778 non-mated comparisons (reference of each subject with probes of all other subjects).

For the fuzzy vault scheme, a fusion of four fingerprints is performed. To this end, the MCYT-100 fingerprint dataset [48] is used, which contains fingerprints from 100 subjects. Specifically, 12 fingerprint images are available for each of a subject's 10 fingers. For fingerprint images, there is no expected variation in terms of sample quality between fingerprints captured during enrolment and authentication. Therefore, images can be divided into reference (presented at enrolment) and probe (presented at authentication) fingerprints as required. Examples of reference and probe images of two pairs of fingerprint images are shown in Fig. 5.8. In order to maximise the number of virtual subjects in the composed multi-biometric dataset, the left and right hands of the MCYT-100 are treated as being from different subjects, resulting in 200 subjects with 4 fingers (fingerprints of the thumbs are discarded). The composed dataset allows for 1,986 mated comparisons. For non-mated comparisons, comparisons between fingerprints of the left and right hands

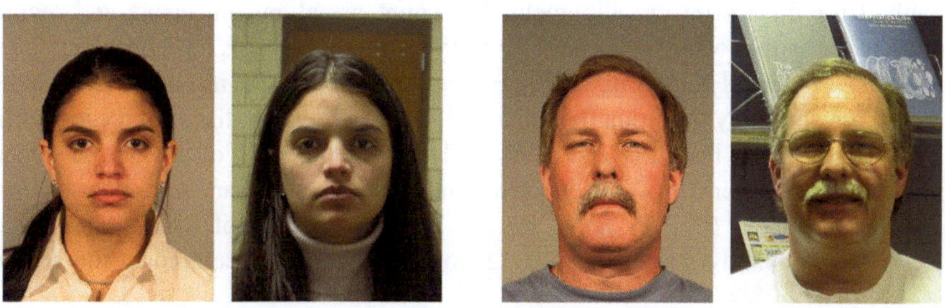

Fig. 5.7 Face image pairs of two different subjects from the FRGCv2 dataset

Fig. 5.8 Fingerprint image pairs of two different fingers from the MCYT-100 dataset

of single subjects are excluded.[12] This results in 196,614 non-mated comparisons (impostors).

3.2 Feature Extraction and Transformation

For face detection, the *dlib* face detector [33] is used, since it works robustly on the employed constrained face images. Feature extraction is performed based on the ResNet100 model from [9], published in the InsightFace repository[13] as LResNet. Applied to a cropped face image, face embeddings consisting of 512 float numbers are extracted. Subsequently, a binarisation is applied to convert float values greater than or equal to zero to one, and any negative numbers to zero, resulting in a feature vector $\mathbf{x} \in \{0, 1\}^{512}$. When calculating the normalised Hamming distance of the newly binarised feature vectors, for mated comparisons, a mean distance of approximately 0.17 is obtained. As expected, non-mated comparisons on average yield a significantly higher Hamming distance (close to 0.5).

For the pre-alignment of fingerprints, the xTARP method [42] is used. The xTARP method is (to the best of the authors' knowledge) the only publicly available method for fingerprint pre-alignment. We count pre-alignment errors and record these in the failure-to-acquire rate (FTA) [25]. Minutiae records have been extracted using the FingerJetFX algorithm [10]. For each fingerprint, the minutiae listed in the record are sorted by their quality value and successively quantised to integers until a predefined upper bound $t_{\max}$ is reached. This results in a set of integers of size at most $t_{\max}$ per fingerprint. This quantisation process is necessary to protect against correlation attacks [67]. In detail, we use a hexagonal grid of which coordinates Λ_i are equidistantly spaced by $\ell = 25$ pixels; the grid is centred in the region

[12] There may be a certain correlation, e.g. the number of minutiae, between fingers of left and right hands of single subjects, which in turn may negatively affect the FMR of the overall system.

[13] https://github.com/deepinsight/insightface/

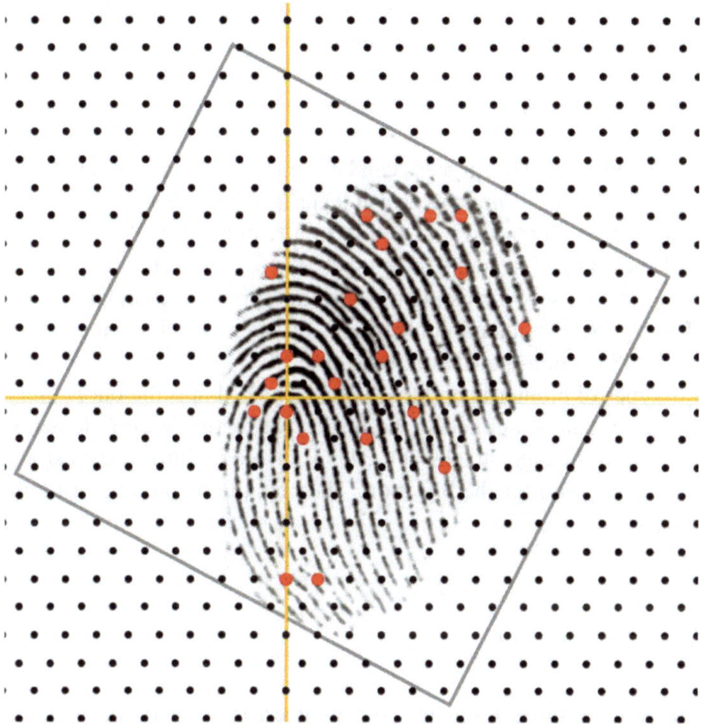

Fig. 5.9 Example of pre-aligned fingerprint with quantised minutiae points

in which absolutely pre-aligned minutiae can occur. Given a minutia (α, β, θ), its quantization is computed by determining the index j of the grid coordinate Λ_j being closest to the coordinates (α, β). An example of a pre-aligned fingerprint and quantised minutiae points is shown in Fig. 5.9. Each minutia angle θ is quantised by $s = 6$ different quanta encoded by $j' = \lfloor s\theta/2\pi \rfloor$. Finally, the quantisations j and j' of the minutia's position and orientation, respectively, are combined to $j' + sj$ as the integer encoding of the quantised minutia.

As mentioned before, for each subject, four integer sets $\mathbf{A}_1, \ldots, \mathbf{A}_4$ are extracted from their four fingerprints. Assuming that $\mathbf{B}_1, \ldots, \mathbf{B}_4$ is the result of a second fingerprint acquisition such that $\mathbf{A}_i$ matches with $\mathbf{B}_i$. Ideally, the two integer sets are fused into new integer sets $\mathbf{A}$ and $\mathbf{B}$, respectively, such that

$$|\mathbf{A}_1 \cap \mathbf{B}_1| + \cdots + |\mathbf{A}_4 \cap \mathbf{B}_4| = |\mathbf{A} \cap \mathbf{B}|. \tag{5.3}$$

In other words, all elements are distinct within the fused integer sets. This can be achieved by attaching a unique index to the elements of each of the integers' sets that together form the fused integer set. For each set, the index is attached to its elements. Let $x \in \mathbf{A}_i$ denote a nonnegative integer; then $i + 4x$ may be used as the feature element to which the index i has been attached. Finally, we can use the union of all elements with attached indices,

$$\mathbf{A} = \{i + 4x | x \in \mathbf{A}_i, i = 0, \ldots, 3\}, \tag{5.4}$$

as the fused integer set. This process can be seen as a concatenation of the different feature sets. Finally, each nonnegative integer $x \in \mathbf{A}$ is encoded as element a of a finite field $\mathbf{F}$ of sufficient size, resulting in a feature set $\mathbf{P}$. In the same way, the feature set $\mathbf{U}$ is obtained from the integer sets $\mathbf{B}_1, \ldots, \mathbf{B}_4$ at the time of verification. The resulting feature sets consisting of four fingerprints contain an average number of 161.45 integers. For mated comparison, on average 89.92, integers match, in contrast to 21.48 for non-mated comparisons.

For both types of biometric cryptosystems, a record-specific but public bijection, i.e. permutation, can be applied to the respective feature vector elements with the goal of preventing linkage attacks [11, 31]. To avoid additional data storage, $H(\kappa)$ can be used as the seed for the bijection. Thereby, the requirement of unlinkability can be achieved.

3.3 Error Correction

For the fuzzy commitment scheme, different error correction configurations are tested. Firstly, the sole use of bit-level error correction is investigated. To this end, the key κ consisting of k bits is encoded with a Hadamard code such that the encoded key consists of 512 bits, same as the binary feature vector $\mathbf{x} \in \{0, 1\}^{512}$ it is going to be bound to. As the Hadamard code encodes k bits into a codeword $\mathbf{c}$ of 2^{k-1} bits, the key size is estimated as $k = \log_2(512) + 1$. If the key is divided into b blocks where each is encoded separately, the key size is determined as

$$k = b\left(\log_2(512/b) + 1\right). \tag{5.5}$$

In a codeword $\mathbf{c}$ of length 512, up to $512/4 - 1 = 127$ errors can be corrected, which is the error correction capacity of the used Hadamard code (see Sect. 2.3). Accordingly, $(512/4b) - 1$ errors are correctable in each block if the key is divided into b blocks. Note that the overall number of correctable errors slightly decreases if the number of blocks is increased.

Alternatively, a combination of error correction mechanisms can be applied, as suggested in [22]. For this purpose, a Reed-Solomon code $RS(4, 2)$ is applied, i.e. the error correction encoding results in four blocks consisting of $b = 2$ data blocks and $r = 2$ redundancy blocks. The resulting four 8-bit blocks are Hadamard encoded, summing up to $4 \times 2^7 = 512$ bits. After Hadamard decoding, this allows for the additional correction of $(4 - 2)/2 = 1$ block error.

Regarding the fuzzy vault, an improved version of the Guruswami-Sudan list decoding algorithm [21], published by Trifonov [68], is employed. This list decoder returns a list of candidate polynomials. From these, the correct polynomial can be determined by checking its hash value. The Guruswami-Sudan algorithm will recover κ from $\mathbf{U}$ in a single step with probability

$$P(u, \omega, k, c) = \binom{u}{c}^{-1} \sum_{j=\lceil\sqrt{c\cdot(k-1)}\rceil}^{\min(\omega,c)} \binom{\omega}{j} \cdot \binom{u-\omega}{c-j}, \tag{5.6}$$

where u is the size of the unlocking set, ω is the number of genuine points, and c is referred to as multiplicity (which is set to 1). The latter parameter provides a trade-off between computational efficiency and the number of errors that are correctable. The higher the multiplicity, the more errors the algorithm can tolerate while also being more inefficient. For instance, for a multiplicity of 1, the number of correctable errors is approximately $u - \sqrt{2u(k-1)}$. This strategy is expected to outperform the iterated Lagrange as well as the Reed-Solomon strategies.

3.4 Metrics

Biometric performance is measured in terms of genuine match rate (GMR)[14] and false match rate (FMR) [24]. Obviously, there is a relationship between the FMR and the security of a biometric cryptosystem [70]. The false accept security (FAS) provides a good approximation of the security of a biometric cryptosystem as the false accept attack[15] is typically one of the most efficient attacks. In a false accept attack, the adversary iteratively simulates non-mated authentication trials until a false match is reached. According to [23], this refers to a general attack model, i.e. an adversary is assumed to possess full knowledge of the underlying algorithm. In addition, the adversary may have access to one or more protected templates from one or more datasets. The adversary may also possess knowledge of the statistical properties of biometric features. The FAS is often estimated as FAS = 1/FMR. However, it should be noted that an attacker can deviate from the parameters corresponding to the operational FMR. For example, for a GMR of approximately 95%, an FAS above 50 bits was reported for a fuzzy vault based on four fingerprints in [66]. This was achieved primarily by using a classical Reed-Solomon decoder during authentication. However, if an attacker uses a more efficient Guruswami-Sudan decoder, the chances of successfully recovering the correct key significantly increase, leading to a reduced FAS (as also shown in the experiments of this chapter). Additionally, the time required for performing a single-key-retrieval attempt should be taken into account when estimating the FAS. As explained earlier, the FAS relates to the security of the biometric cryptosystem. At

[14] The GMR is also referred to as true match rate (TMR).

[15] In the term false accept security, false accept can also be interpreted as false match.

this point, it is important to note that, in most relevant biometric cryptosystems, e.g. fuzzy commitment or fuzzy vault, the irreversibility might as well be broken in case a false attack is successful. That is, if the key can be reconstructed, the unprotected (or transformed) biometric feature vector can also be recovered. This would only be possible in an offline attack, where the attacker has access to the protected template. Therefore, the FAS also relates to privacy protection, which is associated with the irreversibility requirement of biometric template protection.

Many published works report the Brute Force Security (BFS) as a measure of security. Usually, the BFS is derived from the size of the secret key space and often overestimates the effective security of a biometric cryptosystem. That is, for an attacker, it is usually much easier to find a feature vector based on which the secret key can be retrieved, than to guess the secret key. Furthermore, it is important to note that false accept and brute force attacks are only feasible in offline systems, while in practice a system might block a user after a small number of unsuccessful authentication attempts.

In the presented fuzzy commitment scheme, the error correction decoding can be performed efficiently. That is, the time required for key retrieval is negligible. Following the approach in [57], the FAS of the fuzzy commitment scheme is estimated as

$$\log(0.5)/\log(1-\text{FMR}) \tag{5.7}$$

as the number of operations that an attacker requires to succeed with a probability of 50% (alternatively, the FAS could be estimated as t/FMR, i.e. the expected number of steps until an attack succeeds). Accordingly, the FAS of the fuzzy vault scheme is estimated as

$$t \cdot \log(0.5)/\log(1-\text{FMR}), \tag{5.8}$$

where t is the average number of operations for a non-mated verification attempt. Note that t depends on k, i.e. decoding times vary depending on the size of the chosen key. Moreover, t is measured relative to a Lagrange interpolation. Specifically, the estimated decoding time is divided by that of single Lagrange interpolation, which is seen as a single attack iteration (analogous to a single guess of a password or PIN).

3.5 Performance

The obtained results for the face-based fuzzy commitment scheme are summarised in Table 5.2. It can be observed that by dividing the binary feature vector $\mathbf{x}$ into more bit blocks, i.e. larger values of b in Table 5.2, the size of κ can be increased. However, this also implies a decrease in biometric performance in terms of GMR, e.g. $b = 4$, since errors within all b blocks have to be corrected to finally retrieve

Table 5.2 Performance of the fuzzy commitment scheme based on face

k	b	r	GMR (in %)	FMR (in %)	FAS (in bits)
10	1	0	99.61	0.0021	15.01
18	2	0	97.91	0.0014	15.60
16	2	2	98.28	0.0014	15.60
32	4	0	89.81	0.0014	15.60

Table 5.3 Performance of the fuzzy vault scheme based on four fingerprints

k	GMR (in %)	FMR (in %)	FAS (in bits)
8	100.00	19.0808	7.17
12	99.80	3.42464	9.77
16	99.29	0.46672	12.74
20	98.58	0.05400	15.85
24	97.82	0.00746	18.73
28	95.85	0.00026	23.61

the correct key. Further, it can be seen that adding another layer of Reed-Solomon error correction to the Hadamard-based bit-level error correction can improve the biometric performance at the cost of a decreased key size. For instance, a division of the key into two blocks and the addition of two redundancy blocks by the Reed-Solomon encoding, i.e. $b = 2$ and $r = 2$, achieves a good trade-off between biometric performance and key size. The estimated FMRs yield FAS values of approximately 15 bits. Also, note that for some parameter configurations, the estimated FAS can be higher than the key size k. That is, a brute force attack on the key would be a more effective attack.

Biometric performance rates of the multi-fingerprint fuzzy vault are listed in Table 5.3. Failure-to-enrol rate (FTE) for the combination of four fingerprints is 1.1%, due to errors in the pre-alignment process. It is observable that the GMR and FMR decrease with an increase in the key size, which directly contributes to an increase in the FAS. For example, using an 8-bit key results in GMR of 100% and FMR of around 19%, compared to GMR of 95.85% and FMR of close to 0 obtained using a 28-bit key. Consequently, the FAS increases from 7.17 to 23.61 bits when the key size increases from 8 to 28 bits. These results are considerably worse than those reported in [66], due to the use of the efficient Guruswami-Sudan decoder from [68].

Unlinkability is not explicitly evaluated. However, regarding both evaluated biometric cryptosystems, public random permutations can be incorporated to meet the requirement of unlinkability. Here, the stored hash can be used as a seed for such a random permutation. Regarding the biometric performance, the application of a random permutation can be beneficial for the fuzzy commitment scheme since it may break up burst errors. With respect to the fuzzy vault, the application of random permutations will not impact the biometric performance as the overlap size of feature sets remains unaltered after permuting feature elements.

In summary, the presented results are comparable to those reported in other published works. Biometric performance obtained in both cryptosystems is suitable for practical applications. However, it can also be observed that the sizes of keys retrieved in the constructed biometric cryptosystems are quite small and the achieved FAS values are rather low. In other words, the effective entropy of the employed biometric characteristics is not high enough to provide practical security from a cryptographic point of view, i.e. above 100 bits. As a consequence, brute force and false accept attacks may be feasible.

4 Open Challenges

A major issue with biometric cryptosystems is recognition accuracy. It is well-known that biometric cryptosystems generally achieve inferior biometric performance compared to unprotected biometric systems [45]. This decrease in biometric performance is caused by various factors, including template alignment and feature-type transformations, among others. For instance, during key retrieval, the protected biometric template is not "seen" and, therefore, templates cannot be aligned in a pair-wise way. For biometric characteristics that cannot be trivially pre-aligned, e.g. fingerprints, this can result in a decrease in performance. Deteriorated biometric performance may also be due to feature-type transformation processes. As mentioned earlier, coarse quantisation can result in information loss and decreased recognition accuracy.

From the experimental results presented in the previous section, it becomes clear that the security levels of biometric cryptosystems are significantly lower than what is currently considered secure in the field of cryptography, i.e. security levels beyond 128 bits. Therefore, several researchers have proposed multi-biometric template protection systems [52], e.g. in [44], which utilise biometric templates obtained from multiple characteristics or multiple instances of a single characteristic. Thereby, the overall security of the biometric cryptosystem can be significantly increased. In contrast to unprotected biometric systems, where fusion may also take place at score or decision level, the fusion in multi-biometric cryptosystems should be performed at the feature level to achieve high security levels [41]; otherwise, the protected templates of the individual characteristics can be attacked separately. That is, two or more separately protected templates could be attacked in parallel. This would significantly reduce the number of operations and hence time required by the attacker, resulting in essentially the same overall security as that of a biometric cryptosystem based on a single characteristic.

If a multi-biometric cryptosystem is constructed based on different instances of a single biometric characteristic, e.g. multiple fingerprints or two irises of the same subject, the fused feature vectors are expected to exhibit similar properties (see Sect. 3). In case a fusion of different biometric characteristics is performed, two important issues that may negatively impact the overall system security are expected to arise [58]. The first issue is that feature vectors may exhibit varying biometric variances (intra- and interclass), i.e. an attacker could focus on launching a false accept attack on a single characteristic for which it is known that non-mated comparisons result in a large number of matching elements. The second issue is that, in a fusion, an implicit weighting is introduced according to the set sizes, i.e. larger sets are weighted more strongly and vice versa, which can in turn have a negative impact on the overall security of a multi-biometric cryptosystem. Again, an attacker could merely focus on launching a false accept attack on the biometric characteristic that constitutes the largest relative part of the fused template.

A possible way of avoiding the aforementioned issues in a multi-biometric cryptosystem would be to harmonise the feature extraction methods. In particular, deep neural networks have been applied to extract fixed-length float vectors from various biometric characteristics [63], including fingerprints [15].

A (multi-)biometric cryptosystem can be further extended with a password or PIN in order to improve its security. In contrast to the biometric features, the password is required to match perfectly. The main idea behind this so-called password hardening is that the security of the biometric cryptosystem (in bits) is increased by the entropy of the added password. If the entropy of the password fully contributes to the security, the FAS of the biometric cryptosystem is increased by the sum of the entropy of the password and the entropy of the biometric data. This was first suggested in [47], which proposed the application of a random transformation function derived from the user password to the biometric template. The transformed template is then secured by the biometric cryptosystem, i.e. fuzzy vault. Finally, the vault is encrypted using a key derived from the password. Such a scheme can be seen as a hybrid template protection scheme, combining a biometric cryptosystem with traditional cryptographic techniques. Similar approaches are suggested in [58, 66].

5 Conclusion

Biometric template protection has been an active field of research for more than two decades. Among the proposed concepts, biometric cryptosystems represent the most thoroughly investigated category of template protection schemes. Regarding the aforementioned requirements of biometric template protection, biometric cryptosystems provide privacy protection, i.e. achieve irreversibility, while the corresponding authentication procedures are considerably complex and computationally costly compared to unprotected biometric systems. Unlinkability can also be achieved within biometric cryptosystems by adding randomness to the protection mechanism. The construction of biometric cryptosystems involves several processing steps that need to be applied. Depending on the employed biometric characteristics and their representations, certain pitfalls must be adequately addressed to achieve a good trade-off between privacy protection and recognition accuracy in biometric cryptosystems. However, proposals of biometric cryptosystems have generally reported inferior biometric performance compared to unprotected systems, i.e. the requirement of performance preservation is usually not fulfilled. This chapter provided a comprehensive overview of the constituent parts of relevant biometric cryptosystems. Detailed descriptions of how to implement a face-based fuzzy commitment scheme and a fingerprint-based fuzzy vault were provided, along with experimental evaluation results and their corresponding discussion.

To gain a deeper understanding of biometric cryptosystems, the interested reader is referred to published overview articles, e.g. [3, 39, 45, 54, 59]. In order to obtain further insights, it is recommended to implement the main components of biometric cryptosystems, including error correction codes or feature-type transformations. As a starting point for implementation, the THIMBLE research library[16] for development and analysis of fingerprint-based biometric cryptosystems is recommended.

6 Summary

- Biometric cryptosystems enable the retrieval of keys using biometric data through error-tolerant key-generation/binding processes.
- Biometric cryptosystems are commonly categorised as key-generation and key-binding schemes, with the latter being of greater importance in the literature.
- The two most popular biometric cryptosystems are the fuzzy commitment and the fuzzy vault schemes, which employ error correction codes to overcome biometric variance.
- Feature-type transformations are often required to make biometric feature vectors compatible with a biometric cryptosystem.
- Biometric cryptosystems have been well-studied in the scientific literature and are capable of fulfilling biometric information protection requirements, albeit at the cost of reduced recognition accuracy and increased complexity.
- Biometric cryptosystems have been applied for various biometric characteristics, with multi-biometric cryptosystems achieving the most competitive results in terms of accuracy and security.

7 Study Questions

1. What are the main advantages/disadvantages of biometric cryptosystems compared to other types of biometric template protection mechanisms (e.g. cancellable biometrics and homomorphic encryption)?
2. Can fixed-length real-valued biometric feature vectors, e.g. extracted by deep neural networks, be protected with a fuzzy commitment or fuzzy vault scheme? Which processing steps would be necessary in each case?
3. How can multiple biometric characteristics be protected in biometric cryptosystems? Which issues need to be addressed when constructing such multi-biometric cryptosystems?

[16] https://github.com/btams/thimble

4. Research one-time pad (OTP) encryption and explain which biometric cryptosystem it is related to.
5. Why do biometric samples have to be pre-aligned before protecting them via biometric cryptosystems?
6. A biometric cryptosystem provides a security level of 35 bits. This biometric cryptosystem is further hardened with a 3-digit PIN. What is the overall security (in bits) provided by the hardened system?

Acknowledgments This research work has been funded by the German Federal Ministry of Education and Research and the Hessian Ministry of Higher Education, Research, Science and the Arts within their joint support of the National Research Center for Applied Cybersecurity ATHENE.

References

1. Acar, A., Aksu, H., Uluagac, A.S., Conti, M.: A survey on homomorphic encryption schemes: theory and implementation. ACM Comput. Surv. **51**(4), 1–35 (2018)
2. Aguilar-Melchor, C., Fau, S., Fontaine, C., Gogniat, G., Sirdey, R.: Recent advances in homomorphic encryption: a possible future for signal processing in the encrypted domain. IEEE Signal Process. Mag. **30**(2), 108–117 (2013)
3. Barni, M., Droandi, G., Lazzeretti, R.: Privacy protection in biometric-based recognition systems: a marriage between cryptography and signal processing. IEEE Signal Process. Mag. **32**(5), 66–76 (2015)
4. Billeb, S., Rathgeb, C., Reininger, H., Kasper, K., Busch, C.: Biometric template protection for speaker recognition based on universal background models. IET Biom. **4**, 116–126 (2015)
5. Bringer, J., Chabanne, H., Cohen, G., Kindarji, B., Zemor, G.: Theoretical and practical boundaries of binary secure sketches. IEEE Trans. Inf. Forensics Secur. **3**, 673–683 (2008)
6. Cao, Z., Long, M., Wang, J., Yu, P.S.: HashNet: Deep learning to hash by continuation. In: International Conference on Computer Vision (ICCV), pp. 5609–5618 (2017)
7. Cappelli, R., Ferrara, M., Maltoni, D.: Minutia cylinder-code: A new representation and matching technique for fingerprint recognition. IEEE Trans. Pattern Analy. Mach. Intell. **32**(12), 2128–2141 (2010)
8. Clancy, T.C., Kiyavash, N., Lin, D.J.: Secure smartcard-based fingerprint authentication. In: SIGMM Workshop on Biometrics Methods and Applications (WBMA), pp. 45–52 (2003)
9. Deng, J., Guo, J., Xue, N., Zafeiriou, S.: ArcFace: Additive angular margin loss for deep face recognition. In: Conference on Computer Vision and Pattern Recognition (CVPR), pp. 4685–4694 (2019)
10. DigitalPersona: FingerJetFX OSE – Fingerprint Feature Extractor, Open Source Edition. https://github.com/FingerJetFXOSE/FingerJetFXOSE (2011). Last accessed: December 13, 2025
11. Dodis, Y., Ostrovsky, R., Reyzin, L., Smith, A.: Fuzzy extractors: how to generate strong keys from biometrics and other noisy data. SIAM J. Comput. **38**(1), 97–139 (2008)
12. Dong, X., Kim, S., Jin, Z., Hwang, J.Y., Cho, S., Teoh, A.B.J.: Secure chaff-less fuzzy vault for face identification systems. ACM Trans. Multimedia Comput. Commun. Appl. **17**(3), 1–22 (2021)
13. Drozdowski, P., Struck, F., Rathgeb, C., Busch, C.: Benchmarking binarisation schemes for deep face templates. In: International Conference on Image Processing (ICIP), pp. 1–5. IEEE (2018)

14. Drozdowski, P., Rathgeb, C., Busch, C.: Computational workload in biometric identification systems: an overview. IET Biom. **8**(6), 351–368 (2019)
15. Engelsma, J.J., Cao, K., Jain, A.K.: Learning a fixed-length fingerprint representation. IEEE Trans. Pattern Analy. Mach. Intell. **43**(6), 1981–1997 (2021)
16. European Parliament: Regulation (EU) 2016/679. Official J. Europ. Union **L119**, 1–88 (2016)
17. Gao, S.: A new algorithm for decoding Reed-Solomon codes. In: Communications, Information and Network Security, pp. 55–68 (2002)
18. Gilkalaye, B.P., Rattani, A., Derakhshani, R.: Euclidean-distance based fuzzy commitment scheme for biometric template security. In: Proceedings of the IEEE International Workshop on Biometrics and Forensics (IWBF), pp. 1–6 (2019)
19. Gomez-Barrero, M., Galbally, J.: Reversing the irreversible: a survey on inverse biometrics. Comput. Secur. **90**, 101700 (2020)
20. Gray, F.: Pulse code communications (1953). U.S. Patent 2,632,058
21. Guruswami, V., Sudan, M.: Improved decoding of Reed-Solomon and algebraic-geometric codes. IEEE Trans. Inf. Theory **45**, 1757–1767 (1998)
22. Hao, F., Anderson, R., Daugman, J.: Combining Cryptography with Biometrics Effectively. IEEE Trans. Comput. **55**(9), 1081–1088 (2006)
23. ISO/IEC JTC1 SC37 Biometrics: ISO/IEC 30136:2018. Information technology – Performance testing of biometric template protection. In: International Organization for Standardization (2018)
24. ISO/IEC JTC1 SC37 Biometrics: ISO/IEC 19795-1:2021. Information Technology – Biometric Performance Testing and Reporting – Part 1: Principles and Framework. In: International Organization for Standardization and International Electrotechnical Committee (2021)
25. ISO/IEC JTC1 SC37 Biometrics: ISO/IEC 2382-37:2022 Information Technology - Vocabulary - Part 37: Biometrics. In: International Organization for Standardization (2022)
26. ISO/IEC JTC1 SC27 Security Techniques: ISO/IEC 24745:2022. Information Technology - Security Techniques - Biometric Information Protection. International Organization for Standardization (2022)
27. Jindal, A.K., Chalamala, S., Jami, S.K.: Face Template Protection Using Deep Convolutional Neural Network. In: 2018 IEEE/CVF Conference on Computer Vision and Pattern Recognition Workshops (CVPRW), pp. 575–5758 (2018). https://doi.org/10.1109/CVPRW.2018.00087
28. Juels, A., Sudan, M.: A fuzzy vault scheme. In: IEEE International Symposium on Information Theory (ISIT), p. 408 (2002)
29. Juels, A., Sudan, M.: A fuzzy vault scheme. Designs Codes Cryptograp. **38**(2), 237–257 (2006)
30. Juels, A., Wattenberg, M.: A fuzzy commitment scheme. In: 6th ACM Conference on Computer and Communications Security (CCS), pp. 28–36 (1999)
31. Kelkboom, E.J.C., Breebaart, J., Kevenaar, T.A.M., Buhan, I., Veldhuis, R.N.J.: Preventing the decodability attack based cross-matching in a fuzzy commitment scheme. IEEE Trans. Inf. Forensics Secur. **6**(1), 107–121 (2011)
32. Kholmatov, A., Yanikoglu, B.: Realization of correlation attack against the fuzzy vault scheme. In: Security, Forensics, Steganography, and Watermarking of Multimedia Contents X, vol. 6819. SPIE (2008)
33. King, D.E.: Dlib-ml: A machine learning toolkit. J. Mach. Learn. Res. **10**, 1755–1758 (2009)
34. Krivokuća, V., Abdulla, W.H., Swain, A.: A dissection of fingerprint fuzzy vault schemes. In: Image and Vision Computing New Zealand (IVCNZ), pp. 256–261 (2012)
35. Kumar, M., Kumar, N.: Cancelable biometrics: a comprehensive survey. Artif. Intell. Rev. **53**, 3403–3446 (2019)
36. Lee, Y.J., Bae, K., Lee, S.J., Park, K.R., Kim, J.: Biometric key binding: Fuzzy vault based on iris images. In: International Conference on (ICB), pp. 800–808 (2007)
37. Lim, M.H., Teoh, A.B.J.: A novel encoding scheme for effective biometric discretization: linearly separable subcode. IEEE Trans. Pattern Analy. Mach. Intell. **35**(2), 300–313 (2013)
38. Lim, M.H., Teoh, A.B.J., Kim, J.: Biometric feature-type transformation: Making templates compatible for secret protection. IEEE Signal Process. Mag. **32**(5), 77–87 (2015)

39. Melzi, P., Rathgeb, C., Tolosana, R., Vera-Rodriguez, R., Busch, C.: An overview of privacy-enhancing technologies in biometric recognition. arXiv preprint arXiv:2206.10465 (2022)
40. Merkle, J., Tams, B.: Security of the improved fuzzy vault scheme in the presence of record multiplicity (full version). arXiv (2013). http://arxiv.org/abs/1312.5225
41. Merkle, J., Kevenaar, T., Korte, U.: Multi-modal and multi-instance fusion for biometric cryptosystems. In: International Conference of Biometrics Special Interest Group (BIOSIG), pp. 1–6 (2012)
42. Merkle, J., Tams, B., Dieckmann, B., Korte, U.: xTARP: Improving the tented arch reference point detection algorithm. In: International Conference of the Biometrics Special Interest Group (BIOSIG), pp. 1–7 (2017)
43. Nagar, A., Nandakumar, K., Jain, A.K.: A hybrid biometric cryptosystem for securing fingerprint minutiae templates. Pattern Recogn. Lett. **31**, 733–741 (2010)
44. Nagar, A., Nandakumar, K., Jain, A.K.: Multibiometric cryptosystems based on feature-level fusion. IEEE Trans. Inf. Forensics Secur. **7**(1), 255–268 (2012). https://doi.org/10.1109/TIFS.2011.2166545
45. Nandakumar, K., Jain, A.K.: Biometric template protection: Bridging the performance gap between theory and practice. IEEE Signal Process. Mag. - Special Issue on Biom. Secur. Privacy **32**, 1–12 (2015)
46. Nandakumar, K., Jain, A.K., Pankanti, S.: Fingerprint-based fuzzy vault: implementation and performance. IEEE Trans. Inf. Forensics Secur. **2**(4), 744–757 (2007)
47. Nandakumar, K., Nagar, A., Jain, A.K.: Hardening fingerprint fuzzy vault using password. In: International Conference on Biometrics (ICB), pp. 927–937 (2007)
48. Ortega-Garcia, J., Fierrez-Aguilar, J., Simon, D., Gonzalez, J., Faundez-Zanuy, M., et al.: MCYT baseline corpus: a bimodal biometric database. IEE Proc. Vision Image Signal Process. **150**(6), 395–401 (2003)
49. Patel, V.M., Ratha, N.K., Chellappa, R.: Cancelable biometrics: a review. IEEE Signal Process. Mag. **32**(5), 54–65 (2015). https://doi.org/10.1109/MSP.2015.2434151
50. Phillips, P., Flynn, P., Scruggs, T., Bowyer, K., Chang, J., Hoffman, K., Marques, J., Min, J., Worek, W.: Overview of the face recognition grand challenge. In: Conference on Computer Vision and Pattern Recognition (CVPR) (2005)
51. Ponce-Hernandez, W., Blanco-Gonzalo, R., Liu-Jimenez, J., Sanchez-Reillo, R.: Fuzzy vault scheme based on fixed-length templates applied to dynamic signature verification. IEEE Access **8**, 11152–11164 (2020)
52. Rathgeb, C., Busch, C.: Multibiometric template protection: Issues and challenges. In: New Trends and Developments in Biometrics, pp. 173–190. InTech, London (2012)
53. Rathgeb, C., Uhl, A.: An iris-based interval-mapping scheme for biometric key generation. In: International Symposium on Image and Signal Processing and Analysis (ISPA) (2009)
54. Rathgeb, C., Uhl, A.: A survey on biometric cryptosystems and cancelable biometrics. EURASIP J. Inf. Secur. **2011**, 1–25 (2011)
55. Rathgeb, C., Uhl, A.: Statistical attack against fuzzy commitment scheme. IET Biom. **1**(2), 94–104 (2012)
56. Rathgeb, C., Tams, B., Wagner, J., Busch, C.: Unlinkable improved multi-biometric iris fuzzy vault. EURASIP J. Inf. Secur. **2016**(1), 26 (2016)
57. Rathgeb, C., Merkle, J., Scholz, J., Tams, B., Nesterowicz, V.: Deep face fuzzy vault: implementation and performance. Comput. Secur. **113**, 102539 (2022)
58. Rathgeb, C., Tams, B., Merkle, J., Nesterowicz, V., Korte, U., Neu, M.: Multi-biometric fuzzy vault based on face and fingerprints. In: 2023 IEEE International Joint Conference on Biometrics (IJCB), pp. 1–10 (2023)
59. Sandhya, M., Prasad, M.V.N.K.: Biometric template protection: a systematic literature review of approaches and modalities. In: Biometric Security and Privacy, pp. 323–370. Springer, Cham (2017)
60. Scheirer, W.J., Boult, T.E.: Cracking fuzzy vaults and biometric encryption. In: Biometrics Symposium, pp. 1–6 (2007)

61. Simoens, K., Tuyls, P., Preneel, B.: Privacy weaknesses in biometric sketches. In: Proceedings of the 30th IEEE Symposium on Security and Privacy, pp. 188–203 (2009)
62. Stoianov, A., Kevenaar, T., van der Veen, M.: Security issues of biometric encryption. In: 2009 IEEE Toronto International Conference on Science and Technology for Humanity (TIC-STH), pp. 34–39 (2009)
63. Sundararajan, K., Woodard, D.L.: Deep learning for biometrics: a survey. Comput. Surv. **51**(3), 1–34 (2018)
64. Talreja, V., Valenti, M.C., Nasrabadi, N.M.: Deep hashing for secure multimodal biometrics. IEEE Trans. Inf. Forensics Secur. **16**, 1306–1321 (2021)
65. Tams, B.: Decodability attack against the fuzzy commitment scheme with public feature transforms. CoRR **abs/1406.1154** (2014)
66. Tams, B.: Unlinkable minutiae-based fuzzy vault for multiple fingerprints. IET Biom. **5**(3), 170–180 (2016)
67. Tams, B., Mihăilescu, P., Munk, A.: Security considerations in minutiae-based fuzzy vaults. IEEE Trans. Inf. Forensics Secur. **10**(5), 985–998 (2015)
68. Trifonov, P.: Efficient interpolation in the Guruswami-Sudan algorithm. IEEE Trans. Inf. Theory **56**(9), 4341–4349 (2010)
69. Uludag, U., Pankanti, S., Prabhakar, S., Jain, A.K.: Biometric cryptosystems: issues and challenges. Proc. IEEE **92**(6), 948–960 (2004)
70. Veldhuis, R.N.: The relation between the secrecy rate of biometric template protection and biometric recognition performance. In: International Conference on Biometrics (ICB), pp. 311–318 (2015)

Chapter 6
Homomorphic Encryption for Biometric Template Protection

Vishnu Naresh Boddeti

Abstract Biometric systems are witnessing widespread adoption driven by (1) significant advances made in AI and, more specifically, deep learning, (2) growth in application scenarios that adopt biometrics technology, and (3) growth in cloud services that host biometric applications. This trifecta of changes calls for re-evaluating the threat model related to biometrics system operation—for example, the threats and risks when a biometrics system is hosted on a cloud increase significantly. Similarly, the underlying deep model training and deployment introduces new types of attacks. Therefore, it is imperative to consider the challenges that now come to the fore, including privacy and security. In this chapter, we extend well-known past biometrics threat models to include attacks that may be attributed to deep machine learning models and the associated cloud services. The chapter outlines the critical security and privacy vulnerabilities of modern biometric systems and the role of homomorphic encryption in mitigating these vulnerabilities. Specifically, we elucidate the opportunities and challenges of employing homomorphic encryption to secure biometric templates.

1 Introduction

In 2014, a hack on the US Office of Personnel Management (OPM) exposed 22 million user records, including millions of fingerprint records. Data breaches, like the OPM hack, could have untold consequences for those whose personally identifiable information (PII[1]) was compromised, including identity theft, robbery,

[1] https://bit.ly/2HD83Pq

V. N. Boddeti (✉)
Department of Computer Science and Engineering, Michigan State University, East Lansing, MI, USA
e-mail: vishnu@msu.edu

V. Krivokuća Hahn et al. (eds.), *Handbook of Biometric Template Protection*,
https://doi.org/10.1007/978-981-95-0995-9_6

unauthorized access to secure facilities, and blackmail. Unfortunately, in today's day and age, data breaches like these are not isolated incidents.[2,3,4]

The consequences of such security breaches on biometric systems go beyond interfering with the services that rely on biometric authentication or access control due to the nature of biometric characteristics, namely users' physical and behavioral information. The loss or unauthorized access to this type of personal information may lead to long-standing consequences for the users of biometric systems. Thus, there is a dire need to design biometric template protection (BTP) schemes with solid guarantees for privacy preservation and security of the underlying data *at all times*. Many regulations, such as HIPAA [1] and GDPR [54], mandate strict rules regarding storage and access to sensitive information, including biometric data. Given the proliferation of large-scale applications of biometric systems, failure to follow the rules set out by privacy regulations can lead to deep societal problems such as loss of user privacy, propagation or amplification of bias against specific individuals or demographic subgroups, and, ultimately, loss of trust in biometric systems.

While biometric systems have been operational for a long time, they have witnessed impressive empirical performance gains across many biometric modalities and applications. Much of this progress is fueled by the availability of large-scale biometric datasets for training, coupled with the adoption of deep neural-network-based end-to-end learning algorithms. However, the complexity and opaqueness of deep-learning-based solutions introduce many new and unique challenges from a privacy and security perspective. For instance, deep learning systems are exposed to more vulnerabilities that malicious entities can exploit. For example, deep learning models are vulnerable to backdoor attacks, where an attacker can insert hidden vulnerabilities into the model that are not apparent to the user [24].

One of the most promising solutions for securing machine learning systems is to employ homomorphic encryption (HE), a class of cryptographic systems that allow algebraic operations such as addition and multiplication on encrypted data. This way, parties holding encrypted data may perform calculations without learning the unencrypted values. Such a scheme is especially suitable for mitigating the vulnerabilities in biometric systems by preventing unauthorized access to user data or the underlying biometric system components, for example, by encrypting the system's parameters like the feature extraction model weights and the reference templates. An attacker cannot access the underlying user data and system components without decryption keys, thwarting potential security breaches.

This chapter seeks to accomplish the following three goals: (1) introduce homomorphic encryption for BTP, (2) discuss prior work on employing homomorphic encryption for BTP, and (3) elucidate the opportunities and limitations of employing

[2] https://wapo.st/39PQuaT

[3] https://wapo.st/2V3kHPS

[4] https://bit.ly/2OQhlM3

homomorphic encryption as a robust solution for securing biometric templates against security and privacy violations.

2 Biometric Privacy and Security

The topic of security and privacy of biometric templates is not new. Over the past two decades, many privacy and security concerns have been identified with biometric templates. Consequently, many solutions have been specifically tailored to overcome such concerns. However, the technology that underpins biometric systems has witnessed a rapid transformation, especially in terms of (1) the adoption of learned, as opposed to handcrafted, biometric features, (2) the rapid expansion of services and applications that adopt biometric technology as an authentication mechanism, and (3) the growth in cloud services that host large-scale biometric systems. This trifecta of factors introduces new challenges for biometric template privacy and security that existing solutions need to be equipped to address. Therefore, it is imperative to revisit the threat model related to BTP systems and explore the opportunities presented by modern cryptographic solutions to mitigate such threats.

In this section, we outline the various possible vulnerabilities in modern biometric templates. Across all biometric modalities, the templates are increasingly just high-dimensional features extracted from deep neural networks.

Figure 6.1 shows an overview of the inference/deployment process of biometric systems and the possible privacy and security vulnerabilities during this process. This chapter will focus on attacks that target the templates, i.e., either the probe or reference biometric templates, or the communication channel between the probe template and the reference template database. These attacks correspond to attacks 5, 7, and 8 in Fig. 6.1.

Feature Tampering Once a feature representation is extracted from the biometric data, it is sent to the matcher. As seen in attack 5 of Fig. 6.1, an adversary may intercept that feature and modify it to prevent proper matching. However, knowing the feature representation of biometric data is enough to compromise user information privacy. As discussed in Chap. 1 of Part I of this book, it is possible to reconstruct the original image from just the feature representation [35]. Additionally, traits of the biometric data (such as hair color and other features) can be ascertained with reasonable accuracy [37].

Template Database Tampering An adversary who breaches the template database containing feature representations and identities may perform the same kinds of feature representation attacks as mentioned above—namely leaking private information or editing templates [43]. This corresponds to attack 7 in Fig. 6.1. Adversaries who can edit the template database may also insert their own feature representations with new identities, circumventing the need for enrollment altogether.

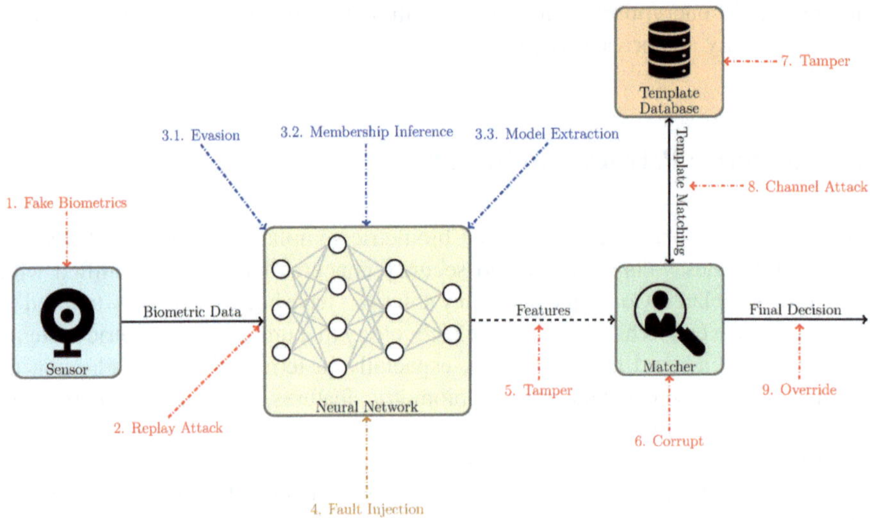

Fig. 6.1 Biometrics Pipeline with Vulnerabilities. An overview of the authentication pipeline from biometric sample capture to authentication. The solid black arrows represent the regular flow of operation over networks. Depending on the system setup, a dotted arrow shows information that may not travel over a network, e.g., when the respective system components are colocated. Red text and arrows denote traditional biometrics attacks (i.e., 1, 2, 5, 6, 7, 8, and 9). Blue text and arrows denote possible neural network test time attacks (i.e., 3.1, 3.2, and 3.3). The brown text and arrow denote an attack that falls under no other major category: the fault injection attack (i.e., 4)

Template Matching Channel Attack Figure 6.1 attack 8 represents the possible attacks when the matcher performs its matching functions, sending feature representations to and from the database. The types of attacks possible at this step are identical to those of Fig. 6.1 attack 5.

3 Homomorphic Encryption: A Primer

Cryptosystems are an attractive solution for protecting biometric templates. However, cryptosystem-based BTP solutions are rarely used in operational biometric systems. Generic encryption schemes cannot directly support basic arithmetic operations necessary for standard biometric authentication operations (e.g., template matching) in the encrypted domain. As such, the encrypted templates must be decrypted during the comparison/matching stage, which exposes them to attacks. Such schemes are also discussed in Part I Chap. 2 of this book. Other biometric cryptosystems, such as fuzzy vault and fuzzy commitment schemes, have also been

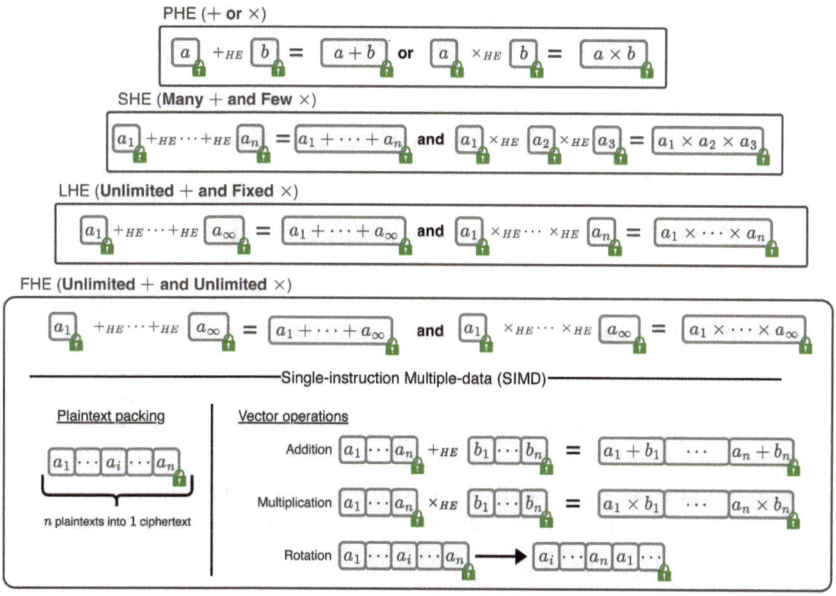

Fig. 6.2 Comparison of encrypted operations supported by four types of homomorphic encryption schemes, namely, partially homomorphic encryption (PHE), somewhat homomorphic encryption (SHE), leveled homomorphic encryption (LHE), and fully homomorphic encryption (FHE)

employed in the literature, but these schemes often sacrifice matching accuracy for increased privacy.

On the other hand, homomorphic cryptosystems are a special class of cryptosystems that allow data owners to encrypt their data and let a third party perform computations directly on the *encrypted data* without the need for prior decryption [23]. The result of the computations on encrypted data can then be sent back to the data owner, who alone can decrypt the encrypted result. Therefore, this remarkable property of encrypting the data and directly operating on it without decryption allows us to prevent unauthorized access to users' data while maintaining its utility.

Homomorphic encryption schemes typically fall under the umbrella of *public key cryptography*. In public key cryptography, pairs of keys (public and private) are used for encryption and decryption, respectively. While anyone can encrypt a message using the public key, only the owner possesses the private key necessary for decryption.

There are *four primary types* of homomorphic encryption schemes, each with varying levels of security and complexity as shown in Fig. 6.2.

Partially Homomorphic Encryption (PHE) PHE permits the evaluation of *specific mathematical operations* on encrypted data. These operations typically include *addition or multiplication but not both*. An example of an *additive partially* *homomorphic cryptosystem* is the *Paillier cryptosystem* [41]. PHE is relatively straightforward to design, but its applications are somewhat limited due to the constraint of supporting only one type of operation. Specifically, Paillier encryption is defined as $[\![x]\!] = g^x r^T \text{mod } T^2$, where $[\![x]\!]$ is the encryption of x, the pair of values (g, T) is an encryption key, and r is a random number generated per encryption. Let x and y be two messages. Given $[\![x]\!] = g^x(r)^T \text{mod } T^2$ and $[\![y]\!] = g^y(r^{(2)})^T \text{mod } T^2$, the encrypted sum is derived as follows: $[\![x]\!][\![y]\!] = g^{x+y}(rr^{(2)})^T \text{mod } T^2 = [\![x+y]\!]$. Further details can be found in [23, 41]. Thus, Paillier cryptosystems can only support homomorphic additions. As with most cryptosystems, the security of PHE schemes like the Paillier cryptosystem depends on the computational hardness of carefully constructed mathematical problems. For example, the security of the popular RSA [45] scheme, which is a PHE cryptosystem that supports homomorphic multiplications, depends on the hardness of prime factorization. While most PHE schemes are secure against attacks based on classical computing, they may not withstand attacks based on quantum computing, which is believed to possess significantly more computational capabilities than classical computing. As such, PHE schemes are not considered post-quantum secure.

Somewhat Homomorphic Encryption (SHE) SHE extends the capabilities of PHE by allowing *multiple types of operations* on encrypted data. However, there is a *limited number of allowed operations* on a *limited number of function types or boolean circuits*. Examples of SHE include the *ElGamal cryptosystem* [20] and the *Goldwasser-Micali cryptosystem*. Although SHE provides more flexibility than PHE in terms of the number of allowed operations (for instance, they allow for a fixed number of addition or multiplication operations), it still falls short of fully homomorphic encryption.

Leveled Homomorphic Encryption (LHE) LHE extends the capabilities of SHE by allowing for a limited number of supported operations (addition and multiplication) without restrictions on the type of function or boolean circuit. Examples of LHE include the *Brakerski-Gentry-Vaikuntanathan* (BGV) [16], *Brakerski/Fan-Vercauteren* (BFV) [22], and *Cheon, Kim, Kim and Song* (CKKS) [17]. These schemes are based on the hardness of the *learning with errors* problem. In most LHE schemes, the plaintext message is encrypted as $[\![m]\!] =< a, s > +e + \Delta m$, where a is a random public ring element, s is the secret key, $<, >$ is the dot product, Δ is a scaling factor, and e is the added noise, typically sampled from a discrete Gaussian distribution. Although LHE provides more flexibility than SHE, each arithmetic operation accumulates and enhances the noise e in the result, which limits the number of sequential operations they can perform. More specifically, beyond a certain number of operations, typically multiplications, the noise dominates the data, leading to decryption failure. As such, LHE schemes still fall short of fully homomorphic encryption.

Fully Homomorphic Encryption (FHE) FHE is the pinnacle of homomorphic encryption, enabling an *unlimited number of operations* on encrypted data. With FHE, one can perform *addition, subtraction, and multiplication* without decrypting the data. In contrast, other operations, like division, square root, etc., cannot be performed directly without approximations through additions and multiplications. Achieving FHE, in theory, was groundbreaking, as it allows computations on encrypted data to be as versatile as those on plaintext data. However, FHE schemes are computationally intensive and require careful selection of the encryption parameters.

Practical realizations of FHE are extensions of LHE schemes by employing a *bootstrapping* operation, by which a ciphertext is homomorphically re-encrypted without decryption. As alluded to above, noise growth in LHE schemes allows for a limited number of homomorphic multiplications, called *levels*, with each multiplication consuming one level due to rescaling. Once a ciphertext's level reaches zero, a bootstrapping operation is required to reset the noise level, refresh the ciphertext to a higher level, and allow for further multiplications. The bootstrapping operation is computationally expensive and is a significant bottleneck in FHE schemes.

Among the different homomorphic encryption schemes, FHE-based BTP offers many attractive properties:

1. One of the highest levels of cryptographic security and post-quantum security for an appropriate choice of encryption parameters, as outlined in the homomorphic encryption standard [3].
2. Unlike classical BTP schemes (e.g., through geometric distortion or fuzzy vaults), they do not suffer from a security-utility trade-off since arithmetic computations on encrypted data are exact, i.e., HE-protected biometric systems can maintain the recognition accuracy of their unprotected counterparts.
3. Unlike secure multiparty computation, another commonly employed cryptographic scheme for secure computations based on multiple communicating parties, FHE-based BTP schemes do not suffer from security-communication cost trade-off since the interaction between multiple parties is not required to execute computations.

In summary, these homomorphic encryption systems offer a trade-off between generalization and computational complexity. Ergo, while the latter (e.g., LHE and FHE) are more general in that they allow for more operations to be performed in the encrypted domain, they are significantly more computationally demanding than the former systems (e.g., PHE).

4 Homomorphic Encryption for Biometric Security

This section will discuss existing applications of homomorphic encryption for biometric template security. We will start with the threat model for securing biometric templates and then discuss existing work that applies homomorphic encryption for this purpose. We will then discuss some of these solutions' security vulnerabilities and plausible directions to mitigate them. Finally, we will discuss

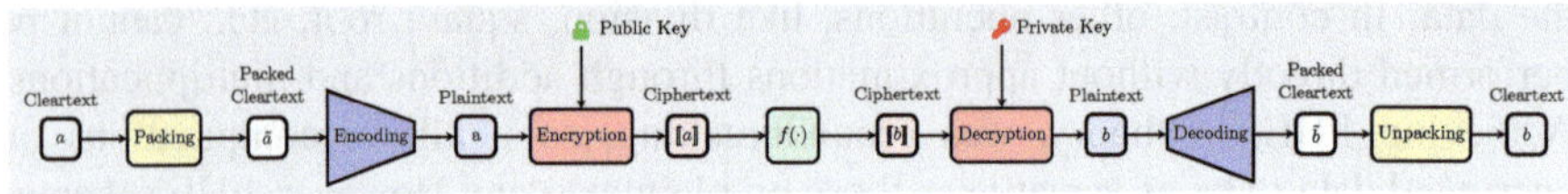

Fig. 6.3 Sequence of operations for homomorphically processing encrypted data

some limitations and challenges of existing homomorphic encryption technology for secure and privacy-preserving biometric systems.

4.1 Problem Setup

Overview of Encrypted Computation Figure 6.3 outlines the processing steps involved in performing encrypted computations using homomorphic encryption. These include *packing*, *encoding*, *encryption*, *function evaluation*, *decryption*, *decoding*, and *unpacking*. The data is first packed, i.e., organized into a suitable structure. Then, the data is encoded into a suitable format for encryption, typically involving transforming real-valued data into polynomial representations. Once encoded, the data is encrypted using a homomorphic encryption scheme, which allows computations to be performed directly on the encrypted data. The desired function can be homomorphically evaluated directly on the encrypted data without requiring decryption, and the encrypted result is decrypted to obtain the plaintext result. The plaintext result is then decoded and unpacked into the original data format. This process ensures that sensitive data remains secure throughout the computation, as it is never exposed in its unencrypted form during processing. Among these operations, *packing* is primarily relevant for the LHE and FHE schemes described in Sect. 3. It is the operation that the user has the most control over and, thus, is often critical in mitigating the computational burden of encrypted function evaluations.

Terminology We will use the following terminology from cryptography through the rest of this chapter. These terms are also labeled in Fig. 6.3:

- **Cleartext:** Standard data that is not encrypted
- **Plaintext:** Unencrypted data which is specifically formatted for encryption
- **Ciphertext:** Encrypted version of the plaintext data
- **Private Key:** A key used to decrypt data
- **Public Key:** A key used to encrypt data

Biometric Template Matching Functions A typical biometric matching (comparison) task involves a database of m reference templates (d-dimensional feature vectors) $\boldsymbol{P} = [\boldsymbol{p}_1, \ldots, \boldsymbol{p}_m] \in \mathbb{R}^{d \times m}$ against which a probe template $\boldsymbol{q} \in \mathbb{R}^d$ is compared. The comparison process results in a score determining the degree of similarity between $\boldsymbol{q}$ and each template in $\boldsymbol{P}$. A common metric adopted for template matching is the Euclidean distance or the cosine similarity. The Euclidean distance between two feature vectors $\boldsymbol{p}$ and $\boldsymbol{q}$ is defined as

$$\begin{aligned} dist(\boldsymbol{p}, \boldsymbol{q}) &= \|\boldsymbol{p} - \boldsymbol{q}\|_2^2 \\ &= (\boldsymbol{p} - \boldsymbol{q})^T (\boldsymbol{p} - \boldsymbol{q}) \\ &= \sum_{i=1}^{d} (p_i - q_i)^2 . \end{aligned} \tag{6.1}$$

Hence, the template matching process comprises d scalar multiplications and d scalar additions. Similarly, the cosine similarity between the same feature vectors is defined as

$$r(\boldsymbol{p}, \boldsymbol{q}) = \frac{\boldsymbol{p}^T \boldsymbol{q}}{\|\boldsymbol{p}\| \|\boldsymbol{q}\|} = \tilde{\boldsymbol{p}}^T \tilde{\boldsymbol{q}} = \sum_{i=1}^{d} \tilde{p}_i \tilde{q}_i . \tag{6.2}$$

At the core, both of these metrics involve matrix-vector products of the form: $r(\boldsymbol{P}, \boldsymbol{q}) = \boldsymbol{P}^T \boldsymbol{q}$. Hence, the biometric reference-probe template matching/comparison process comprises md scalar multiplications and md scalar additions.

Encrypted Evaluation of Biometric Matching Functions We devise a solution to cryptographically guarantee the security of the database $\boldsymbol{P}$ as well as the probe $\boldsymbol{q}$ to prevent leakage of any private information. This can be achieved through a parameterized function that transforms a representation $\boldsymbol{z}$ from the original space into an alternate space, i.e., $[\![\boldsymbol{z}]\!] = f(\boldsymbol{z}; \boldsymbol{\theta}_{pk})$, where $f(\cdot; \boldsymbol{\theta}_{pk})$ is the encryption function with public key $\boldsymbol{\theta}_{pk}$, and $\boldsymbol{z} = g([\![\boldsymbol{z}]\!]; \boldsymbol{\theta}_{sk})$, where $g(\cdot; \boldsymbol{\theta}_{sk})$ is the decryption function with private key $\boldsymbol{\theta}_{sk}$. The key idea is to adopt an encryption function to secure the database and the probe while retaining the ability to compute their matching score efficiently at scale and without any loss of accuracy, i.e.,

$$r(\boldsymbol{P}, \boldsymbol{q}) \approx g\left(r(f(\boldsymbol{P}, \boldsymbol{\theta}_{pk}), f(\boldsymbol{q}, \boldsymbol{\theta}_{pk})); \boldsymbol{\theta}_{sk}\right) . \tag{6.3}$$

Homomorphic encryption satisfies this property and enables us to preserve user privacy. Even if a malicious attacker can gain access to the reference template database or the probe template, without access to the private key $\boldsymbol{\theta}_{sk}$, the attacker cannot recover the underlying template (e.g., $\boldsymbol{p}$ or $\boldsymbol{q}$) nor, therefore, reconstruct the corresponding biometric sample (e.g., face image). An illustration of this approach is shown in Fig. 6.4.

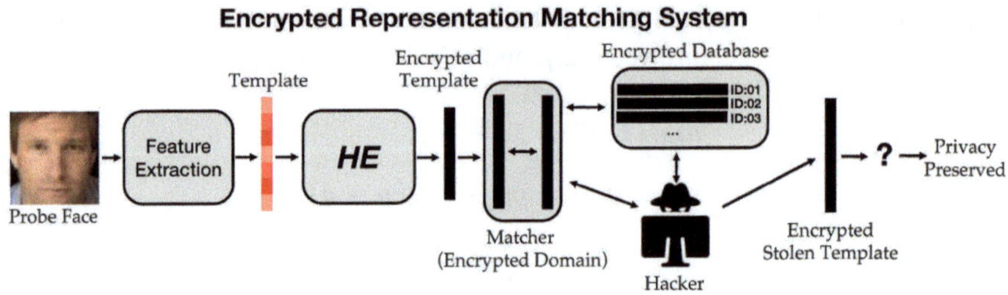

Fig. 6.4 The biometric template security is achieved as follows: (i) The templates are encrypted during database enrollment, and (ii) the templates are matched *within the encrypted domain*. As such, a hacker cannot exploit any meaningful information from stolen templates

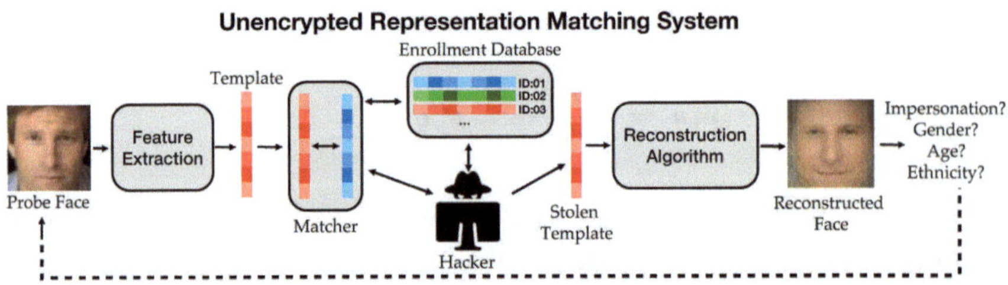

Fig. 6.5 Standard biometric identification system. Given a biometric template (e.g., face representation), it is either (i) stored in a database (enrollment) or (ii) passed to the matcher for searching. Both the database and the matcher are potential points of attack. An attacker can steal a template from an unencrypted database, launching an impersonation attack. Or, if the database were encrypted using non-HE algorithms (e.g., AES), the hacker could attack the matcher, where templates are decrypted for comparison

4.2 *Threat Model for Biometric Template Security*

There is ample evidence that biometric templates contain significant sensitive private information. It is possible to infer this personal information (e.g., gender, age, health condition, ethnicity, occupation, etc.) [18, 35] and reconstruct raw biometric samples (e.g., facial images) of individuals, a process known as template inversion attacks [46, 47, 57].[5] An illustration of the threat model is shown in Fig. 6.5. The plaintext (i.e., unencrypted) access to biometric feature vectors (templates) enables, on the one hand, an undesirable personal information inference that intensifies the severity of social issues, such as gender inequality and discrimination, due to biased decision-making models. Such models violate the privacy of individuals by performing classification tasks other than recognition. On the other hand, it permits the reconstruction of the raw biometric sample from a given reference or probe template, which leads to security issues such as identity

[5] See Part I Chap. 1 of this book for more details.

fraud and impersonation attacks. Therefore, feature vectors extracted from deep neural networks are vulnerable and require strong protection.

4.3 Enrollment and Verification Protocols

We now describe a user enrollment and verification protocol for a face recognition system using homomorphic encryption. We consider a scenario with two entities, a *device* and a *database*.

Enrollment During this phase, the following actions are performed (for a user) on the *device*: (1) generate three keys, a public encryption key $\boldsymbol{\theta}_{pk}$, a private (secret) decryption key $\boldsymbol{\theta}_{sk}$ (ideally each user should have their own keys), and a public evaluation key $\boldsymbol{\theta}_{ev}$ (necessary to perform secure computations), (2) transmit the evaluation key $\boldsymbol{\theta}_{ev}$ to the *database*, (3) capture an image of the face, (4) extract the representation (template) of the acquired face image $\boldsymbol{p}^c$ for the c-th identity, (5) encrypt the face image using the public key $\boldsymbol{\theta}_{pk}$, and (6) transmit the encrypted template to the database along with the identity label. The encrypted template, the evaluation key $\boldsymbol{\theta}_{ev}$, and the identity label are added to the database. Figure 6.6a illustrates this process

Verification During this phase, the *device* seeks to verify the identity of the user through the following process: (1) acquire the user's facial image and extract the template (feature vector) $\boldsymbol{q}$, (2) encrypt $\boldsymbol{q}$ using the public key $\boldsymbol{\theta}_{pk}$, (3) transmit the encrypted template $[\![\boldsymbol{q}]\!]$ and the claimed identity (c'). At the database, (4) compute the dissimilarity score(s) $dist([\![\boldsymbol{q}]\!], [\![\boldsymbol{p}]\!]_k^{c'})$ for all the potentially $n > 1$ templates of the c'-th identity using the evaluation key $\boldsymbol{\theta}_{ev}$, and (5) transmit the score(s) back to the device. Finally, the encrypted scores are decrypted at the device using the secret decryption key $\boldsymbol{\theta}_{sk}$ to verify the user's identity by comparing to a predetermined threshold to determine a match or no match decision, i.e., the thresholding is performed in the plaintext domain. Figure 6.6b illustrates this procedure. Note that releasing the raw score in verification scenarios is not recommended since the templates can be recovered. A detailed discussion of this limitation and potential mitigation strategies is provided in Sect. 4.7.

4.4 Existing Solutions

Multiple HE-based BTP techniques have been developed in the literature. These include early methods that were based on PHE schemes, such as the Paillier cryptosystem, and more recent methods that leverage LHE schemes, such as the Brakerski-Gentry-Vaikuntanathan (BGV) and Cheon-Kim-Kim-Song (CKKS) schemes. Table 6.1 provides a summary of the existing solutions for BTP using

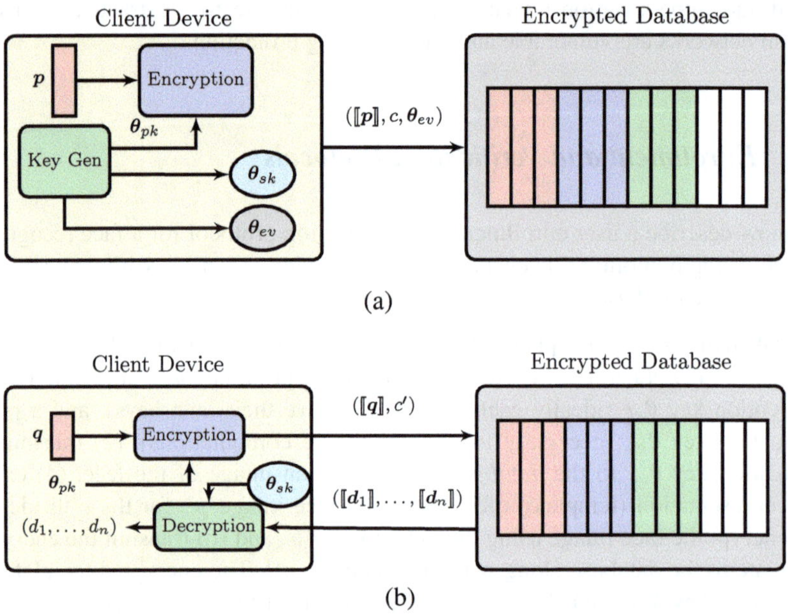

Fig. 6.6 Enrollment and verification protocols for secure face matching using fully homomorphic encryption. (**a**) **Enrollment:** During this phase, the user generates the keys ($\boldsymbol{\theta}_{pk}, \boldsymbol{\theta}_{sk}, \boldsymbol{\theta}_{ev}$), encrypts feature vector $\boldsymbol{p}$ with the public key $\boldsymbol{\theta}_{pk}$, and transmits the encrypted feature vector $[\![\boldsymbol{p}]\!]$, the user identity c, and the evaluation key $\boldsymbol{\theta}_{ev}$ to the database. However, the private key $\boldsymbol{\theta}_{sk}$ remains on the client device and is protected through standard key management techniques. (**b**) **Verification:** During this phase, a user seeks to get verified, encrypts the probe feature vector $\boldsymbol{q}$ with the public key $\boldsymbol{\theta}_{pk}$, and transmits $[\![\boldsymbol{q}]\!]$ to the database along with the claimed identity c'. The database computes the dissimilarity scores over the encrypted features from n samples of the claimed identity c' using the evaluation key $\boldsymbol{\theta}_{ev}$ and transmits the matching scores to the client, where they are decrypted with the private key $\boldsymbol{\theta}_{sk}$

homomorphic encryption. The table lists the method, the homomorphic encryption scheme used, whether the probe and reference templates are encrypted, whether it is optimized for verification or identification, and the efficiency focus of the method. The table is divided into three sections: The first section lists methods where the probe is unencrypted, the second section lists methods where only the probe is encrypted, and the third section lists methods where both the probe and the reference database are encrypted.

4.4.1 Partially Homomorphic Encryption

Initial homomorphic encryption [26]-driven biometric verification approaches [5, 33] were primarily based on partial homomorphic encryption (PHE) schemes and in the context of matching binarized templates. Upmanyu et al. [52, 53] proposed

Table 6.1 Comparison of existing HE-based BTP solutions

Method	HE scheme	Encrypted probe	Encrypted reference	Optimized for	Efficiency focus
Bassit et al. [7]	Additive ElGamal	×	✓	Verification (1:1)	NA
Bassit et al. [8, 10]	BFV	×	✓	Verification (1:1)	Removing multiplications
Bassit [6]	BFVrns	×	✓	Identification (1:N)	Removing multiplications
Upmanyu et al. [52, 53]	Paillier	✓	NA	Verification (1:1)	NA
Barni et al. [4, 5]	Paillier	✓	×	Verification (1:1)	NA
Troncoso-Pastoriza et al. [50]	G11	✓	✓	Verification (1:1)	NA
Boddeti [12]	BFV	✓	✓	Verification (1:1)	SIMD packing along each template
Engelsma et al. [21]	BFV	✓	✓	Identification (1:N)	Template compression, SIMD packing along each dimension
Drozdowski et al. [19]	BFV	✓	✓	Identification (1:N)	Reference database preprocessing, tree search
Bauspieβ et al. [11]	BFV, CKKS	✓	✓	Verification (1:1)	Dimensionality reduction, k-packing
Sperling et al. [49]	CKKS	✓	✓	Template fusion	Linear feature projection
				Verification (1:1)	Feature normalization

Client		Server
Request authentication of user uID Extract user's probe $\boldsymbol{P} = (\hat{f}_1, \cdots, \hat{f}_k)$	uID $\longrightarrow$	Check if uID is registered If not **abort**
For each row: Select the $\hat{f}_i^{\text{th}}$ component	$\longleftarrow$ $[\![\boldsymbol{T}_{u\text{ID}}]\!]$	Fetch the encrypted template $[\![\boldsymbol{T}_{u\text{ID}}]\!]$
Compute $[\![S]\!] = \prod_{i=1}^{k} [\![s^i_{f_i,\hat{f}_i}]\!]$ Re-randomize $[\![S]\!] = [\![S]\!] \cdot [\![0]\!]$	$[\![S]\!]$ $\longrightarrow$	Encrypt $[\![t]\!]$ for all $t \in [\theta, S_{max}]$ Compute $[\![\boldsymbol{C}]\!] = (([\![S]\!] - [\![t]\!]))_t$ $= ([\![c_i]\!])_{i \in [1,len]}$ Choose $\boldsymbol{a} = (a_i)_{i \in [1,len]}$ st $a_i \neq 0$ Blind $[\![\boldsymbol{C}]\!]$ with $\boldsymbol{a}$ such that $[\![\boldsymbol{aC}]\!] = ([\![a_i c_i]\!])_{i \in [1,len]}$ Permute using π such that $[\![\boldsymbol{aC}]\!] := \pi([\![\boldsymbol{aC}]\!])$ Partially decrypt $[\![\boldsymbol{aC}]\!]$: $[\boldsymbol{aC}]_{ser} = ([a_i c_i]_{ser})_{i \in [1,len]}$
Run final decryption $a_i c_i = [[a_i c_i]_{ser}]_{clt}$ $\forall i \in [1, len]$ If $\exists i \in [1, len] : a_i c_i == 0$ Output 1 (i.e. Match) Otherwise 0 (i.e. No Match)	$\longleftarrow$ $[\boldsymbol{aC}]_{ser}$	

Fig. 6.7 A ElGamal-based biometric verification protocol secure against semi-honest adversaries [7]. Such PHE schemes often require multiple rounds of communication between the client and the server

a biometric matching system based on a PHE scheme. Barni et al. [4, 5] leverage a Paillier cryptosystem, a PHE system that supports addition over encrypted data. This system was used for matching fingerprints using finger code templates, where the probe is encrypted, while the database remains unencrypted, providing no security to the fingerprint database. Penn et al. [42] also leverage a Paillier cryptosystem [41] for matching binary iris templates. Most recently, Bassit et al. [7] proposed a PHE-based BTP scheme that uses the additive homomorphic ElGamal encryption scheme for matching face and dynamic signature templates (see Fig. 6.7 for the detailed protocol). Since biometric matching requires more than one arithmetic operation, the above PHE-based schemes require repeated rounds of communication between the client and the database to compute the match score, suffering from significant communication overhead and computational complexity.

4.4.2 Leveled Homomorphic Encryption

The majority of the BTP schemes based on LHE use the Fan-Vercauteren (FV) scheme [22]. Plaintext space of the FV scheme is represented as a polynomial ring over a finite field $R_t = \mathbb{Z}_t[x]/\boldsymbol{\Phi}_n(x)$, where $t \in \mathbb{Z}$ is an integer that represents the size of the plaintext space and $\boldsymbol{\Phi}_n(x)$[6] is an irreducible polynomial of degree at most n, where n is the ring dimension. Upon encrypting the plaintext polynomial, the encrypted numbers (ciphertext) are encoded as polynomials in the ring R_q. The FV scheme utilizes three keys: (1) a private decryption key $\boldsymbol{\theta}_{sk}$, (2) a public encryption key $\boldsymbol{\theta}_{pk}$, and (3) evaluation keys $\boldsymbol{\theta}_{ev}$ which are utilized by LHE schemes to perform multiplications over encrypted data. Adding and multiplying two ciphertexts translates to polynomial addition and dyadic multiplication in R_q. As long as the coefficients of the resulting polynomials do not exceed q, correctness is ensured. This homomorphic encryption system is based on modular arithmetic. The security of this scheme is cryptographically guaranteed by the hardness of the *ring learning with errors* problem [14]. The exact description of the entire scheme, including encryption, decryption, ciphertext addition, and ciphertext multiplication, is deferred to Appendix section "Fully Homomorphic Encryption".

LHE schemes like *Brakerski/Fan-Vercauteren* (BFV) [22] and *Cheon, Kim, Kim, and Song* (CKKS) [17] can be directly utilized for template matching by encrypting each feature dimension, but they suffer from high computational requirements. Supporting computations involving many high-precision real values requires prohibitively large values of n and t, the encryption key size, and the size of the plaintext space, respectively. For a 512-dimensional template and a desired security level of 128 bits (i.e., the probability of successfully decrypting a ciphertext without the decryption key is 2^{-128}), naively encrypting each dimension requires 16.5 MB of storage space for each encrypted template and 0.6 seconds for matching a pair of such templates. Boddeti [12] presented a few different solutions to address these limitations: first, a quantization scheme to encode templates in R_t and then, using the Chinese Remainder Theorem, a batching scheme for encoding a vector of real values into a single polynomial. This encoding allows us to amortize multiple homomorphic multiplications within a single homomorphic multiplication (single-instruction multiple data), thereby providing significant computational efficiencies.

Next, we will look at two main considerations for using LHE schemes for BTP, namely, data representation and leveraging SIMD capabilities of LHE schemes.

Data Representation The efficiency of homomorphic additions and multiplications is critically dependent on the encoding scheme chosen to represent the real-valued elements of the template within a polynomial ring R_t. The space of ring R_t is significantly different from the space of real values $\mathbb{R}$ or the space of integers $\mathbb{Z}$. Hence, to maintain the integrity of the homomorphic computations, the chosen encoding scheme needs to ensure that the range of values after the desired homomorphic operations remains within the ring. Pursuantly, Boddeti [12] encoded the real-valued face features into integers with a precision of two decimal digits and then represented these integers in base w. Thus, a real number a_r is first converted into an integer with a precision of two decimal digits i.e., $a = \lceil a_r \times 100 \rceil$. This

[6] Almost always chosen to be $x^n + 1$, where n is typically a power of 2, since it enables efficient polynomial multiplication via the discrete Fourier transform (DFT) or the number-theoretic transform (NTT).

integer is then represented in base w and encoded as

$$Encoding(a) = sign(a)(a_{n-1}x^{n-1} + \cdots + a_1 x + a_0). \tag{6.4}$$

Accordingly, this encoding scheme can represent any integer in $-(w^n - 1) \leq a \leq (w^n - 1)$. As a numerical example, let us consider a real-valued feature $a_r = 123.452$. To encode this feature using the described scheme, we first convert it into an integer with a precision of two decimal digits i.e., 123.452×100, resulting in $a = 12345$. Next, we represent this integer in base w. Let us choose $w = 10$ and $n = 5$ for simplicity. The integer 12345 can be represented as

$$Encoding(12345) = 1 \cdot 10^4 + 2 \cdot 10^3 + 3 \cdot 10^2 + 4 \cdot 10^1 + 5 \cdot 10^0. \tag{6.5}$$

Thus, the encoded polynomial is

$$Encoding(12345) = x^4 + 2x^3 + 3x^2 + 4x + 5. \tag{6.6}$$

This polynomial can now be used for homomorphic operations within the ring R_t.

SIMD Encoding The main computational bottleneck of template matching over encrypted data is the number of homomorphic multiplications necessary for computing the dissimilarity score. Brakerski et al. [15] and Smart et al. [48] proposed techniques for homomorphic encryption and decryption over an array of numbers instead of a single number at a time. These techniques leverage the Chinese Remainder Theorem (CRT).

Informally, the CRT roughly states that the R_t for a large number t can be represented as a tuple of numbers $(t_1, t_2, \ldots, t_k)$, i.e., $t = \prod_{i=1}^{k}(t_i \bmod p_i)$, with each $t_i \equiv t \bmod p_i$ for some choices of primes p_i (they must be co-prime, and their product must be larger than x). We can reconstruct the original large number x from the tuple, and a residue number system represents numbers in terms of their "residues" (the modulo tuples). Amazingly, with the residue number system, we can still perform computations. Adding or multiplying the tuples entry-wise (followed by the relevant modular reduction in each entry) is equivalent to adding or multiplying the original number. The computations for each prime are independent and can be implemented in parallel.

The CRT extends to a similar statement about polynomial quotient rings that factor as a direct product of smaller quotient rings. Thus, by leveraging the CRT, we can encode multiple numbers within the same polynomial. For instance, given ξ, the primitive $2n$-th root of unity modulo t, we have $x^n + 1 = (x - \xi)(x - \xi^3)\ldots(x - \xi^{2n-1}) \bmod t$.

Given two vectors $\boldsymbol{x}$ and $\boldsymbol{y}$, the sum and Hadamard product of the two vectors can be computed as element-wise addition and multiplication, respectively, of the encrypted vectors. By batching k numbers into a single encrypted block, we can perform k homomorphic additions or multiplications at the block level for the computational cost of a single operation. Therefore, we can realize significant

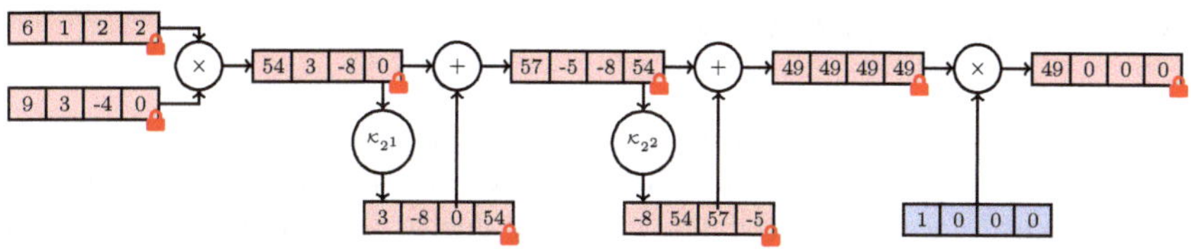

Fig. 6.8 Homomorphic computation of inner product between vectors using SIMD encoding, where multiple elements are encrypted into a single encrypted block. The SIMD encoding does not allow access to each element of the encrypted block. Therefore, after the Hadamard product, the sum of the elements within the encrypted block can be computed through repeated cyclic rotations and additions. The unencrypted hand-designed vector in blue is used for isolating the match score in the first slot of the vector. $\mathcal{K}_{21}$ and $\mathcal{K}_{22}$ correspond to cyclic rotations by 2^1 and 2^2 slots, respectively

computational efficiency as the batch size gets larger. However, the main drawback of this scheme is the inability to access the individual elements of the packed encrypted vector.[7] This prevents us from computing the sum of the components, an operation that is necessary for computing the dissimilarity score (Eqs. 6.1 and 6.2). This limitation can be addressed by leveraging the observation made by Gentry et al. [25]; namely, it is possible to cyclically rotate the encrypted vectors without decryption. Therefore, the sum of the encrypted values can be computed by cyclically rotating and adding the encrypted vectors $l = \log_2 d$ times. Figure 6.8 and Algorithm 1 provide a pictorial illustration and algorithmic description of this process.

Algorithm 1 Homomorphic inner product

procedure ENCRYPTEDINNERPRODUCT($\boldsymbol{m}, \boldsymbol{m}'$)
  $\mathcal{E}(\boldsymbol{x}) \leftarrow f(\boldsymbol{x}, \boldsymbol{\theta}_{pk})$ ▷ CRT Encoding
  $\mathcal{E}(\boldsymbol{y}) \leftarrow f(\boldsymbol{y}, \boldsymbol{\theta}_{pk})$ ▷ CRT Encoding
  $\boldsymbol{ct} \leftarrow Multiply(\mathcal{E}(\boldsymbol{x}), \mathcal{E}(\boldsymbol{y}))$ ▷ Batch Multiply
  for $i = \{0, \ldots, l\}$ **do**
    $\boldsymbol{ct} \leftarrow \boldsymbol{ct} + \mathcal{K}_{g^i}(\boldsymbol{ct})$ ▷ Cyclic Rotation
  end for
  return $\boldsymbol{ct}$ ▷ The element in the first slot is the desired inner product.
end procedure

[7] See Fig. 6.8, Sect. 4.5, and Fig. 6.9 for more details.

4.5 Computational Efficiency

The computational overhead is a key challenge in employing homomorphic encryption for BTP. Homomorphic encryption schemes are significantly more complex than traditional encryption schemes, primarily due to the complex computations necessary for homomorphic operations. As such, several attempts have been proposed to mitigate the computational burden of homomorphic encryption schemes for BTP.

Template Compression The approach from Boddeti [12] was designed for biometric verification (1:1 matching). It is not readily scalable to large reference template sizes due to two key reasons: (1) the data-packing scheme, where each feature vector is packed into a single ciphertext, wastes a significant number of slots if the feature dimension is small, and (2) it requires multiple ciphertext rotations, which are computationally very expensive when scaling to a large number of reference-probe template comparisons. Bauspieβ et al. [11] proposed a k-packing scheme that packs k feature vectors into a single ciphertext to improve the computational efficiency of 1:1 verification. Figure 6.9 illustrates the different packing schemes.

Engelsma et al. [21] proposed the first HE-based BTP scheme focusing on scalable search, i.e., identification (1:N matching) for large-scale biometric systems. They employed two key ideas to reduce the computational burden when scaling to large reference sizes: a packing scheme customized for large-scale search and reducing the dimensionality of the features.

Ciphertext Packing Given a reference of m templates each with d dimensions, Boddeti's [12] horizontal packing scheme yields m ciphertexts. This scheme is inefficient when the number of features d is small, and the reference template database size m is large since it requires m homomorphic multiplications. Engelsma et al. [21] proposed the vertical packing scheme to pack each dimension of the feature across multiple reference templates into a single ciphertext, yielding d ciphertexts, thus requiring d homomorphic multiplications.

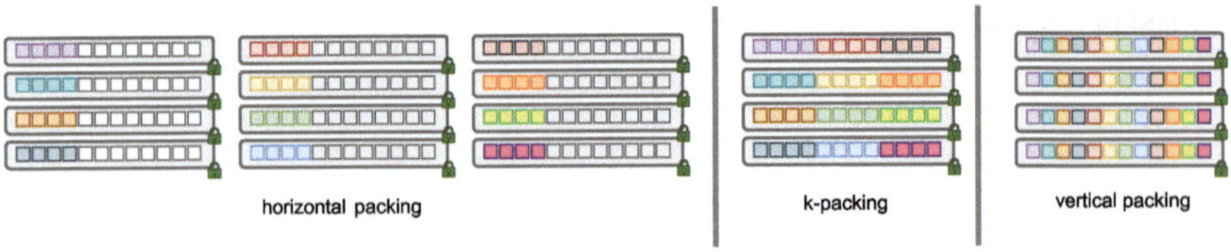

Fig. 6.9 Illustration of different packing schemes. Horizontal packing [12] (left) encodes one feature vector into a single cleartext, an advanced version of horizontal packing that encodes multiple feature vectors into a single cleartext called k-packing [11] (center), and vertical packing [21] (right) encodes each feature vector dimension from many users into a single cleartext. So, the latter has as many cleartexts as the number of dimensions

Dimensionality Reduction For the vertical packing scheme, the number of homomorphic multiplications is equal to the number of features d. Therefore, reducing the dimensionality translates to direct computational savings. For example, reducing the dimensionality of the features from 256 to 32 results in an eight-fold reduction in the number of homomorphic multiplications. Consequently, Engelsma et al. [21] sought to reduce the dimensionality of the templates as much as possible while still retaining the matching accuracy. Specifically, they attempted to map the templates from the ambient space to its intrinsic dimensionality.[8] This solution was built upon the growing evidence [28] that representations learned by deep convolutional neural networks are highly redundant, i.e., they lie on a low-dimensional manifold whose intrinsic dimensionality is $20\times$ to $30\times$ smaller than the ambient space that the representation is embedded in.

Multiplication-Free Homomorphic Score Computation A key bottleneck of the LHE scheme employed by Boddeti [12] and Engelsma [21] is the computational complexity of the homomorphic multiplication operation. Bassit et al. [6–8, 10] proposed log-likelihood-ratio classifier-based matching that can be performed over homomorphically encrypted templates without the need for homomorphic multiplications. Instead, the match scores are estimated through precomputed look-up tables and homomorphic rotations and additions. While reducing the number of multiplications yields modest gains in the latency of the matching process, it also leads to a significant increase in the template size due to the need to store entire rows of the look-up tables for each template.

Preprocessing Reference Templates Prior work on homomorphically encrypted biometric search (i.e., 1:N) has focused on a linear scan through the entire reference template database. As such, the computational complexity of the matching process is proportional to the size of the reference template database. Preprocessing the reference template database can significantly reduce the computational complexity of the matching process. For instance, Drozdowski et al. [19] proposed a method for indexing and retrieval of biometric templates using a tree search structure. The reference templates are preprocessed to create a tree search structure that fuses similar templates. The matching score is computed on the preprocessed templates. This technique significantly reduces the computational complexity of the matching process. Preprocessing the reference templates, however, enhances the vulnerability of the system to template inversion attacks, as the attacker can exploit the tree's structure to infer the underlying templates more efficiently.

[8] Intrinsic dimensionality [28] is the minimum number of dimensions needed to maintain the information present in the ambient representation.

4.6 Comparison of Existing Solutions

Table 6.2 compares the theoretical and empirical performances of existing HE-based BTP schemes for 1:N biometric search, i.e., identification. The table shows two groups of approaches, one where both the probe and reference templates are secured through encryption, and another where the probe and reference templates are secured through permutation and encryption, respectively. The latter group of methods can completely eliminate the need for homomorphic multiplications, which can lead to significant gains in runtime at the cost of diminished security for the probe, and increased memory requirements. We also observe that tailoring the plaintext packing scheme (compare row 2 and row 4) for the search problem leads to a significant runtime speedup. Lastly, feature compression schemes also lead to significant gains in runtime as shown in Fig. 6.10.

4.7 Security Vulnerabilities and Opportunities

The common security assumption in cryptography is that of *semi-honesty*, i.e., the entities in the system (client and server) "follow the protocol properly with the exception that the participants keep a record of all their intermediate computations" [40]. Under these assumptions, the security of HE-based BTP schemes is built upon the security of the HE schemes like BFV, BGV, and CKKS, which in turn is based on the hardness of the *ring learning with errors* problem [36]. Practically, this means that the security of the entire protocol hinges upon the fact that the ciphertext cannot be decrypted without access to the private (secret) decryption key, which resides only with the client. An attractive property of the aforementioned HE schemes is that they offer post-quantum security for an appropriate choice of encryption parameters as outlined in the homomorphic encryption standard [3]. Most HE-based BTP schemes choose the encryption parameters (n, t, q) corresponding to 128 bits of post-quantum security.

The BTP scheme in Fig. 6.6 has three sources of vulnerability to attackers, namely, (1) the client device which holds the secret keys, (2) the communication channel between the client and server (database), and (3) the database which holds the encrypted representations and performs score computation in the encrypted domain. The physical and digital security of the client is critical to protecting the secret keys. Indeed, if the secret key were obtained from the client, the encrypted templates could be inverted and exposed. However, commonly employed HE schemes such as BFV and CKKS guarantee the security of the communication channel and the database server.

Table 6.2 Computational complexity of matching a d-dimensional encrypted probe template against an encrypted reference template database of size m (i.e., consisting of m d-dimensional encrypted templates) is $\mathcal{O}(K \cdot (\text{HE-Mult} + \text{HE-Rot} + \text{HE-Add}))$. Runtime is measured for 1:1 million reference template search. Packing schemes correspond to those in Fig. 6.9

Method	Packing	K	HE-Mult	HE-Rot	HE-Add	Memory	Ref.	Probe	Runtime
Naïve	None	m	$d-1$	0	$d-1$	md	Enc.	Enc.	N/A
SecureFace [12]	Horizontal	m	1	$\log_2\left(\frac{RingDim}{2}\right)$	$\log_2\left(\frac{RingDim}{2}\right)$	$d \cdot m$	Enc.	Enc.	8.67 h
BOK+'22 [11]	k-packing	$\left\lceil\frac{d \cdot m}{c}\right\rceil$	1	$d-1$	d	$\left\lceil\frac{d \cdot m}{c}\right\rceil$	Enc.	Enc.	12.86 h
HERS [21] w/o compression	Vertical	$\left\lceil\frac{m}{c}\right\rceil$	d	0	$d-1$	$d \cdot \left\lceil\frac{m}{c}\right\rceil$	Enc.	Enc.	38.37 s
HERS [21] w/ 4× compression	Vertical	$\left\lceil\frac{m}{c}\right\rceil$	$\frac{d}{4}$	0	$\left\lceil\frac{d-1}{4}\right\rceil$	$\frac{d}{4} \cdot \left\lceil\frac{m}{c}\right\rceil$	Enc.	Enc.	9.35 s
MFIPv2 [10]	Horizontal	m	0	$\log_2\left(\frac{RingDim}{2}\right)$	$\log_2\left(\frac{RingDim}{2}\right)$	$\left(\sum_{i=1}^{d} N_i\right) \cdot m$	Enc.	Perm.	4.7 h
BHV+'24 [6]	Vertical	$\left\lceil\frac{m}{c}\right\rceil$	0	0	$d-1$	$\left(\sum_{i=1}^{d} N_i\right) \cdot \left\lceil\frac{m}{c}\right\rceil$	Enc.	Perm.	1.28s

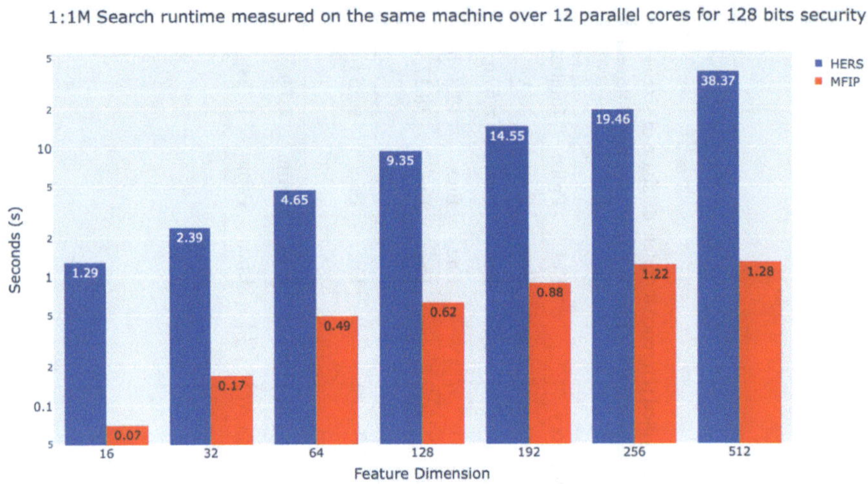

Fig. 6.10 Runtime comparison of HERS [21] and MFIP [6] as the feature vector is compressed for biometric search against a reference template database of size 1 Million. The former secures the probe template through encryption, while the latter is a multiplication-free method that secures the probe template through permutation

Table 6.3 Template inversion attacks from raw verification match score

Method	Number of probe templates	Number of reference templates	Attack success (raw score)	Attack success (perturbed score)
Engelsma et al. [21]	1	$n > 1$	×	×
Bassit et al. [9]	$n > 1$	1	✓	×

4.7.1 Template Inversion Attacks from Raw Verification Match Scores

We now consider two different attack scenarios in the context of biometric verification, i.e., 1:1 matching with a claimed identity. The first scenario aims to recover an unknown biometric template from the match scores across multiple reference templates. The second scenario aims to recover an unknown biometric template from matching scores obtained through multiple representative features. Table 6.3 summarizes the two attack scenarios.

Scenario 1 [21] From an adversary's perspective, recovering the unknown feature $\boldsymbol{q} \in \mathbb{R}^d$ from matching scores $\boldsymbol{r} = \boldsymbol{P}^T\boldsymbol{q}$ against multiple reference templates $\boldsymbol{P}$ of the claimed identity can be expressed as an optimization problem,

$$\begin{aligned} \min_{\boldsymbol{q}} \quad & \|\boldsymbol{r} - \boldsymbol{P}^T\boldsymbol{q}\|_2^2 \\ s.t. \quad & \boldsymbol{q}^T\boldsymbol{q} = 1, \end{aligned} \tag{6.7}$$

where we assume that the unknown feature is normalized. If the feature is not normalized, the constraint can be removed. The solution of this optimization problem is $\boldsymbol{q} = \left(\boldsymbol{P}\boldsymbol{P}^T + \lambda \boldsymbol{I}\right)^{-1} \boldsymbol{P}\boldsymbol{r}$. Observe that the solution depends on accessing the database's raw features $\boldsymbol{P}$ for the claimed identity. However, without access to the secret decryption key, the database $\boldsymbol{P}$ is available only in the encrypted form. Therefore, the unknown feature cannot be recovered even with access to the unencrypted scores. An alternative to accessing the database's raw features is to solve the optimization problem in the encrypted domain. However, there are no known solutions to compute the matrix inverse required for the solution in the encrypted domain.

Scenario 2 [9] From an adversary's perspective, recovering the unknown feature $\boldsymbol{q} \in \mathbb{R}^d$ from matching scores $\boldsymbol{r} = \boldsymbol{F}^T\boldsymbol{q}$ through multiple probe templates $\boldsymbol{F}$ can be expressed as an optimization problem,

$$\begin{aligned} \min_{\boldsymbol{q}} \quad & \|\boldsymbol{r} - \boldsymbol{F}^T\boldsymbol{q}\|_2^2 \\ s.t. \quad & \boldsymbol{q}^T\boldsymbol{q} = 1, \end{aligned} \tag{6.8}$$

where we assume that the unknown feature is normalized. If the feature is not normalized, the constraint can be removed. The solution of this optimization problem is $\boldsymbol{q} = \left(\boldsymbol{F}\boldsymbol{F}^T + \lambda \boldsymbol{I}\right)^{-1} \boldsymbol{F}\boldsymbol{r}$. Unlike *Scenario 1* above, the solution depends only on the probe templates employed for the attack, which the attacker will have access to. Bassit et al. [9] showed that 60–165 fake templates are necessary for a 50% attack success rate. Therefore, this attack can successfully recover the unknown reference template of the claimed identity with a sufficient number of attempts.

In summary, it is not recommended that the raw match score be released for biometric authentication.

4.7.2 Defenses Against Template Inversion Attacks

Two solutions can be used to defend against the above-described template inversion attacks. The first is to perturb the match scores before releasing them to the client. The second is to design a secure biometric verification protocol that is provably secure against malicious clients and servers.

Score Perturbation A simple *perturbation* of the score is sufficient to prevent template recovery while performing biometric verification. The perturbed score can be computed as

$$r_{perturb}^{(i)} = (r^{(i)} - t)w^{(i)}, \tag{6.9}$$

where $w^{(i)} \in \mathbb{R}^+$ is a random nonnegative number. The perturbed score $r^{(i)}_{perturb}$ can still facilitate biometric verification (1:1)—$r^{(i)}{}_{perturb} > 0$ indicates a match, while $r^{(i)}{}_{perturb} < 0$ indicates a no match—without leaking sufficient information for recovering the unknown template.

Secure Protocol Design The security of HE-based BTP schemes depends on the so-called *honest but curious* nature of the participants, i.e., all participating parties (client and server) honestly following the cryptographic protocols without collusion. However, when the participants do not follow the protocol, the security of the protocol is compromised. Bassit et al. [7] designed a custom biometric verification protocol that is provably secure against malicious clients and servers, ensuring both the correctness of the comparison outcome and zero-biometric information leakage (see Fig. 6.7 for an illustration of the protocol). This solution, however, is based on the additive homomorphic ElGamal encryption scheme (i.e., PHE) and thus requires multiple rounds of communication between the client and server for each biometric template comparison. The scalability of this solution to large-scale biometric systems is yet to be investigated.

4.8 Publicly Available HE Libraries

Several open-source HE libraries are available that can be employed for BTP. They span a range of homomorphic encryption schemes, including BFV, BGV, CKKS (with or without bootstrapping), and TFHE. Each library supports one or more homomorphic encryption schemes (see Table 6.4).

Employing HE-based BTP requires the following desired properties:

1. **Computational Efficiency:** Large-scale biometric systems must perform significant computations over the biometric templates. As such, the homomorphically encrypted operations should be efficient. However, a major shortcoming of homomorphic encryption is its steep computation expense compared to plaintext computations.
2. **Comparison Operator:** Comparison ($\leq$, $\geq$) is an elementary operation necessary for any biometric matching computations, e.g., to compare the match

Table 6.4 Homomorphic encryption libraries and supported HE schemes

Name	BGV	CKKS	BFV	CKKS bootstrapping	TFHE
SEAL (github.com/microsoft/SEAL)	✓	✓	✓	×	×
OpenFHE (www.openfhe.org)	✓	✓	✓	✓	✓
HEAAN (github.com/snucrypto/HEAAN)	×	✓	×	✓	×
TFHE-rs (github.com/zama-ai/tfhe-rs)	×	×	×	×	✓
Lattigo (github.com/tuneinsight/lattigo)	✓	✓	✓	✓	×

score to a threshold. As such, homomorphic encryption schemes must directly or approximately support such operations. For instance, TFHE natively supports comparison operations, while schemes like BFV, BGV, and CKKS do need to approximate the comparison operator through polynomials.
3. **Ciphertext Packing:** Biometric templates are typically vector-valued, and computing Euclidean distance or cosine similarity involves multiple scalar multiplications and additions. However, operations on homomorphically encrypted scalars are computationally expensive, and executing them serially is computationally prohibitive for practical applications. As such, homomorphic encryption schemes need to support ciphertext packing, i.e., the ability to simultaneously perform operations on multiple plaintexts at the cost of one operation is paramount. Except for TFHE, the other schemes (BFV, BGV, CKKS) support ciphertext packing.
4. **Multithreading:** Modern computational platforms, such as CPUs, GPUs, *etc.,* natively support parallel processing. As such, homomorphic encryption libraries must take advantage of these computational platforms. TFHE-rs and OpenFHE natively support multithreading.
5. **Floating-Point Arithmetic:** Biometric templates are usually represented in terms of floating-point values, and tasks like matching are also typically performed in the floating-point domain. As such, homomorphic encryption implementations need to support floating-point operations. Only CKKS natively supports floating-point arithmetic through fixed-point arithmetic.
6. **Bootstrapping:** Practical applications that operate on biometric templates often require multiple sequential operations. Executing arbitrarily deep circuits (e.g., deep neural network) necessitates bootstrapping to refresh zero noise level ciphertexts and facilitate additional multiplication operations. However, the computational expense of bootstrapping is significantly higher than that of other arithmetic operations like multiplication and addition.

The libraries above support a different set of features and code optimizations. We compare these in Table 6.5.

Among the above-mentioned library implementations, OpenFHE is the recommended library for BTP. It supports all the desired properties and is actively maintained. The library is written in C++ and supports both BGV and CKKS schemes. It also supports bootstrapping, SIMD operations, and fixed-point arithmetic. The library is designed to be user-friendly and is well-documented. The library is also designed to be scalable and can support large-scale biometric systems. A few open-source implementations of HE-based BTP schemes are available. These are listed below:

1. Secure face matching using HE:
    - https://github.com/human-analysis/secure-face-matching
2. Multiplication-free biometric matching using HE:
    - https://github.com/aminabassit/improvedMFBR

Table 6.5 Properties of well-supported HE libraries

Property	OpenFHE [2]	SEAL [38]	HEAAN [17]	Lattigo [39]	TFHE-rs [56]
Language	C++	C++	C++	Go	Rust
Bootstrapping	✓	×	✓	✓	✓
Ciphertext packing (SIMD)	✓	✓	✓	✓	×
Multithreading	✓	×	×	×	✓
Comparison operator	Approx	Approx	Approx	Approx	Exact
Integer arithmetic	✓	✓	×	✓	✓
Fixed-point arithmetic	✓	✓	✓	✓	×
Boolean operations	✓	×	×	×	✓

3. Biometric privacy and security tutorial:
   - https://biometric-privacy-security.github.io

5 Cryptographic Versus Non-cryptographic BTP Schemes

This section provides a qualitative discussion of the similarities and differences between the homomorphic encryption (HE)-based BTP schemes described in this chapter and the non-HE-based BTP schemes discussed in Part II (Chaps. 4 and 5) of this handbook, where the latter includes non-HE cryptographic and non-cryptographic BTP schemes. While all of these solutions seek to protect biometric templates, they adopt distinct approaches for doing so. HE-based and non-HE-based cryptographic BTP schemes seek to achieve privacy through cryptographic security, whereas non-cryptographic schemes seek to achieve privacy through statistical approaches. Understanding the fundamental differences between these concepts is essential for distinguishing the roles of these BTP schemes and comprehending how they potentially complement each other. Table 6.6 summarizes the similarities and differences between these BTP schemes in terms of the following properties:

1. **Provable Security:** The ability to provide provable security guarantees on the privacy and security of biometric templates. This often involves proving that breaking the scheme would require solving a difficult mathematical problem (such as factoring large numbers) and showing that no better attack exists than solving that problem directly:
   (a) HE-based schemes, discussed in this chapter, afford privacy through secure computation, i.e., protect data as we perform downstream computations without loss of functionality. So these solutions allow for deferring large

Table 6.6 Comparison of handcrafted cryptographic and non-cryptographic biometric template protection schemes

Category	Method	Provable security	Security level (bits)	Accuracy	Efficiency
Non-cryptographic	PolyProtect [32]	✗	FMR[b]	Preserved[d]	High
	Bloom filters [27]	✗	FMR[b]	Preserved[d]	High
	Feature transform [13, 44]	✗	FMR[b]	Degrades	High
	BioHashing [31]	✗	FMR[b]	Preserved[d]	High
	IronMask [30]	✓	115[e]	Degrades[c]	Medium
Non-HE cryptographic	Fuzzy vault [51]	✓	69	Degrades	Medium
	Secure sketch [34]	✓	≤ 128	Degrades	Low
	Fuzzy commitment [29]	✓	79	Degrades[c]	Medium
HE cryptographic	Partially homomorphic encryption [53]	✓	≥ 128	Preserved	Low
	Fully homomorphic encryption [12, 21]	✓ [a]	≥ 128	Preserved	Medium

[a] Post-quantum security
[b] Estimated from FMR
[c] Depends on the error-correcting capacity
[d] Usually preserved (or even improved) only when the transformation parameters are properly tuned (e.g., user-specific parameters). Accuracy often degrades in other cases (e.g., system-specific parameters)
[e] Estimate is based on the ambient dimensionality of the features, 512 in this case. However, the intrinsic dimensionality is much lower [28], around 32. So the real security level is likely to be lower

computations, like template matching or search through encryption, to the cloud while preserving privacy. They provide strong theoretical guarantees. Since the underlying sensitive data remains intact, it can be accessed with the decryption key. So, these schemes cannot meet the irreversibility requirement under the *full disclosure threat model*, where attackers are assumed to know the algorithm and decryption keys. However, they can meet the irreversibility requirement under the *partial disclosure threat model*, where attackers are assumed to know the algorithm but not the decryption keys.

(b) Just like the HE-based BTP schemes, the non-HE-based cryptographic schemes provide provable security guarantees. However, they do not provide the same level of security as HE-based schemes. For example, the security of the fuzzy vault scheme is based on the polynomial reconstruction problem, which is considered easier to solve than the lattice-based problems on which LHE/FHE schemes are based. So, the security level of these schemes is lower than that of HE-based schemes.

(c) Non-cryptographic BTP schemes, such as PolyProtect [32] and Bloom Filters [27], achieve privacy through data transformation, i.e., protect data by transforming it through a many-to-one function in a way that preserves the data's utility. So, this makes it challenging to reverse-engineer the original data since the inverse is a one-to-many function. However, unlike cryptographic schemes, these schemes do not relate the difficulty of reverse-engineering to a known hard mathematical problem nor provide provable guarantees on the minimum size or cardinality of the inverse function for a given choice of parameters. As such, these schemes do not provide provable guarantees on the difficulty of irreversibility, neither under the *full* nor *partial* disclosure threat models.

2. **Security Level:** The level of security of the BTP method is expressed in terms of the number of bits of security. It corresponds to the minimum difficulty of the mathematical problem that an attacker must solve to break the scheme:

   (a) HE-based BTP schemes afford one of the highest levels of security, typically at least 128 bits or more. Some HE-based schemes, like those based on FHE, provide post-quantum security.
   (b) Non-HE-based cryptographic BTP schemes have a lower security level, typically less than 128 bits, which is the minimum desired security level for high-stakes applications of biometric authentication. For example, the security level of the fuzzy vault scheme is estimated to be around 69 bits.
   (c) In non-cryptographic BTP schemes, which rely on the nonuniqueness of the inverse transformation function, the security level corresponds to the size or cardinality of the inverse function space for a given set of parameters. However, it is challenging to analytically or numerically estimate this quantity exactly or obtain a provably tight lower bound. In practice, the security level has been approximately estimated from false match rates instead.

3. **Accuracy:** Whether the biometric authentication accuracy is affected by the BTP method under consideration:

   (a) Since computations are exact in HE-based BTP schemes, the accuracy of biometric authentication is preserved.
   (b) Since the non-HE-based cryptographic BTP schemes are not explicitly designed for lossless secure computation, they typically suffer from a loss of accuracy.
   (c) When using subject-specific parameters, non-cryptographic BTP schemes, such as PolyProtect [32], can preserve (or even improve) the accuracy of biometric authentication. However, when using global parameters, non-cryptographic BTP schemes typically suffer from a loss of accuracy.

4. **Efficiency:** The computational efficiency of the BTP method:

   (a) The primary drawback of HE-based BTP schemes is the steeper cost of computation compared to non-cryptographic BTP schemes. However, several approaches [6, 21] have been developed to enhance the computational efficiency of these schemes.

(b) Non-HE-based cryptographic BTP schemes have not been developed with efficiency as a primary goal. For instance, unlike the FHE-based BTP schemes that leverage SIMD for parallel computations, the non-HE-based cryptographic BTP schemes have not been designed for parallel computations. As such, they are computationally less efficient than HE-based BTP schemes.
(c) Since non-cryptographic BTP schemes operate directly on the transformed data, they are computationally very efficient.

Hybrid approaches that combine HE with non-cryptographic methods are also being developed. The goal is to overcome the limitations of individual schemes and provide a more effective BTP scheme. For instance, since HE-based schemes reveal the original data when the decryption key is known, incorporating a non-cryptographic method that transforms the original data and renders reverse-engineering the original data difficult is an attractive solution. Such a solution also enhances the security of the corresponding non-cryptographic BTP scheme by providing theoretical guarantees of privacy under the partial disclosure threat model. For example, Yalavarthi et al. [55] proposed a hybrid approach combining PolyProtect [32], a non-cryptographic BTP scheme, with LHE. They demonstrated that this hybrid scheme could maintain high accuracy while addressing the limitations of PolyProtect and HE.

6 Conclusions

With the rapid growth in deep learning and cloud deployments of biometric services, as well as significant growth in the adoption of biometrics, there is a critical need to reassess the threats to biometric templates. Concurrent advances in cryptographic technology now allow biometric operations to be carried out on encrypted data using FHE. This chapter discussed the role of modern HE in securing biometric templates.

The key criteria of a BTP scheme are recognition accuracy, irreversibility, and renewability/unlinkability. The HE-based BTP schemes discussed in this chapter satisfy all of these criteria. Recognition accuracy is maintained since the computations on the ciphertext are exact to a large extent, they are irreversible without access to the secret decryption key, and renewability/unlinkability is achieved by simply changing the encryption and decryption keys and re-encrypting the ciphertext.

However, HE-based BTP schemes are computationally expensive and require significant computational resources. This chapter also discussed the limitations of HE and the opportunities for enhancing privacy. We also provided a comparison of existing solutions and publicly available HE libraries. We hope this chapter will be a valuable resource for researchers and practitioners interested in securing biometric templates using HE.

7 Summary

Below, we list the salient lessons learned from this chapter:

- The key desiderata of a BTP scheme are recognition accuracy, irreversibility, and renewability/unlinkability.
- The HE-based BTP schemes discussed in this chapter satisfy all these criteria.
- HE-based BTP schemes are computationally expensive and require significant computational resources when applied naively.
- Careful choice of a data-packing scheme is crucial for improving the computational efficiency of these BTP schemes. For example, the elementary horizontal packing scheme from Boddeti [12] is computationally efficient for 1:1 matching, while the vertical packing scheme from Engelsma [21] is better suited for 1:N matching.
- Leveraging machine learning ideas, such as feature compression, or using likelihood-ratio-based classifiers with look-up tables can significantly improve the practical efficiency of these schemes.
- It is feasible to perform a search on an encrypted reference template database of 1 million records in under 10 seconds without loss of accuracy on commodity hardware.
- It is crucial to protect not just the biometric templates but also match scores to prevent template inversion attacks.

8 Study Questions

1. Name the different types of HE schemes.
2. What are the limitations of each HE scheme?
3. What are the key desiderata of a BTP scheme?
4. Do HE-based BTP schemes satisfy all BTP criteria?
5. What are the different data-packing schemes used in HE-based BTP schemes?
6. Which data-packing scheme is better suited for 1:N matching?
7. Which data-packing scheme is better suited for 1:1 matching?
8. What role can machine learning play in improving the practicality of HE-based BTP schemes?
9. What is bootstrapping in HE schemes, and why is it necessary?
10. What are the limitations of LHE- or FHE-based BTP schemes?

Acknowledgments Vishnu Naresh Boddeti would like to thank Dr. Nalini Ratha, Dr. Arun Ross, and Dr. Amina Bassit for their helpful discussions and NSF CITeR for their financial assistance.

Appendix

Fully Homomorphic Encryption

For completeness, we describe the Fan-Vercauteren [22] scheme and the associated homomorphic operations, i.e., ciphertext addition and multiplication. These operations will be used in the enrollment and search phase.

Mathematical Notation For $t \in \mathbb{Z}$, a ring $R_t = \mathbb{Z}_t[x]/(x^n + 1)$ represents polynomials of degree less than n with the coefficients modulo t. The operators $\lfloor\cdot\rfloor$, $\lceil\cdot\rceil$, and $\lfloor\cdot\rceil$ denote rounding down, up, and to the nearest integer, respectively. The operator $[\cdot]$ denotes the reduction of an integer by modulo t, where the reductions are performed on the symmetric interval $[-t/2, t/2)$. When applied to a polynomial, the operators are assumed to act independently on the polynomial coefficients. $a \overset{\$}{\longleftarrow} \mathcal{S}$ denotes that a is sampled uniformly from the finite set $\mathcal{S}$. Similarly, $a \longleftarrow \chi$ denotes that a is sampled from a discrete truncated Gaussian. We note the plaintext polynomial (also called message) as $\boldsymbol{m}$ and the ciphertext polynomial as $\boldsymbol{ct}$.

Fan-Vercauteren Scheme [22] The FV scheme encodes integers to polynomials in a ring R_t referred to as plaintext. Given such a polynomial plaintext, the FV scheme defines the encryption and decryption protocols for such polynomials. The ciphertext is encoded as polynomials in a different ring R_q.

Let λ be the desired level of security, w the base to represent numbers in, and $l = \lfloor \log_w q \rfloor$ the number of terms in the decomposition of q into base w. Below are the details of the FV scheme regarding key generation, encryption, decryption, addition, and multiplication over encrypted integers.

Algorithm 2 Key generation

procedure GETKEYS(λ, l, w, q)
    Sample: $\boldsymbol{\theta}_{sk} \leftarrow R_2$ ▷ private (secret) key
    Sample: $\boldsymbol{a} \leftarrow R_q$ and $\boldsymbol{e} \leftarrow \chi$
    $\boldsymbol{\theta}_{pk} = ([-(\boldsymbol{a}\boldsymbol{\theta}_{sk} + \boldsymbol{e})]_q, \boldsymbol{a})$ ▷ public key
    $\boldsymbol{\theta}_{ev} = \emptyset$
    for $i = 1$ to l **do** ▷ generate evaluation keys
        Sample: $\boldsymbol{a}_i \leftarrow R_q, \boldsymbol{e}_i \leftarrow \chi$
        $\boldsymbol{\theta}^i_{ev} = ([-(\boldsymbol{a}_i\boldsymbol{\theta}_{sk} + \boldsymbol{e}_i) + w^i\boldsymbol{\theta}^2_{sk}]_q, \boldsymbol{a}_i)$
        $\boldsymbol{\theta}_{ev} = \boldsymbol{\theta}_{ev} \cup \{\boldsymbol{\theta}^i_{ev}\}$
    end for
    return $\boldsymbol{\theta}_{pk}, \boldsymbol{\theta}_{sk}, \boldsymbol{\theta}_{ev}$ ▷ return all the keys
end procedure

Algorithm 3 Encryption

procedure ENCRYPT($\boldsymbol{m}, \boldsymbol{\theta}_{pk}, q, t$)
  Sample: $\boldsymbol{u} \longleftarrow R_2, \boldsymbol{e}_1 \longleftarrow \chi$ and $\boldsymbol{e}_2 \longleftarrow \chi$
  $\Delta = \lfloor \frac{q}{t} \rfloor$
  $\boldsymbol{ct} = ([\Delta \boldsymbol{m} + \boldsymbol{\theta}_{pk}[0]\boldsymbol{u} + \boldsymbol{e}_1]_q, [\boldsymbol{\theta}_{pk}[1]\boldsymbol{u} + \boldsymbol{e}_2]_q) = (\boldsymbol{ct}[0], \boldsymbol{ct}[1])$
  return $\boldsymbol{ct}$
end procedure

Algorithm 4 Decryption

procedure DECRYPT($\boldsymbol{ct}, \boldsymbol{\theta}_{sk}, q, t$)
  $\boldsymbol{pt} = \left[\left\lfloor \frac{t}{q} [\boldsymbol{ct}[0] + \boldsymbol{ct}[1]\boldsymbol{\theta}_{sk}]_q \right\rceil\right]_t$
  return $\boldsymbol{pt}$
end procedure

Algorithm 5 Ciphertext addition

procedure CIPHERADD($\boldsymbol{ct}_0, \boldsymbol{ct}_1, q$)
  $\boldsymbol{ot} = ([\boldsymbol{ct}_0[0] + \boldsymbol{ct}_1[0]]_q, [\boldsymbol{ct}_0[1] + \boldsymbol{ct}_1[1]]_q)$
  return $\boldsymbol{ot}$
end procedure

Algorithm 6 Ciphertext multiplication

procedure CIPHERMULTIPLY($\boldsymbol{ct}_0, \boldsymbol{ct}_1, w, l, q, t$)
  $\boldsymbol{c}_0 = \left[\left\lfloor \frac{t}{q} (\boldsymbol{ct}_0[0]\boldsymbol{ct}_1[0]) \right\rceil\right]_q$
  $\boldsymbol{c}_1 = \left[\left\lfloor \frac{t}{q} (\boldsymbol{ct}_0[0]\boldsymbol{ct}_1[1] + \boldsymbol{ct}_0[1]\boldsymbol{ct}_1[0]) \right\rceil\right]_q$
  $\boldsymbol{c}_2 = \left[\left\lfloor \frac{t}{q} (\boldsymbol{ct}_0[1]\boldsymbol{ct}_1[1]) \right\rceil\right]_q$
  $\boldsymbol{c}_2 = \sum_{i=0}^{l} \boldsymbol{c}_2^{(i)} w^i$ and compute
  $\boldsymbol{c}_0' = \boldsymbol{c}_0 + \sum_{i=1}^{l} \boldsymbol{\theta}_{ev}[i][0]\boldsymbol{c}_2^{(i)}$
  $\boldsymbol{c}_1' = \boldsymbol{c}_1 + \sum_{i=1}^{l} \boldsymbol{\theta}_{ev}[i][1]\boldsymbol{c}_2^{(i)}$
  return $(\boldsymbol{c}_0', \boldsymbol{c}_1')$
end procedure

Protocols

Here, we describe the detailed algorithms of the two phases of biometric matching, namely, *enrollment* (Algorithm 7) and *search* (Algorithm 8). These algorithms are built upon the cryptographic primitives described in section "Fully Homomorphic Encryption".

Enrollment

Algorithm 7 Enrollment

1: **Encryption Parameters:** coefficient bit length b_c, plaintext modulus t, ciphertext modulus q, ring dimension n
2: Server initializes empty database $\mathcal{D}_i \leftarrow \emptyset \ \forall i \in \{1, \ldots, d\}$, label set $\mathcal{I} \leftarrow \emptyset$ and database index $k = 0$, $v = 0$
3: $\boldsymbol{\theta}_{pk}, \boldsymbol{\theta}_{sk}, \boldsymbol{\theta}_{ev} = GetKeys(\lambda, l, w, q)$ ▷ client generates keys
4: **Inputs:** $\boldsymbol{id} \in \mathbb{N}^m$ and $\boldsymbol{q} \in \mathbb{R}^{d \times m}$ ▷ m feature vectors of dimension d each
5: **for** $i = 1$ to d **do**
6: $\quad v \leftarrow k \bmod n$
7: $\quad \boldsymbol{m} \leftarrow BatchEncode(\boldsymbol{q}_{i,:}; v)$ ▷ i-th dim to v-th index of plaintext
8: $\quad \boldsymbol{ct}_i = Encrypt(\boldsymbol{m}; \boldsymbol{\theta}_{pk}$,q,t)
9: **end for**
10: $k \leftarrow k + m$ ▷ increment database index
11: Send $(\{\boldsymbol{ct}_1, \ldots, \boldsymbol{ct}_d\}, \boldsymbol{id})$ to the server

▷ enrollment at server

12: $\mathcal{I} \leftarrow \mathcal{I} \cup \{\boldsymbol{id}\}$
13: $\tilde{v} \leftarrow \lceil \frac{k}{n} \rceil$
14: **if** $\tilde{v} > v$ **then**
15: $\quad \mathcal{D} \leftarrow \mathcal{D} \cup \{\boldsymbol{r}_1, \ldots, \boldsymbol{r}_d\}$
16: $\quad v \leftarrow \tilde{v}$
17: $\quad \boldsymbol{r}_i \leftarrow Encrypt(\boldsymbol{0}; \boldsymbol{\theta}_{pk}$,q,t) $\forall i \in \{1, \ldots, d\}$ ▷ initialize all zero ciphertext
18: **else**
19: $\quad$ **for** $i = 1$ to d **do** ▷ enrollment at server
20: $\quad\quad \boldsymbol{r}_i \leftarrow CipherAdd(\boldsymbol{r}_i, \boldsymbol{ct}_i$;q)
21: $\quad$ **end for**
22: **end if**

Algorithm 7 describes HERS's entire enrollment procedure. The algorithm is designed to handle the scenario where the number of samples in the database m is larger than the ring dimension n (degree of the polynomial). The algorithm also considers a more practical scenario of online enrollment, i.e., we may wish to enroll one reference feature vector at a time in the encrypted database. For this purpose, we first encrypt an all-zero feature representation and update it with each new reference we wish to enroll. This is implemented in Lines 12–22 of Algorithm 7.

Algorithm 8 Search

Inputs: $\boldsymbol{q} \in \mathbb{R}^d$, $\mathcal{T}$, $\mathcal{D}$, database index k, ring dimension n ▷ unencrypted probe and encrypted database

▷ authentication at client

for $i = 1$ to d **do**
  $\boldsymbol{m} \leftarrow BatchEncode(\boldsymbol{q}_{i\cdot}; 0)$ ▷ i-th dim to all indices of plaintext
  $\boldsymbol{ct}_i = Encrypt(\boldsymbol{m}; \boldsymbol{\theta}_{pk}$,q,t)
end for
Send $(\{\boldsymbol{ct}_1, \ldots, \boldsymbol{ct}_d\})$ to the server

▷ authentication at server

$\mathcal{S} \leftarrow \emptyset$
for $v = 1$ to $\lceil \frac{k}{n} \rceil$ **do**
  $\boldsymbol{s} \leftarrow Encrypt(\boldsymbol{0}; \boldsymbol{\theta}_{pk}$,q,t) ▷ initialize all zero score ciphertext
  for $i = 1$ to d **do**
    $\boldsymbol{p} \leftarrow CipherMultiply(\boldsymbol{ct}_i, \mathcal{D}_i^v$;w,l,q,t)
    $\boldsymbol{s} \leftarrow CipherAdd(\boldsymbol{s}, \boldsymbol{p}$;q)
  end for
  $\mathcal{S} \leftarrow \mathcal{S} \cup \{\boldsymbol{s}\}$
end for
Send encrypted scores $\mathcal{S}$ back to client

▷ authentication at client

$\mathcal{R} \leftarrow \emptyset$
for $l = 1$ to $\lceil \frac{k}{n} \rceil$ **do**
  $\boldsymbol{r} \leftarrow Decrypt(\mathcal{S}_l; \boldsymbol{\theta}_{sk}$,q,t)
  $\mathcal{R} \leftarrow \mathcal{R} \cup \{\boldsymbol{r}\}$
end for
nearest neighbor $\leftarrow \arg\max \mathcal{R}$

Search

Algorithm 8 describes HERS's entire search procedure. This includes probe encryption, encrypted score computation, score decryption, and argmax on the decrypted scores to find the nearest match. The search process is illustrated in Fig. 6.11.

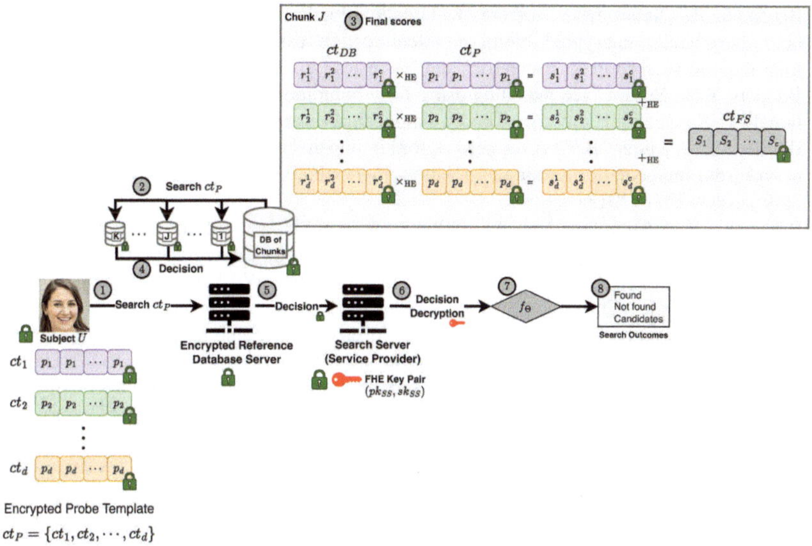

Fig. 6.11 HERS search process

References

1. Act, A.: Health insurance portability and accountability act of 1996. Public law **104**, 191 (1996)
2. Al Badawi, A., Bates, J., Bergamaschi, F., Cousins, D.B., Erabelli, S., Genise, N., Halevi, S., Hunt, H., Kim, A., Lee, Y., et al.: OpenFHE: Open-source fully homomorphic encryption library. In: Workshop on Encrypted Computing & Applied Homomorphic Cryptography (2022)
3. Albrecht, M.R., Chase, M., Chen, H., Ding, J., Goldwasser, S., Gorbunov, S., Halevi, S., Hoffstein, J., Laine, K., Lauter, K.E., et al.: Homomorphic encryption standard. In: IACR Cryptology ePrint Archive (2019)
4. Barni, M., Bianchi, T., Catalano, D., Di Raimondo, M., Donida Labati, R., Failla, P., Fiore, D., Lazzeretti, R., Piuri, V., Scotti, F., et al.: Privacy-preserving fingercode authentication. In: ACM Workshop on Multimedia and Security (2010)
5. Barni, M., Droandi, G., Lazzeretti, R.: Privacy protection in biometric-based recognition systems: A marriage between cryptography and signal processing. IEEE Signal Process Mag **32**(5), 66–76 (2015)
6. Bassit, A.: Fast and accurate biometric search under encryption (2023)
7. Bassit, A., Hahn, F., Peeters, J., Kevenaar, T., Veldhuis, R., Peter, A.: Fast and accurate likelihood ratio-based biometric verification secure against malicious adversaries. IEEE Trans. Inf. Forens. Security **16**, 5045–5060 (2021)
8. Bassit, A., Hahn, F., Veldhuis, R., Peter, A.: Multiplication-free biometric recognition for faster processing under encryption. In: IEEE International Joint Conference on Biometrics (2022)
9. Bassit, A., Hahn, F., Rezgui, Z., Kelly, U., Veldhuis, R., Peter, A.: Template recovery attack on homomorphically encrypted biometric recognition systems with unprotected threshold comparison. In: IEEE International Joint Conference on Biometrics (2023)
10. Bassit, A., Hahn, F., Veldhuis, R., Peter, A.: Improved multiplication-free biometric recognition under encryption. IEEE Trans. Biom. Behav. Identity Sci. **6**, 314–325 (2023)

11. Bauspieß, P., Olafsson, J., Kolberg, J., Drozdowski, P., Rathgeb, C., Busch, C.: Improved homomorphically encrypted biometric identification using coefficient packing. In: IEEE International Workshop on Biometrics and Forensics (2022)
12. Boddeti, V.N.: Secure face matching using fully homomorphic encryption. In: IEEE International Conference on Biometrics Theory, Applications and Systems (2018)
13. Boddeti, V.N., Kumar, B.V.: A framework for binding and retrieving class-specific information to and from image patterns using correlation filters. IEEE Trans. Pattern Analy. Mach. Intell. **35**(9), 2064–2077 (2013)
14. Brakerski, Z., Vaikuntanathan, V.: Fully homomorphic encryption from Ring-LWE and security for key dependent messages. In: Annual Cryptology Conference (2011)
15. Brakerski, Z., Gentry, C., Halevi, S.: Packed ciphertexts in LWE-based homomorphic encryption. In: Public-Key Cryptography–PKC 2013 (2013)
16. Brakerski, Z., Gentry, C., Vaikuntanathan, V.: (leveled) fully homomorphic encryption without bootstrapping. ACM Trans. Comput. Theory **6**(3), 1–36 (2014)
17. Cheon, J.H., Kim, A., Kim, M., Song, Y.: Homomorphic encryption for arithmetic of approximate numbers. In: International Conference on the Theory and Applications of Cryptology and Information Security (2017)
18. Dantcheva, A., Elia, P., Ross, A.: What else does your biometric data reveal? A survey on soft biometrics. IEEE Trans. Inf. Forens. Security **11**(3), 441–467 (2015)
19. Drozdowski, P., Stockhardt, F., Rathgeb, C., Osorio-Roig, D., Busch, C.: Feature fusion methods for indexing and retrieval of biometric data: Application to face recognition with privacy protection. IEEE Access **9**, 139361–139378 (2021)
20. ElGamal, T.: A public key cryptosystem and a signature scheme based on discrete logarithms. IEEE Trans. Inf. Theory **31**(4), 469–472 (1985)
21. Engelsma, J.J., Jain, A.K., Boddeti, V.N.: HERS: homomorphically encrypted representation search. IEEE Trans. Biom. Behav. Identity Sci. **4**(3), 349–360 (2022)
22. Fan, J., Vercauteren, F.: Somewhat practical fully homomorphic encryption. In: IACR Cryptology ePrint Archive (2012)
23. Fontaine, C., Galand, F.: A Survey of Homomorphic Encryption for Nonspecialists. EURASIP J. Inf. Secur. **2007**(15), 1–10 (2007). https://doi.org/10.1155/2007/13801. http://jis.eurasipjournals.com/content/2007/1/013801
24. Gao, Y., Doan, B.G., Zhang, Z., Ma, S., Zhang, J., Fu, A., Nepal, S., Kim, H.: Backdoor attacks and countermeasures on deep learning: A comprehensive review. arXiv preprint arXiv:2007.10760 (2020)
25. Gentry, C., Halevi, S., Smart, N.P.: Fully homomorphic encryption with polylog overhead. In: Annual International Conference on the Theory and Applications of Cryptographic Techniques (2012)
26. Goldreich, O.: Foundations of Cryptography: Volume 2, Basic Applications. Cambridge University Press, Cambridge (2009)
27. Gomez-Barrero, M., Rathgeb, C., Galbally, J., Busch, C., Fierrez, J.: Unlinkable and irreversible biometric template protection based on bloom filters. Inf. Sci. **370**, 18–32 (2016)
28. Gong, S., Boddeti, V.N., Jain, A.K.: On the intrinsic dimensionality of image representations. In: IEEE/CVF Conference on Computer Vision and Pattern Recognition (2019)
29. Juels, A., Wattenberg, M.: A fuzzy commitment scheme. In: 6th ACM Conference on Computer and Communications Security (CCS), pp. 28–36 (1999)
30. Kim, S., Jeong, Y., Kim, J., Kim, J., Lee, H.T., Seo, J.H.: Ironmask: Modular architecture for protecting deep face template. In: IEEE/CVF Conference on Computer Vision and Pattern Recognition (2021)
31. Kong, A., Cheung, K.H., Zhang, D., Kamel, M., You, J.: An analysis of biohashing and its variants. Pattern Recogn. **39**(7), 1359–1368 (2006)
32. Krivokuća Hahn, V., Marcel, S.: Towards protecting face embeddings in mobile face verification scenarios. IEEE Trans. Biom. Behav. Identity Science. **4**(1), 117–134 (2022). https://doi.org/10.1109/TBIOM.2022.3140472

33. Lagendijk, R.L., Erkin, Z., Barni, M.: Encrypted signal processing for privacy protection: Conveying the utility of homomorphic encryption and multiparty computation. IEEE Signal Process. Mag. **30**(1), 82–105 (2013)
34. Li, Q., Sutcu, Y., Memon, N.: Secure sketch for biometric templates. In: International Conference on the Theory and Application of Cryptology and Information Security (2006)
35. Liu, Z., Luo, P., Wang, X., Tang, X.: Deep learning face attributes in the wild. In: IEEE/CVF International Conference on Computer Vision (2015)
36. Lyubashevsky, V., Peikert, C., Regev, O.: On ideal lattices and learning with errors over rings. In: International Conference on the Theory and Applications of Cryptographic Techniques (2010)
37. Mai, G., Cao, K., Yuen, P.C., Jain, A.K.: On the reconstruction of face images from deep face templates. IEEE Trans. Pattern Analy. Mach. Intell. **41**(5), 1188–1202 (2018)
38. Microsoft SEAL (release 4.1). https://github.com/Microsoft/SEAL (2023). Microsoft Research, Redmond, WA
39. Mouchet, C.V., Bossuat, J.P., Troncoso-Pastoriza, J.R., Hubaux, J.P.: Lattigo: A multiparty homomorphic encryption library in go. In: Workshop on Encrypted Computing and Applied Homomorphic Cryptography (2020)
40. Oded Goldreich: Foundations of Cryptography: Basic Applications. Cambridge University Press, Cambridge (2004). https://doi.org/10.1561/0400000001
41. Paillier, P.: Public-key cryptosystems based on composite degree residuosity classes. In: Advances in Cryptology, EUROCRYPT. Lecture Notes in Computer Science, vol. 1592, pp. 233–238. Springer, Berlin (1999)
42. Penn, G.M., Pötzelsberger, G., Rohde, M., Uhl, A.: Customisation of Paillier homomorphic encryption for efficient binary biometric feature vector matching. In: International Conference of the Biometrics Special Interest Group (2014)
43. Ratha, N.K., Connell, J.H., Bolle, R.M.: Enhancing security and privacy in biometrics-based authentication systems. IBM Syst. J. **40**(3), 614–634 (2001)
44. Ratha, N.K., Chikkerur, S., Connell, J.H., Bolle, R.M.: Generating cancelable fingerprint templates. IEEE Transa. Pattern Analy. Mach. Intell. **29**(4), 561–572 (2007)
45. Rivest, R.L., Shamir, A., Adleman, L.: A method for obtaining digital signatures and public-key cryptosystems. Commun. ACM **21**(2), 120–126 (1978)
46. Shahreza, H.O., Marcel, S.: Template inversion attack using synthetic face images against real face recognition systems. IEEE Trans. Biom. Behav. Identity Sci. **6**, 374–384 (2024)
47. Shahreza, H.O., Krivokuća Hahn, V., Marcel, S.: Vulnerability of state-of-the-art face recognition models to template inversion attack. IEEE Trans, Inf. Forens. Secur. **19**, 4585–4600 (2024)
48. Smart, N.P., Vercauteren, F.: Fully homomorphic SIMD operations. Designs Codes Cryptograp. **71**(1), 57–81 (2014)
49. Sperling, L., Ratha, N., Ross, A., Boddeti, V.N.: HEFT: Homomorphically encrypted fusion of biometric templates. In: IEEE International Joint Conference on Biometrics (2022)
50. Troncoso-Pastoriza, J.R., González-Jiménez, D., Pérez-González, F.: Fully private noninteractive face verification. IEEE Trans. Inf. Forensics Secur. **8**(7), 1101–1114 (2013)
51. Uludag, U., Pankanti, S., Jain, A.K.: Fuzzy vault for fingerprints. In: International Conference on Audio-and Video-Based Biometric Person Authentication (2005)
52. Upmanyu, M., Namboodiri, A.M., Srinathan, K., Jawahar, C.: Efficient biometric verification in encrypted domain. In: International Conference on Biometrics (2009)
53. Upmanyu, M., Namboodiri, A.M., Srinathan, K., Jawahar, C.: Blind authentication: a secure crypto-biometric verification protocol. IEEE Trans. Inf. Forensics Secur. **5**(2), 255–268 (2010)
54. Voigt, P., Von dem Bussche, A.: The EU general data protection regulation (GDPR). In: A Practical Guide, vol. 10, no. 3152676, pp. 10–5555, 1st edn. Springer International Publishing, Cham (2017)
55. Yalavarthi, B., Kaushik, A.R., Ross, A., Boddeti, V.N., Ratha, N.K.: Enhancing privacy in face analytics using fully homomorphic encryption. In: International Conference on Automatic Face and Gesture Recognition (2024)

56. Zama: TFHE-rs: A Pure Rust Implementation of the TFHE Scheme for Boolean and Integer Arithmetics Over Encrypted Data (2022). https://github.com/zama-ai/tfhe-rs
57. Zhang, Y., Jia, R., Pei, H., Wang, W., Li, B., Song, D.: The secret revealer: Generative model-inversion attacks against deep neural networks. In: IEEE/CVF Conference on Computer Vision and Pattern Recognition (2020)

Chapter 7
Using Neural Networks to Learn Biometric Template Protection

Vedrana Krivokuća Hahn, Matthew Valenti, Veeru Talreja, Nasser Nasrabadi, Tiong-Sik Ng, and Andrew Beng Jin Teoh

Abstract This chapter presents a discussion of the approaches toward *learning* protected biometric templates using neural networks. Learned biometric template protection (BTP) methods are different to the *handcrafted* techniques from Chaps. 4–6 of this book, in that the handcrafted algorithms are explicitly defined by humans, while the *learned* approaches rely on neural networks to learn how to generate a protected template from its unprotected version. Learned BTP methods have been studied mainly for *face* template protection, so this will be the primary context in which these methods will be investigated in this chapter; however, the presented techniques are by no means exclusive to the face modality. The chapter consists of three main sections, which build upon each other to track the development of Learned BTP research. The first section introduces the earliest approaches, which train a neural network to learn a mapping from the biometric template to a *predefined* (random) code. The second section explores the move toward a more flexible approach, where neural networks are trained to learn their *own representation* of a protected template instead of learning a mapping to a predefined code. The third section discusses the most recent Learned BTP approaches, which incorporate additional *randomness* into the learning process to allow for the renewal of the learned protected templates in the event of compromise.

V. Krivokuća Hahn (✉)
Biometrics Security & Privacy Group, Idiap Research Institute, Martigny, Switzerland
e-mail: vkrivokuca@idiap.ch

M. Valenti · V. Talreja · N. Nasrabadi
Lane Department of CSEE, West Virginia University, Morgantown, WV, USA
e-mail: Matthew.Valenti@mail.wvu.edu; veerutalreja@gmail.com; Nasser.Nasrabadi@mail.wvu.edu

T.-S. Ng · A. B. J. Teoh
School of Electrical and Electronic Engineering, Yonsei University, Seoul, Republic of Korea
e-mail: ngtiongsik@yonsei.ac.kr; bjteoh@yonsei.ac.kr

V. Krivokuća Hahn et al. (eds.), *Handbook of Biometric Template Protection*,
https://doi.org/10.1007/978-981-95-0995-9_7

1 Protected Template Is a Predefined Code

The earliest approaches toward Learned BTP methods involve training a neural network to learn a mapping from a biometric template to a *predefined* (randomly generated) binary code. A cryptographic hash of the predefined code then serves as the protected template, and during the recognition stage, the probe and reference codes are compared in the hashed domain.

This type of Learned BTP approach has been investigated primarily for the protection of face templates, and examples include: [3, 9, 13, 14, 27, 28]. Of these, [3, 27, 28] adopt an *image-level* approach, whereby the neural network is trained in an end-to-end manner to map face *images* to their corresponding predefined codes. Alternatively, [9, 13, 14] adopt a *feature-level* approach, where the network training starts from the extracted face *features* as opposed to the raw images.

Most of these BTP methods build upon the approach proposed in [27, 28], which involves assigning a random, maximum-entropy binary (MEB) code to every user of the target face recognition system, and then training a convolutional neural network (CNN) to map each user's face image to their corresponding MEB code. During the training stage, illustrated in Fig. 7.1, the input to the CNN is a face image, and the output consists of n floating-point values produced by n sigmoid activation functions. Each of these outputs is compared to the corresponding bit in the predefined n-bit code, and the training continues until the n-valued output is as close as possible to the n-bit code. This process is repeated for every user that is to be enrolled in the face recognition system (although Fig. 7.1 illustrates the training for only one person). Once the training has been completed, each user's predefined MEB code is cryptographically hashed and stored in the system's database as a representation of their protected face template.

During the inference or recognition stage, also illustrated in Fig. 7.1, the input (probe) face image is passed through the trained CNN to produce the n sigmoid outputs, which are then binarized (by setting values above 0.5 to 1, and the rest to 0)

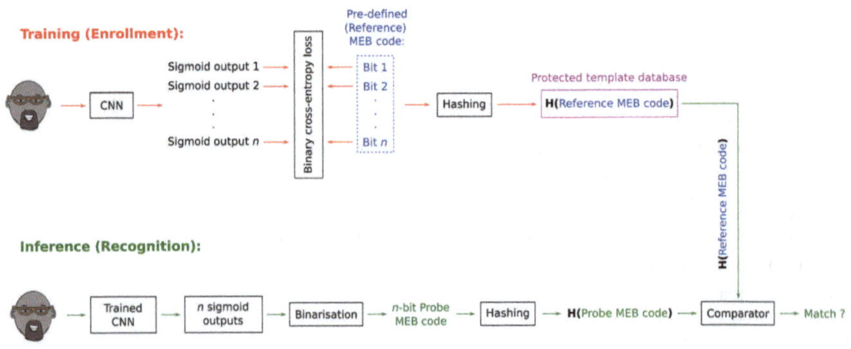

Fig. 7.1 The training/enrollment and inference/recognition stages in a face recognition system that learns protected face templates using the MEB codes BTP method (Image adapted from [16])

to generate the corresponding n-bit binary code. This code is then cryptographically hashed and compared to the hash of the claimed user's MEB code (assuming a claimed identity in a verification scenario), which is stored in the protected template database. If the CNN is well trained, it should be able to deal with natural variations across different face images acquired from the same user, thereby producing *exactly the same code* during each recognition attempt, and the generated code should match exactly the code that was assigned to this user during enrollment. This exactness is a necessary requirement, because template comparison is based on an exact match between the cryptographic hashes of the reference and probe codes. Since cryptographic hashing is extremely sensitive to small changes in the input,[1] even a 1-bit difference between the reference and probe codes would produce very different hashes. So, in order for the MEB-code-based face recognition system to work in practice, the MEB codes and thus hashes from the same person would need to match 100%, while hashes from different people should be very different.

The need to be able to reproduce MEB codes with 100% accuracy during each recognition attempt is one of the main challenges in the adoption of this BTP method in practice due to the intraclass variance in face recognition systems[2] (e.g., changes in lighting conditions or head pose during face image acquisition). This presents an issue for the MEB codes method because, if the trained CNN is unable to achieve this level of accuracy, the false reject rate (FRR) or false non-match rate (FNMR) of the protected face recognition system would be impractically high. So, the main focus of the proposed improvements to the MEB codes method in the literature has been to boost the capability of the CNN to generate the correct code for a given user's face image.

One idea [3] is to encode the predefined codes into error-correcting codes (ECCs) during training, such that the CNN learns the mapping between a user's face image and their corresponding ECC. During recognition, the ECC obtained for the probe image is then decoded to recover the underlying binary code, and the cryptographic hashes of the probe and reference binary codes are compared. This approach aims to use the error-correction capabilities of the adopted ECCs to improve the CNN's robustness to intraclass variations.

Another proposed improvement [13], illustrated in Fig. 7.2, is to adopt a deeper CNN consisting of two components: a pretrained deep neural network (DNN) that is used to extract face features from the input face images, followed by a second network that maps the extracted face features to the user's predefined binary code. Since network training now starts from the extracted face template (i.e., it does not involve changes to the pretrained DNN), we may consider this improvement as a *feature-level* version of the MEB codes BTP method. Indeed, the main idea behind this work is to take advantage of the robust feature extraction capabilities of the adopted DNN to improve the CNN's ability to deal with both intraclass and

[1] See Part I Chap. 2 of this handbook, where properties of cryptographic hashes are explained.

[2] All types of biometric systems, not only face recognition systems, must deal with intraclass variance.

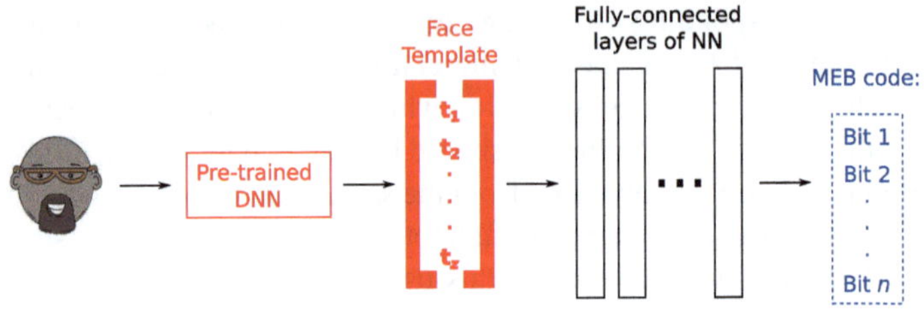

Fig. 7.2 A proposed improvement to the MEB codes method [13], using a pretrained DNN to extract a face template from the user's face image, and then using a second neural network (NN) to map the extracted template to the user's predefined MEB code

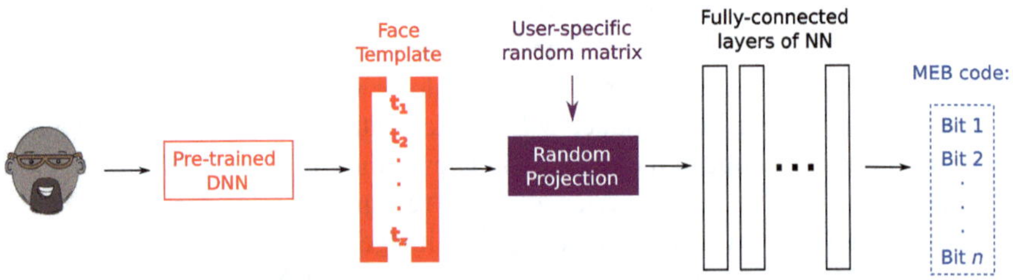

Fig. 7.3 Another proposed improvement to the MEB codes method [14], which builds on top of the improvement from [13] to incorporate a user-specific random projection step before mapping the user's face template to their predefined MEB code

interclass variations among the input face images, thereby increasing the recognition accuracy in the protected template domain.

Further improvements to the MEB codes BTP approach in [27, 28], also based on *feature-level* neural network training, were proposed in [9, 14]. Both suggestions for improvement mainly focus on the addition of extra, user-specific information to incorporate more complexity into the mapping between a user's face features and their predefined MEB code. Specifically, [14] builds on top of [13], proposing a random projection step following the feature extraction, as illustrated in Fig. 7.3. In this case, the extracted face template is projected to a lower-dimensional code (where the projection is defined by a random, user-specific matrix), after which the neural network learns to map this projected code to the user's predefined MEB code. The random projection step is motivated by its potential to: (i) increase recognition accuracy by removing redundancies in the face feature vector, (ii) improve security due to the added difficulty in recovering a user's feature vector or face image from their protected template, and (iii) enable the revocability of compromised templates by replacing the user's projection matrix.

The addition of user-specific randomness is also proposed as an improvement to the MEB codes method in [9], except that this time the additional user-specific information is incorporated through random perturbations (instead of random projections, as in [14]). Specifically, [9] proposes applying random, user-specific perturbations to the pre-extracted face template and then training the neural network to map the perturbed feature vector to its predefined binary code. The perturbations are stored as a user-specific key, which is used to apply the same perturbations to the probe face template obtained during the recognition stage.

There are two main advantages of the type of Learned BTP approach proposed by the MEB codes method. The first is that the MEB codes are randomly generated and subsequently assigned to the users of the biometric recognition system, so the codes themselves are fundamentally unrelated to the users' biometric templates. The second important advantage is that the randomly generated binary codes are protected using a cryptographic hashing function. Since cryptographic hashing algorithms are designed to be non-invertible,[3] it should be practically impossible to recover an MEB code from its hash. So, even if an attacker were to gain access to the hashes stored in the biometric system's protected template database, they should be unable to reverse the hashing algorithm to recover the underlying MEB codes. Furthermore, even in the unlikely scenario where the attacker somehow manages to invert a hash, the obtained MEB code would reveal no information about the biometric template to which it had been randomly assigned. Of course, this is based on the assumption that access to the parameters of the trained neural network would not help the adversary uncover any hints on the link between a biometric template and its hash; however, such an assumption may not hold in practice, especially if we consider the worst-case scenario of a fully informed attacker.

Despite the aforementioned advantages of the MEB codes method, as well as the proposed enhancements to improve the accuracy of the mapping between a biometric template and the predefined codes, there is one important limitation of this type of Learned BTP method that renders it difficult to deploy in practice. The main issue with approaches like the MEB codes method, which rely on predefined outputs, is that the neural network would need to be retrained (either fully or partially) each time a new user wishes to enroll into the biometric recognition system or when a compromised user needs to be re-enrolled with a new protected template. Considering the time and resource requirements of network retraining, the scalability of this type of Learned BTP method in practice is questionable.

So, overall, Learned BTP approaches like the MEB codes method may be suitable for biometric template protection in stable, smaller-scale systems, where the users are unlikely to change frequently and where template renewability is unlikely to be a regular occurrence. However, the rigidity of exact, predefined outputs, while highly attractive from a security and privacy point of view (particularly due to the use of cryptographic hashing), would very likely be seen as an insurmountable barrier to the adoption of this type of Learned BTP method in most practical biometric recognition systems.

[3] See Part I Chap. 2 of this handbook for more details on the properties of cryptographic hash functions.

2 Protected Template Is a Learned Representation

While there are many convenient benefits of implementing BTP using predefined codes, there are several drawbacks as well. Predefined codes are static representations of biometric data, and if accessed by an adversary, could be used to bypass security measures and gain unauthorized access. Without strong cryptographic hashing, malicious actors with access to both the neural network's parameters and the predefined code may attempt to reconstruct the original biometric data from the stored template, posing a significant threat to privacy and security [26]. Moreover, with predefined codes, the system must typically be retrained when a new user is enrolled. If a user's code is compromised, it can be handled by issuing a new code to the user, but that would also require retraining.

Fortunately, advancements in deep learning have led to the development of a more secure and robust approach to biometric template protection: neural-network-generated codes, which is referred to here as *Adaptive BTP* [37, 38]. This innovative method leverages the power of artificial neural networks to create unique and non-invertible codes for each user. Unlike predefined templates, which are static representations and designed independently of specific biometric inputs, in Adaptive BTP, a code generated by the neural network is dynamically learned during training. Predefined templates are typically created using neural networks trained on fixed datasets or processes, and these templates follow a fixed structure and transparent algorithms. This means that the mapping between a user's biometric data and their assigned template is predetermined and consistent across all users, making the process more predictable. In contrast, in Adaptive BTP, codes rely on nonlinear, high-dimensional mappings learned during training, which distribute the biometric features across multiple neurons and layers. Unlike predefined templates, these learned representations lack explicit, fixed rules, making it computationally difficult to reconstruct the original input from the generated code. This introduces an additional layer of flexibility and adaptability, making Adaptive BTP codes even more difficult to reverse-engineer, thus enhancing the security and privacy of biometric data. Further improvements to the Adaptive BTP codes can be obtained by leveraging the power of *deep hashing*, which is the application of deep learning to generate compact binary vectors from raw image data and is generally used for fast image retrieval [1, 2, 19, 20, 35, 36, 40, 41].

In this section, an example Adaptive BTP system that operates in two stages is detailed. First, a multibranch deep biometric hashing (DBH) component leverages a margin-based loss function to generate concise binary codes. These codes are designed to maintain similarity between user representations in the Hamming space. Essentially, the DBH component ensures that similar users have similar codes, fostering effective authentication.

However, as explained in Sect. 1, the accuracy of each biometric recognition attempt is imperfect owing to variations in factors like lighting and pose. Just as predefined codes can benefit from ECC, so can Adaptive BTP. Recent work has shown that the same kinds of neural network architectures used for classification can also be used to decode ECC codes [7, 21, 23, 25]. The example therefore includes a neural error-correcting decoder (NECD) [23], integrated into the deep biometric hashing architecture as an ECC component to address potential errors. This neural network acts as a safeguard, rectifying any errors that might occur in the initial hash codes generated by the DBH component. The NECD is specifically trained to handle errors within a defined range, ensuring accurate user identification even with slight variations in the biometric data. The advantage of using an NECD instead of a conventional ECC decoder is that implementing the decoder as a neural network provides the benefit of using a similar architecture as the DBH component that generates the binary code, and hence, it can be more efficiently jointly optimized and implemented within a common framework. Another advantage of using the NECD is that it provides an opportunity to jointly learn and optimize with respect to biometric datasets, which are not necessarily characterized by Gaussian noise as is assumed by a conventional decoder.

Finally, and similar to systems that use predefined codes, the generated binary code undergoes a cryptographic hashing process for added security and is then stored as the user's biometric template.

2.1 Example Adaptive BTP System

In this subsection, an example Adaptive BTP system called *Deep Neural Network Decoding for Biometric Security (DNNDBS)* is presented. A schematic of DNNDBS is shown in Fig. 7.4. The DNNDBS architecture consists of two important components: (1) a "deep biometric hashing" (DBH) architecture, which contains two image convolutional neural networks (Image-CNNs), and (2) a neural error-correcting decoder (NECD).

As illustrated in Fig. 7.4, the entire DNNDBS network is trained end to end by implementing an alternating minimization algorithm in two stages.

Stage 1 is divided into parts 1(a) and 1(b). In stage 1(a), the algorithm learns DBH parameters by utilizing a novel multimodal loss function that employs margin-based distance logistic loss (DLL) to train the DBH parameters, thereby generating intermediate hash codes. This loss function aims to push representations of images from the same subject closer in the embedding space while maintaining separation between images from different subjects.

It is important to clarify that the DNNDBS system is trained on several images from each subject, not just two. In practice, multiple images (e.g., five to ten) of the same subject are used during training, depending on the dataset. These images capture variations in pose, lighting, or expression to improve robustness. During training, images are typically processed in pairs, where each pair consists of two images from the same subject, which are treated as positive samples, and other images from different subjects are treated as negative samples. This pairwise handling allows the system to learn discriminative features by pushing positive

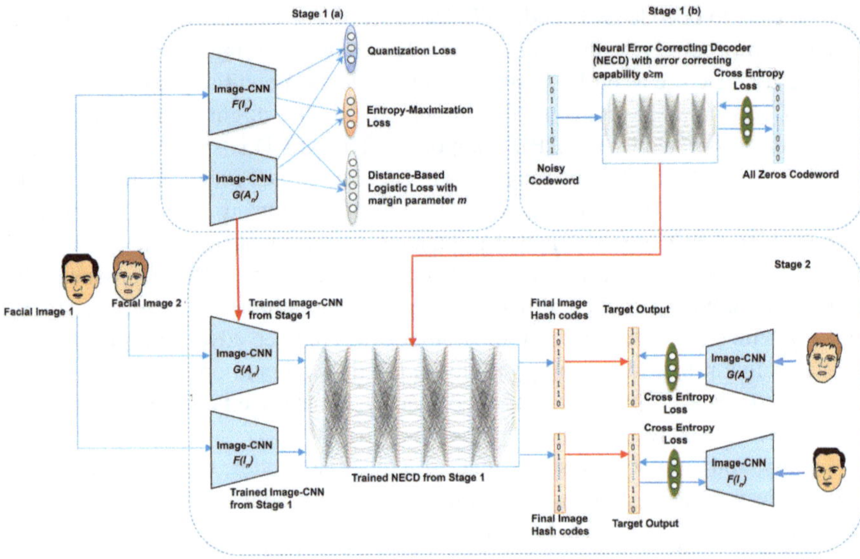

Fig. 7.4 A schematic diagram of the DNNDBS framework, which comprises two main components: the deep biometric hashing (DBH) network shown in Stage 1(a) and the neural error-correcting decoder (NECD) shown in Stage 1(b). In Stage 2, the same training data from Stage 1(a) is input into the already trained DBH network. The DBH network produces real-valued outputs, which are then passed through the trained NECD to generate the final hash codes. These final hash codes are subsequently used as target outputs (they are identical, as shown by the red arrows) to further optimize the trained DBH network

samples (same subject) closer together in the embedding space, while keeping negative samples (different subjects) further apart.

Stage 1(b) involves learning an NECD by correlating the error-correcting capability e of the ECC used to create the NECD with the margin m used in the distance logistic loss for training the DBH parameters in stage 1(a). Specifically, in stage 1(b), to ensure that intermediate hash codes of two images of the same subject are pushed closer and decoded to the same codeword, an ECC associated with the NECD is selected such that the error-correcting capability e is greater than or equal to m, where m represents the margin parameter used in the distance logistic loss for training the DBH parameters in stage 1(a).

In *Stage 2* of the alternating minimization algorithm, the intermediate hash codes (real-valued vectors) generated by DBH (from stage 1(a)) are fed to the trained NECD network (from stage 1(b)) to identify the closest correct codeword (binary) to the intermediate hash codes. The cross-entropy loss between the correct codeword and the intermediate codes is backpropagated only to the DBH network to update its parameters. Stages 1(a) and 2 are performed iteratively until there is no significant improvement in retrieval efficiency with respect to the training. The details of each stage are provided in the next section.

2.1.1 Stage 1(a): Learning Intermediate Hash Codes

In Stage 1(a), the deep biometric hashing (DBH) network, which is a coupled deep neural network (DNN), is trained to learn the intermediate hash codes. DBH has three main objectives:

1. Cross-Modal Similarity Preservation: The DBH network aims to learn a distance-based logistic loss function to preserve similarity between samples from different biometric images encoded in the similarity matrix **S**. As with the previous discussion, samples from the same subject should be mapped to closer representations in the embedding space, while those from different subjects should be further apart.
2. Minimizing Quantization Error: The DBH network is trained to minimize the quantization error that arises when real-valued network outputs are converted into binary hash codes. This ensures that the discrete hash codes retain as much information as possible from the continuous representations.
3. Maximizing Entropy: The DBH network incorporates an entropy maximization term in its objective function. This encourages the generated hash codes to have an approximately equal distribution of 1s and -1s for each bit. This property improves the discriminative power of the hash codes, leading to better performance.

The DBH network comprises two image convolutional neural networks (Image-CNNs). An Image-CNN extracts deep features from the raw pixel data of the images. A tanh activation is applied to the last layer of both networks to ensure outputs are within the range $[-1,1]$. The objective function for DBH comprises three parts: margin-based distance logistic loss, quantization loss, and entropy maximization loss.

The total objective function for DBH is defined as follows:

$$
\begin{aligned}
\mathcal{J} = & \sum_{i=1}^{n}\sum_{j=1}^{n} \ell_c(p(\mathbf{P}_{*i}, \mathbf{Q}_{*j}), S_{ij}) \\
& - \frac{\theta}{c}\left(\sum_{i=1}^{n} ||\mathbf{P}_{*i}||^2 + \sum_{j=1}^{n} ||\mathbf{Q}_{*j}||^2\right) \\
& + \lambda\left(\sum_{e=1}^{c} ||(\mathbf{P}^{\mathsf{T}})_{*e}||^2 + \sum_{f=1}^{c} ||(\mathbf{Q}^{\mathsf{T}})_{*f}||^2\right),
\end{aligned}
\tag{7.1}
$$

where $\mathbf{P} \in \mathbb{R}^{c\times n}$ represents the image feature matrix of one Image-CNN constructed by placing the CNN features of the training samples columnwise and $\mathbf{P}_{*i} = p(\mathbf{w}_x, \mathbf{x}_\mathrm{i})$ is the CNN feature corresponding to sample $\mathbf{x}_\mathrm{i}$. $(\mathbf{P}^{\mathsf{T}})_{*e}$ is a column vector, representing the e-th bit of all the training samples. Likewise, $\mathbf{Q} \in \mathbb{R}^{c\times n}$ represents a corresponding image feature matrix from the other Image-CNN and

$\mathbf{Q}_{*j} = q(\mathbf{w}_y, \mathbf{y}_j)$ is the image feature for the image sample $\mathbf{y}_j$; $(\mathbf{Q}^{\mathrm{T}})_{*f}$ is a column vector, which represents the f-th bit of all the training samples. The objective function in (7.1) needs to be minimized with respect to parameters $\mathbf{w}_x, \mathbf{w}_y$. For objective function details, please refer to [36].

2.1.2 Stage 1(b): Training the Neural Error-Correcting Decoder

As previously discussed, there is an opportunity to enhance cross-modal retrieval efficiency by minimizing the Hamming distance between the intermediate hash codes of different biometric images pertaining to the same subject. This optimization can be achieved through the implementation of an error-correcting code (ECC) decoder. The functionality of an ECC decoder is demonstrated in Fig. 7.5a. As depicted, if the received or corrupted codewords (represented as green solid circles) fall within the error-correcting capability e of the ECC, the ECC decoder rectifies them to the correct codeword (depicted as a black solid circle).

The intermediate hash codes generated by DBH can be regarded as corrupted codewords, situated within a certain distance d from the correct codeword of an ECC. If this distance d falls within the error-correcting capability e of the ECC, the ECC decoder rectifies the intermediate hash codes to the corresponding correct codeword. However, merely decoding the intermediate hash codes to a correct codeword does not guarantee an enhancement in cross-modal retrieval

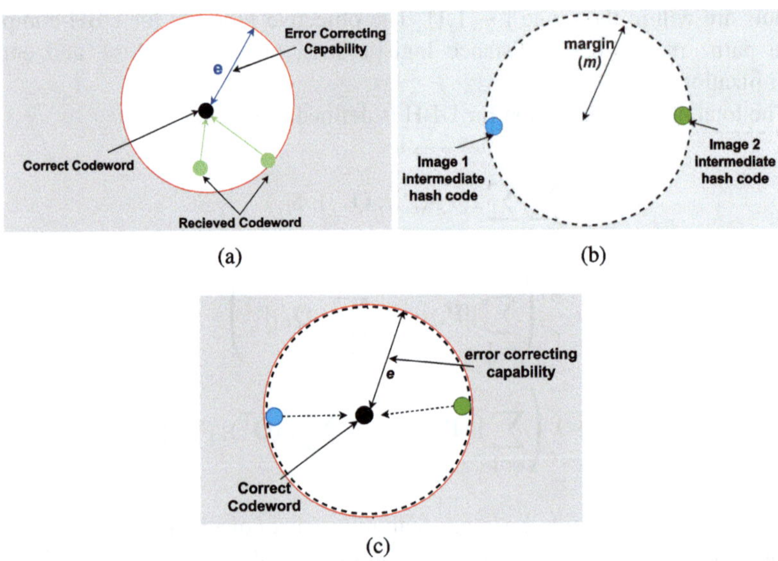

Fig. 7.5 Relating the error-correcting capability of ECC to the margin of DLL. (**a**) Error-correcting capability. (**b**) Margin of DLL. (**c**) Margin of DLL and the error-correcting capability

efficiency, which quantifies the speed and accuracy at which the system finds relevant information in one type of data (like an image) using something else (like a text description); although in the above architecture, it is being used for the same kind of data (facial images). To achieve improved efficiency, it is imperative not only for the intermediate hash codes to be decoded to the correct codeword of the ECC but also for the intermediate hash codes of the same subject to be decoded to the same codeword.

To meet the aforementioned criterion, the error-correcting capability of the ECC decoder is leveraged and correlated with the margin m utilized in training the DBH during stage 1(a). Figure 7.5b illustrates the margin circle representing the DLL loss in stage 1(a). The blue and green circles on the margin depict the intermediate hash codes for images from the two Image-CNNs, respectively, belonging to the same subject. Now, examine Fig. 7.5c, portraying the margin circle (depicted as a black dashed line) alongside the Hamming sphere of the ECC (represented by a red solid line) with an error-correcting capability of e. It is evident that the blue and green circles (i.e., intermediate hash codes for the two images) fall within the ECC's error-correcting capability. Consequently, the image intermediate hash codes will be decoded to the same correct codeword (indicated by the small black circle at the center) by the ECC decoder. This scenario is feasible only when the error-correcting capability e of the ECC decoder is at least equal to the margin m employed for DLL. Thus, an ECC decoder is selected such that the error-correcting capability of the ECC (e) is greater than or equal to m.

Recently, several neural-network-based ECC decoders [21, 23, 24] with outstanding performance, nearly approaching the maximum likelihood (ML) performance for ECC,[4] have been proposed. These methods can be harnessed to produce high-quality and efficient hash codes. Hence, such a neural-network-based ECC decoder can be adapted, trained, and employed as an auxiliary component to refine the intermediate hash codes generated by DBH.

Neural Error-Correcting Decoder The NECD is a non-fully-connected neural network that works like a smart map (trellis) of all possible ways to fix errors, similar to how traditional decoding methods (like belief propagation decoding) work. Inside the NECD network, its hidden layers correspond to the connections in a special kind of error-correcting map (Tanner graph) that is used in belief propagation decoding [36]. In Stage 1(b), the NECD is built and trained for correcting the intermediate hash codes generated by DBH in stage 1(a). In this regard, the ECC to build the NECD is selected in such a way that the error-correcting capability e of the ECC is at least equal to the margin m. To train the NECD network, it is sufficient to use a dataset which is constructed by using noisy versions of a single codeword [25]. For convenience, the all-zeros codeword is used, and the dataset captures different channel outputs when the all-zeros codeword is transmitted.

[4] ML performance for ECC refers to how well the error-correcting code can recover the original message as accurately as possible by selecting the most likely (maximum likelihood) option based on the received data.

2.1.3 Stage 2: Correcting the Intermediate Hash Codes

The trained DBH network from Stage 1(a) and the trained NECD from Stage 1(b) are leveraged in Stage 2, as depicted by the red unidirectional arrows in Fig. 7.4. Using the same dataset as in Stage 1(a), the real-valued vector outputs from the trained Image-CNNs (from Stage 1(a)) are obtained without applying the sign function for thresholding. These outputs from both networks are then fed into the trained NECD from Stage 1(b) to derive the corresponding image binary hash codes. Subsequently, these final image hash codes serve as target outputs (i.e., ground truths) to fine-tune the Image-CNNs from Stage 1(a). In the fine-tuning process, illustrated in Fig. 7.4, the intermediate hash codes (real-valued vector output of the trained Image-CNNs) and the corresponding final hash codes (binary) are utilized as predicted outputs and ground truths, respectively. Cross-entropy is employed as the loss function for fine-tuning the Image-CNNs in Stage 2.

The cross-entropy loss function $L_C(y, p)$ is given by

$$L_C(y, p) = -\frac{1}{N}\sum_{i=1}^{N}\sum_{j=1}^{k} y_j^{(i)} \log\left(p_j^{(i)}\right) + \left(1 - y_j^{(i)}\right)\log\left(1 - p_j^{(i)}\right). \tag{7.2}$$

Here, $y_j^{(i)}$ represents the final hash code value for the i-th training sample and the j-th element in the output layer, while $p_j^{(i)}$ denotes the intermediate hash code value for the i-th training sample and the j-th element in the output layer. N denotes the number of training samples in a mini-batch, k signifies the hash code length, and $L_C(y, p)$ characterizes the cross-entropy loss function between the intermediate hash code vector p and the final hash code vector y.

In this stage of the training algorithm, the focus is on updating the parameters of the DBH network (i.e., $\mathbf{w}_x$ and $\mathbf{w}_y$) based on the cross-entropy loss between the intermediate hash codes generated by DBH and the corrected codewords obtained by NECD. The alternating optimization algorithm is iterated, performing stage 1(a) and stage 2 in sequence until the cross-entropy loss in stage 2 shows no significant improvement. The same trained NECD from stage 1(b) is used in stage 2 for both Image-CNNs. Thus, if the NECD in stage 1(b) has an error-correcting capability of $e \geq m$, where m is the margin used for DLL in stage 1(a), the final hash codes will be identical for both images at the end of the training. Consequently, only one Image-CNN is used for enrollment and authentication. The complete algorithm is detailed in Fig. 7.4.

2.2 *Enrollment and Authentication*

Following the completion of training DNNDBS until it reaches convergence (i.e., no further improvement in accuracy on the training set), a straightforward method is employed for generating the error-corrected hash code of a new instance not present in the training set. This process involves utilizing a single Image-CNN.

During the enrollment phase, the biometric image of the user $\mathbf{x}_i$ undergoes resizing and is then input into the Image-CNN of the trained DNNDBS. The output of the Image-CNN yields its final binary hash code, represented as: $\mathbf{c}_i = \text{sign}(p(\mathbf{w}_x, \mathbf{x}_i))$. Subsequently, this final binary code undergoes cryptographic hashing using SHA3-512, creating the user's enrollment biometric template $\mathbf{T}_e$, which is stored securely in the database. It is essential to note that the final binary code is neither exposed to the user nor stored without protection. Only the cryptographic hash of the final binary code is maintained as a template in the database.

During the authentication process, a fresh biometric image sample from the enrolled user is passed through the Image-CNN to obtain the final binary code $\mathbf{c}_p$ for the probe. This resultant binary code undergoes cryptographic hashing using SHA3-512 to produce the probe template $\mathbf{T}_p$, which is subsequently compared with the enrollment template $\mathbf{T}_e$ by the matcher. This comparison generates a binary score of an accept/reject nature.

2.3 *Reference Infrastructure Implementation*

In this subsection, a comprehensive reference implementation is presented to demonstrate the effectiveness and robustness of the DNNDBS architecture in the domain of facial biometrics. This implementation is detailed to provide a clear and practical example of how the DNNDBS framework can be applied to real-world biometric tasks.

As described earlier, DNNDBS utilizes two image convolutional neural networks (Image-CNNs) for feature extraction from biometric images. The Image-CNNs are initialized with weights pretrained on the ImageNet [5] dataset using a VGG-19 network [34]. The original VGG-19 architecture consists of five convolutional layers ("conv1-conv5") and three fully connected layers ("fc6-fc8"). For DNNDBS, the VGG-19 architecture is modified by discarding the final fully connected layer ($fc8$). The second-to-last layer ($fc7$) is also replaced with a new layer (f_{ch}) containing c hidden nodes, where c represents the desired intermediate hash code length. ReLU activation is used for all convolutional layers and the $fc6$ layer, while the f_{ch} layer employs a tanh activation function. The intermediate hash code length is set to match the codeword size used in the NECD network. The training is optimized using the Adam optimizer [17] with its default hyperparameters.

An alternating minimization approach is used for training, and a fixed batch size of 128 samples is maintained throughout the experiments. The entire DNNDBS implementation is written in Python using TensorFlow's API, and all training is conducted on two NVIDIA GeForce GTX TITAN X GPUs with 12 GB of memory each.

The NECD network can be trained using a database containing noisy versions of a single codeword [23]. For simplicity, noisy versions of the zero codeword are utilized. The training data encompasses various channel output realizations when transmitting the zero codeword. The NECD's goal is to learn to produce an N-dimensional output word that is as close as possible to the zero codeword. The NECD network is trained with various Bose-Chaudhuri-Hocquenghem (BCH) codes, including BCH(31,21), BCH(63,45), and BCH(127,92).[5] This translates to intermediate and target hash code lengths of 31, 63, and 127 for the experiments. However, the specific codeword size (N, k) depends on the required error-correcting capability e of the NECD. This capability, in turn, is influenced by the margin m used in the distance-based logistic loss (DLL) function during DNNDBS training, ensuring $e \geq m$. In practice, for a given error-correction capability e, the parameters N (codeword length) and k (data length) in BCH codes are selected based on the desired balance between error correction and transmission efficiency. N should be large enough to accommodate both the data and the necessary redundancy to correct e errors. The difference $N - k$ represents the number of parity bits added for error correction; increasing this difference allows the code to correct more errors but reduces data efficiency. Typically, N is chosen as $2^m - 1$, where m is an integer, and k is adjusted to provide the required error correction.

2.4 An Operational Example

In this operational example, the focus is on face biometrics. A set of experiments was conducted to demonstrate the performance of the Deep Neural Network Decoding for Biometric Security (DNNDBS).

The proposed framework is evaluated using four datasets, allowing for a comprehensive assessment of its performance. The first three datasets have been used for a fair comparison with the state of the art in face template protection. The last dataset is used to test the system on a modern large-scale face recognition dataset. Here is a breakdown of the datasets utilized:

1. **CMU PIE Database**: This dataset comprises 41,368 images of 68 subjects, captured under various conditions including 13 different poses, 43 illumination variations, and 4 expressions. Fifty subjects are utilized for training the DBH network in Stage 1(a), while 12 subjects are reserved for fine-tuning the system in Stage 2, and six subjects are used for testing.
2. **Extended Yale Face Database**: With 2,432 images of 38 subjects captured under different illumination conditions, this dataset serves as another valuable resource. A subset of 22 subjects is employed for training the DBH network, and 10 subjects are allocated for system fine-tuning, along with six subjects for testing.

[5] In a BCH(N, k) code, k represents the block of actual data bits and $N - k$ extra bits are added for error correction, creating a total of N bits. This helps detect and fix errors during transmission, ensuring that the original data can be recovered even if some bits get corrupted.

3. **CMU Multi-PIE Database**: Comprising a vast collection of 750,000 images corresponding to 337 subjects under various conditions, this dataset is utilized to assess system robustness. 125 subjects are selected for DBH network training, 53 subjects for system fine-tuning, and 20 subjects for testing.
4. **WVU Multimodal Dataset**: Collected at West Virginia University, this dataset contains facial images from 2012 and 2013, totaling 131,400 images across 2,263 subjects. A subset of 769 subjects from the 2013 dataset is used for DBH network training, and the remaining 294 common subjects are used for system fine-tuning.

For data augmentation, specific techniques to enhance the training dataset are employed. Each facial image undergoes horizontal flipping and scaling to various proportions (60%, 70%, 80%, and 90%). Additionally, all possible crops of size 221×221 are extracted from the augmented images, resulting in an expanded dataset for training the deep learning algorithm. This augmentation strategy significantly increases the diversity of the training data, enhancing the robustness and generalization capabilities of the model.

The genuine accept rate (GAR) at different false accept rates (FAR) is used as the evaluation metric, and the equal error rate (EER) is also reported. Since the train-test splits are randomly generated, the mean and standard deviation of the results for five random splits are provided.

As discussed in Sect. 2.2, authentication is based on binary accept/reject by comparing the probe template $\mathbf{T}_\mathrm{p}$ with the enrolled template $\mathbf{T}_\mathrm{e}$. However, this is not an ideal scenario for an experimental testing of a biometric recognition system as a tunable metric is needed to adjust the false accept rate (FAR) and false reject rate (FRR) of the system. To address this, several augmented images of each image presented for authentication are used, and $\mathbf{T}_\mathrm{p}$ is calculated for each augmented image, resulting in a set of templates $\mathscr{T}$. Therefore, as given in [28], the final match score can be defined by the number of templates $\mathbf{T}_\mathrm{p}$ in $\mathscr{T}$ that match the stored template $\mathbf{T}_\mathrm{e}$, scaled by the cardinality of $\mathscr{T}$. A threshold can then be applied to the match score to achieve a desired value of FAR/FRR.

Before explaining the experimental results, it is important to understand the concepts of *zero-shot, one-shot, and multi-shot enrollment*. In *zero-shot* enrollment, the system can recognize or classify new users without having seen any prior examples during the training phase. In *one-shot* enrollment, strictly only one image is used during enrollment and training, while in *multi-shot* enrollment, multiple images are used during enrollment and training of the network.

For the experiments, the mean and standard deviation of the EER, and the GAR at 0.01% FAR for five different train-test splits, with zero-shot, one-shot, and multi-shot enrollment, using binary code dimensions $K = \{255, 1023\}$, have been reported in Table 7.1. With zero-shot enrollment, GARs of up to $\approx$83% on CMU-PIE, $\approx$86% on Extended Yale, $\approx$81% on Multi-PIE, and $\approx$88% on WVU Multimodal are achievable with up to $K = 1023$ at the strict operating point of 0.01% FAR. Higher GARs, in the range of 98–99%, are observed for one-shot and multi-shot enrollment across all datasets.

Table 7.1 Recognition accuracy results for different datasets

Dataset	Enrollment type	K	GAR@0.01%FAR	EER
PIE	Zero-shot	255	$83.6 \pm 2.1\%$	$14.71 \pm 0.83\%$
		1023	$82.8 \pm 1.83\%$	$14.89 \pm 0.77\%$
	One-shot	255	$96.2 \pm 0.98\%$	$0.99 \pm 0.12\%$
		1023	$96.0 \pm 1.12\%$	$1.32 \pm 0.40\%$
	Multi-shot	255	$99.9 \pm 0.06\%$	$0.051 \pm 0.022\%$
		1023	$99.0 \pm 0.88\%$	$0.078 \pm 0.016\%$
Yale	Zero-shot	255	$87.4 \pm 1.46\%$	$12.5 \pm 0.98\%$
		1023	$85.1 \pm 1.98\%$	$14.65 \pm 1.23\%$
	One-shot	255	$99.9 \pm 0.03\%$	$0.052 \pm 0.023\%$
		1023	$99.1 \pm 0.18\%$	$0.072 \pm 0.034\%$
	Multi-shot	255	$99.98 \pm 0.005\%$	$0.049 \pm 0.015\%$
		1023	$99.8 \pm 0.09\%$	$0.039 \pm 0.012\%$
Multi-PIE	Zero-shot	255	$81.4 \pm 2.32\%$	$15.43 \pm 1.08\%$
		1023	$81.2 \pm 2.18\%$	$16.69 \pm 1.21\%$
	One-shot	255	$98.7 \pm 0.99\%$	$0.263 \pm 0.10\%$
		1023	$97.4 \pm 0.94\%$	$0.34 \pm 0.13\%$
	Multi-shot	255	$99.8 \pm 0.17\%$	$0.93 \pm 0.11\%$
		1023	$98.5 \pm 0.43\%$	$1.14 \pm 0.13\%$
WVU multimodal	Zero-shot	255	$88.7 \pm 1.87\%$	$10.32 \pm 0.83\%$
		1023	$88.1 \pm 1.68\%$	$11.32 \pm 0.92\%$
	One-shot	255	$97.5 \pm 0.98\%$	$0.42 \pm 0.14\%$
		1023	$97.23 \pm 0.89\%$	$0.51 \pm 0.11\%$
	Multi-shot	255	$99.7 \pm 0.16\%$	$0.11 \pm 0.02\%$
		1023	$98.5 \pm 0.57\%$	$0.48 \pm 0.10\%$

The observed poorer performance of zero-shot enrollment, when compared to one-shot/multi-shot enrollment, can be attributed to the network's lack of exposure to user-specific biometric features. In zero-shot cases, the lack of such data leads to poorer generalization, while one-shot and multi-shot enrollments provide the model with enough information to adapt effectively to new users. Compared to predefined code methods, adaptive codes offer flexibility and adaptability but are more sensitive to the availability of training data. To improve zero-shot performance with adaptive codes, techniques such as incorporating auxiliary data, applying domain adaptation, or using a hybrid approach with predefined codes could be explored.

It can be observed from Table 7.1 that the results are stable with respect to parameter K as there is no drastic change in the GAR or EER as K changes from 255 to 1023. Therefore, this makes the parameter K totally selectable purely on the basis of the required template security.

The ability to select K in the range of 255 to 1023 bits gives a biometric security system significant control over the level of irreversibility. Larger values of K result in stronger protection against attacks, making it more difficult to reverse-engineer the original biometric data from the template. This enhances the overall security of the system by ensuring that even if a template is compromised, it cannot be used to reconstruct the original biometric data, safeguarding the user's privacy. In essence, the irreversibility of this method relies heavily on the choice of K, with higher values providing more robust protection, making the biometric template more secure and reducing the possibility of deriving the original biometric information from the hash code.

2.5 Renewability and Unlinkability in Adaptive BTP

In Adaptive BTP methods that rely on neural networks to generate a protected code (or template), these systems typically learn a representation of the biometric data without incorporating any user-specific randomness (such as a user-specific key or random noise) into the generation of the template. While this allows the system to create a reliable and repeatable code, it introduces challenges related to renewability and unlinkability.

In traditional BTP methods, *renewability* is achieved by incorporating a random user-specific key or factor into the template generation process. This ensures that if a template is compromised, a new template can be generated from the same biometric data, making the old template useless to attackers. However, in Adaptive BTP methods, where the neural network learns a static mapping from the biometric data to the code, the template is largely deterministic. Without incorporating randomness or user-specific factors, it becomes difficult to regenerate a new template for the same user, limiting the method's renewability.

Unlinkability refers to the inability to correlate or link a user's biometric template across different systems or databases. In methods that use learned codes without randomization, the same biometric input will always produce the same output (or code), which can be recognized across multiple systems. Without user-specific randomness, this means that if the same user enrolls in different systems, the learned code (or template) may be identical, allowing for potential cross-linking between systems. This weakens the unlinkability of the method and could expose the user to privacy risks.

While Adaptive BTP methods provide flexible and robust protection by learning biometric representations, they may lack renewability and unlinkability because they do not integrate user-specific randomness in the template generation process. Addressing these limitations by introducing random factors or user-specific keys would strengthen the overall security and privacy of such systems.

3 Protected Template Is a Learned Representation with Randomness

Section 2 discussed an approach referred to as Adaptive BTP, which utilizes machine learning algorithms such as deep learning to learn a suitable representation of a protected template. In contrast to the predefined code approach delineated in Sect. 1, Adaptive BTP is designed to directly transform biometric data into a protected template, eliminating the need to retrain the trained neural network for each new enrollment, (i.e., it allows for zero-shot enrollment). This approach enhances the scalability of the protected biometrics recognition system.

However, it is worth noting that for the types of Adaptive BTP methods discussed in Sect. 2, achieving revocability and renewability for compromised protected templates appears challenging. Integrating external information like user-specific or application-specific random keys into the protected template is necessary to renew compromised protected templates. By including such external data, if the protected template is compromised, it becomes possible to invalidate it and replace it with a new protected template generated from the same user's biometrics but incorporating new external information.

The development of the Learned BTP with randomness methods (which we will refer to as Learned Random BTP methods), [4, 6, 8, 11, 18, 22, 30, 31, 33], took renewability into account during the design phase. Most of these approaches incorporate user-specific randomness into the process of learning the protected template.

Similarly to the predefined code method, the design of a Learned Random BTP method can also be implemented at either the image [8, 22, 30, 33] or feature level [6, 18, 31], as shown in Fig. 7.6. In the former approach, a neural network is trained end to end to learn a representation of a protected template from raw biometric signals. Conversely, the feature-level approach involves learning a protected template based on extracted biometric features. Randomness is incorporated through *salting, permutation, or shuffling* or possibly non-invertible transformation mechanisms. These methods draw inspiration from the handcrafted feature transformation approach.

3.1 Randomness via Salting

Various salting approaches, such as random noise injection, random projection, and random convolution, have been employed to integrate user-specific randomness into the learned protected template, encompassing methods from [8, 30, 31], and [33]. Roh et al. [31] mark an early instance of a salted Learned Random BTP method at the feature level. This work uses a pretrained convolutional neural network (CNN) as a face feature extractor. Subsequently, the extracted feature vector and random noises are inputs to a recurrent neural network (RNN) for training. The RNN's

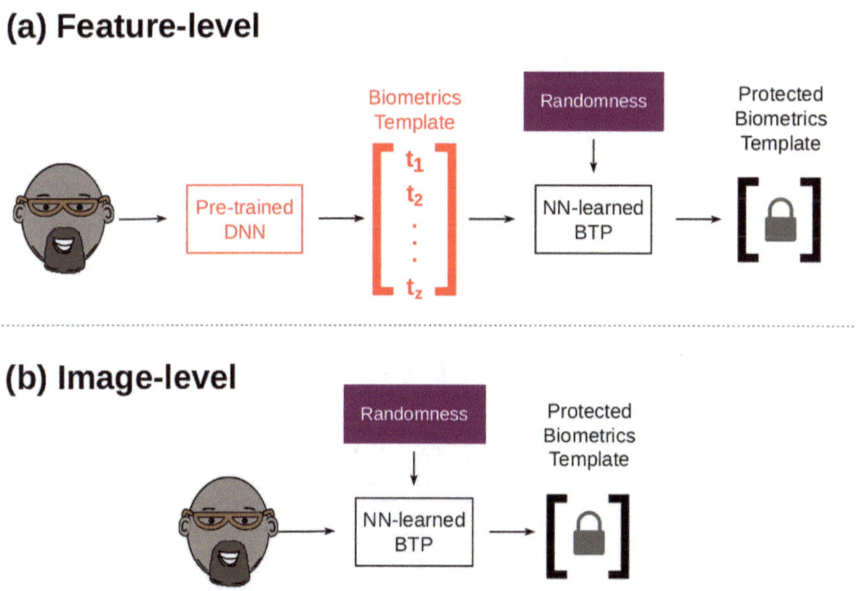

Fig. 7.6 Learned Random BTP Methods. (**a**) The feature-level approach utilizes a pretrained neural network or handcrafted feature extractor for biometrics feature extraction, and the protected template is learned with randomness. (**b**) The image-level approach adopts an end-to-end trained network with randomness to learn protected templates

output undergoes correction through Reed-Solomon error correction, ultimately forming the protected template in binary string form. However, the training of RNN did not comply with the open-set protocol, wherein the identities within the training and testing sets are mutually exclusive. Consequently, the feasibility of zero-shot enrollment is precluded. Additionally, there is a lack of adequate justification for satisfying the unlinkability and irreversibility criteria.

Pinto et al. [30] propose an image-level Learned Random BTP method that utilizes a biometric modality customized pretrained network to extract a feature vector from ECG signals and face images. This vector is *concatenated* with a user-specific random key and passed through two fully connected layers. The training process involves a secure triplet loss (STL) function specifically designed to minimize the distance between triplet pairs derived from the same identity and key, while maximizing the distance between pairs from the same identity with different keys and from different identities with different keys.

Specifically, unlike the conventional triplet loss setup that utilizes the triplet inputs (x_A, x_P, and x_N) as illustrated in Fig. 7.7a, they introduce a mechanism involving two distinct keys (k_1 and k_2) integrated with the inputs by the network itself. The inputs are sequentially combined with k_1 and k_2. Specifically, the anchor x_A is exclusively associated with k_1. Consequently, this results in five distinct representations: $(z_A = f(x_A, k_1))$, $(z_{P1} = f(x_P, k_1))$, $(z_{P2} = f(x_P, k_2))$,

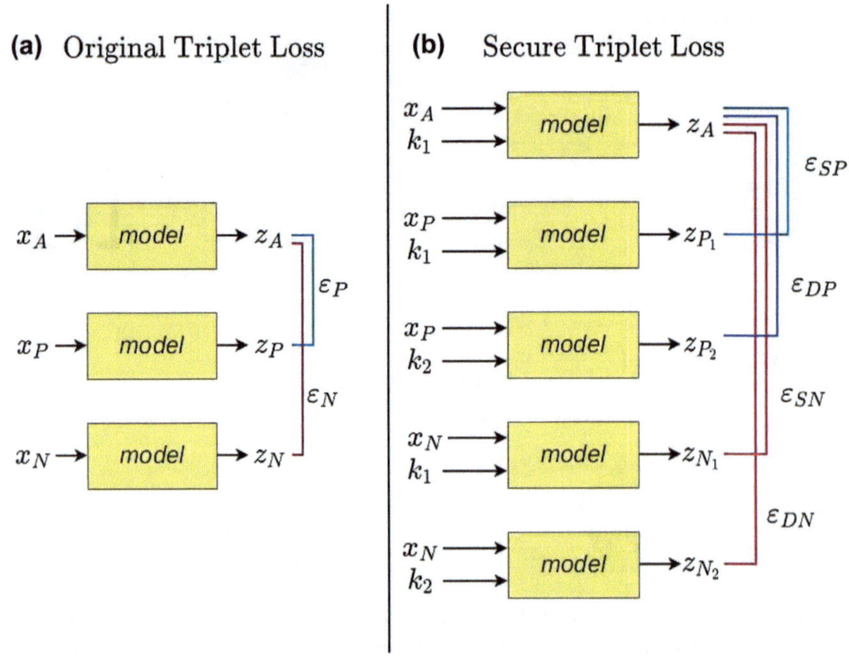

Fig. 7.7 (**a**) Original triplet loss and (**b**) secure triplet loss

$(z_{N1} = f(x_N, k_1))$, and $(z_{N2} = f(x_N, k_2))$, where f is the network model. From these representations, we compute four key distances: $(\varepsilon_{SP} = \varepsilon(z_A, z_{P1}))$ (with matching identities and keys), $(\varepsilon_{DP} = \varepsilon(z_A, z_{P2}))$ (with matching identities but different keys), $(\varepsilon_{SN} = \varepsilon(z_A, z_{N1}))$ (with different identities but matching keys), and $(\varepsilon_{DN} = \varepsilon(z_A, z_{N2}))$ (with non-matching identities and keys).

So, the STL function is instrumental in regulating linkability between protected templates. Unlinkability is achieved by comparing protected templates generated using different keys to ensure similar distance values are obtained. Notably, the renewal of a compromised template and the enrollment of a new user do not necessarily require the retraining of the network.

While [30] assert enhanced security by incorporating user-specific keys with minimal performance degradation, as these keys are effectively integrated with the pretrained network without quantization-induced information loss, [10] introduce a notable challenge. The authors of [10] present an impersonation attack algorithm targeting the model proposed by Pinto et al. [30]. Specifically, the adversary is assumed to have access only to similarity scores between adversarial queries and the target template within a black-box model. The attacker selects an arbitrary facial image, independent of the target's facial image, and assigns a randomly generated key as the initial key. This pair of the fixed facial image and the initial key is then input into the black-box target system, allowing the attacker to obtain similarity scores between the target template and the template resulting from the queried pair. The study demonstrates the attacker's ability to successfully impersonate the subject with a high probability using similarity scores obtained from the black-box target system.

On the other hand, [33] introduced an image-level Learned Random BTP method with a model based on convolutional autoencoder (CAE) for feature extraction. The network is trained explicitly with typical mean square error (MSE) loss function on palm vein, wrist vein, and palm print images. Random noise serves as salt and is added to the feature vector obtained from the CAE to satisfy renewability and unlinkability. A randomly generated kernel with dimensions 7×7 is then applied to the salted feature vector through convolution. Subsequently, median filtering is employed to derive the cancelable template.

3.2 *Randomness via Permutation or Shuffling*

Besides salting, another prominent way to introduce randomness to a Learned BTP method is by permutation or shuffling [4, 6, 18]. In [4], the feature vector obtained from a pretrained face recognition model undergoes permutation using a user-specific permutation matrix. Subsequently, it is fed into a subnetwork trained to emulate the handcrafted IoM hashing algorithm [12]. The resulting protected template is a hash code comprising the indices of maximum values obtained through multiple random projections of the permuted feature vector.

An improvement over the method in [4] is introduced in [18], where the architecture is termed the SoftmaxOut Transformation Permutation Network, depicted in Fig. 7.8. Unlike [4], where permutation is directly applied to the feature vector, this novel approach applies permutation prior to the SoftmaxOut process. In both methods, template renewability is facilitated by altering the user-specific

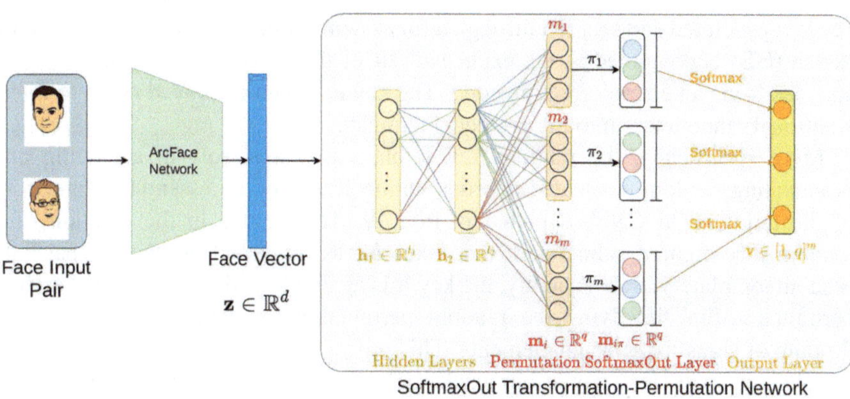

Fig. 7.8 The schematic for SoftmaxOut Transformation Permutation Network

permutation matrix, serving as the origin of non-face-related randomness. Zero-shot enrollment is possible as the IoM hashing subnetwork [18] adheres to the open-set protocol.

In [8], a modification is made to a pretrained network, adapting it to acquire discriminative multiscale features from face images. Subsequently, the extracted feature vector is salted by adding Gaussian random noise, followed by normalization to mitigate noise bursts. The network is trained further to quantize normalized feature vectors. This involves mapping each quantized segment to the nearest binary codeword within a randomly generated codebook. The resulting codeword indices are then binarized and concatenated to form the protected template. While the salting introduces diversity to the protected templates, its role in template renewability is not explicitly emphasized. Instead, the renewability of protected templates is asserted to be attainable through reordering codewords in the codebook. Despite the network being trained end to end using the open-set protocol, concerns arise regarding the scalability of this approach, especially prior to the mandatory retraining of the neural network with new codebooks. Consequently, the feasibility of zero-shot enrollment remains ambiguous.

ProFace is a Learned Random BTP method for face templates introduced by Garg et al. [6]. This scheme operates at the feature level, employing end-to-end training following an open-set evaluation protocol. This provides the advantage of zero-shot enrollment. ProFace permutes face embeddings through user-specific secret keys and utilizes an enhanced center triplet loss function for optimization. This approach guarantees resilience against both interclass and intraclass variations. The resulting permuted face embeddings, derived from the optimized network, serve as protected templates.

Mai et al. [22] introduce a randomized CNN through the integration of user-specific randomness. The proposed randomized CNN comprises a feature extraction network, deriving a discriminative feature vector $\boldsymbol{b}$ from facial images. The first level of randomness is introduced by randomly permuting the feature vector using a user-specific permutation vector $\boldsymbol{p}_{rpt}$. Subsequently, the permuted vector is divided into two components, denoted as $\boldsymbol{b}_A$ and $\boldsymbol{b}_B$. To fortify the user's security, a random key $\mathbf{k}$ is generated and secured through a fuzzy commitment framework. The secure sketch (SS) is computed as the exclusive OR of the $\mathbf{c}$ and the $\boldsymbol{b}_B$, where $\mathbf{c}$ is the encoded $\mathbf{k}$ via an error-correction code. The key $\mathbf{k}$ is then employed twice to inject additional randomness into the protected template.

More specifically, the random key $\mathbf{k}$ plays a crucial role in activating and deactivating randomly selected neurons within RandNet, an essential subnetwork of the randomized CNN, depicted in Fig. 7.9. This results in the creation of a randomly configured subnetwork that takes $\boldsymbol{b}_A$ as input and produces a partially random template $\boldsymbol{y}$. Subsequently, the key $\mathbf{k}$ is again utilized to perform a "random permutation-flip" involving the random permutation of elements in $\boldsymbol{y}$ and the flipping of signs for selected elements. This process yields the renewable protected template $\boldsymbol{y}_p$, which is stored alongside SS and $\boldsymbol{p}_{rpt}$ in the database during the enrollment phase. During the verification, the query protected template $\boldsymbol{y}_p^*$ is generated using the key $\mathbf{k}$, which is decoded from the secure sketch SS.

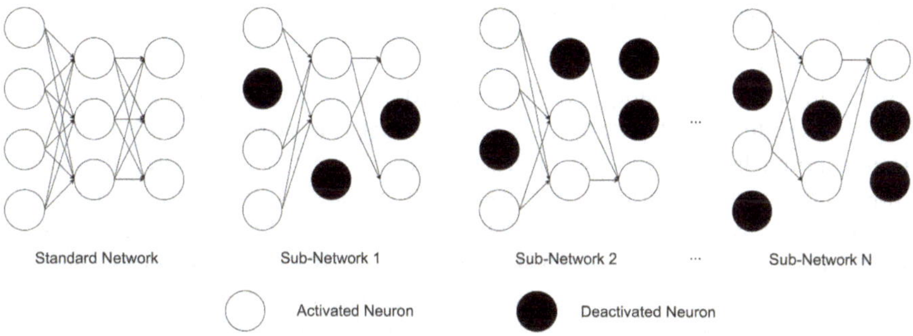

Fig. 7.9 An overview of RandNet: subnetworks differentiated by the activation and deactivation of random neurons dictated by the random key **k**

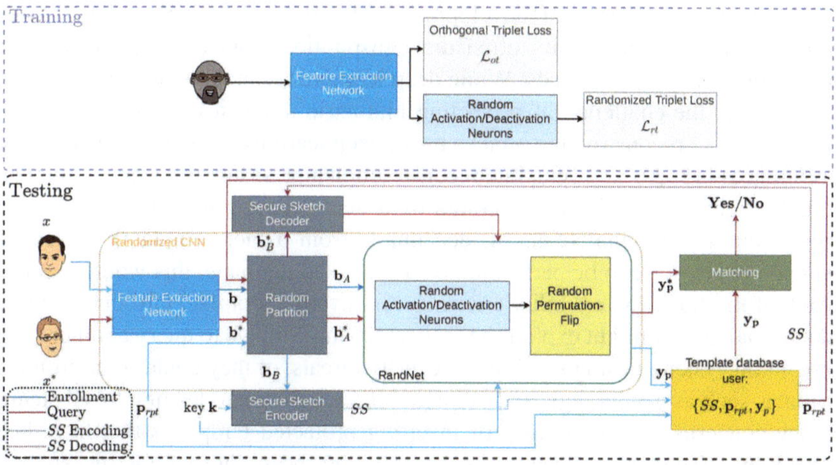

Fig. 7.10 An overview of the randomized CNN

The training of the randomized CNN involves two distinct loss functions: randomized triplet loss and orthogonal triplet loss. The former aims to minimize the distance between templates generated by the same user with the same key, while maximizing the distance between templates generated using different keys. The latter contributes to enhancing the entropy of the resulting templates. Notably, the randomized CNN is trained following an open-set protocol that enables zero-shot enrollment. The working flow of the randomized CNN is illustrated in Fig. 7.10.

3.3 Summary and Challenges

Among the existing techniques, only a limited number can be categorized as “true” Learned Random BTP methods, such as the methods proposed in [30] and [22]. These approaches holistically consider feature discrimination, renewability, and unlinkability during learning. For instance, the STL function introduced in [30] optimizes for discriminative features and template unlinkability, while the approach in [22] incorporates random activation/deactivation of network neurons, and thus random modifications to the network architecture, to achieve renewability and unlinkability. Conversely, the approaches outlined in [6, 8, 18, 31, 33] introduced randomness either into the extracted feature vector or into the outputs of specific layers of the neural network.

However, it is essential to note that the field of Learned Random BTP methods is still in its early stages of development. The strategies employed to achieve unlinkability and renewability often draw inspiration from or adapt handcrafted feature transformation methods. While deep learning technology aids in preserving performance, the challenge of protecting biometric templates intensifies with the rise of template reconstruction attacks using deep learning techniques, as indicated in references [15, 29, 32]. Template reconstruction attacks aim to reverse-engineer a biometric template, typically generated by a deep learning model, to retrieve the original biometric signal (e.g., a face image from a face template). If such an inversion attack were to be performed on a protected template, this would signify a breach of the BTP irreversibility criterion. An inverted template introduces several risks: An adversary might exploit the recovered (face) image to query another (face) recognition system, posing significant security threats, or they could infer protected attributes such as gender, age, and ethnicity of the individual, leading to substantial privacy concerns. The feasibility of inverting protected templates that have been learned by (deep) neural networks has not yet been thoroughly investigated. Furthermore, there remains work to be done on exploring the leakage of information about biometric templates in different layers of the neural network that has been trained to generate protected templates. Additionally, challenges like zero-shot enrollment and scalability remain significant, because model discrimination tends to deteriorate as the number of enrolled users increases. The scalability of Learned Random BTP methods in relation to the growing number of enrolled users is still an under-explored area.

Furthermore, it is worth emphasizing that Learned Random BTP methods are typically relevant for one-to-one matching tasks, i.e., verification. This suitability arises from the requirement for two-factor inputs, biometrics and user-specific randomness, usually provided as tokens or passwords. The security of such a scheme heavily relies on maintaining the secrecy of the user-specific randomness, making protecting this information a critical concern. As exemplified by Mai et al. [22], the existing literature employs biometric cryptosystems [39] such as fuzzy commitment and digital lockers to secure user-specific randomness, but this approach introduces complexities to the algorithm and may potentially increase the false reject rate

(FRR). Addressing this challenge necessitates exploring more effective solutions for protecting user-specific randomness in the context of Learned Random BTP methods.

4 Conclusions

This chapter explored Learned BTP methods, which transform an unprotected biometric template to a protected template using a neural network that has been explicitly trained for this purpose. Three categories of Learned BTP approaches were discussed.

The earliest Learned BTP methods train a neural network to learn a mapping from the biometric template to a *predefined* (and randomly generated) code. Most of these methods build upon the maximum-entropy binary (MEB) codes approach, which involves assigning a random code to every user of the biometric system and then training a CNN to map each user's biometric sample to their corresponding MEB code. A cryptographic hash of the predefined code serves as the protected template, and during recognition the probe and reference codes are compared in the hashed domain. The main advantages of this type of Learned BTP method are related to its irreversibility properties, in that: (i) The codes are randomly generated and subsequently assigned to the users of the biometric system, so the codes themselves are fundamentally unrelated to the users' biometric templates and can thus not be "inverted" to recover the biometric templates to which they have been assigned; (ii) The codes are protected using a cryptographic hashing function, so it should be practically impossible to recover a code from its hash. The main disadvantages of this type of Learned BTP method are related to its recognition accuracy and renewability/unlinkability properties, in that: (i) The (predefined) codes must be reproduced with 100% accuracy during each recognition attempt, which might result in a high FRR/FNMR if the neural network is not well-trained to deal with intraclass variance; (ii) Since the codes (and thus protected templates) are predefined for each user of the biometric system, the neural network would need to be retrained each time a compromised user needs to be re-enrolled with a new protected template (or when a new user wishes to enroll into the biometric system).

A more flexible approach toward Learned BTP involves training a neural network to learn its *own representation* of a protected template, instead of learning a mapping to a predefined code. This approach was referred to as Adaptive BTP in this chapter. An example of an Adaptive BTP system was introduced, which uses the Deep Neural Network Decoding for Biometric Security (DNNDBS) architecture. The DNNDBS architecture consists of two main components: the deep biometric hashing (DBH) network, which generates binary hash codes from biometric data, and the neural error-correcting decoder (NECD), which corrects errors in these codes. The DBH network uses a margin-based loss function to push similar representations closer together, while separating different ones. The NECD adds error correction to ensure accuracy, even with slight variations in the input biometric data. The Adaptive BTP system, as demonstrated by DNNDBS, combines deep learning and error correction to create a robust method for biometric template protection, which allows for the generation of reliable and repeatable protected templates. However, since such Adaptive BTP methods tend to learn a protected template without incorporating any user-specific randomness (such as a user-specific key or random noise) into the template generation process, the same (or very similar) protected template would be produced for every instance of a biometric sample from the same identity. Consequently, protected templates generated using Adaptive BTP methods are typically *not renewable*.

The most recent Learned BTP approaches incorporate additional *randomness* into the learning process to allow for the *renewal* of the learned protected templates in the event of compromise. This category of approaches was referred to as Learned Random BTP in this chapter. In Learned Random BTP methods, deep learning algorithms are harnessed to convert raw biometric data into templates that are both protected and renewable. The renewability aspect is satisfied by integrating user-specific randomness into the learning process, via operations such as salting, permutation, or shuffling. Learned Random BTP methods thus bolster template security by ensuring that protected templates are renewable, unlinkable, and non-invertible. Despite the promising advancements that have been made, however, Learned Random BTP methods are still in their developmental stage. In particular, challenges, such as zero-shot enrollment, scalability, and the confidentiality of user-specific randomness, have yet to be considered from a practical point of view. Furthermore, the irreversibility of the learned protected templates, including any potential leakage of information in different layers of the trained neural network, has yet to be fully explored (for Learned BTP methods in general). Addressing these issues may necessitate the implementation of hybrid BTP solutions, for example, by combining Learned BTP methods with other types of BTP approaches and/or integrating them with cryptographic protection mechanisms, thereby paving the way toward more robust and secure biometric systems.

5 Summary

- Learned BTP methods employ neural networks to learn protected templates from unprotected templates.
- The earliest Learned BTP methods train a neural network to learn a mapping from the biometric template to a *predefined* code:
  - Mostly influenced by the MEB codes method, which:
    1. Assigns a random code to every user of the biometric system.
    2. Trains a CNN to map each user's biometric sample to their corresponding MEB code.
    3. Stores a cryptographic hash of the MEB code as the protected template.
    4. Compares the probe hash to a reference hash during verification.

- Advantages:
  - Codes are random, so they cannot be easily "inverted" to recover the (unprotected) biometric templates to which they have been assigned.
  - Codes are protected using a cryptographic hashing function, so it should be impossible to recover a code from its hash.
- Disadvantages:
  - Very sensitive to intraclass variance, because verification fails if probe and reference code hashes do not match 100%.
  - Since codes are predefined for all users of the biometric system, enrolling new users or renewing compromised protected templates would necessitate retraining of the neural network.

• A more flexible approach toward Learned BTP involves training a neural network to learn its *own representation* of a protected template, instead of learning a mapping to a predefined code:
  - Referred to as Adaptive BTP.
  - An example is the Deep Neural Network Decoding for Biometric Security (DNNDBS) architecture, which consists of two main components:
    1. Deep biometric hashing (DBH) network: generates binary hash codes from biometric data.
    2. Neural error-correcting decoder (NECD): corrects errors in these codes.
  - Advantages:
    - Can generate reliable and repeatable protected templates.
    - Can enroll new biometric system users without necessarily retraining the neural network, since protected templates are not predefined.
  - Disadvantages:
    - Protected templates are not renewable, because no (user-specific) randomness is incorporated into the template generation process.

• The most recent Learned BTP approaches incorporate additional *randomness* into the learning process to allow for the *renewal* of the learned protected templates in the event of compromise:
  - Referred to as Learned Random BTP.
  - Harness deep learning algorithms to convert raw biometric data into templates that are both protected and renewable.
  - Template renewability is enabled by integrating user-specific randomness into the learning process, via operations such as salting, permutation, or shuffling.
  - Advantages:

  - Can generate protected templates that are renewable, unlinkable, and non-invertible.
- Disadvantages:
  - Practical challenges like zero-shot enrollment, scalability, and confidentiality of user-specific randomness must be further addressed.
  - Thorough investigation into irreversibility of protected templates is currently lacking (applies to Learned BTP method in general).

6 Study Questions

1. Why are predefined codes, like MEB codes, cryptographically hashed before being stored in the biometric system's database during enrollment? What might be the consequences of storing the codes as they are (i.e., without hashing)?
2. Assume that an adversary gains access to: (i) the neural network that has been trained to generate MEB codes from the face images of the users of a specific face recognition system, (ii) the hashes of those users' MEB codes, stored in the system's protected template database, and (iii) the cryptographic hashing function. Do you think that it would be possible for the adversary to learn an "inverse" mapping from the hashes to the original (unprotected) face templates to which the MEB codes were assigned during enrollment?
3. Considering a neural network that has been trained to learn the mapping from a person's biometric template to a predefined code, why would this network need to be retrained in the event that the protected template (i.e., cryptographically hashed code) is compromised?
4. Describe how deep biometric hashing (DBH) in Adaptive BTP systems enhances the accuracy and robustness of biometric authentication. How does the use of margin-based distance logistic loss (DLL) contribute to the system's ability to differentiate between biometric data from the same user and different users?
5. Explain how the use of an error-correction code with a neural error-correcting decoder (NECD) enhances the accuracy and security of the Adaptive BTP approach. In your explanation, describe the role of the error-correcting capability e and its relationship to the margin m used in training the deep biometric hashing (DBH) parameters. How does this correlation improve cross-modal retrieval efficiency and contribute to the robustness of the system in real-world biometric scenarios?
6. In the context of Adaptive BTP methods, explain the challenges related to renewability and unlinkability when neural networks generate biometric templates without incorporating user-specific randomness. How do these challenges impact the security and privacy of the system? What potential solutions could be implemented to address these limitations and enhance both renewability and unlinkability?

7. Explain the difference between image-level and feature-level approaches in Learned Random BTP methods. How does each approach contribute to the security and scalability of biometric systems?
8. Discuss the role of randomness in enhancing the security of protected biometric templates. How do methods such as salting and permutation ensure renewability and unlinkability, and what are the potential vulnerabilities associated with these methods?
9. Identify and analyze the primary challenges faced by current Learned Random BTP methods, particularly concerning zero-shot enrollment and scalability. What innovative solutions or advancements in technology could potentially address these challenges, and how might they impact the future of biometric security?

References

1. Cao, Z., Long, M., Wang, J., Yu, P.S.: HashNet: deep learning to hash by continuation. In: International Conference on Computer Vision (ICCV), pp. 5609–5618 (2017)
2. Chen, Z., Yuan, X., Lu, J., Tian, Q., Zhou, J.: Deep hashing via discrepancy minimization. In: Proceedings of the IEEE Conference on Computer Vision and Pattern Recognition (CVPR), pp. 6838–6847 (2018)
3. Chen, L., Zhao, G., Zhou, J., Ho, A.T.S., Cheng, L.M.: Face template protection using deep LDPC codes learning. IET Biomet. **8**(3), 190–197 (2019)
4. Cui, J., Teoh, A.B.J.: Deep index-of-maximum hashing for face template protection. In: 2020 5th International Conference on Computer and Communication Systems (ICCCS), pp. 413–418. IEEE, Piscataway (2020)
5. Deng, J., Dong, W., Socher, R., Li, L.J., Li, K., Fei-Fei, L.: ImageNet: a large-scale hierarchical image database. In: Proceedings of the IEEE Conference on Computer Vision and Pattern Recognition (CVPR), pp. 248–255 (2009)
6. Garg, S., Jindal, A.K., Rajan, M., Chalamala, S.R.: Proface: a cancelable face template protection approach. In: 2023 15th International Conference on COMmunication Systems & NETworkS (COMSNETS), pp. 147–152. IEEE, Piscataway (2023)
7. Gruber, T., Cammerer, S., Hoydis, J., ten Brink, S.: On deep learning-based channel decoding. In: Proceedings of the IEEE Annual Conference on Information Sciences and Systems (CISS) (2017)
8. Jang, Y.K., Cho, N.I.: Deep face image retrieval for cancelable biometric authentication. In: 2019 16th IEEE International Conference on Advanced Video and Signal Based Surveillance (AVSS), pp. 1–8. IEEE, Piscataway (2019)
9. Jami, S.K., Chalamala, S.R., Jindal, A.K.: Biometric Template Protection Through Adversarial Learning. In: 2019 IEEE International Conference on Consumer Electronics (ICCE), pp. 1–6 (2019). https://doi.org/10.1109/ICCE.2019.8661905
10. Jeong, B., Kim, S., Paik, S., Seo, J.H.: Analysis on secure triplet loss. IEEE Access **10**, 124355–124362 (2022)
11. Jin, A.T.B., Ling, D.N.C., Goh, A.: Biohashing: two factor authentication featuring fingerprint data and tokenised random number. Pattern Recognit. **37**(11), 2245–2255 (2004)
12. Jin, Z., Hwang, J.Y., Lai, Y.L., Kim, S., Teoh, A.B.J.: Ranking-based locality sensitive hashing-enabled cancelable biometrics: Index-of-max hashing. IEEE Trans. Inf. Forensics Secur. **13**(2), 393–407 (2017)
13. Jindal, A.K., Chalamala, S., Jami, S.K.: Face template protection using deep convolutional neural network. In: 2018 IEEE/CVF Conference on Computer Vision and Pattern Recognition Workshops (CVPRW), pp. 575–5758 (2018). https://doi.org/10.1109/CVPRW.2018.00087

14. Jindal, A.K., Chalamala, S.R., Jami, S.K.: Securing face templates using deep convolutional neural network and random projection. In: 2019 IEEE International Conference on Consumer Electronics (ICCE), pp. 1–6 (2019). https://doi.org/10.1109/ICCE.2019.8662094
15. Kim, S., Tan, Y.K., Jeong, B., Mondal, S., Khin, M.M.A., Seo, J.H.: Scores tell everything about Bob: non-adaptive face reconstruction on face recognition systems. In: 2024 IEEE Symposium on Security and Privacy (SP), pp. 161–161. IEEE Computer Society, Los Alamitos (2024)
16. Krivokuća Hahn, V.: Biometric template protection for face recognition systems: A behind-the-scenes look at the motivation, methods, and metrics. Tutorial presented at IJCB2022 (2022). https://drive.switch.ch/index.php/s/wNlOfS1LX00pXkl
17. Kingma, D.P., Ba, J.: Adam: a method for stochastic optimization. Preprint. arXiv:1412.6980 (2014)
18. Lee, H., Low, C.Y., Teoh, A.B.J.: Softmaxout transformation-permutation network for facial template protection. In: 2020 25th International Conference on Pattern Recognition (ICPR), pp. 7558–7565. IEEE, Piscataway (2021)
19. Lin, K., Lu, J., Chen, C.S., Zhou, J.: Learning compact binary descriptors with unsupervised deep neural networks. In: Proceedings of the IEEE Conference on Computer Vision and Pattern Recognition (CVPR) (2016). https://doi.org/10.1109/CVPR.2016.133
20. Liu, H., Wang, R., Shan, S., Chen, X.: Deep supervised hashing for fast image retrieval. In: Proceedings of the IEEE Conference on Computer Vision and Pattern Recognition (CVPR), pp. 2064–2072 (2016)
21. Lugosch, L., Gross, W.J.: Neural offset min-sum decoding. In: Proceedings of the IEEE International Symposium on Information Theory, pp. 1361–1365 (2017)
22. Mai, G., Cao, K., Lan, X., Yuen, P.C.: SecureFace: face template protection. IEEE Trans. Inf. Forensics Secur. **16**, 262–277 (2021). https://doi.org/10.1109/TIFS.2020.3009590
23. Nachmani, E., Be'ery, Y., Burshtein, D.: Learning to decode linear codes using deep learning. In: Proceedings of the 54th Annual Allerton Conference on Communication, Control, and Computing (Allerton), pp. 341–346 (2016). https://doi.org/10.1109/ALLERTON.2016.7852251
24. Nachmani, E., Marciano, E., Burshtein, D., Be'ery, Y.: RNN decoding of linear block codes. Preprint. arXiv:1702.07560 (2017)
25. Nachmani, E., Marciano, E., Lugosch, L., Gross, W.J., Burshtein, D., Be'ery, Y.: Deep learning methods for improved decoding of linear codes. IEEE J. Select. Top. Signal Proces. **12**(1), 119–131 (2018)
26. Nagar, A., Nandakumar, K., Jain, A.K.: Multibiometric cryptosystems based on feature-level fusion. IEEE Trans. Inform. Forensics Secur. **7**(1), 255–268 (2012). https://doi.org/10.1109/TIFS.2011.2166545
27. Pandey, R.K., Zhou, Y., Kota, B.U., Govindaraju, V.: Maximum entropy binary encoding for face template protection. Preprint. arXiv:1512.01691 (2015)
28. Pandey, R.K., Zhou, Y., Kota, B.U., Govindaraju, V.: Deep secure encoding for face template protection. In: 2016 IEEE Conference on Computer Vision and Pattern Recognition Workshops (CVPRW), pp. 77–83 (2016). https://doi.org/10.1109/CVPRW.2016.17
29. Park, H., Park, J., Dong, X., Teoh, A.B.J.: Towards query efficient and generalizable black-box face reconstruction attack. In: 2023 IEEE International Conference on Image Processing (ICIP), pp. 1060–1064. IEEE, Piscataway (2023)
30. Pinto, J.R., Correia, M.V., Cardoso, J.S.: Secure triplet loss: Achieving cancelability and non-linkability in end-to-end deep biometrics. IEEE Trans. Biomet. Behav. Identity Sci. **3**(2), 180–189 (2020)
31. Roh, J.h., Cho, S., Jin, S.H.: Learning based biometric key generation method using CNN and RNN. In: 2018 10th International Conference on Information Technology and Electrical Engineering (ICITEE), pp. 136–139. IEEE, Piscataway (2018)
32. Shahreza, H.O., Marcel, S.: Face reconstruction from facial templates by learning latent space of a generator network. In: Thirty-seventh Conference on Neural Information Processing Systems (2023)

33. Siddhad, G., Khanna, P., Ojha, A.: Cancelable biometric template generation using convolutional autoencoder. In: International Conference on Computer Vision and Image Processing, pp. 303–314. Springer, Berlin (2020)
34. Simonyan, K., Zisserman, A.: Very deep convolutional networks for large-scale image recognition. CoRR abs/1409.1556 (2014)
35. Taherkhani, F., Talreja, V., Kazemi, H., Nasrabadi, N.: Facial attribute guided deep cross-modal hashing for face image retrieval. In: International Conference of the Biometrics Special Interest Group (BIOSIG). IEEE, Piscataway (2018)
36. Taherkhani, F., Talreja, V., Valenti, M.C., Nasrabadi, N.M.: Error-corrected margin-based deep cross-modal hashing for facial image retrieval. IEEE Trans. Biomet. Behav. Identity Sci. **2**(3), 279–293 (2020)
37. Talreja, V., Soleymani, S., Valenti, M.C., Nasrabadi, N.M.: Learning to authenticate with deep multibiometric hashing and neural network decoding. In: Proceedings of the IEEE International Conference on Communications (ICC) (2019)
38. Talreja, V., Valenti, M.C., Nasrabadi, N.M.: Zero-shot deep hashing and neural network based error correction for face template protection. In: Proceedings of the IEEE International Conference on Biometrics Theory, Applications and Systems (BTAS) (2019)
39. Uludag, U., Pankanti, S., Prabhakar, S., Jain, A.K.: Biometric cryptosystems: issues and challenges. Proc. IEEE **92**(6), 948–960 (2004)
40. Yuan, X., Ren, L., Lu, J., Zhou, J.: Relaxation-free deep hashing via policy gradient. In: The European Conference on Computer Vision (ECCV) (2018)
41. Zhu, H., Long, M., Wang, J., Cao, Y.: Deep hashing network for efficient similarity retrieval. In: Proceedings of the AAAI Conference on Artificial Intelligence, pp. 2415–2421 (2016)

Part III
Metrics

Chapter 8
On the Evaluation of Recognition Performance in Protected Biometric Systems

Hatef Otroshi Shahreza and Sébastien Marcel

Abstract Biometric recognition systems are widely used for automatic authentication in different applications. The main goal of each biometric system is to accurately recognize individuals in verification or identification tasks. Biometric template protection (BTP) schemes provide protection for biometric templates against different security and privacy attacks. In addition to the protection provided by these schemes, it is important that the protected system has satisfying recognition accuracy. However, compared to unprotected biometric systems, we can consider different scenarios for a protected biometric system, and therefore we need to evaluate the recognition performance of the system in these different scenarios. This chapter presents an overview of the evaluation of protected biometric systems. We focus on standardized evaluation of biometric systems and discuss different scenarios in which the performance of a protected system should be evaluated, for both verification and identification (open-set and closed-set) tasks. Moreover, we discuss other criteria, such as complexity and memory consumption, as well as recognition bias, that should be taken into account when evaluating protected systems.

H. Otroshi Shahreza (✉)
Biometrics Security & Privacy Group, Idiap Research Institute, Martigny, Switzerland

School of Engineering, École Polytechnique Fédérale de Lausanne (EPFL), Lausanne, Switzerland
e-mail: hatef.otroshi@idiap.ch

S. Marcel
Biometrics Security & Privacy Group, Idiap Research Institute, Martigny, Switzerland

School of Criminal Justice, Université de Lausanne (UNIL), Lausanne, Switzerland
e-mail: sebastien.marcel@idiap.ch

V. Krivokuća Hahn et al. (eds.), *Handbook of Biometric Template Protection*,
https://doi.org/10.1007/978-981-95-0995-9_8

1 Introduction

Biometric recognition systems are broadly deployed in various large-scale and everyday applications, from border control to online banking or unlocking smartphones. Considering increasing concerns about the sensitivity of biometric data, biometric template protection (BTP) mechanisms have been proposed to protect the sensitive information in biometric templates and thus alleviate the security and privacy threats faced by unprotected systems. However, even in protected biometric systems, the reliable authentication of individuals is the main objective. In particular, biometric systems are currently used in applications that require very accurate recognition, and therefore the recognition performance of the protected biometric system should still satisfy the required accuracy. But, what if the recognition performance of these systems is far from the performance of the state-of-the-art unprotected systems?

The recognition performance of protected systems is undoubtedly one of the most important criteria in both evaluating the systems themselves and benchmarking different biometric systems. Considering the high importance of recognition performance, how should we evaluate and benchmark protected systems? Should we use the same approach as for evaluating an unprotected system or are there any special considerations to take into account when evaluating the recognition performance of protected systems? In fact, a template protection scheme is designed to provide protection (in terms of irreversibility, unlinkability, etc., as defined in the ISO/IEC 24745:2022 standard [10]), but is there a trade-off with, or a cost to, the resulting recognition accuracy?

In a protected biometric system, there are often some secrets used for the BTP mechanisms. Hence, the recognition performance of the system may be affected by these secrets in either a positive way (e.g., by increasing the "entropy" of the system's users if the secrets are user-specific) or in a negative way (e.g., if the secrets are partially or completely leaked to an adversary). Compared to unprotected biometric systems, which have only a single (normal) operating scenario, we can define different scenarios for a protected system (for example, based on whether user-specific or system-specific secrets are used, whether the secrets are leaked, etc.). Accordingly, for a complete evaluation of the security of a protected biometric system, it is necessary to evaluate the recognition performance of the system under various applicable scenarios. This chapter explains typical techniques for evaluating the recognition performance in protected biometric systems, including a discussion of different evaluation scenarios.

In the remainder of the chapter, we first review the evaluation of recognition performance in an unprotected system for verification and identification (open set and closed set) tasks in Sect. 2. Then, we describe different scenarios to evaluate the performance of a protected biometric system in Sect. 3. In Sect. 4, we discuss how to evaluate the performance of a protected system in terms of other performance criteria that are complementary to recognition accuracy. Finally, the chapter is concluded in Sect. 5.

2 Evaluating the Recognition Performance of Unprotected Biometric Systems

To evaluate the recognition performance of an unprotected biometric system, we need to have a dataset with identity labels and use a protocol (predefined) to create pairs of mated (positive or genuine) and non-mated (negative or zero-effort impostor) samples. Then, we can compute the comparison scores for mated and non-mated pairs, and the resulting scores can be used to generate histograms of mated and non-mated scores. In an ideal case, the histograms of scores for mated and non-mated pairs should be completely separated, enabling recognition based on comparison scores by selecting a threshold between the two histograms to determine match decisions. However, in practice there is usually an overlap between the two histograms, introducing recognition errors for the system. Using these histograms, we can adjust the decision threshold of the system and find the false match rate (FMR) and the corresponding false non-match rate (FNMR) at different thresholds. Then, we can choose a threshold that achieves the most acceptable trade-off between the two types of errors (FMR and FNMR). The FMR is the ratio of the number of false match pairs to the total number of non-mated pairs:

$$\text{FMR} = \frac{\#\,\text{False Match}}{\#\,\text{Non-Mated Pairs}} = \frac{\#\,\text{False Match}}{\#\,\text{False Match} + \#\,\text{True Non-Match}}. \tag{8.1}$$

Similarly, the FNMR is the ratio of the number of false non-match pairs to the total number of mated pairs:

$$\text{FNMR} = \frac{\#\,\text{False Non-Match}}{\#\,\text{Mated Pairs}} = \frac{\#\,\text{False Non-Match}}{\#\,\text{False Non-Match} + \#\,\text{True Match}}. \tag{8.2}$$

The value of FNMR is considered as the recognition error[1] of the system at the corresponding FMR value. By varying the threshold of the system, we can plot the FNMR vs. FMR in a detection error trade-off (DET) curve. The ISO/IEC 19795-1:2021 standard [9] suggests the DET curve as a standardized approach to evaluate the recognition performance of biometric systems. The DET curve can also be used to benchmark the recognition error of different systems, while considering different FMR values. For example, Fig. 8.1 illustrates the histograms of mated (a.k.a. genuine) and non-mated (a.k.a. zero-effort impostor) scores for an ArcFace [5] face recognition model on the IARPA Janus Benchmark-C (IJB-C) dataset [16]. As can be seen, the histograms of mated and non-mated scores are almost disjoint, but there is some overlap between the two score distributions. Figure 8.2 depicts the DET curve of this system on the same dataset. The DET curve provides the FNMR

[1] As recommended by the ISO/IEC 19795-1:2021 standard [9], it is common to report recognition errors (i.e., FMR and FNMR) instead of recognition accuracy (e.g., true match rate (TMR), etc.) for the recognition performance of biometric systems.

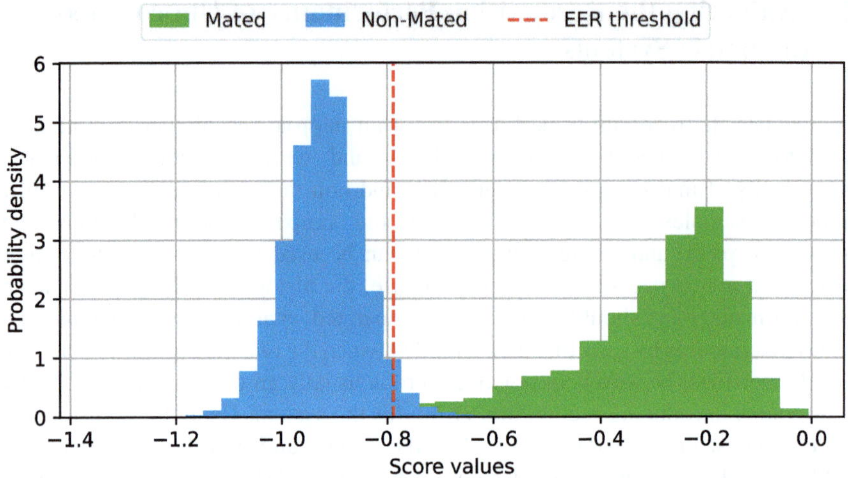

Fig. 8.1 Histograms of comparison scores for an unprotected system

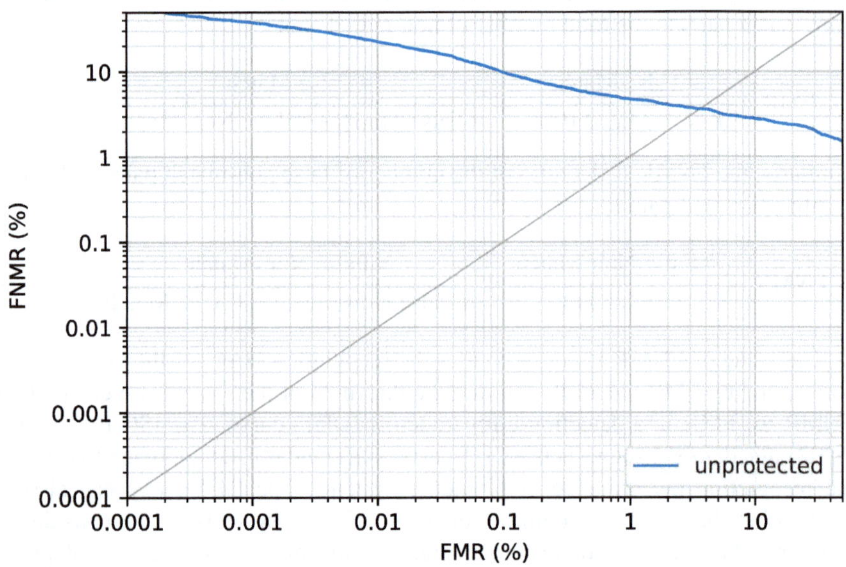

Fig. 8.2 Detection error trade-off (DET) of an unprotected system

of the system at different thresholds corresponding to different FMR values. We can see that the lower the FMR the higher the FNMR, and vice versa. Hence, we can use the DET curve to set the decision threshold of the biometric system such that we achieve the desired balance between FMR and FNMR.

The DET curve can be used to report the recognition error of the biometric system in a verification task. In an identification task, we can use the cumulative match

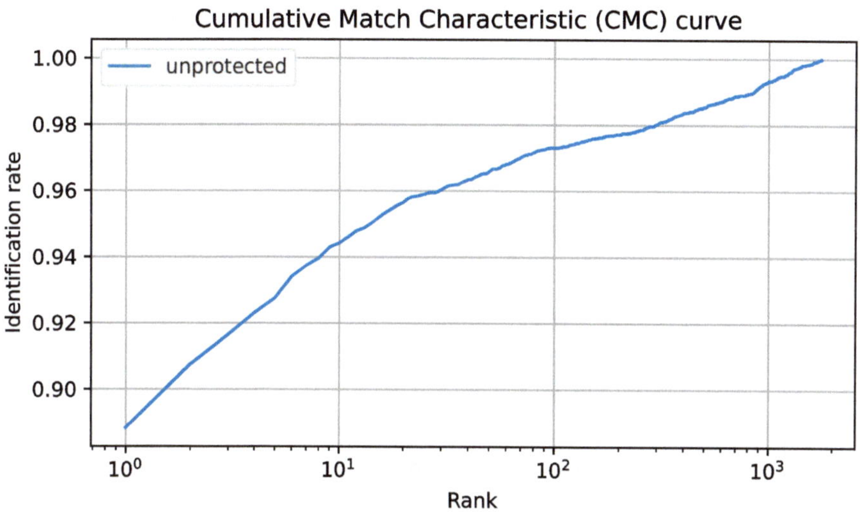

Fig. 8.3 Cumulative match characteristic (CMC) curve of an unprotected system

characteristic (CMC) curve and detection and identification rate (DIR) curve for closed-set and open-set identification tasks, respectively. The CMC curve estimates the probability that the correct subject is among the N enrolled subjects with the highest similarity to the given probe template. For a rank n, represented on the horizontal axis in the CMC plot, the vertical axis in the CMC plot reports the probability that the correct identity of the probe subject is among the top-n returned identities (corresponding to the top-n scores), when comparing the probe against all subjects in the gallery for closed-set identification. The DIR curve shows the number of correctly classified in-gallery probe items. The horizontal axis in the DIR plot shows the false positive identification rate (FPIR), which is the ratio of incorrect matches out of all identification attempts. The vertical axis reports the true positive identification rate (TPIR), which is the ratio of correct matches out of all identification attempts. Similarly to the DET curve, by changing the system threshold, we can set our biometric system to operate at different values of FPIR, which will determine the corresponding TPIR.

Figures 8.3 and 8.4 illustrate CMC and DIR plots for a face recognition system in closed-set and open-set identification tasks, respectively. The CMC plot in Fig. 8.3 tells us that, at a rank of 1, the identification rate is close to 89%. This suggests that, in 89% of the identification attempts, the correct identity of the probe will be returned as the highest-ranking identity from the database. On the other hand, if we increase our tolerance to a rank of 10, the correct identity of the probe subject will be in the top-10 returned identities over 94% of the time. The DIR plot in Fig. 8.4 tells us that, if we set our system threshold to an FPIR of 10^{-3}, which corresponds to a 1 in 1,000 chance of achieving a false positive, then we can expect a TPIR of about 0.1 (corresponding to a 10% chance of achieving a true positive). However,

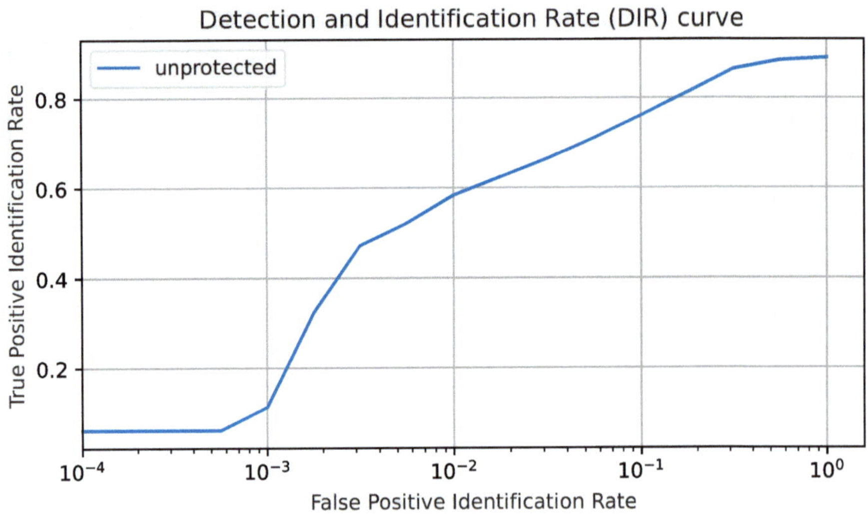

Fig. 8.4 Detection and identification rate (DIR) curve of an unprotected system

increasing the FPIR threshold to 10^{-1}, which corresponds to a 1 in 10 chance of a false positive, we can achieve a TPIR of about 0.75 (corresponding to a 75% chance of achieving a true positive).

3 Evaluating the Recognition Performance of Protected Biometric Systems

In a protected biometric system, a template protection scheme is used. The protection mechanism often contains some secrets, which are not expected to be disclosed to an adversary. Therefore, it is necessary to evaluate the recognition performance of the biometric system under the normal operation of the system (i.e., secrets are not disclosed or used by the adversary) and compare the performance with any of the possible scenarios where the adversary gains some access to secrets and tries to enter the system. These scenarios can be defined based on the design of the template protection scheme.

For example, consider cancelable BTP methods, such as BioHash [11], MLP-Hash [24], Bloom Filter [19], etc. which usually apply user-specific keys or secrets (assumed to be stored on some sort of token), and which have mainly been studied in the context of verification tasks. We can consider the scenario where the adversary steals the user-specific token and uses it with their own biometric sample (e.g., adversary's own face) to impersonate the subject whose token was stolen. Therefore, we need to evaluate the performance of the system under the stolen-token scenario

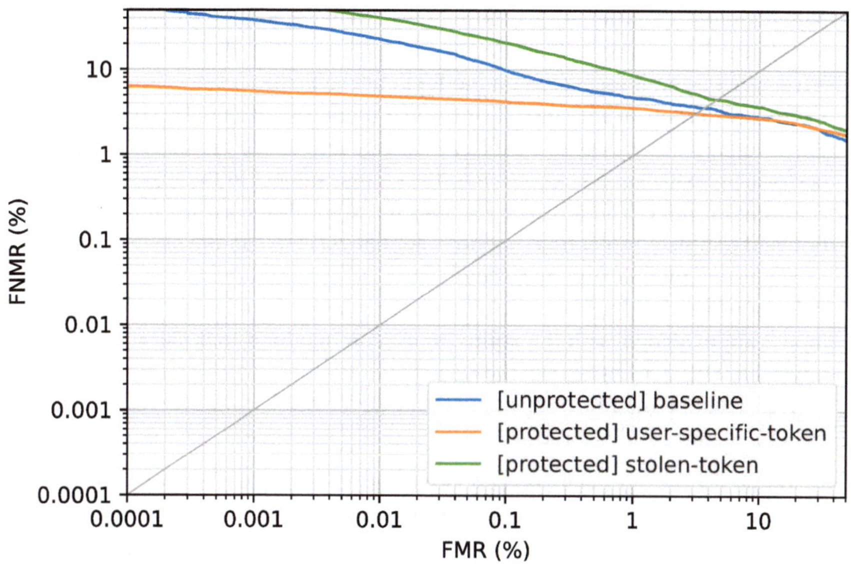

Fig. 8.5 Detection error trade-off (DET) of a protected versus unprotected system

too and benchmark it with the performance in the expected situation (normal scenario, i.e., no secrets being leaked).

Figure 8.5 shows an example of using a DET plot to evaluate the verification performance of a face recognition system, which uses the ArcFace model as the feature extractor and is protected using BioHash. This figure depicts DET curves for user-specific token (i.e., normal) and stolen-token scenarios, which are also compared to the unprotected system as a baseline. As we can see, the protected system in the normal scenario achieves better performance than the unprotected system. This is because, in the normal scenario, the system is using user-specific tokens, and therefore the protected biometric system is operating as a two-step verification system. However, when the token is leaked, the performance of the system drops significantly. Degradation of the recognition performance in the stolen-token scenario is due to the fact that the representation of unprotected templates is distorted when they are mapped to the protected space with the same tokens. In summary, we observe that the recognition performance of the system is improved in the user-specific token configuration, but is decreased in the stolen-token scenario. In [23], the recognition performance of cancelable biometric systems is investigated for verification and identification tasks in different scenarios. More examples of such analyses for the verification task can be found in [13, 18, 20, 21, 25].

The ISO/IEC 30136:2018 standard [8] defined several threat models to evaluate the performance of protected biometric systems:

- **Naive model**: The adversary is assumed to have access to leaked protected templates. The protected system is a black box for the adversary, and the adversary has no information on the BTP mechanism.
- **Collision model**: In this model, the naive model is extended to the case where the adversary has access to a dataset of a large amount of biometric data, and can perform an exhaustive search to find the closest subject in their own dataset.
- **Standard model**: The adversary knows the algorithm used for template extraction and template protection, but does not know secrets in the system and cannot execute such modules in the system.
- **Advanced model**: In this model, the capabilities of the adversary in the standard model are extended with the ability to execute modules that use secrets, but the adversary still does not know the secrets.
- **Full disclosure model**: In this model, the adversary knows everything about the system, including all secrets.

In summary, in the evaluation of protected systems, we need to consider the recognition performance of protected systems in the normal scenario and compare it with different scenarios corresponding to possible threat models.[2] We should also consider, as a baseline, the recognition performance of the corresponding unprotected system, where the template protection is applied as an additional module. However, this may not always be feasible, since in some template protection schemes, such as [15], the template protection and feature extraction modules are integrated and are trained simultaneously as a single module. In such cases, we can consider the closest possible system without template protection as a baseline, against which to compare the accuracy of the protected system.

4 Other Criteria to Evaluate the Performance of Protected Biometric Systems

In addition to evaluating the recognition accuracy of protected systems, we also need to consider the efficiency of the system according to the application. One important criterion is the complexity of template protection and runtime of recognition in

[2] Some publicly available implementations for the evaluation of recognition performance in protected biometric systems include [13, 14, 21–25]:

- https://github.com/otroshi/benchmark_cb
- https://gitlab.idiap.ch/bob/bob.paper.eusipco2023_mlphash
- https://gitlab.idiap.ch/bob/bob.paper.biosig2023_remote_cb
- https://gitlab.idiap.ch/bob/bob.paper.ijcb2022_hybrid_btp
- https://gitlab.idiap.ch/bob/bob.paper.tbiom2021_protect_vascular_dnn_biohash
- https://gitlab.idiap.ch/bob/bob.chapter.fingerveins_biohashing
- https://gitlab.idiap.ch/bob/bob.paper.polyprotect_2021

protected biometric systems. For example, in the identification scenario, we have a 1-to-N comparison, and therefore, in order to use the system in a large-scale application, it is necessary to calculate the comparison scores of N pairs within a reasonable time, e.g., a fraction of a second in many applications. However, the comparison operation is a bottleneck in some template protection mechanisms, such as homomorphic encryption (HE). For this reason, there are some works on using indexing mechanisms to reduce the workload in the identification scenario (such as [7, 17]). Moreover, some other works have proposed methods for reducing the computation in HE schemes by dimensionality reduction (such as [3, 22]) or designing new functions (such as [1, 2]), which can increase speed in both verification and identification tasks.[3]

In addition to the execution speed, there might be some other criteria that need to be considered when evaluating the efficiency of the protected system. For example, the required memory to store each protected template can also be important, especially in applications with limited resources such as edge devices [3, 6, 7, 13].

Last but not least, for evaluating the recognition performance of protected systems, we discussed calculating the performance on a dataset using different metrics (e.g., FNMR at a specific FMR) and plots (e.g., DET). However, such evaluations are based on average recognition performance on a single dataset and do not show the performance across different demographic groups. While bias in recognition accuracy has been extensively studied for unprotected systems [4, 12, 26], similar studies can be deployed for bias in recognition performance of protected systems.

5 Conclusion

The recognition performance of protected biometric systems is a critical property for reliable authentication. In this chapter, we discussed different aspects of evaluating this criterion. We first reviewed the evaluation of recognition accuracy for unprotected biometric systems. Since most template protection schemes incorporate some secrets in their design, it is essential to investigate different situations where these secrets may or may not be leaked and explore their effect on the recognition performance. Therefore, we extended our discussion to the evaluation of protected biometric systems and explained the necessity of considering different evaluation scenarios. Finally, we provided a brief discussion of criteria other than recognition accuracy, such as runtime, memory consumption, and bias in the evaluation of the recognition performance of protected biometric systems.

[3] Part II Chap. 6 of this book also discusses the computational efficiency of HE.

6 Summary

- A BTP method must satisfy the recognition accuracy criterion, i.e., not degrade the accuracy of the biometric system.
- Recognition accuracy of an unprotected biometric system can be evaluated using different metrics (FMR, FNMR, FPIR, TPIR, etc.) and curves (DET, CMC, DIR, etc.).
- Evaluation of the recognition accuracy of protected biometric systems can be performed in a similar way, but under different evaluation scenarios, e.g., normal versus stolen-token scenario.
- Different threat models should be considered when assessing the recognition accuracy of protected biometric systems.
- In addition to recognition accuracy, other performance criteria should also be evaluated, such as runtime, memory consumption, bias, and fairness.

7 Study Questions

1. What are the differences between evaluating protected versus unprotected biometric systems?
2. Which metrics should be used to evaluate protected biometric systems in a verification task?
3. Which metrics should be used to evaluate protected biometric systems in an identification task? What are the differences between the evaluation of open-set and closed-set identification?
4. Which threat models should be considered when evaluating the recognition performance of protected biometric systems?
5. What are some other criteria to be considered when evaluating the recognition performance of the protected system?

Acknowledgments This research is based upon work supported by the H2020 TReSPAsS-ETN Marie Skłodowska-Curie early training network (grant agreement 860813).

References

1. Bassit, A., Hahn, F., Veldhuis, R., Peter, A.: Multiplication-free biometric recognition for faster processing under encryption. In: IEEE International Joint Conference on Biometrics (2022)
2. Bassit, A., Hahn, F., Veldhuis, R., Peter, A.: Improved multiplication-free biometric recognition under encryption. IEEE Trans. Biomet. Behav. Identity Sci. **6**(3), 314–325 (2023)
3. Boddeti, V.N.: Secure face matching using fully homomorphic encryption. In: IEEE International Conference on Biometrics Theory, Applications and Systems (2018)

4. de Freitas Pereira, T., Marcel, S.: Fairness in biometrics: a figure of merit to assess biometric verification systems. IEEE Trans. Biomet. Behav. Identity Sci. **4**(1), 19–29 (2021)
5. Deng, J., Guo, J., Xue, N., Zafeiriou, S.: ArcFace: additive angular margin loss for deep face recognition. In: Conference on Computer Vision and Pattern Recognition (CVPR), pp. 4685–4694 (2019)
6. Drozdowski, P., Buchmann, N., Rathgeb, C., Margraf, M., Busch, C.: On the application of homomorphic encryption to face identification. In: Proceedings of the IEE International Conference of the Biometrics Special Interest Group (BIOSIG), pp. 1–5 (2019)
7. Drozdowski, P., Stockhardt, F., Rathgeb, C., Osorio-Roig, D., Busch, C.: Feature fusion methods for indexing and retrieval of biometric data: application to face recognition with privacy protection. IEEE Access **9**, 139361–139378 (2021)
8. ISO/IEC JTC1 SC37 Biometrics: ISO/IEC 30136:2018. Information technology – Performance testing of biometric template protection. International Organization for Standardization (2018)
9. ISO/IEC JTC1 SC37 Biometrics: ISO/IEC 19795-1:2021. Information Technology – Biometric Performance Testing and Reporting – Part 1: Principles and Framework. International Organization for Standardization and International Electrotechnical Committee (2021)
10. ISO/IEC JTC1 SC27 Security Techniques: ISO/IEC 24745:2022. Information Technology - Security Techniques - Biometric Information Protection. International Organization for Standardization (2022)
11. Jin, A.T.B., Ling, D.N.C., Goh, A.: Biohashing: two factor authentication featuring fingerprint data and tokenised random number. Pattern Recognit. **37**(11), 2245–2255 (2004)
12. Kotwal, K., Marcel, S.: Fairness index measures to evaluate bias in biometric recognition. In: International Conference on Pattern Recognition, pp. 479–493. Springer, Berlin (2022)
13. Krivokuća, V., Marcel, S.: On the recognition performance of BioHash-protected finger vein templates. Handbook of Vascular Biometrics, pp. 465–480 (2020)
14. Krivokuća Hahn, V., Marcel, S.: Towards protecting face embeddings in mobile face verification scenarios. IEEE Trans. Biomet. Behav. Identity Sci. **4**(1), 117–134 (2022). https://doi.org/10.1109/TBIOM.2022.3140472
15. Mai, G., Cao, K., Lan, X., Yuen, P.C.: SecureFace: face template protection. IEEE Trans. Inf. Forensics Secur. **16**, 262–277 (2021). https://doi.org/10.1109/TIFS.2020.3009590
16. Maze, B., Adams, J., Duncan, J.A., Kalka, N., Miller, T., Otto, C., Jain, A.K., Niggel, W.T., Anderson, J., Cheney, J., et al.: IARPA Janus Benchmark-C: face dataset and protocol. In: 2018 International Conference on Biometrics (ICB), pp. 158–165. IEEE, Piscataway (2018)
17. Osorio-Roig, D., Rathgeb, C., Drozdowski, P., Busch, C.: Stable hash generation for efficient privacy-preserving face identification. IEEE Trans. Biomet. Behav. Identity Sci. **4**(3), 333–348 (2021)
18. Otroshi Shahreza, H.: On the information in deep biometric templates: from vulnerability of unprotected templates to leakage in protected templates. Ph.D. thesis, EPFL (2024)
19. Rathgeb, C., Breitinger, F., Busch, C.: Alignment-free cancelable iris biometric templates based on adaptive bloom filters. In: 2013 International Conference on Biometrics (ICB), pp. 1–8. IEEE, Piscataway (2013)
20. Shahreza, H.O., Krivokuća Hahn, V., Marcel, S.: On the recognition performance of biohashing on state-of-the-art face recognition models. In: Proceedings of the IEEE International Workshop on Information Forensics and Security (WIFS), pp. 1–6. IEEE, Piscataway (2021)
21. Shahreza, H.O., Marcel, S.: Towards protecting and enhancing vascular biometric recognition methods via biohashing and deep neural networks. IEEE Trans. Biomet. Behav. Identity Sci. **3**(3), 394–404 (2021)
22. Shahreza, H.O., Rathgeb, C., Osorio-Roig, D., Krivokuća Hahn, V., Marcel, S., Busch, C.: Hybrid protection of biometric templates by combining homomorphic encryption and cancelable biometrics. In: 2022 IEEE International Joint Conference on Biometrics (IJCB), pp. 1–10. IEEE, Piscataway (2022)

23. Shahreza, H.O., Bassit, A., Marcel, S., Veldhuis, R.: Remote cancelable biometric system for verification and identification applications. In: 2023 International Conference of the Biometrics Special Interest Group (BIOSIG), pp. 1–5. IEEE, Piscataway (2023)
24. Shahreza, H.O., Krivokuća Hahn, V., Marcel, S.: MLP-Hash: protecting face templates via hashing of randomized multi-layer perceptron. In: Proceedings of the 31st European Signal Processing Conference (EUSIPCO). IEEE, Piscataway (2023)
25. Shahreza, H.O., Melzi, P., Osorio-Roig, D., Rathgeb, C., Busch, C., Marcel, S., Tolosana, R., Vera-Rodriguez, R.: Benchmarking of cancelable biometrics for deep templates. Preprint. arXiv:2302.13286 (2023)
26. Terhörst, P., Kolf, J.N., Huber, M., Kirchbuchner, F., Damer, N., Moreno, A.M., Fierrez, J., Kuijper, A.: A comprehensive study on face recognition biases beyond demographics. IEEE Trans. Technol. Society **3**(1), 16–30 (2021)

Chapter 9
Evaluating Irreversibility of Biometric Template Protection Schemes

Shantanu Rane

Abstract Irreversibility refers to the degree of difficulty faced by an adversary in recovering the unprotected biometric features from the protected templates stored in a Biometric Template Protection (BTP) system. Irreversibility is a vital privacy consideration in the design of BTP systems. In this chapter, we attempt to characterize irreversibility in a systematic way. We explain the concept of irreversibility, justify its importance, and describe approaches to measure it. We begin with theoretical measures of irreversibility derived from information theory. We argue that a suitable information-theoretic irreversibility metric is the number of bits of information about the unprotected template revealed by the protected template. Next, we consider measures of irreversibility based on cryptography, particularly for BTP systems enabled by homomorphic cryptosystems. We then discuss irreversibility of BTP systems based on feature transformations applied to the unprotected template. These transformations include salting-based transformations, non-invertible transformations, and neural network-based mappings. In practice, few BTP implementations lend themselves to a clean, theoretical characterization of irreversibility, and the property has to be measured empirically. We review challenges associated with empirical measurements of irreversibility, and we also describe some best practices to ensure that the empirical irreversibility metrics are meaningful and applicable. Finally, we consider irreversibility in cases where a given user has protected templates stored on several BTP systems.

1 Introduction

As we have seen in the earlier chapters, the primary motivation behind designing and deploying biometric template protection is to protect the privacy of the human agent, while enabling the use of biometric recognition for security-critical applications.

S. Rane (✉)
Computer Science Laboratory, SRI, Menlo Park, CA, USA
e-mail: shantanu.rane@sri.com

V. Krivokuća Hahn et al. (eds.), *Handbook of Biometric Template Protection*,
https://doi.org/10.1007/978-981-95-0995-9_9

Therefore, it should be difficult for an adversary to take a protected template and use it to extract either the unprotected template or the underlying biometric characteristic[1]—the fingerprint image, iris scan, face image, etc.–from which that template was derived. The greater this difficulty is, the more privacy-preserving is the template protection scheme. In this chapter, we attempt to characterize this difficulty of recovering the unprotected template from the protected template in a systematic way. Intuitively, since the unprotected template is a collection of features derived from the biometric characteristic, the difficulty of recovering the biometric characteristic is, in general, higher than the difficulty of recovering the unprotected template. The central concept in our development is termed "irreversibility."

In biometric template protection, irreversibility refers to a property of a biometric reference extracted from a biometric characteristic provided by an individual, whereby it is impossible to recover the biometric characteristic or an unprotected biometric template given the (protected) biometric reference. In practice it is often difficult to guarantee perfect irreversibility. Therefore, it is more useful to characterize irreversibility as the *degree of difficulty* of extracting an individual's biometric characteristic, or the individual's unprotected biometric template, given the protected biometric reference. As we have seen in the previous chapters, in a biometric template protection system, the biometric reference comprises auxiliary data (AD) extracted from the biometric characteristic or provided in the form of external transformation parameters and a pseudonymous identifier (PI) that facilitates biometric recognition in the absence of the unprotected enrollment (reference) biometric characteristic or the unprotected enrollment biometric template. Irreversibility is an important design consideration of a biometric template protection approach and for the specific implementation of that approach. In this chapter, we will explain the concept of irreversibility, justify its importance, and describe techniques to measure it.

As biometrics is, inherently, an applied science, there are many ways to characterize irreversibility based on the particular flavor of biometric template protection scheme used. To establish the concept and to build intuition, we will begin with theoretical measures derived from information theory. We shall argue that a suitable information-theoretic irreversibility metric is the number of bits of information about the unprotected template revealed by the biometric reference. This measure is readily applicable to the information-theoretically motivated template protection systems, namely fuzzy commitments and secure biometric sketches. In our view, this metric—the bits of information that the adversary needs to guess—also provides a good framework for thinking about the security and privacy of biometric template protection schemes in general, even when they are not directly based on fuzzy commitments or secure sketches.

---

[1] When we talk about the recovery of a *biometric characteristic*, we are technically referring to the reconstruction of a *digital sample* of that characteristic (e.g., an image of a face), not to the recovery of the underlying physical trait (e.g., the face itself).

Our discussion will also include measures of irreversibility based on cryptography. These measures are useful in biometric template protection systems enabled by hashing algorithms and encrypted-domain computation. In this class of systems, irreversibility is related to the difficulty of performing a computationally intractable task, e.g., guessing a decryption key of a certain length, or reversing a cryptographic hash function.

We will also discuss irreversibility in BTP systems based on feature transformations and machine learning. We cover the classes of salting-based transformations and non-invertible transformations, as well as BTP approaches that use deep neural networks to transform an unprotected template into a protected template. In such systems, irreversibility is related to the difficulty of reversing the transformation to recover the unprotected biometric features.

In practice, few template protection implementations lend themselves to a clean theoretical characterization of irreversibility. This can be due to complexities introduced by feature extraction algorithms, nonideal statistics of biometric characteristics, dependence on specific biometric datasets, and implementation trade-offs made in security protocols. For example, information-theoretic guarantees of irreversibility might only be approximately true because of unavoidable correlations between bits of a biometric feature vector. As another example, if biometric references are derived using complex algorithms such as deep neural networks, it becomes difficult to establish concrete guarantees about the difficulty of inverting the template, given varying levels of knowledge about the algorithm. Therefore, it is necessary to conduct an empirical evaluation of the irreversibility. We will review challenges associated with empirical measurements of irreversibility. We will also describe some best practices to ensure that the obtained empirical irreversibility metrics are meaningful and applicable.

Finally, we will consider irreversibility in the less investigated but practically relevant use-case of multiple systems, i.e., the user has reference templates in multiple biometric recognition systems, where these templates have possibly been generated using different template protection approaches. This is a comparatively less explored topic and an interesting area for future exploration. In particular, the question we would like to answer is the following: Does compromising more and more template protection systems leak more and more information about the underlying biometric characteristic, or does compromising any one system give the adversary all the information they need to know? The answer depends on how the template protection systems have been designed, both individually and jointly. We will attempt an explanation of these design considerations to stimulate readers to think about this topic, as it has significant practical relevance.

2 Analysis Framework and Notation

To understand irreversibility as a concept applicable to all biometric template protection systems—irrespective of their particular implementation or underlying

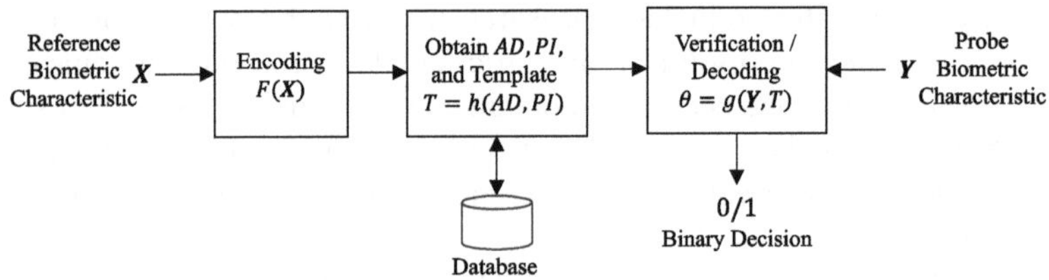

Fig. 9.1 General template protection system, consisting of an encoding operation that generates a template and a decoding operation that performs biometric recognition based on the template and a probe biometric signal. All implementations of biometric template protection can be cast into this basic framework

principles—we will present a simple analysis framework. This framework is general in that it encompasses a variety of template protection architectures, including information theory-motivated systems, cryptography-based systems, cancelable biometrics, etc. We will define irreversibility for this general framework. In the subsequent sections, we will specialize the analysis framework to specific architectures, and we will provide definitions of irreversibility that apply to those architectures. Our development is based on the framework presented in [33], with some modifications made to the terminology to reflect standard practice in the template protection literature.

Consider the general template protection system shown in Fig. 9.1. A biometric template protection system can be viewed as a combination of (1) an encoding function F applied to a reference biometric characteristic $\mathbf{X}$, which produces a biometric reference T, and (2) a decoding function g that takes a probe biometric characteristic $\mathbf{Y}$ as input and produces a verification or identification decision. The encoding operation, in turn, consists of (a) deriving from the biometric characteristic or external data (e.g., a randomly generated user-specific key) some Auxiliary Data (AD), and (optionally), (b) binding a Pseudonymous Identifier (PI) to the AD or generating a PI from the biometric characteristic and the AD (depending on the BTP method). The AD and the PI are assumed to be stored in a biometric database. In our notation, we make no distinction between a biometric characteristic captured at enrollment and the unprotected biometric template, i.e., the biometric features extracted from that signal. Both are denoted by $\mathbf{X}$. We are not explicitly concerned with the signal processing methods applied to the reference biometric characteristic in order to extract reference features, which can then be encoded into the reference T. In other words, the reader is free to absorb the biometric feature extraction process into the encoding function F. Similarly, we make no distinction between a probe biometric characteristic captured for the purpose of biometric recognition and the biometric features extracted from the probe biometric characteristic. Both are denoted by $\mathbf{Y}$. Note that, as far as measuring irreversibility is concerned, this is a conservative assumption. This is because, given the reference T, it is easier to extract the unprotected template, i.e., the features, than it is to extract the entire biometric characteristic.[2]

Note that a biometric template protection system can be used for *identification*, i.e., to determine the identity of the person providing their biometric, by comparing their biometric against templates of several "identities" enrolled in the database. It can also be used for *verification*, i.e., to determine whether the person claiming to be a certain identity in the biometric database can be recognized based on the template that they have provided at enrollment. Verification is less complex because the decoding operation described above has to be run only once using the AD and the PI corresponding to the claimed identity. Identification, in general, will require the decoding operation to be run more than once. For simplicity, we will focus on biometric *verification* systems in this chapter.

Definition Given an enrolled biometric reference $T = F(\mathbf{X}) = h(AD, PI)$, the irreversibility of the employed biometric template protection scheme is defined as the degree of difficulty faced by an adversary in their attempt to recover the original biometric characteristic[3] $\mathbf{X}$. The notation $h(\cdot, \cdot)$ indicates that the encoding $F(\cdot)$ produces a result which is a mathematical function of the AD and PI. □

Irreversibility is one of the three key aspects of privacy defined in the ISO/IEC 24745 standard on Biometric Information Protection [26]. While the processes of encoding, storage, and decision-making are common to most biometric recognition systems, it is the presence of the *AD* and *PI* that distinguishes a template protection system from conventional recognition systems. The ISO/IEC 24745 standard includes formal definitions of *AD* and *PI*, with the two items being defined in relation to each other.

Definition Auxiliary Data (*AD*): The *AD* is defined as a portion of an individual's enrollment information that may be used to reconstruct a *PI* during the biometric recognition process. □

Definition Pseudonymous Identifier (*PI*): Complementarily, the *PI* is defined as the portion of the enrollment information that uniquely represents the individual, wherein uniqueness can be established based on a captured biometric sample and the correct *AD*. □

Ideally, it would be beneficial if the *PI* could not be used to recover any information about the biometric characteristic or the identity of its owner. In

---

[2] An information-theoretic way of justifying that this claim is conservative is to note that the biometric characteristic, the (unprotected) biometric template, and the (protected) biometric reference form a Markov chain.

[3] For ease of exposition, we do not distinguish between the biometric characteristic and the unprotected biometric template, i.e., the biometric features, and denote both by $\mathbf{X}$. Note that, given only the biometric reference, it is—in general—easier to recover the biometric features than it is to recover the biometric characteristic. Thus, by not differentiating between the biometric features and the biometric characteristic in our definition, we are being *conservative* in our definition of irreversibility.

practice, this is not the case, and the amount of information leaked by the *PI* depends on the template protection architecture and the threat model. We elaborate on the threat model and its connection to the employed template protection architecture at the end of this section. For example, in schemes based on cryptography, we can guarantee that it is "computationally infeasible" for an adversary to recover sensitive information from the *PI*. On the other hand, for feature transformation-based template protection schemes, the mathematical construction of the scheme might result in some information leakage based on, for example, the invertibility of a matrix vector product given the matrix. The reader should note these characteristics of the *AD* and the *PI* and use them to evaluate the different template protection architectures considered in this and other chapters.

As described above, a function of the *AD* and *PI* constitutes the protected biometric reference. In the above definition, we have written $h(AD, PI)$ for generality. There are various ways to combine the *AD* and the *PI*. One simple approach is for function $h(\cdot)$ to be a simple concatenation, i.e., $h(AD, PI) = AD \| PI$. In such systems, the AD and the PI are just stored in a biometric database, to be used by the decision function as needed. Later on, when an individual claiming to be a certain identity provides a probe biometric characteristic, the decision module will use the probe biometric characteristic and the *AD* to generate an estimate of the *PI*. Recognition is deemed successful if and only if the estimated *PI* matches that stored in the device's database of *PI*s.

The specific metric used to measure irreversibility, i.e., the difficulty of recovering the biometric characteristic, depends on the specific implementation of template protection. Clearly, irrespective of the implementation, it is desirable that this metric represents a high difficulty of recovering the biometric characteristic. In the following sections, we will define irreversibility for specific implementations. Another aspect to note at the outset is that it is possible to use a second factor—typically a secret key or secret parameters chosen independently of the biometric characteristic. When the second factor is unknown to the adversary, it is possible to significantly increase the irreversibility of the biometric verification system.

Finally, we remark that a very important consideration while evaluating irreversibility is the threat model, i.e., the capabilities and limitations of the adversary, that is being assumed for the system. Indeed, evaluation of the irreversibility only makes sense in the context of the assumed threat model. Furthermore, in the sections that follow, the reader should note that different implementations or architectures are necessarily associated with different threat models. For example, an implementation based on cryptographic techniques would assume a threat model based on computational intractability of reversing encryption schemes in the absence of a key, but this model would be insufficient protection for a threat model that allows a computationally unbounded adversary.

3 Information-Theoretic Characterization of Irreversibility for Biometric Cryptosystems

To facilitate understanding, we first consider information-theoretic metrics for irreversibility of a template protection system. Such metrics are particularly appropriate for template protection systems that have been constructed using the principle of a fuzzy vault [14], fuzzy extractors [7], and secure sketches [7]. These are information theory-based constructions and can be realized in practice using error-correcting codes. We will use fuzzy commitment and secure sketches in our explanation below. We begin with a caveat: The threat model strictly consistent with information theory-based systems should assume a computationally unbounded adversary. However, in the interest of describing systems that are practically realizable, we have chosen to combine considerations of (a) the information-theoretic difficulty of extracting information from parity or syndrome symbols of error-correcting codes and (b) the computational difficulty of reversing cryptographic hashes.

In particular, fuzzy commitment-based constructions are based on the idea that there is an imaginary error-prone channel between the reference biometric features and the probe biometric features. We make a simplifying assumption that the reference feature vector $\mathbf{X}$ consists of independent bits that are equally likely to be 0 or 1. In practice, enrollment (reference) features are seldom independent or identically distributed and may not be binary. We show a simple but complete implementation of a fuzzy commitment scheme in Fig. 9.2 based on block error-correcting codes. Consider a block error-correcting code characterized by a generator matrix $\mathbf{G}$. Typically, $\mathbf{G}$ is a $k \times n$ matrix with elements that belong to a finite field.[4] Note that $k < n$, and denote $n - k = m$. An example of a finite field of size 2 is $\{0, 1\}$ which yields a binary matrix. In the development below, consider this binary field for simplicity.

Now, for a randomly chosen binary message $\mathbf{Z}$ of length k, we can obtain an n-bit codeword of that error-correcting code as $\mathbf{G}^T\mathbf{Z}$. Next, compute a bitwise-XOR of the codeword and the n-bit reference biometric feature vector $\mathbf{X}$. This perturbed codeword is stored as the AD, while a cryptographic hash of the message $\mathbf{Z}$ is stored as the PI. Here, we have assumed that $\mathbf{Z}$ consists of k independent bits, each equally likely to be 0 or 1. The first step of the decoding, i.e., the recognition process, is to compute a bitwise XOR of the AD with the n-bit probe biometric feature vector $\mathbf{Y}$. The reader will notice that $\mathbf{X} \oplus \mathbf{Y}$ represents precisely the bit errors in the codeword

[4] A block error-correcting code is characterized by a $k \times n$ generator matrix $\mathbf{G}$ and an $n - k \times n$ parity check matrix $\mathbf{H}$. These matrices are related, i.e., $\mathbf{G}^T\mathbf{H} = \mathbf{0}$, i.e., a matrix of zeros. Given a k-bit message $\mathbf{Z}$, we obtain the corresponding n-bit codeword of the error-correcting code as $\mathbf{G}^T\mathbf{Z}$. Given a received n-bit codeword $\mathbf{A}$, we obtain an $(n - k)$-bit syndrome of the error-correcting code as $\mathbf{HA}$. We will further elaborate on the meaning of the syndrome later in the section. For a comprehensive introduction to the topic of error-correcting codes, see [34]. For now, we note that if $\mathbf{B}$ is a valid codeword derived from a message $\mathbf{K}$, then its syndrome is the $(n - k)$-bit zero vector because $\mathbf{HB} = \mathbf{HG}^T\mathbf{Z} = \mathbf{0}$.

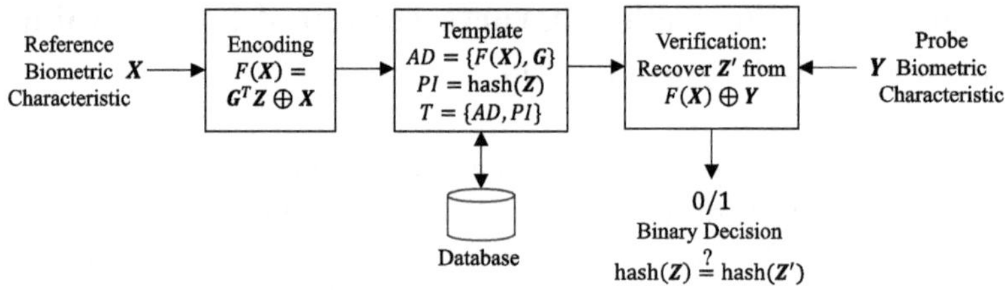

Fig. 9.2 A template protection system based on fuzzy commitment can be constructed by generating a bitwise XOR of the reference biometric with a codeword of an error-correcting code generated from a random message. This results in a perturbed codeword. Successful verification then involves XORing the perturbed codeword with the probe biometric—resulting in an error-prone codeword—and then recovering the original message

$\mathbf{G}^T\mathbf{Z}$ corresponding to the message $\mathbf{Z}$. Successful verification implies that these bit errors can be corrected and the k-bit message $\mathbf{Z}$ can be correctly recovered. The correct recovery of $\mathbf{Z}$ can be verified by hashing the recovered message and comparing it with the PI. The parameters of the error correcting code, e.g., the elements of the generator matrix $\mathbf{G}$, are also stored as helper information and may be considered as part of the AD.

In this approach to template protection, the irreversibility is closely related to the privacy leakage, i.e., the number of bits of information leaked by the reference template $T = \{AD, PI\}$ about the reference biometric characteristic $\mathbf{X}$. To compute the privacy leakage explicitly for the case of the linear systematic error correcting code with generator matrix $\mathbf{G}_{k\times n}$, with $k < n$, we determine the mutual information, I, as follows:

$$
\begin{aligned}
I(\mathbf{X}; AD) &= I(\mathbf{X}; \mathbf{G}^T\mathbf{Z} \oplus \mathbf{X}) \\
&= H(\mathbf{G}^T\mathbf{Z} \oplus \mathbf{X}) - H(\mathbf{G}^T\mathbf{Z}) \qquad (9.1) \\
&= n - k = m = n(1 - R) \qquad (9.2)
\end{aligned}
$$

where $R = k/n = 1 - m/n$ is the rate of the channel code. To see why this is the case, note that the mutual information $I(\mathbf{X}; AD)$ measures the *reduction in uncertainty*[5] about $\mathbf{X}$ when we are given the AD. We evaluate this reduction in uncertainty by writing out mutual information as a difference between entropies as shown in (9.1). In the second equality, $H(\cdot)$ is the information-theoretic entropy, which measures the bits of uncertainty in its argument [6]. Since $\mathbf{X}$ consists of n independent and equally likely bits, the first term in (9.1) contributes n bits of entropy. Since $\mathbf{Z}$ consists of k independent bits and $\mathbf{G}^T$ is a skinny matrix, i.e.,

[5] To be absolutely precise, we should be considering the mutual information, $I(\mathbf{X}; T)$. However, since the PI in this architecture is the cryptographic hash of $\mathbf{Z}$, the bits of the PI are independent of the bits of $\mathbf{X}$. Thus it suffices to evaluate $I(\mathbf{X}; AD)$.

$n > k$, the second term in (9.1) contributes k bits of entropy. The reduction in uncertainty is then given by $m = n - k = n(1 - k/n) = n(1 - R)$ bits. This means that the presence of *AD* reduces the uncertainty in $\mathbf{X}$ by $m = n - k$ bits. This privacy leakage is an explicit measure of irreversibility in the sense that the smaller the value of m, the harder it is for an adversary to guess the n bits of $\mathbf{X}$.

The *PI* is a cryptographic hash; thus it is pertinent to ask if one or more $\mathbf{Z}' \neq \mathbf{Z}$ could be found such that they generate the same PI. This is the problem of finding a specific hash collision for $\mathbf{Z}$. This is related—but not identical—to the birthday attack.[6] A negative consequence of finding a collision for $\mathbf{Z}$ is that, by construction, finding such a $\mathbf{Z}'$ enables the adversary to verify successfully without discovering the reference biometric characteristic (or feature vector) $\mathbf{X}$. However, it is important to note that this attack does not compromise irreversibility since $\mathbf{Z}' \neq \mathbf{Z}$. The difficulty of finding a $\mathbf{Z}' \equiv \mathbf{Z}$, for a particular $\mathbf{Z}$, is referred to as the pre-image resistance of the cryptographic hash function. For an ℓ-bit cryptographic hash function (e.g., $\ell = 256$ for SHA-256), which has 2^ℓ possible outputs, an attacker will have to try out 2^ℓ hash computations on average, to discover $\mathbf{Z}$. Thus, we can say that the irreversibility is related to the pre-image resistance of the cryptographic hash.[7]

In a related vein, secure sketch-based constructions treat biometric features as messages from which a syndrome[8] of an error correcting code can be extracted. Again, we show a simple implementation of a secure sketch scheme in Fig. 9.3, based on block error-correcting codes. Here, a syndrome corresponding to the

[6] The difficulty of finding a specific hash collision, i.e., finding a $\mathbf{Z}' \neq \mathbf{Z}$ such that hash($\mathbf{Z}'$) = hash($\mathbf{Z}$), is called the *second* pre-image resistance of a cryptographic hash code [18]. Breaking the second pre-image resistance for an idealized ℓ-bit cryptographic hash requires 2^ℓ operations on average. This is stronger than the difficulty of finding a birthday attack, i.e., finding *any* pair of inputs that map to the same hash, which is termed as a hash collision. A birthday attack ideally requires an average of $2^{(\ell/2)}$ operations. For practical hash functions, the pre-image resistance, the second pre-image resistance, and collision resistance may be lower because an adversary can carry out analytic attacks on the hash function.

[7] Note the subtle difference between the birthday attack (any collision), the second pre-image resistance (specific collision), and the pre-image resistance (reversing the hash). The latter two aspects of pre-image resistance, while technically different, have the same level of difficulty, i.e., 2^ℓ operations on average for an ideal hash function. They both are stronger than the birthday attack, which requires $2^{\ell/2}$ operations on average.

[8] In the language of error correcting codes, a syndrome is a collection of bits (or symbols, in general) that provides clues about which bits in a received codeword might be erroneous. They are closely related to the parity symbols of the error correction code [34]. By itself, the syndrome does not reveal the error-free codeword. However, given a syndrome and an error-prone codeword, a decoding operation can be used to recover the error-free codeword and hence the underlying message contained in the codeword. Typically, the decoding operation has a higher probability of succeeding when there are enough syndrome symbols, i.e., enough clues, available. For block error-correcting codes, such as Reed-Solomon codes, the decoding operation always succeeds when the number of syndrome symbols is higher than a well-defined threshold for the code being used. Finally, for every valid codeword in the codebook of an error-correcting code, the syndrome is a zero vector.

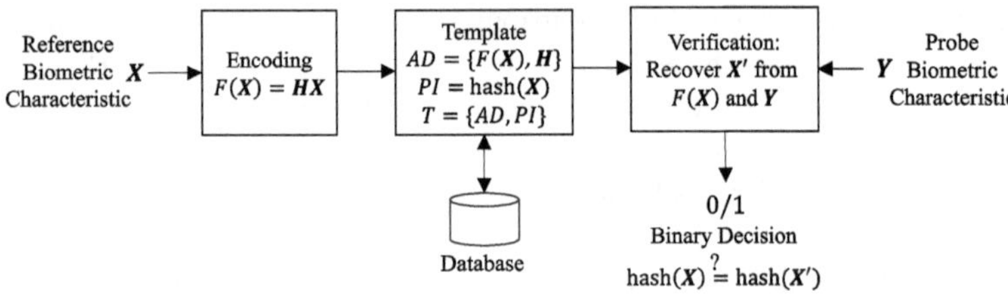

Fig. 9.3 A template protection system based on a secure sketch can be constructed by generating a syndrome of the reference biometric feature vector based on the parity check matrix of an error correcting code. Successful verification then involves recovering the reference biometric feature vector using the probe biometric feature vector, where successful verification is determined using a hash comparison, as the reference biometric is never stored in the database

reference vector **X** is obtained by multiplying **X** by a parity check matrix **H**, and it is stored as the *AD*, while a cryptographic hash of **X** is stored as the *PI*. Biometric recognition then involves attempting to recover **X**, using the *AD*, i.e., the syndrome, and the probe **Y**, which is assumed to be a noisy version of **X**. Note the similarities and differences with respect to the fuzzy commitment approach of Fig. 9.2. Both approaches are based on error-correcting codes. In fuzzy commitment, the *AD* is a codeword perturbed by the biometric features. In a secure sketch-based approach, the *AD* is constructed by computing the syndrome symbols extracted directly from the biometric features. As in the case of the fuzzy commitment setting, the parameters of the error correcting code, e.g., the elements of the parity check matrix **H**, are also stored as helper information and may be considered as part of the *AD*.

As the reader might guess, the fuzzy commitment and secure sketch settings are closely related. In fact, for the example with a block error-correcting code with generator matrix **G** and parity check matrix **H** considered here, it can be shown that the implementations are equivalent in terms of the privacy leakage and other performance metrics, including the FMR, FNMR, and the successful attack rate [33]. Consequently, they are also equivalent in terms of irreversibility. To see this, observe that the irreversibility here is also related to the privacy leakage, i.e., the number of bits of **X** revealed by the syndrome, i.e., the *AD*. For our linear error-correcting code with a parity check matrix $\mathbf{H}_{m\times n}$, with $m = n - k < n$, we again determine the privacy leakage using mutual information, I, as

$$I(\mathbf{X}; AD) = I(\mathbf{X}; \mathbf{HX}) = H(\mathbf{HX}) = m = n(1 - R)$$

To see why this is the case, note again that the mutual information measures the reduction in the uncertainty of guessing the biometric features **X** given the *AD*. This is identical to the entropy of the syndrome, given by $H(\mathbf{HX})$. Since **X** has independent and equally likely 0 or 1 bits, this entropy is just the entropy of an m bit vector of equally likely 0 or 1 bits. Thus, knowing the *AD* reduces the uncertainty in **X** from n bits to $n - m = k$ bits. Another intuitive way of seeing this is that revealing the AD to the adversary gives them access to m simultaneous equations in n unknowns, which are the bits of $\mathbf{X}$. Clearly, if the number of equations is small, the uncertainty still remaining in $\mathbf{X}$ is large, and hence the irreversibility of the system is large.

Thus the irreversibility of the secure sketch system is the same as that for fuzzy commitment, i.e., $m = n - k$ bits, so long as they used the same error-correcting code. The reader should note that this equivalence relies on having the ideal distribution for $\mathbf{X}$ for the secure sketch system. In practice, researchers have found that for many biometric modalities and feature extraction approaches, we cannot guarantee independent and identically distributed Bernoulli-0.5 bits for $\mathbf{X}$. In such situations, this equivalence may not hold. The fuzzy commitment system, on the other hand, requires the random message $\mathbf{Z}$, but not the biometric $\mathbf{X}$, to possess this idealized Bernoulli-0.5 distribution—while $\mathbf{X}$ merely needs to have independent bits—to achieve an irreversibility metric of $n - m$ bits. The idealized requirement on the bits of $\mathbf{Z}$ is easier to approximate because $\mathbf{Z}$ is synthetically generated and does not depend on the biometric modality or on the feature extraction algorithm. Therefore, theoretical equivalence notwithstanding, evaluators of the irreversibility of fuzzy commitments and secure sketches should be attentive to this subtle distinction.

From the perspective of privacy leakage and irreversibility, rather than biometric verification performance, it is particularly interesting to examine two-factor versions of these schemes. Since the two approaches are information-theoretically equivalent, assuming the idealized distribution of the bits of $\mathbf{X}$, it suffices to examine the privacy leakage and irreversibility of one of these approaches, say the two-factor fuzzy commitment scheme, shown in Fig. 9.4.

For the purpose of explanation, our two-factor scheme builds on the single-factor scheme in Fig. 9.2. The single-factor scheme is augmented by a secret key $\mathbf{K}$ that is provided at enrollment. Now, a codeword corresponding to a randomly chosen message $\mathbf{Z}$ is obtained, and bitwise-XOR is computed using the codeword, the reference biometric feature vector $\mathbf{X}$, and the key $\mathbf{K}$. Note that the bits of $\mathbf{K}$ are

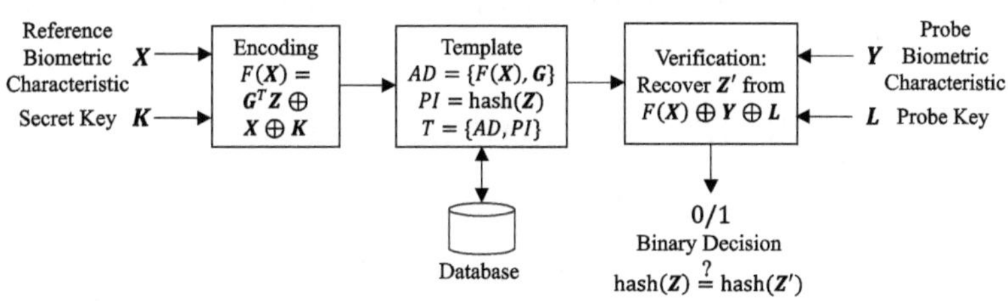

Fig. 9.4 A two-factor template protection system based on fuzzy commitment can be constructed by generating a bitwise XOR of the reference biometric feature vector, a codeword of an error-correcting code corresponding to a random message, and a randomly generated secret key. This results in a perturbed codeword. Successful verification then involves XORing the perturbed codeword with the probe biometric feature vector and with the probe key—resulting in an error-prone codeword—and then recovering the original message

independent of the bits of $\mathbf{Z}$ and the bits of the reference biometric $\mathbf{X}$. As before, the perturbed codeword is stored as the AD, while a cryptographic hash of the message $\mathbf{Z}$ is stored as the PI. The first step of the decoding, i.e., the recognition process, is to compute a bitwise XOR of the AD, the probe biometric feature vector $\mathbf{Y}$, and a probe key $\mathbf{L}$ provided by the user. The reader will notice that $\mathbf{X} \oplus \mathbf{K} \oplus \mathbf{Y} \oplus \mathbf{L}$ represents precisely the bit errors in the codeword corresponding to the message $\mathbf{Z}$. Successful verification implies that these bit errors can be corrected, and the message $\mathbf{Z}$ can be correctly recovered, a situation that can—as before—be verified by hashing the recovered message and comparing it with the *PI*. The parameters of the error correcting code, e.g., the elements of the generator matrix $\mathbf{G}$, are also stored as helper information and may be considered as part of the *AD*.

For the two-factor scheme, we are concerned with privacy leakage and irreversibility in cases where some or all of the *AD* is compromised. We again assume that, since the *PI* is a cryptographic hash, it is computationally hard for the adversary to extract $\mathbf{Z}$. We examine cases in which (1) only the AD is compromised, (2) only the secret key $\mathbf{K}$ is compromised, and (3) both the AD and the secret key are compromised. In other words, we want to derive the *reduction in uncertainty* involved in guessing $\mathbf{X}$ in these three cases. For the first case,

$$I(\mathbf{X};\, AD) = I(\mathbf{X};\, \mathbf{G}^T\mathbf{Z} \oplus \mathbf{X} \oplus \mathbf{K}) = 0.$$

Thus, if we write out the *AD* in the expression for the mutual information, we find that the second term contains the key $\mathbf{K}$, which makes the entire second argument independent of the first argument. This means that the *AD* is statistically independent of biometric feature vector $\mathbf{X}$ and cannot reduce the uncertainty in guessing $\mathbf{X}$. For the same reason, we can write, for the second case in which only the secret key $\mathbf{K}$ is compromised,

$$I(\mathbf{X};\, \mathbf{K}) = 0$$

This means that a compromised key does not leak any information about the biometric feature vector $\mathbf{X}$. For the third case, in which both the *AD* and the secret key are compromised, we write the reduction in uncertainty as

$$I(\mathbf{X};\, \mathbf{K}, AD) = I(\mathbf{X};\, \mathbf{K}, \mathbf{G}^T\mathbf{Z} \oplus \mathbf{X} \oplus \mathbf{K})$$

$$= I(\mathbf{X};\, \mathbf{K}) + I(\mathbf{X};\, \mathbf{G}^T\mathbf{Z} \oplus \mathbf{X} \oplus \mathbf{K}|\mathbf{K}) \tag{9.3}$$

$$= 0 + I(\mathbf{X};\, \mathbf{G}^T\mathbf{Z} \oplus \mathbf{X}) \tag{9.4}$$

$$= m = n(1 - R) \tag{9.5}$$

To see why these relationships hold, note that in (9.3), we are using the property of joint mutual information $I(\mathbf{A};\, \mathbf{B}, \mathbf{C}) = I(\mathbf{A};\, \mathbf{B}) + I(\mathbf{A};\, \mathbf{C}|\mathbf{B})$. Intuitively, this means that the reduction in uncertainty in $\mathbf{A}$ is the sum of the reduction in uncertainty due to knowledge of $\mathbf{B}$ and the reduction in uncertainty due to *additional* knowledge of **C** assuming that knowledge of **B** has already been accounted for. Due to the independence of the key **K**, the expression then reduces to the one we already encountered in the single-factor analysis[9] in (9.1).

Thus, if either the AD or the secret key **K** is compromised, there is no privacy leakage, i.e., the irreversibility is explicitly the difficulty of guessing all n bits of the biometric feature vector **X**. If *both* the AD and the secret key **K** are compromised, the two-factor scheme effectively reduces to a single-factor scheme with privacy leakage m bits, and irreversibility is explicitly the difficulty of guessing the remaining $n - m$ bits of the biometric feature vector **X**.

4 Cryptography-Based Characterization of Irreversibility for Systems Based on Homomorphic Cryptosystems

An emerging approach for biometric template protection is to encrypt the biometric characteristic—or the biometric features—and then utilize encrypted-domain computation to determine whether a probe biometric represents the claimed identity. Encrypted-domain computation is accomplished by means of homomorphic cryptosystems [1]. These are cryptosystems that allow certain computations to be performed in the encrypted domain. According to the operations allowed, these cryptosystems can be additively homomorphic [19], multiplicatively homomorphic [2], and fully homomorphic [31]. A variant called Somewhat Homomorphic Encryption (SHE) allows a limited number of homomorphic operations [3]. SHE constructions allow encrypted domain computation to be performed with lower computational complexity compared to fully homomorphic constructions.[10] The threat model for this class of systems assumes a computationally bounded adversary.

A notional template protection scheme based on homomorphic encryption is shown in Fig. 9.5. In this class of approaches, a biometric feature vector is encrypted (usually element-wise) using a homomorphic encryption scheme, based on a public key provided by the recognition system. Biometric verification involves encrypting

[9] The discerning reader will inquire why we refer to information-theoretic characterization of irreversibility while also including a cryptographic hash in our constructions. This has to do primarily with the threat model. While the fuzzy commitment and secure sketch constructions are undoubtedly motivated by information-theoretic concepts and are analyzed in that vein, we chose to assume that the adversary is still computationally bounded. The reason for this assumption is that practical template protection systems must necessarily have computationally bounded adversaries, for whom reversing properly designed cryptographic hash functions is computationally intractable. If we had assumed a computationally unbounded adversary, as is common in purely information-theoretic analyses, we would have to assume that the hash would be broken. This does not alter the irreversibility analysis we have presented but does alter other properties, e.g., probability of a successful verification without having to guess **X**. For more details, we refer the reader to [33].

[10] Please refer to Part II, Chap. 6 of this book for a detailed description of template protection systems based on homomorphic encryption, including performance evaluations. In this section, we restrict our development to the characterization of irreversibility.

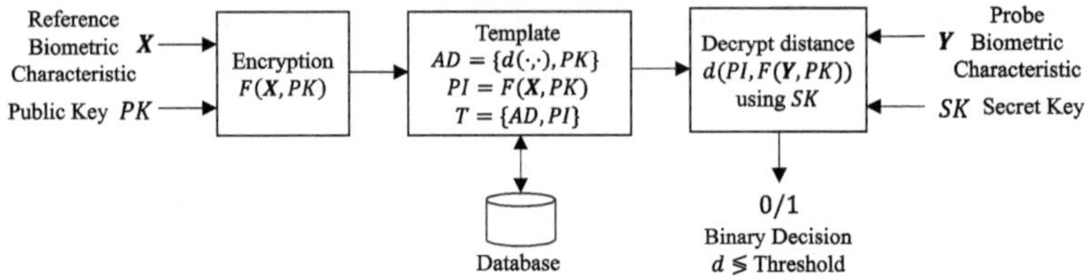

Fig. 9.5 A homomorphic cryptosystem enables a template protection scheme based on encrypted computation of a distance metric between the reference and probe feature vectors. The irreversibility of such schemes relies on the computational hardness of reversing the encryption, in order to reveal the reference feature vectors

the probe biometric feature vector, computing a distance metric between the reference and probe biometrics in the encrypted domain, and then comparing that distance to a known threshold. The threshold can be unique for each user, or we could employ a common threshold for the whole database. We assume that the public/private key pair is furnished by the user. The public key can be stored on the system without loss of security. A scheme designed in this way is, by construction, a two-factor approach in which the private (decryption) key (also called the secret key) is the second factor.[11]

In this approach, the *PI* is essentially the encrypted biometric feature vector as shown in Fig. 9.5. The *AD* contains information necessary to perform the verification process. In this example, the distance metric $d(\cdot, \cdot)$ and the user-specific public key PK serve as the AD. If the distance metric is parameterized differently for each user, then the AD can be made user-specific by including the distance function and the parameter values for each user. In this chapter, we assume that the same distance metric is used for each enrolled user.

Given that the *PI* is a homomorphic encryption of the biometric feature vector, the irreversibility of this approach is dominated by the computational hardness of reversing the encryption scheme. Once again, the threat model assumes a computationally bounded adversary. The computational difficulty of reversing the encryption scheme in the absence of the decryption key, in turn, depends on the mathematical "hard problem" on which the homomorphic cryptosystem is based. For example, Paillier encryption is based on the composite residuosity

[11] We could have constructed a single-factor template protection scheme in which all users' biometrics are encrypted using the same public key, and the distance between the respective reference and probe biometrics for all users is decrypted using the same secret key. However, this would require the public-private key pair to be stored at the recognition system. This is only secure if the recognition system is trusted or honest. Since we cannot readily make this assumption and since the principal feature of template protection is to preserve the privacy of biometric templates, we cannot make the assumption that the recognition system is trusted; it can, for example, be compromised by an adversary that will then trivially access all reference biometric feature vectors. In that situation, the system would not possess irreversibility.

problem [19].[12] As another example, some fully homomorphic encryption schemes are based on the problem of Learning With Errors (LWE) [9].[13]

Since reversing the encryption is computationally intractable, the adversary is reduced to guessing the decryption key so that they can decrypt the *PI*. One way to numerically specify the irreversibility for such template protection approaches is to provide the key size for the encryption scheme. Thus, for example, we could specify that a Paillier-based biometric cryptosystem uses a 2048-bit modulus and employs the Hamming distance computation between encrypted binary biometric feature vectors; we then say that the system has 2048 bits of security. In other words, irreversibility is equivalent to guessing the secret key of the homomorphic cryptosystem. Intuitively, each extra bit in the secret key makes the adversary's search space twice as large, thus doubling the difficulty of guessing the key. In practice, the adversary can resort to cryptanalysis, which involves trying to use the properties of the encryption and decryption systems to reduce this difficulty. For problems that are known to be hard, such as the examples above, the computational effort of cryptanalysis is large enough that it is impractical for the adversary.[14]

Under the above threat model, the adversary has access to the public key used for encryption, but the secret key that is used to decrypt the distance metric is available only to a legitimately enrolled user. From a practical standpoint, it is natural to ask how the user is furnished with the (public) encryption key and the (private) decryption key. One possibility is to generate these user-specific keys at enrollment. However, it must be ensured that these keys—after they are provided to

[12] Let $N = pq$, where p and q are prime numbers. Then, a number z is considered a composite residue modulo N^2 if we can express it as $z = x^N \mod N^2$ for some integer x. To solve the composite residuosity problem, we are given z, and we must determine whether it is a residue modulo N^2. When p and q are large primes, this is believed to be computationally intractable. The difficulty of this problem is closely related to the hardness of factorizing a large composite number N into its component primes.

[13] To obtain the intuition behind the LWE problem, let $\mathbb{Z}_q$ be the ring of integers modulo q, where q is a prime number. Then $\mathbb{Z}_q^n$ is the set of n-vectors over $\mathbb{Z}_q$. Consider the system of equations $b_i = \mathbf{a}_i \cdot \mathbf{x} + e_i \mod q$, where $\mathbf{a}_i \in \mathbb{Z}_q^n$ and e_i are (small) scalar noise terms from a suitable noise distribution. We have to solve for a vector $\mathbf{x}$ that satisfies all pairs $(\mathbf{a}_i, b_i)$. The number of equations is a polynomial in n. Solving these simultaneous equations in the absence of the noise terms is easy and can be performed in polynomial time using Gaussian elimination. With the noise terms, however, this problem is hard especially in high-dimensional space. The difficulty of this problem is related to the difficulty of the Shortest Vector Problem (SVP), which is the problem of finding the vector with the smallest norm in a lattice, that is not the zero vector. The hardness of LWE underpins the design of fully homomorphic cryptosystems.

[14] This is a reasonable assumption to make for traditional computing. If quantum computing becomes a practical reality, this assumption would not hold for several cryptosystems in use today. In particular, for the examples discussed above, the problem of factorizing a large number into its component primes can be solved efficiently by a quantum computer using Shor's algorithm [27]. Therefore, schemes like the Paillier cryptosystem would not remain secure. On the other hand, due to the addition of the noise terms in the system of simultaneous equations, there is no known efficient quantum algorithm to solve the LWE problem. Therefore, cryptosystems based on LWE would remain secure against quantum computing attacks.

the user—are securely deleted from the system. Failure to do so creates a significant vulnerability: An adversary that is present at the enrollment stage, and obtains access to the decryption key, can trivially reverse the encryption to obtain the user's unprotected reference biometric. In that case, we can no longer claim that irreversibility is determined by the computational hardness of the homomorphic cryptosystem.

5 Irreversibility of Template Protection Scheme Based on Feature Transformations and Machine Learning

Feature transformation-based schemes were among the earliest implementations of template protection systems in the literature [22, 23]. With the increased popularity of neural networks, these schemes have experienced a resurgence. In keeping with the categorization from the earlier chapters, we will classify feature transformations into two major categories: salting-based transformations and non-invertible transformations. The first category includes approaches such as BioHashing and its variants [5, 21, 29, 30, 35], Index-of-Max Hashing [12], and the Partial Hadamard Transformations [32]. The second category consists of geometric transformations [22], Bloom filters [10, 11], and polynomial transformations [16]. All these approaches involve a transformation of the reference biometric characteristic by mapping it into a different subspace. The transformed feature vector functions as the *PI*. To perform biometric verification, the probe biometric characteristic is also transformed using the correct mapping functions, and the transformed probe biometric feature vector is compared against the *PI*. If the distance in the target subspace is lower than the threshold, then verification is deemed to be successful.[15]

A key property of salting-based transformations is that they are invertible, given knowledge of the mapping parameters and the mapping functions. Therefore, if an adversary knows the mapping function and parameters or keys, they can derive the unprotected biometric feature vector (or at least a close approximation of it). For example, in a BioHashing scheme, the adversary can attempt to reverse a matrix vector product **AX** to obtain **X**, given a matrix **A** consisting of independent random variables from a known distribution. Similar approaches can be used to recover the unprotected biometric features for other kinds of salting transforms. To avoid this situation, one can consider a two-factor cancelable biometrics setup in which the transform parameters and keys are not part of the *AD*, and have to be separately carried by the user, for e.g., on a smart card. This approach is depicted in Fig. 9.6.

A contrasting key property of non-invertible transformations is that, even if the mapping parameters are revealed, the adversary cannot exactly recover the

[15] Please refer to Part II, Chap. 4 of this book for a detailed description of template protection systems based on feature transformations. In this section, we restrict our development to the characterization of irreversibility.

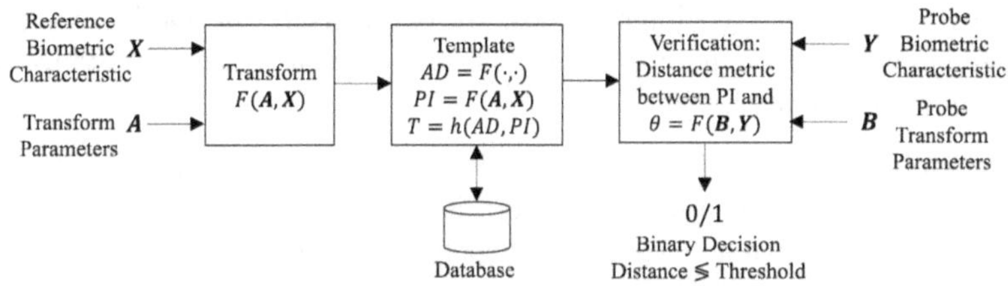

Fig. 9.6 To provide irreversibility for salting-based transformations, as well as some neural network-based transformations, a two-factor approach can be devised wherein the user is assigned their own transform parameters on a smart card and then provides it along with the probe biometric characteristic at the time of verification. If the transformation parameters are compromised or reverse engineered by an adversary, they can often be replaced by another transformation

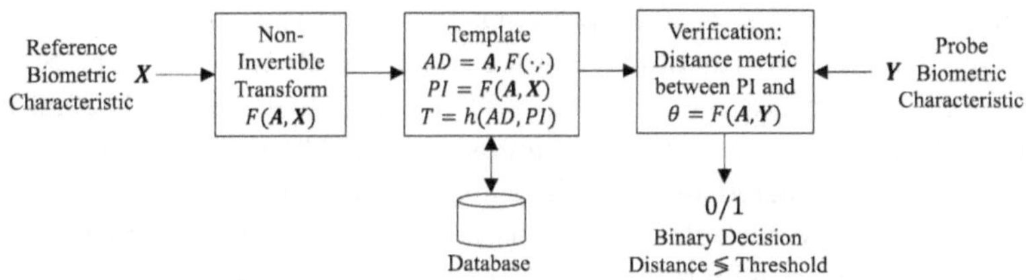

Fig. 9.7 In the case of non-invertible transformation-based template protection schemes, the specification of the transformation function, along with its parameters and/or keys, serves as the *AD*, while the result of the transformation is stored as the *PI*. During the verification process, a probe biometric characteristic is transformed and compared against the *PI*. If compromised, the *AD* can be replaced by another transformation

unprotected biometric feature vector from the *PI*. In this case, the *AD* can consist of a specification of the mapping function, as well as all the mapping parameters and keys. In other words, a single factor scheme, as shown in Fig. 9.7, suffices. This is not to say that a theoretical calculation of irreversibility is always possible. The irreversibility may often have to be measured empirically depending on the side information available to the adversary. What is clear is that these systems can operate in a much stronger threat model, referred to as the *full disclosure* model, which assumes that the algorithms and all secrets necessary for operation (parameters and keys) are made available to the adversary.

A salient characteristic of some feature transformation-based template protection systems is that if the protected template (stored as the *PI*) is compromised, a new template can be issued by changing the *AD* and any other parameters used to derive the *PI*. For some of the approaches discussed above, such as BioHashing, it is possible to estimate the irreversibility based on the inversion of a matrix-vector product **AX**, where **A** is a matrix of independent and identically distributed entries. For most other approaches, it is not possible to express the irreversibility of the transformation in the form of a concrete metric. In such cases, irreversibility must be measured empirically, as described in Sect. 6.

For neural network-based approaches, we will consider primarily systems that leverage neural networks to create the protected template.[16] These systems can be classified into two main kinds:[17]

1. Systems in which a protected template is a vector that is predefined for a given user. In such systems, a neural network is trained such that a user's biometric characteristic or feature vector is mapped by the network to that predefined vector [13, 20]. A cryptographic hash of the predefined vector is then stored as the *PI*. The vector itself is not stored.
2. Systems in which a user's biometric characteristic or feature vector is mapped by a neural network (or a combination of neural networks) into a vector representation that has desired properties [25]. Typically, the desired properties include (a) semantic similarity, i.e., similar input biometric characteristics or feature vectors result in similar vector representations, and (b) statistical properties, e.g., the output vector consists of bits that are equally likely to be 0s or 1s. Since the network learns a representation for a user, we expect that there will be intra-class variations, i.e., the vector representations generated by different impressions of the biometric characteristic from the same user will differ slightly. In order to compensate for the intra-class variations, a second neural network may be trained to correct the errors with respect to the reference vector provided at enrollment. Successful error correction at the time of verification may then be verified by computing a cryptographic hash of the generated vector and comparing it against a cryptographic hash computed from the vector representation generated at the time of enrollment. The reader should note the similarities between this approach and the use of error-correcting codes to account for intra-class variations in fuzzy commitment and secure sketch systems.

Both of the above forms may be implemented either as a single-factor system (Fig. 9.7) or as a two-factor system (Fig. 9.6). In a single-factor system, the *AD* consists of (a) the mapping function F which is a cascade of the neural network mapping and the hashing operation and (b) the parameter matrix $\mathbf{A}$ which contains the parameters of the trained neural network and the cryptographic hash. In a two-factor implementation, the *AD* consists only of the mapping function F and the cryptographic hash function, but the neural network parameters are withheld from the adversary and presented by the user as a second factor during verification. Irreversibility of both single-factor and two-factor approaches is determined empir-

[16] As described in the earlier chapters, there exist template protection schemes in which the feature extraction step separately employs neural networks. We do not consider those approaches in this section. Our rationale is that biometric features extracted using neural networks do not necessarily have to be protected using transformation-based or learning-based approaches, which are the subject of this section. Indeed, they can be protected using any of the other template protection architectures that we have discussed in this chapter. Therefore, in this section, we specifically consider approaches in which neural networks are used to obtain the *protected template*.

[17] Please refer to Part II, Chap. 7 of this book for a detailed description of template protection systems based on neural networks.

ically. Though there is less work on the subject, it is reasonable to inquire about the incremental information leakage along the layers of a neural network. Concretely, different from determining the difficulty of obtaining the unprotected feature vector **X** given the *PI*, which is the output of an N-stage neural network, we consider the difficulty of reversing each individual layer and obtaining the intermediate $N - 1$ representations. This could provide a richer description of information leakage—and hence the irreversibility—and the manner in which it evolves as an adversary works backward through the neural network.[18]

6 Empirical Characterization of Irreversibility

As we have seen, there are many ways to implement biometric template protection systems. Some of these approaches admit a theoretical analysis, and in these approaches it is possible to assign a concrete meaning to irreversibility, e.g., number of bits of the reference biometric leaked by the template, hardness of the quadratic residuosity problem for a homomorphic encryption algorithm with 2048-bit keys. For other approaches, no such concrete meaning is available, and irreversibility should be estimated. Even in the approaches that admit a theoretical measure, empirical irreversibility might be less than theoretical irreversibility due to a variety of reasons. We discuss these challenges in this section.

6.1 Concerns over Information-Theoretic Characterization

A chief concern with measuring irreversibility using metrics such as bits leaked is that the metric relies on assumptions that are difficult to meet in practice. To make the analysis tractable, it is often assumed that the elements of the reference biometric feature vector **X** are independent and identically distributed; this leads to a straightforward computation of the entropy of **X**. In [33], for instance, **X** consists of independent Bernoulli-0.5 bits. In practice, **X** consists of numbers, bits, or vectors extracted from human biometrics, which exhibit significant spatial correlations

[18] This consideration applies primarily to the case in which the neural network weights are included in the *AD* rather than being provided as a second factor. It arises from the fact that, given the network weights, each layer of the neural network essentially implements a matrix-vector product followed by a usually nonlinear activation function. The matrix consists of the neural network weights, while the vector is the input to the layer under consideration. Given the output of the tth layer, how difficult is it to derive the input to that layer? This depends on the size of the input vector, width of the network, i.e., the number of neurons in the tth layer, and the form of the activation function. Intuition suggests that this inversion is still quite difficult, though examining the per-layer dimensions and activation functions can provide useful hints on which layers of the network are likely to be vulnerable. Furthermore, thinking about per-layer invertibility can drive the choice of the width, depth, and activation functions of the neural network.

and location-dependent statistics; in other words, they are neither independent nor identically distributed. There have been attempts in the literature to design the feature extraction algorithm such that these dependencies can be shaped and their effect can be analyzed accurately. For example, rather than relying on individual fingerprint minutiae, developing feature vectors based on the aggregate number of minutiae in a neighborhood allows a system designer to determine which bits in the feature vector are independent and to characterize noise in biometric measurements in a tractable fashion, e.g., as a binary symmetric channel with a small cross-over probability $p \ll 0.5$ [28]. This has the advantage of making the theoretical leakage metrics a good approximation to the actual leakage observed in practice.

Another challenge is that it is quite difficult to extract too many statistically independent and identically distributed (i.i.d.) symbols from a human biometric. While a feature vector extracted from a face or fingerprint minutiae can be quite long, the corresponding i.i.d. feature encoding is a smaller number of bits. This has implications for the system implementation: An error-correcting code, such as one used in fuzzy commitment, approaches the Shannon performance bound only when the messages are extremely long. In other words, if the biometric feature vectors are very long, then the code approaches ideal performance and prescribes the number of parity (or syndrome) bits that will be sufficient to correct errors introduced because of the inherent noisiness of biometric measurements. Note that this is precisely the type of error that is corrected by the error-correcting codes in the fuzzy commitment approach in Sect. 3. As the number of useful, nonredundant features one can practically extract from a biometric characteristic is limited, the lengths of the codewords and messages we consider in these information theory-based systems are also limited. Therefore, error-correcting codes applied to these features are inefficient, i.e., they require more parity bits (than the number of bits specified by the Shannon performance bound) to be stored in the AD. Therefore, more privacy is leaked when the AD is compromised.

It bears mentioning that template protection systems based exclusively on information theoretic concepts are not generally used in practice. See, for example, the fuzzy commitment and secure sketch constructions described in this chapter. The decision for successful or failed recognition is made using a comparison of a cryptographic hash, such as SHA-256. For the information-theoretic portion of the system, the irreversibility is given by the parameters of the error correcting code, i.e., $n - m$ bits as we saw in Sect. 3. For the cryptographic hash portion, the irreversibility is given by the difficulty of reversing the hash to exactly recover the reference biometric feature vector. For an ℓ-bit hash, this requires 2^ℓ operations on average, i.e., provides an average of ℓ bits of security. We have assumed that $n \geq \ell$. Combining the irreversibility characterization from the information-theoretic and cryptographic portions of the system, the worst-case irreversibility would be $\min(n - m, \ell)$. If n is much larger than ℓ and the number of bits revealed by the AD is small such that $m < n - \ell$, then we can quantify the irreversibility as $\min(n - m, \ell) = \ell$. This is the difficulty of finding a specific hash collision for an ℓ-bit hash. In Sect. 3, we called this the *second* pre-image resistance of the cryptographic hash. On the other hand, if the AD reveals too many bits such that

$m > n - \ell$, the adversary can be more efficient in their attempt to find a specific hash collision, by attempting to guess $n - m$ bits and computing the cryptographic hash, rather than reversing the ℓ-bit hash on its own. In that case, the irreversibility would be $n - m$.

6.2 Concerns over Cryptographic Characterization

As explained in Sect. 4, the single point of failure for cryptography-based template protection systems is the revelation of the secret key (also known as the private key or the decryption key). Typically, this key unlocks a homomorphically encrypted ciphertext and reveals the underlying biometric features. In two-factor systems, these keys can be carried by the user on a smart card, which is less user-friendly and counteracts the ease of use afforded by biometrics. Another possibility is for the secret keys to be stored in a secure enclave and accessed by a password or a PIN code known to the user. From an ease-of-use perspective, this might be preferable, however, it creates a vulnerability. It is possible for a skilled adversary to trick a user into revealing the password by using phishing and social engineering attacks. Thus, when we claim that the cryptosystem has c-bit keys, an irreversibility metric of c bits might be overly optimistic because the metric does not take into account the possibility that the user might have protected the key using a weak password or a reused password that might have been revealed during an unrelated data breach.

This also highlights another aspect of the difficulty of an empirical characterization of irreversibility. Phishing and social engineering attacks rely on the creativity of the adversary and the strength and uniqueness of the password. The threat model for such attacks should be clearly stronger than just assuming a computationally bounded attacker who must guess keys or passwords from scratch. However, what this threat model should precisely be is difficult to characterize and standardize. Assuming an information-theoretic, i.e., a computationally *unbounded*, adversary is not useful, because encryption-based systems are inherently insecure against this attacker. On the other hand, assuming a computationally bounded but fully informed attacker is not useful either, because knowledge of the keys and passwords renders the encryption-based approaches trivially insecure.

6.3 More Challenges with Empirical Characterization

In order to determine irreversibility empirically, it is necessary to set up a suitable experiment. This experiment should provide the adversary with the template $T = \{AD, PI\}$ and any reasonable data that can help them construct a privacy attack in the real world. The type and amount of data available to the adversary depends on the threat model under which security guarantees for the template protection system are provided. While the threat model is usually specified quite rigorously in terms of the adversary's computational capability, there is often no consensus on what type and amount of available data the adversary can be assumed to access. Is it reasonable, for example, to provide an adversary with a large corpus of biometric signals (or biometric features extracted from the signals) supplied by people who are *not* users of the template protection system? If all users' biometric signals were included in such a corpus, then the attack is trivially accomplished by trying all possible biometrics as the probe biometric, and the attack complexity is just linear in the size of the corpus. By choosing a corpus which does not contain the enrolled users, we still afford the adversary the opportunity to try a number of probe biometrics, examine the output of the recognition system, and employ iterative techniques to modify one or more biometrics in the corpus, so as to force successful recognition.[19] If the adversary succeeds, then there needs to be an additional step that checks whether they have successfully derived a user's reference biometric, or if they have discovered a specific hash collision, i.e., found an alternative biometric which authenticates as the enrolled user.

This raises another fundamental question: Should the definition of irreversibility only permit exact reconstruction of a user's reference biometric features, or should an approximation error be tolerated? Concretely, if the adversary finds an $\mathbf{X}' \neq \mathbf{X}$ that forces successful verification according to the criterion when supplied to the given template protection system, then should we consider that the template protection system has been shown to be reversible? How can we characterize irreversibility while noting that a successful attack on the verification system does not necessarily compromise the privacy of the enrolled user? One way to achieve this is to construct a definition of irreversibility that allows for the possibility of discovering a biometric feature vector that forces successful verification while also being *close* (but not necessarily equal) to a given user's unprotected reference biometric according to a suitable distance metric, e.g., Hamming distance. Mathematically, this defines irreversibility as the computational effort (in CPU cycles, time, etc.) for the adversary to discover a feature vector $\mathbf{X}'$ such that the decoding operation outputs $\theta = g(\mathbf{X}', T) = 1$ and $d(\mathbf{X}, \mathbf{X}') < \epsilon$ for a distance metric $d(\cdot, \cdot)$ for some $\mathbf{X}$ in the enrolled database of users.[20]

A final challenge in empirical characterization is related to modern mechanisms used to construct templates. In order to achieve high recognition accuracy, i.e.,

[19] With that said, it is desirable that the corpus of biometric data be *representative* of the enrolled data, even if it does not directly contain data from the enrolled subjects. For example, in the case of face images, the images that the adversary has access to should be similar in terms of their characteristics—cooperative versus uncooperative captures, comparable environmental conditions, comparable camera noise statistics, etc.–to the face images used to generate the reference templates. Otherwise, we may underestimate the attacker's ability.

[20] Note that the metric for closeness is computed on the unprotected features, while the verification itself is for a template protection system. This means that if the discovered $\mathbf{X}'$ is close enough to the unprotected $\mathbf{X}$, then when $\mathbf{X}'$ is provided at the time of verification, the template protection system utilizes the *AD*, the *PI*, and $\mathbf{X}'$ to generate a positive verification result for the user possessing the unprotected feature vector $\mathbf{X}$.

low FMR, low FNMR, low equal error rates (EER), biometric feature extraction algorithms use modern AI approaches based on deep neural networks. It is known that these approaches exhibit *algorithmic bias* with respect to the subject's gender, ethnicity, and other relevant characteristics [4, 8]. For example, owing to biased representation of people from disadvantaged demographics in a training corpus, the biometric recognition performance, measured by the FNMR and FMR, can be inferior to the reported FNMR and FMR guarantees for that system. Does a similar challenge exist for irreversibility, i.e., are irreversibility guarantees for some demographics measurably worse for machine learning-based template protection schemes? As of this writing, there has not been sufficient research on this topic. For machine learning-based template protection schemes, any conclusions made about irreversibility must take algorithmic bias into account. This makes it difficult to construct an experiment to determine irreversibility and to fully trust its results.

6.4 Best Practices for Empirical Measurement of Irreversibility

Measuring irreversibility amounts to measuring the difficulty of an attack that will reveal the reference biometric features. To provide a conservative metric for irreversibility, it is necessary to ensure that the attack experiment is set up in accordance with well-founded security practices. A key consideration is Kerckhoff's Principle, which states that all aspects of a security algorithm must be revealed to the adversary, except the decryption key(s) if they happen to be used [15]. Adherence to this principle means that we never rely on security through obscurity. A security guarantee—in our case, irreversibility guarantee—based on this principle implies that, as long as we are able to keep the key secret from the adversary, any other information that the adversary can utilize about the system will not increase their advantage. Note that Kerckhoff's Principle accommodates two-factor schemes, i.e., the second factor—**K** in Figs. 9.4 and 9.5—is a key that can be kept secret from the adversary without violating the principle. Note that the full disclosure model—discussed as a threat model for some non-invertible feature transformation-based template protection systems—is strictly stronger than the requirement imposed by Kerckhoff's Principle, because it explicitly allows all secrets (keys) to be revealed to the adversary.

To make the irreversibility metric a usable rather than utopian concept, it is important to establish key properties for the experiment in which the adversary attempts to "reverse the template T." Concretely, it is desirable to (1) specify a credible threat model, (2) define the vector space in which the reference biometric feature vector lives, (3) establish a distance metric $d(\cdot, \cdot)$ which allows the adversary to measure the effectiveness of a privacy attack that seeks to reveal the reference biometric features, (4) establish a stopping criterion ϵ, as described above, which will indicate that the adversary has successfully reversed the template, and (5) account for the effect of multiple compromised templates on irreversibility. The definitions of the vector space, distance measure, and the stopping threshold will depend on the specific biometric characteristic in question, the biometric sensing equipment, the quality of the extra datasets assumed to be accessed by the adversary, the intrinsic variability in biometric features within and across individuals, and other factors. As an example of a thorough consideration of all of the above requirements, we refer the reader to the empirical evaluation of the irreversibility of PolyProtect [16].[21]

To provide the adversary with a starting point for an attack, it is reasonable to provide them with a corpus of biometric features that are compatible with the template protection system under consideration. As argued above, the corpus should not contain the biometric features of any of the users legitimately enrolled in the system. One approach is to generate the corpus synthetically, rather than using real biometric data. It is a valid attack strategy for the adversary to iteratively modify one or more of the feature vectors in the corpus, until they gain access, i.e., until the system recognizes the adversary's modified feature vector as belonging to a specific enrolled user.[22] If carried out with appropriate cost functions and modification criteria, iterative attacks are likely to have some success with approaches based on cancelable biometrics and information theory, but not cryptographic approaches. This is because well-designed encryption schemes generate completely different ciphertexts, when provided with biometric features from iteration to iteration.

7 Understanding Irreversibility for the Multiple Systems Case

We now consider a use-case for template protection that is extremely relevant but has received very little attention from the research community—the multiple systems case. Simply put, this use-case refers to a situation in which a user (e.g., Alice) has provided the same (or similar) reference biometric characteristics to multiple biometric recognition systems. Examples include an apartment complex, a bank, a gym, a laptop, a smartphone, etc. This expands the attack surface available to an adversary. In some cases, the adversary can compromise systems that have lower security and then use the information gathered to attack the more secure systems. This is a kind of Attack on Record Multiplicity (ARM) [17]. Though the ARM notion was introduced for cancelable schemes, the attack can be conceived against other BTP architectures as well, as discussed below.

[21] To access open-source code for the irreversibility evaluation experiments in [16], visit https://gitlab.idiap.ch/bob/bob.paper.polyprotect_2021.

[22] Note our comment on hash collisions and pre-image resistance in Sect. 3. For template protection systems employing a cryptographic hash as shown in this chapter, an adversary gaining access to the system might not necessarily break irreversibility. On the other hand, for systems employing feature transformations, finding $\mathbf{X}'$, a "good-enough" approximation of $\mathbf{X}$, should legitimately be considered as reducing the irreversibility (and hence the privacy) of the system.

Some of these attacks might be able to subvert the authentication systems without requiring the adversary to discover Alice's biometric data. Other attacks would result in the adversary discovering a substantial percentage of Alice's reference biometric features. In a world that increasingly requires authentication technologies, this expansion of the attack surface has significant implications for security, privacy, and hence for irreversibility. We will primarily analyze the multiple systems use-case from the point of view of irreversibility, but for more details the reader should refer to the work of Wang et al. [24, 33].

At the outset, we note that there are various ways in which the multiple template protection systems can be designed and deployed. For example, they might be jointly designed but deployed at various times. Alternatively, they might be incrementally designed and deployed according to availability of resources or need for biometric authentication. For the case of joint design, it is almost always the case that the individual systems are all based on a common architecture. In the incremental approach, it is quite likely that the individual systems are based on a variety of architectures, e.g., some are based on a fuzzy commitment scheme, while others are based on homomorphic encryption. We will focus on the former case, i.e., joint or incremental design wherein all systems are based on the same architecture. The goal is to illuminate interesting trade-offs between security and privacy leakage (hence, irreversibility) that arise when multiple systems based on the same architecture are deployed. It is also a best-case scenario for the adversary, because information revealed about any given system may have more utility since the other systems are known to have the same architecture.

Below, we will describe the case of multiple template protection systems based on information-theoretic concepts, as well as the case of multiple systems based on homomorphic encryption. The reader is encouraged to perform this exercise for various kinds of feature transformation-based and neural network-based BTP systems. In particular, it is useful to ask which of the non-invertible transformation-based approaches scale easily to multiple systems and which ones become vulnerable when reused.

7.1 Multiple Information Theory-Based Systems

Consider first the case of multiple information theory-based systems. For concreteness, assume that Alice has enrolled the same fingerprint in n systems, and each of them implements a single-factor secure sketch-based approach. Since secure sketch-based systems are theoretically equivalent to fuzzy commitment systems, we will not analyze the latter separately. In the ensuing development, we will consider the parity check matrices used by the n secure sketch systems. We will leave a similar argument using generator matrices in fuzzy commitment-based systems as an exercise for the reader.

Let $\mathbf{H}_1, \mathbf{H}_2, \ldots, \mathbf{H}_t$ be the parity check matrices used to construct the secure sketch-based systems for a reference biometric feature vector $\mathbf{X}$. Note that we are making a simplifying argument here that each of the systems uses the same enrollment vector **X**. In practice, this assumption is not met because of the inherently noisy nature of biometrics, which causes the reference vectors at the t systems to be slightly different from each other. We ignore this fact for simplicity. Each $\mathbf{H}_i$ is a binary matrix with dimension $m \times n$. Recalling Fig. 9.3, the AD in each of these systems is given by $AD_i = \mathbf{H}_i\mathbf{X}, i = 1, \ldots, t$. Each AD_i is identically the syndrome corresponding to the codeword **X** according to the ith error-correcting code. A syndrome computed using the parity check matrix can be considered as providing m constraints to linear equations in n unknowns—these n unknowns[23] being the bits of **X**.

Now, we consider the following two cases:

1. $\mathbf{H}_i = \mathbf{H}, i = 1, \ldots, t$, i.e., all systems employ the same error correcting code. If any of these systems is compromised by the adversary, the same m out of n bits of **X** are leaked. However, compromising any further systems does not help the adversary. Thus the privacy leakage, and hence the irreversibility, is capped at m bits. In other words, the adversary does not have any incentive to attack more secure sketch systems, so the irreversibility of the collection of secure sketch systems is no worse than that of any of its component systems.
2. $\mathbf{H}_i \neq \mathbf{H}_j$ in general, and rank is an increasing function of the number of compromised systems. In this case, each of the secure sketch systems uses a different parity check matrix. Suppose, without loss of generality, that the first system is compromised, resulting in privacy leakage of $m_1 < n$ bits. Now, with each successive system being compromised, it is possible that more bits of **X** are revealed to the adversary (see the toy example in Footnote 23). This is because, by construction the rows of $\mathbf{H}_i$ are not all linearly dependent on the rows of $\mathbf{H}_j, i \neq j$. Thus, if the adversary's goal is to discover the biometric **X**, they are incentivized to attack more and more secure sketch systems. Hence, the irreversibility of the collection of secure sketch systems is worse—sometimes

[23] To understand this point better, consider a toy example with a [4, 2] code described by a parity check matrix $\mathbf{H}_1$, where

$$\mathbf{H}_1 = \begin{bmatrix} 1 & 0 & 1 & 1 \\ 0 & 1 & 1 & 1 \end{bmatrix}$$

This code has $m = 2$ and $n = 4$, which means that we have 4-bit codewords and 2-bit syndromes. Suppose that the syndrome stored as AD_1 is $[1, 0]^T$. Let us denote the binary codeword as the vector $\mathbf{X} = [x_1, x_2, x_3, x_4]^T$, where $x_i, i = 1, 2, 3, 4$, are unknown bits. Then, we see that the syndrome imposes a constraint on the bits of **X** given by $\mathbf{H}_1\mathbf{X} = [1, 0]^T$. Thus, we have

$$x_1 + x_3 + x_4 = 1 \quad \text{and} \quad x_2 + x_3 + x_4 = 0 \mod 2$$

Thus there are $m = 2$ equations and $n = 4$ unknowns. As we have seen in Sect. 3, revealing AD_1 to the adversary leaks 2 out of 4 bits. Intuitively, the reader can see that if each successive parity check matrix $\mathbf{H}_i$ provides more independent equations, then more and more information about the bits of **X** is leaked, thus compromising irreversibility.

significantly worse, if the parity check matrices have linearly independent rows—than that of any of its component systems.

This is not intuitively obvious. One would think that it would be better for the systems to possess independent parity check matrices. This desirable property would be restored if one considers two-factor systems, in which Alice enrolls with an *independent* random bit-string—as the second factor—at each of the component systems. As long as the second factor remains hidden, privacy leakage remains zero no matter how many component systems are compromised. We urge the interested reader to prove this rigorously using the results of Sect. 3.

7.2 Multiple Systems Based on Homomorphic Cryptosystems

Next, consider the case of multiple systems based on homomorphic encryption. We reviewed individual systems using this approach in Sect. 4. Assume that Alice has enrolled the same fingerprint in n systems, each based on a homomorphic cryptosystem. We do not insist that the systems employ the same kind of homomorphic encryption, i.e., one of them could use Paillier encryption, the second might be based on a lattice-based encryption scheme, and so on. We again make the simplifying assumption, as above, that each of the systems uses the same reference feature vector $\mathbf{X}$. The threat model is the same as the one used in Sect. 4, i.e., the adversary is computationally bounded, and thus recovering the underlying plaintext from a given ciphertext in the absence of the secret (decryption) key is infeasible for them.

Let the public-private key pairs used in the cryptosystems be represented as $(PK_i, SK_i), i = 1, 2, \ldots, n$, such that $SK_i \neq SK_j$ for all $i \neq j$. Based on the threat model, each individual system is protected from the adversary. Concretely, the templates $T_i = \{AD_i, PI_i\}$ do not reveal anything about $\mathbf{X}$. Even if the adversary is able to obtain possession of multiple templates T_i, the irreversibility is preserved because the adversary does not know any of the secret keys.

Suppose one of the systems—without loss of generality, the first system ($i = 1$)—is compromised by means of a phishing or social engineering attack. In this case, the adversary can trivially decrypt PI_1 and obtain $\mathbf{X}$. Since the reference biometric feature vector is compromised, none of the systems possess the property of irreversibility anymore. At the same time, the reader should note that this privacy compromise does *not* necessarily imply that the systems indexed by $i \neq 1$ have been successfully attacked. As long as the secret keys $SK_i, i \neq 1$ remain secret, the adversary still cannot verify their identity at those systems. Thus, even though privacy is fully compromised, sensitive data or access being protected by any system indexed by $i \neq 1$ remains secure. This is an interesting contrast from traditional biometric systems and some other kinds of template protection systems, wherein a privacy compromise usually implies a security compromise.

8 Conclusion

Irreversibility refers to the degree of difficulty faced by an adversary in recovering the unprotected biometric features from the protected templates stored in a BTP system. Irreversibility is a vital privacy consideration in the design of BTP systems. Using fundamental principles underlying the specific BTP system, it is possible in some cases to derive theoretical guarantees for irreversibility. These include systems based on concepts from information theory, modern cryptography, and the class of salting-based feature transformations. In other BTP systems, e.g., systems that leverage neural networks for feature transformations, or non-invertible transformations, useful theoretical guarantees are not available and irreversibility must be evaluated empirically. Even for systems in which theoretical guarantees are available, empirical measurements are needed to account for deviations of the practical constructions from their idealized behavior. It is necessary for the biometrics research and engineering community to develop consensus around the best practices, the threat models, and experimental conditions for carrying out such empirical measurements.

9 Summary

- **Definition:** Irreversibility is a property of a biometric template protection system that refers to the degree of difficulty faced by the adversary when attempting to recover the unprotected biometric features used to generate the stored (protected) reference template(s).
- **Characterization:** Irreversibility is characterized or measured using a variety of metrics, depending upon the specific principle on which the template protection system is constructed. For example:
  - Information-theoretically motivated architectures, such as fuzzy commitment, and secure sketches, measure irreversibility in terms of the number of bits of the biometric reference features leaked by the template.
  - Cryptographically motivated architectures measure irreversibility in terms of the strength of the cryptographic keys used to encrypt the reference biometric features.
  - In architectures based on feature transformations (e.g., salting or non-invertible transforms), irreversibility is measured in terms of the difficulty of reversing the transformation to recover the unprotected reference biometric features.
- **Measurement:** For some BTP architectures, it is not possible to obtain the irreversibility via a theoretical approach based on the principles underlying the construction of the system. In such cases, irreversibility must be measured empirically. Even when a theoretical measure is available, an empirical measurement

might be needed because of deviation of the implemented systems from ideal behavior. Measuring irreversibility in practice is challenging because of the following factors:

- Ideal statistical distributions of the biometric features cannot always be achieved; thus metrics such as the number of bits leaked are difficult to characterize exactly. Furthermore, it is difficult to know the side information available to the adversary about the feature extraction process, which, in turn, will determine the statistical distribution of the resulting features.
- Often a concrete metric for evaluating irreversibility is unavailable, and the process used by the adversary to recover the reference biometric features from the protected template involves reversing a complex processing pipeline that integrates feature extraction and template protection. In such cases, precise values for irreversibility are difficult to specify.
- It is vital for the research and engineering community to reach a consensus on best practices to be followed during such empirical measurements. We described some best practices and principles in this chapter.
- Providing a more general definition of irreversibility, which allows for approximate recovery of the reference biometric features, would help advance the theory for various template protection architectures and facilitate empirical measurements of irreversibility.

10 Study Questions

1. Discuss the meaning of irreversibility as it applies in colloquial day-to-day usage and as it applies in the context of biometric template protection systems. Compare and contrast the two meanings.
2. If you decide to study the principles behind template protection schemes, you will discover several closely related approaches: secure sketches, fuzzy vaults, fuzzy extractors, and fuzzy commitment. Can you figure out conceptually and/or mathematically how these approaches are related? Are they all equivalent in some sense? From an irreversibility perspective, which would you most prefer to implement in practice?
3. In our discussion of cryptography-based approaches, we cautioned against revealing the secret key to the adversary. Can you think of approaches in which the enrollment system can assign a public-private key pair to each user and then provably forget the secret key? Do these approaches require human supervision, or can they be automated? From an irreversibility perspective, what does your answer say about the prospect of implementing such approaches?
4. You might have noticed that two-factor approaches are desirable because they have better irreversibility properties. Can you think of the disadvantages of such approaches?

5. A formidable competing approach to template protection schemes is to store enrolled biometrics in a secure enclave, as is done in modern smartphones, tablets, and laptops. Try to find out more about how the secure enclave is used. What are the chief vulnerabilities of that approach, from the point of view of an adversary discovering the biometrics? Discuss the pros and cons of these "hardware-driven" approaches vis-a-vis template protection schemes.
6. For the use-case with multiple systems, discuss the use of two-factor approaches. Do these help reduce the potential for exposure of the reference biometric features? What inconvenience does the second factor introduce? How might this inconvenience be mitigated?
7. Consider the case in which a user has multiple enrollments in various biometric recognition systems. We have seen the trade-offs between security and privacy for the various architectures. Discuss the implication of having multiple enrollments for the case of secure enclaves, i.e., when Alice is enrolled on her phone, her laptop, and her tablet. Can we realistically claim that biometrics in enclaves are less reversible than the templates we have studied? Why or why not?

References

1. Acar, A., Aksu, H., Uluagac, A.S., Conti, M.: A survey on homomorphic encryption schemes: theory and implementation. ACM Comput. Surveys **51**(4), 1–35 (2018)
2. Elgamal, T.: A public key cryptosystem and a signature scheme based on discrete logarithms. IEEE Trans. Inf. Theory **31**(4), 469–472 (1985)
3. Brakerski, Z., Vaikuntanathan, V.: Efficient fully homomorphic encryption from (standard) LWE. SIAM J. Comput. **43**(2), 831–871 (2014)
4. Christian, B.: The Alignment Problem: Machine Learning and Human Values. W. W. Norton and Company, New York (2021)
5. Connie, T., Teoh, A., Goh, M., Ngo, D.: Palmhashing: a novel approach for cancelable biometrics. Inf. Proces. Lett. **93**(1), 1–5 (2005)
6. Cover, T., Thomas, J.: Elements of Information Theory. Wiley, Hoboken (2009)
7. Dodis, Y., Reyzin, L., Smith, A.: Fuzzy extractors: how to generate strong keys from biometrics and other noisy data. In: EUROCRYPT, LNCS, vol. 3027, pp. 523–540. Springer, Berlin (2004)
8. Drozdowski, P., Rathgeb, C., Dantcheva, A., Damer, N., Busch, C.: Demographic bias in biometrics: a survey on an emerging challenge. IEEE Trans. Technol. Society **1**(2), 89–103 (2020)
9. Gentry, C., Sahai, A., Waters, B.: Homomorphic encryption from learning with errors: conceptually-simpler, asymptotically-faster, attribute-based. In: Advances in Cryptology–CRYPTO 2013: 33rd Annual Cryptology Conference, Santa Barbara, CA, August 18–22, 2013. Proceedings, Part I, pp. 75–92. Springer, Berlin (2013)
10. Gomez-Barrero, M., Rathgeb, C., Galbally, J., Busch, C., Fierrez, J.: Unlinkable and irreversible biometric template protection based on bloom filters. Inf. Sci. **370**, 18–32 (2016)
11. Gomez-Barrero, M., Rathgeb, C., Li, G., Ramachandra, R., Galbally, J., Busch, C.: Multi-biometric template protection based on bloom filters. Inf. Fus. **42**, 37–50 (2018)
12. Jin, Z., Hwang, J.Y., Lai, Y.L., Kim, S., Teoh, A.B.J.: Ranking-based locality sensitive hashing-enabled cancelable biometrics: Index-of-max hashing. IEEE Trans. Inf. Forens. Secur. **13**(2), 393–407 (2017)

13. Jindal, A.K., Chalamala, S., Jami, S.K.: Face template protection using deep convolutional neural network. In: 2018 IEEE/CVF Conference on Computer Vision and Pattern Recognition Workshops (CVPRW), pp. 575–5758 (2018). https://doi.org/10.1109/CVPRW.2018.00087
14. Juels, A., Sudan, M.: A fuzzy vault scheme. Des. Codes Crypt. **38**(2), 237–257 (2006)
15. Kerckhoffs, A.: La cryptographie militaire (1883)
16. Krivokuća Hahn, V., Marcel, S.: Towards protecting face embeddings in mobile face verification scenarios. IEEE Trans. Biom. Behav. Identity Sci. **4**(1), 117–134 (2022). https://doi.org/10.1109/TBIOM.2022.3140472
17. Li, C., Hu, J.: Attacks via record multiplicity on cancelable biometrics templates. Concurrency Comput. Pract. Exper. **26**(8), 1593–1605 (2014)
18. Menezes, A.J., Van Oorschot, P.C., Vanstone, S.A.: Handbook of Applied Cryptography. CRC Press, Boca Raton (2018)
19. Paillier, P.: Public-key cryptosystems based on composite degree residuosity classes. In: Advances in Cryptology, EUROCRYPT, vol. 1592, pp. 233–238. Springer-Verlag, Berlin, LNCS (1999)
20. Pandey, R.K., Zhou, Y., Kota, B.U., Govindaraju, V.: Deep secure encoding for face template protection. In: 2016 IEEE Conference on Computer Vision and Pattern Recognition Workshops (CVPRW), pp. 77–83 (2016). https://doi.org/10.1109/CVPRW.2016.17
21. Pillai, J.K., Patel, V.M., Chellappa, R., Ratha, N.K.: Sectored random projections for cancelable iris biometrics. In: 2010 IEEE International Conference on Acoustics, Speech and Signal Processing, pp. 1838–1841. IEEE, Piscataway (2010)
22. Ratha, N.K., Connell, J.H., Bolle, R.M.: Enhancing security and privacy in biometrics-based authentication systems. IBM Syst. J. **40**(3), 614–634 (2001)
23. Rathgeb, C., Uhl, A.: A survey on biometric cryptosystems and cancelable biometrics. EURASIP J. Inf. Secur. **2011**, 1–25 (2011)
24. Rane, S., Wang, Y., Draper, S.C., Ishwar, P.: Secure biometrics: concepts, authentication architectures, and challenges. IEEE Signal Process. Mag. **30**(5), 51–64 (2013)
25. Roh, J.h., Cho, S., Jin, S.H.: Learning based biometric key generation method using CNN and RNN. In: 2018 10th International Conference on Information Technology and Electrical Engineering (ICITEE), pp. 136–139. IEEE, Piscataway (2018)
26. SC27 IT Security Techniques: ISO/IEC 24745: Biometric Information Protection. International Standards Organization (2011)
27. Shor, P.W.: Polynomial-time algorithms for prime factorization and discrete logarithms on a quantum computer. SIAM Rev. **41**(2), 303–332 (1999)
28. Sutcu, Y., Rane, S., Yedidia, J.S., Draper, S.C., Vetro, A.: Feature extraction for a Slepian-Wolf biometric system using LDPC codes. In: Proceedings of the IEEE International Symposium on Information Theory, Toronto, pp. 2297–2301 (2008)
29. Teoh, A.B.J., Yuang, C.T.: Cancelable biometrics realization with multispace random projections. IEEE Trans. Syst. Man Cybern. B Cybern. **37**(5), 1096–1106 (2007)
30. Teoh, A., Gho, A., Ngo, D.: Random multispace quantization as an analytic mechanism for biohashing of biometric and random identity inputs. IEEE Trans. Pattern Anal. Mach. Intell. **28**(12), 1892–1901 (2006)
31. Van Dijk, M., Gentry, C., Halevi, S., Vaikuntanathan, V.: Fully homomorphic encryption over the integers. Advances in Cryptology–EUROCRYPT, pp. 24–43 (2010)
32. Wang, S., Deng, G., Hu, J.: A partial Hadamard transform approach to the design of cancelable fingerprint templates containing binary biometric representations. Pattern Recogn. **61**, 447–458 (2017)
33. Wang, Y., Rane, S., Draper, S.C., Ishwar, P.: A theoretical analysis of authentication, privacy and reusability across secure biometric systems. IEEE Trans. Inf. Forensics Secur. **7**(6), 1825–1840 (2012)
34. Wicker, S.B.: Error Control Systems for Digital Communication and Storage. Prentice Hall, Englewood Cliffs (1995)
35. Yang, W., Wang, S., Shahzad, M., Zhou, W.: A cancelable biometric authentication system based on feature-adaptive random projection. J. Inf. Secur. Appl. **58**, 102704 (2021)

Chapter 10
Unlinkability Evaluation of Biometric Template Protection Schemes

Marta Gomez-Barrero and Javier Galbally

Abstract In this chapter, we present a comprehensive overview of how the "renewability/unlinkability" criterion, as defined in ISO/IEC 24745, has been evaluated in the literature. First, we highlight the main difference between the renewability and unlinkability properties: Whereas the former considers different templates in the time dimension (i.e., ability to renew the enrolled template in one specific application at different points in time), the latter focuses on the spatial dimension (i.e., templates enrolled in different applications at the same point in time). We subsequently present a classification of existing evaluation approaches into empirical (qualitative and quantitative) and theoretical methodologies, including representative examples. Then we focus on the main empirical quantitative metrics, as these are the most relevant for general benchmarking of different biometric template protection (BTP) schemes. These metrics are described in a high-level manner, their advantages and disadvantages discussed, and the corresponding links to open-source code repositories included.

1 What Are Unlinkability and Renewability?

As stated in ISO/IEC 24745 on biometric information protection [13], irreversibility of protected biometric templates alone is not enough to protect the underlying biometric data. If a template is compromised, an attacker could use it to gain unlawful access to the biometric system and the related services, even if the template is irreversible. Similarly, through the exposure of biometric templates during storage or transmission, an attacker could identify links between subjects across different applications and various systems, in a so-called linkage attack. Thus, after a data

M. Gomez-Barrero (✉)
RI CODE, Universität der Bundeswehr München, Munich, Germany
e-mail: marta.gomez-barrero@unibw.de

J. Galbally
Capability Building Sector, EU Agency eu-LISA, Tallinn, Estonia
e-mail: javier.galbally@eulisa.europa.eu

V. Krivokuća Hahn et al. (eds.), *Handbook of Biometric Template Protection*,
https://doi.org/10.1007/978-981-95-0995-9_10

breach, there is a strong need to revoke the compromised reference(s) to prevent the attacker from future (or continued) unauthorized access and issue new templates. This is analogous to the case of compromised passwords, with the main difference being that biometric characteristics cannot be revoked and renewed. Thus, in order to generate renewable biometric references (RBRs),[1] the RBR creation process should provide diversification. Let us briefly review these concepts in order to achieve a better understanding of renewability and unlinkability within biometric recognition.

Renewability is defined as the "*property of a transform or process to create multiple, unlinkable transformed biometric references derived from one or more biometric samples obtained from the same data subject and which can be used to recognize the individual while not revealing information about the original reference*" [13]. On the other hand, unlinkability refers to the "*property of two or more biometric references that they cannot be linked to each other or to the subject(s) from whom they were derived*" [13]. Thus, both concepts can be understood as implementations of the diversification process in the time (i.e., renewability of the template within the same system after a data leak) and in the space (i.e., unlinkability across multiple applications) domains. As a consequence, the same metrics can be used to analyze both RBR properties, as pointed out in [23]. In the following, we will refer only to unlinkability for the sake of brevity.

Despite the value of the aforementioned definitions, they are too vague for a mathematical or engineering analysis. Thus, Gomez-Barrero et al. presented a more formal definition in [11], which we will use throughout this chapter.

Prior to providing the formal definition of linkability in the following paragraphs, we should note that, given the inherent noisy nature of biometric data, unlinkability cannot be considered as a binary property. It is rather a continuous property, where two RBRs might be more or less linkable. Keeping this in mind, two RBRs, or templates for short, are defined as linkable to a certain degree if it is more likely that they were extracted from the same instance (e.g., right index fingerprint of a given subject) than from different instances (e.g., right index fingerprint of two different subjects).

Following the concept of linkability as a continuous property presented in the previous paragraph, let us now add some mathematical notation to the intuitive definition introduced above. Two biometric samples $\mathbf{M}_i^1$, with $i = 1, 2$, are acquired from the same instance $\mathbf{I}_1$. Then, the features are extracted, and the *pseudonymous identifier encoder* (*PIE*), taking as input both the samples $\mathbf{M}_i^1$ and some application parameters or keys $\mathbf{K}_i$, computes the corresponding reference templates $\mathbf{T}_i = PIE\left(\mathbf{M}_i^1, \mathbf{K}_i\right)$. This process is depicted in Fig. 10.1.

Building upon this concept, we can assume the existence of a so-called *linkage function*, LF, to provide a linkage score between the analyzed templates: $s = LF\left(\mathbf{T}_1, \mathbf{T}_2\right)$. Examples of linkage functions include the similarity score computed by the BTP scheme or any other function exploiting a vulnerability of the system.

[1] The definition of RBR can be found in Part I Chap. 1 of this book.

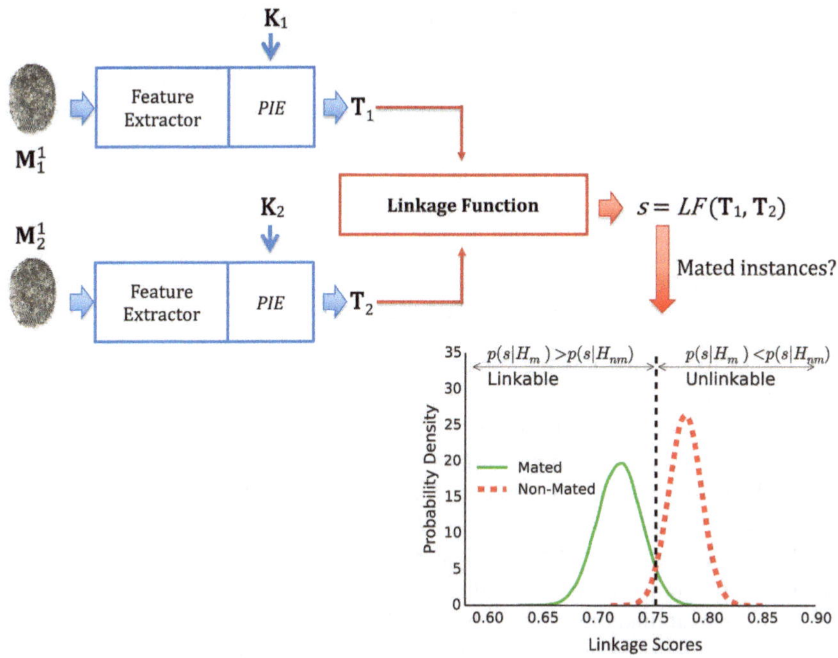

Fig. 10.1 Formal definition of unlinkability, according to [11]. Two samples $\mathbf{M}_i^1$, with $i = \{1, 2\}$, both acquired from the same instance $\mathbf{I}_1$, are presented to a BTP scheme at enrolment. Using different parameters or keys $\mathbf{K}_1, \mathbf{K}_2$, the *pseudonymous identifier encoder* (*PIE*) computes the corresponding reference templates $\mathbf{T}_1, \mathbf{T}_2$. Given a linkage function $s = LF(\mathbf{T}_1, \mathbf{T}_2)$, the templates are considered linkable if $p\,(s|H_m) > p\,(s|H_{nm})$

This score will be used to determine whether both templates stem from the same instance. In other words, a BTP scheme is considered linkable *to some degree* if, given a score $s = LF\,(\mathbf{T}_1, \mathbf{T}_2)$, the likelihood that both templates $\mathbf{T}_1$ and $\mathbf{T}_2$ stem from the same instance is larger than the likelihood that they stem from different instances. This fact can be further formalized using two hypotheses:

$$H_m = \{\text{the two templates come from mated instances}\}$$

$$H_{nm} = \{\text{the two templates come from non-mated instances}\}$$

And two types of score distributions:

- *Mated* instances score distribution: scores s computed from templates that have been extracted from samples acquired from a single instance of the same subject, and protected using different keys:

$$\mathbf{T}_1 = PIE\left(\mathbf{M}_1^1, \mathbf{K}_1\right), \mathbf{T}_2 = PIE\left(\mathbf{M}_2^1, \mathbf{K}_2\right). \qquad (10.1)$$

It represents the conditional probability of obtaining a score s knowing that two templates stem from mated instances, that is, $p\left(s|H_m\right)$.

- *Non-mated* instances score distribution: scores s yielded by templates that have been extracted from samples acquired from different instances, and protected using different keys:

$$\mathbf{T}_1 = PIE\left(\mathbf{M}_1^1, \mathbf{K}_1\right), \mathbf{T}_2 = PIE\left(\mathbf{M}_1^2, \mathbf{K}_2\right). \tag{10.2}$$

It represents the conditional probability of obtaining a score s knowing that two templates stem from non-mated instances, that is, $p\left(s|H_{nm}\right)$.

Thus, the linkability of two given templates, $\mathbf{T}_1$ and $\mathbf{T}_2$, is reduced to the question of whether the linkage score $s = LF\left(\mathbf{T}_1, \mathbf{T}_2\right)$ most likely belongs to the mated or the non-mated instances distribution, as depicted in Fig. 10.1. That is, if for a given score s of the linkage function $p\left(H_m|s\right) > p\left(H_{nm}|s\right)$, then it is more likely that $\mathbf{T}_1$ and $\mathbf{T}_2$ belong to the same instance, and, therefore, the templates are linkable (to some degree). If, on the contrary, $p\left(H_{nm}|s\right) \geq p\left(H_m|s\right)$, then it is more likely that $\mathbf{T}_1$ and $\mathbf{T}_2$ belong to different instances; or, in other words, for that score s, the linkage function would fail to link the two templates. Therefore, it follows that, to have a fully unlinkable system for the whole domain of scores s of the linkage function, there must be a complete overlap between the aforementioned *mated* and *non-mated* instances score distributions.

The question now is how to evaluate such probabilities (i.e., $p\left(H_m|s\right)$ and $p\left(H_{nm}|s\right)$), which will be addressed in the following sections. To that end, we first describe the main unlinkability evaluation methodologies in Sect. 2, both from the perspective of the BTP schemes described in the literature and from the ISO/IEC 30136 standard on performance testing of biometric template protection schemes [16]. We then direct our attention in Sect. 3 to the most common approach, an empirical evaluation, including specific metrics developed following the aforementioned definition of unlinkability. In Sect. 4, we highlight the importance of having standardized evaluation frameworks for biometric template protection schemes. The chapter concludes with a summary in Sect. 5.

2 How to Measure Unlinkability and Renewability?

The ISO/IEC 30136 standard on performance testing of biometric template protection schemes [16] establishes guidelines for the evaluation of biometric template protection schemes, including the unlinkability of protected templates. It differentiates between *theoretical* and *empirical* evaluations.

Theoretical evaluations are inspired by cryptographic proofs: The evaluator shall present a theoretical method to demonstrate unlinkability, for instance, by proving a computational or information-theoretic property limiting the advantage over a random guess of any computationally bounded or unbounded adversary. Existing theoretical evaluation methods proposed in the literature are further reviewed in Sect. 2.2.

On the other hand, in an empirical assessment, the evaluator shall specify an empirical method of demonstrating unlinkability, for example, estimating the adversary's advantage over a random guess in a specific attack scenario. This definition is rather vague, and no further examples of particular empirical metrics are provided in ISO/IEC 30136, which has led to a variety of methods being developed in the literature. Empirical evaluation methods will be reviewed in more detail in Sects. 2.3 and 3.

In addition to the aforementioned evaluation approaches (theoretical and empirical), we can actually find a third type of analysis in some publications, as described by Krivokuća Hahn and Marcel in [23]: *verbal implications*. In this case, only statements are presented implying that unlinkability is satisfied. In general, renewability is claimed to be possible by changing certain (external) parameters, such as the aforementioned **K**, and unlinkability is assumed due to the randomness of these parameters. However, no theoretical or experimental proof is provided to formally validate these implications.

Let us now review the main verbal implications available in the literature, which are summarized in Table 10.1 in the first three rows.

2.1 Verbal Implications

As just mentioned, verbal implications provide less formal or weaker analysis of the unlinkability property than the theoretical and empirical evaluations (that will be reviewed in Sects. 2.2 and 2.3). For instance, systems using homomorphic encryption (HE)[2] to protect biometric templates commonly claim that by changing the key pair, unlinkability is granted [5, 7, 8, 27]. Although the nature of encryption operations suggests that the resulting ciphertexts should be very different, to the best of our knowledge, no formal analysis has been provided to demonstrate the extent of these differences in the context of BTP. Furthermore, the fact that a key leakage would lead to the invertibility of the templates is usually ignored in such approaches.

Newer BTP schemes involve training a neural network[3] or any other form of machine learning algorithm to map a subject's biometric template to a random, predefined binary codeword, which is subsequently cryptographically hashed [18, 28]. Such hashed codewords are thus assumed to have no correlation to the original biometric template, and unlinkability is achieved by changing the user-specific codewords and retraining the neural network. Alternatively, a neural network could be trained to learn its own representation of a protected template, instead of learning

[2] For more information on HE methods for the development of BTP schemes, please read Part II Chap. 6 of this handbook.

[3] For more information on learned BTP methods, please read Part II Chap. 7 of this handbook.

Table 10.1 Summary of the most relevant methodologies reported in the literature for unlinkability assessment and their main properties: (i) type of evaluation that is carried out: verbal implication, theoretical proof, or empirical study (shown vertically on the left-hand side of the table); (ii) whether the evaluation methodology is general enough to be applied to different BTP schemes; (iii) whether linkability is regarded as a continuous characteristic (green tick) or else binary (red cross); (iv) the technical approach behind the proposed metric; and (v) whether the metric is quantitative (✓) or qualitative (✗)

	Ref.	General?	Continuous?	Metric	Quantitative?
Verbal	[8]	✗	✗	Re-encrypt with different keys	✗
	[4]	✗	✗	Retrain DL model	✗
	[35]	✗	✗	No template storage	✗
Theoretical	[33]	✗	✗	Adversary's advantage bio sketches	✓
	[2]	✗	✓	Adversary's advantage QIM	✓
	[3]	✗	✗	Adversary's advantage fuzzy	✓
	[30]	✗	✗	Euclidean distance between fuzzy vaults	✓
Empirical	[1]	✓	–	Score distributions	✗
	[21]	✓	✗	Success rate	✓
	[2]	✓	✗	Accuracy-oriented curves (ROC)	✗
	[19]	✓	✗	Accuracy-oriented curves (ROC)	✗
	[26]	✓	✗	Accuracy-oriented curves (DET)	✗
	[29]	✓	✗	Accuracy-oriented curves (DET)	✗
	[31]	✓	✓	Accuracy-oriented curves (CMC)	✓
	[9]	✓	–	Score distributions	✗
	[36]	✓	–	Score distributions	✗
	[20]	✓	–	Success rate inversion attack	✓
	[11]	✓	✓	Score distributions + LRs	✓
	[32]	✓	✓	Score distributions + ML	✓

a mapping to a predefined code (e.g., [4, 25]). In this case, unlinkability could be achieved by incorporating different user-specific keys or parameters into the learning process, to ensure that the neural network can output different protected templates for the same input (unprotected) template. However, there has been no analysis to demonstrate how scalable the unlinkability effort for neural-network-based BTP methods would be in practice (i.e., in terms of the necessity and frequency of the retraining process, for example, for each new template or after N template renewals). In addition, even if it is usually easy to deduce that using different parameters or assigning new binary codes to a given subject, depending on the specific BTP system under consideration, would result in the generation of a different protected template for the same instance, it is hard to establish whether or not those protected templates would be unlinkable, or the extent of their unlinkability, as in the case of systems based on HE.

Finally, it is claimed in [35] that the lack of template storage means that the protected template cannot be compromised, thereby ensuring unlinkability. However, the possibility of information leakage from the trained model is not considered.

2.2 Theoretical Evaluations

Regarding theoretical evaluations, most case studies have been presented for biometric cryptosystems. In these works, the unlinkability property has been frequently referred to as *indistinguishability* [2, 3, 33], for which the definition is identical to the unlinkability definition included in the corresponding ISO standards [13, 16].

Simoens et al. analyze the unlinkability of biometric sketches in [33], playing the so-called *indistinguishability game*. Assuming the attacker or adversary has obtained a set of sketches, their objective is to identify related sketches. In order to measure their chances of success, they estimate their advantage over a random guess. This is done by setting bounds or computing probabilities that rely on the error correcting codes (ECC) theory, which is fundamental to the development of fuzzy sketches. Therefore, such an analysis cannot be extrapolated to systems based, for instance, on cancelable biometrics approaches. In addition, one of the main limitations of the theoretical derivation is the assumption of handling uniform data, which does not hold for biometric data (since biometric data are not uniform but present high correlation).

A similar approach is followed in [2] for the analysis of quantization index modulation (QIM) biometric cryptosystems. Since "*the concept describes the advantage of an attacker with respect to a perfect indistinguishable system,*" which is hard to achieve in practice due to the inherent correlation of biometric data, the authors propose an alternative practical evaluation in which they benchmark equal error rates (EER) obtained for regular comparisons of templates protected with a single key (i.e., recognition accuracy analysis) against comparisons of templates protected with different keys (i.e., unlinkability analysis). For such comparisons, they adapt the distinguisher function used in [33] for the indistinguishability game. The main drawback of this approach is that, even if an increase of the EER implies some degree of unlinkability of the system (i.e., the system loses discriminative power when different keys are used to protect the templates), the increase in unlinkability is not quantified.

In [3], Buhan et al. consider for the first time a *continuous* value, instead of binary, for the linkability of two given templates for a fuzzy scheme. In other words, unlinkability is regarded as a continuous property, thereby making it possible to assign different *degrees of linkability* to the templates. To that end, they introduce "*a classification function to decide whether the query sketch and the target sketch are related.*" This function is hence used to link templates. Then, the advantage of an eventual attacker over a random guess is theoretically modeled, and a relationship is established with the false match rate (FMR) and false non-match rate (FNMR) of the system. It should be noted that an unrealistic assumption of data uniformity, similar to [33], is made in the theoretical derivation. In addition, the FMR and FNMR are estimated in terms of the verification function of the system, instead of using a linkage function specially tailored to link templates. Thus, such an evaluation would provide an optimistic upper threshold of the real degree of unlinkability.

Simoens et al. proposed in [34] a general framework for the security and privacy analysis of biometric systems. Biometric systems are modeled with four logical entities (i.e., sensor, server, database, and comparator), and security is analyzed assuming different adversary models where some of the aforementioned entities may be malicious. While the information flow and the ability to reconstruct templates are analyzed, no metric or protocol is provided to measure the unlinkability of a given system.

Gilkalaye et al. consider the codewords in a fuzzy commitment scheme as lattice points in [10]. Since those points are spaced sufficiently far apart, the corresponding protected templates (which consist of original templates bound with the codewords) are assumed to be unlinkable. Based on a similar assumption, Rathgeb et al. present in [30] a theoretical analysis showing that the probability of correlating two fuzzy vaults from the same subject using the extended Euclidean algorithm is negligible. Finally, Lee et al. estimate the number of cancelable protected templates that can be generated from a single facial image in [24]. It should be noted, however, that this is probably an over-optimistic upper bound for unlinkability, since there is no test of whether those different templates are truly unlinkable.

2.3 *Empirical Evaluations*

Whereas ad hoc theoretical methodologies, such as the ones described in Sect. 2.2, can be useful to analyze a given BTP scheme, such approaches suffer from a number of disadvantages and are not sufficient to establish a fair benchmark across different systems. Thus, in the following, we focus on general metrics, applicable to any system. To date, these metrics are only of empirical nature.

The first attempts to provide an empirical evaluation of the unlinkability of protected biometric templates were based on specific cross-matching attacks (which can also be considered as a *linkage function*) in order to link templates produced by several template protection schemes, and analyzed the threat posed in terms of their chances of success. For instance, in [1], the score distributions for regular and attacking comparisons are depicted, but no quantitative measure of the linkability is provided. Just a qualitative, visual, estimation can be extracted from the depicted distributions. These kinds of approaches are thus referred to as qualitative in this chapter. In [21], a linkage attack against fuzzy vault schemes is proposed. However, in this case, due to the time-consuming nature of the attack, only ten vaults are analyzed, reporting an attack success rate of 40%.

Kelkboom et al. present a practical evaluation of the robustness of a fuzzy commitment scheme to several linkage attacks in [19]. To that end, and following the approach presented in [2] for the EERs, the receiver operating characteristic (ROC) curves of the system for the accuracy and unlinkability evaluations are compared: If the accuracy shown by the ROC curves decreases, then the system is assumed to be unlinkable. Therefore, the authors assume that there is a direct relationship between FMR and FNMR of the attack and the unlinkability of the templates, rather than analyzing the scores produced by the attacking function directly. In addition, the extracted bits are assumed to be independent with equal bit-error probability, a fact that does not always hold in biometric data due to its inherent correlation. In a similar manner, Nagar et al. analyze the unlinkability of a biometric template protection scheme in [26], where the error rates for the unlinkability analysis are referred to as cross match rate (CMR) and false cross match rate (FCMR).

Following this same concept of using accuracy curves, Piciucco et al. define in [29] the renewable template matching rate (RTMR) as the percentage of correctly linked templates. For the evaluation, a detection error trade-off (DET)-like curve is depicted, where the FNMR is shown for each RTMR for a subset of the database used in the experimental evaluation. In this case, mated scores for the FNMR are computed, comparing templates protected with the *same key* and extracted from the same instance, whereas non-mated scores for the RTMR are obtained from the comparison of templates protected with *different keys* and extracted from different instances. The authors point out that the FNMR *vs*. RTMR curve should be similar to the common DET curve (FNMR *vs*. FMR) to indicate that matching templates protected with different keys are at least as hard as achieving a false match with templates obtained from different subjects. Therefore, if the curves are visually similar, unlinkability is obtained. Whereas this is a valid point, there is again no quantitative evaluation of the degree of unlinkability of the protected templates.

In [31], a linkage function based on principal components regression is defined for fuzzy commitment systems using universal background models (UBM). Building upon this linkage function, the attacker decides what is the identity hidden by both templates. In order to measure linkability, the authors focus on the probability that the attacker chooses the correct identity in a top-N list, and how this probability deviates from a random guess (full unlinkability). In other words, the authors analyze the variation of the cumulative match curves (CMC) used to evaluate the accuracy of closed-set identification biometric systems.

These accuracy-based approaches can hide the degree of template linkability for specific subsets of scores, since they only consider accumulated values or even a single figure for the unlinkability of the whole system. This means that a system might be unlinkable on average, but be very vulnerable for a small set of scores. The subjects whose templates would fall within this set would thus not be adequately protected. In contrast to those approaches, [9, 36] have addressed the problem of unlinkability evaluation by directly analyzing the similarity scores. In [9], Ferrara et al. consider three sets of score distributions resulting from the comparison of templates enrolled in different applications using different secret keys. More specifically, templates were extracted from (i) the same sample of a given instance (e.g., a unique sample of the right index finger of a given subject), (ii) different samples of the same instance (e.g., two different samples of the right index finger of a given subject), or (iii) samples of different instances (e.g., two different samples of two different fingers). The analysis in [36] focuses only on the last two distributions, which are most likely to occur in a real-world scenario. In both works, only a visual benchmark between the score distributions is carried out, presumably due to the lack of an appropriate metric to provide a quantitative analysis.

Continuing this analysis of score distributions, Lee et al. [24] compare genuine, impostor, and mated-impostor distributions. The genuine scores are computed as in a normal verification scenario, using the same transformation parameters for all subjects. The mated-impostor and impostor scores are computed using different parameters, thus corresponding to the mated and non-mated scores described in Sect. 1. Since these two last distributions overlapped to a large extent, the templates were considered unlinkable. Similar evaluations were also presented in [6, 37].

Finally, Keller et al. [20] based their unlinkability analysis of fuzzy commitment schemes on the success rate of an inverse biometrics attack, also known as template inversion attack. Even if such an approach is general, and could be applied to any system, it should be noted that it only provides a lower bound to the unlinkability of the templates: Carrying out an inversion attack is harder than just linking templates without gaining further relevant information about the underlying biometric data.

3 Quantitative Evaluation Frameworks: Likelihood Ratios and Maximal Information Leakage

The two most notable and complete proposals in the literature of quantitative evaluation frameworks to objectively measure linkability of BTP approaches are the likelihood ratios framework presented in [11] and the maximal information leakage framework presented in [32]. Given their relevance, and that these have become, de facto, the two most used approaches for linkability assessment, in this section, we present the two schemes in detail in Sects. 3.1 and 3.2, and we continue with a comparison of their advantages and limitations in Sect. 3.3.

3.1 Likelihood Ratios

Gomez-Barrero et al. proposed in [11] a general framework to evaluate the unlinkability of RBRs, which has been adopted in numerous unlinkability evaluations since its publication, and has been included in ISO/IEC WD 30136 on performance testing of BTP schemes [16] as a set of metrics that can be used for empirical evaluations of the unlinkability criterion. This framework was inspired by the works of Ferrara et al. in [9, 36], considering only the two distributions defined in Sect. 1: The mated $p(s|H_m)$ and the non-mated $p(s|H_{nm})$ instances score distributions. Following the discussion at the end of Sect. 1, two different measures for the linkability of biometric templates are defined:

- Local measure $\mathrm{D}_{\leftrightarrow}(s)$ to evaluate the linkability of the templates on a score-wise basis
- Global measure $\mathrm{D}_{\leftrightarrow}^{sys}$ to give an overall measure of the linkability of the whole system, independent of the score domain of the system at hand, thereby allowing a benchmark across different systems

$\mathrm{D}_{\leftrightarrow}(s) \in [0, 1]$ evaluates the linkability of a system for each *specific linkage score* s. As such, this metric is appropriate to analyze within one system in which segments of the score domain it fails to provide unlinkability. If for a specific score s_1, a system yields $\mathrm{D}_{\leftrightarrow}(s_1) = 1$, it means that, *in case* the linkage function produced s_1, we would be able to link templates $\mathbf{T}_1$ and $\mathbf{T}_2$ to the same instance with almost full certainty. On the other hand, $\mathrm{D}_{\leftrightarrow}(s_0) = 0$ should be interpreted as full unlinkability for that particular score s_0. In other words, *if* s_0 were produced by the linkage function, it would be more likely that the two templates stemmed from different instances, hence failing to link them to a single data subject. All intermediate values of $\mathrm{D}_{\leftrightarrow}(s)$ between 0 and 1 represent an increasing degree of linkability.

The key to the success of linking two templates lies in determining whether, given a score s, it is more likely that the two templates that were compared (and resulted in s) stem from mated instances than from non-mated instances; that is, whether $p(H_m|s) > p(H_{nm}|s)$ for a given score s. Therefore, such linkability can be accounted for in terms of the difference of conditional probabilities of each hypothesis H_m and H_{nm} for a given score s:

$$\mathrm{D}_{\leftrightarrow}(s) = p(H_m|s) - p(H_{nm}|s)\,. \tag{10.3}$$

Since any score s must belong to either the *mated* or the *non-mated* instances distribution, we have $p(H_{nm}|s) = 1 - p(H_m|s)$ and can thus rewrite Eq. 10.3 as

$$\mathrm{D}_{\leftrightarrow}(s) = 2 \cdot p(H_m|s) - 1. \tag{10.4}$$

However, these two conditional a posteriori probabilities are unknown. What can be computed a priori, and is known for each BTP system and linkage function, is the *mated* and *non-mated instances score* distributions (i.e., $p(s|H_m)$ and $p(s|H_{nm})$). Let us thus see how we can compute $\mathrm{D}_{\leftrightarrow}(s) \in [0, 1]$ in terms of these known distributions.

Using Bayes theorem on the definition of likelihood ratios, we obtain the following:

$$LR(s) = \frac{\frac{p(H_m|s)\cdot \cancel{p(s)}}{p(H_m)}}{\frac{p(H_{nm}|s)\cdot \cancel{p(s)}}{p(H_{nm})}} = \frac{p(H_m|s)}{p(H_{nm}|s)} \cdot \frac{p(H_{nm})}{p(H_m)}. \tag{10.5}$$

By defining $\omega = p(H_m)/p(H_{nm})$ as the ratio between the unknown prior probabilities of the *mated instances* and *non-mated instances* score distributions, Eq. 10.5 can be formulated as follows:

$$p(H_m|s) = LR(s) \cdot p(H_{nm}|s) \cdot \omega = LR(s) \cdot (1 - p(H_m|s)) \cdot \omega \Leftrightarrow \tag{10.6}$$

$$p(H_m|s) = \frac{LR(s) \cdot \omega}{1 + LR(s) \cdot \omega}. \tag{10.7}$$

Combining Eqs. 10.4 and 10.7, the local linkability measure is computed as

$$\mathrm{D}_{\leftrightarrow}(s) = 2\frac{LR(s) \cdot \omega}{1 + LR(s) \cdot \omega} - 1. \tag{10.8}$$

It should now be noted that, if $LR(s) \cdot \omega \le 1$ (i.e., $p(H_m|s) \le p(H_{nm}|s)$), we can deduce, with some certainty, that the two templates do *not* belong to the same instance. As a consequence, we cannot link both templates to the same data subject. In that case, $\mathrm{D}_{\leftrightarrow}(s)$ yields a negative value, and hence, the system is not linkable for that score. However, in order to have a single measure for template unlinkability, a single value for this range of scores would be desired: $\mathrm{D}_{\leftrightarrow}(s) = 0 \quad \forall s \mid LR(s) \cdot \omega \le 1$. This leads to the final definition of $\mathrm{D}_{\leftrightarrow}(s)$ in [11] as a two-part function, depending on the value of the corresponding $LR(s) \cdot \omega$, as follows:

$$\mathrm{D}_{\leftrightarrow}(s) = \begin{cases} 0 & \text{if } LR(s) \cdot \omega \le 1 \\ 2\frac{LR(s) \cdot \omega}{1 + LR(s) \cdot \omega} - 1 & \text{if } LR(s) \cdot \omega > 1. \end{cases} \tag{10.9}$$

Building upon this local measure, a global metric $\mathrm{D}_{\leftrightarrow}^{sys} \in [0, 1]$ is also introduced in [11], which gives an estimation of the global linkability of a system, *independently* of the score. This way, if a system has $\mathrm{D}_{\leftrightarrow}^{sys} = 1$ (i.e., case in which the *mated instances* and *non-mated instances* score distributions have no overlap, as shown in Fig. 10.2c), it means that it is fully linkable for all the scores of the *mated instances* score distribution domain (i.e., where $\mathrm{D}_{\leftrightarrow}(s) = 1$). That is, if we evaluate the linkage function on two protected templates $\mathbf{T}_1$ and $\mathbf{T}_2$, we can decide (with almost full certainty) whether or not they correspond to the same instance. Similarly, $\mathrm{D}_{\leftrightarrow}^{sys} = 0$ (i.e., Fig. 10.2a, where the two score distributions totally overlap) means that the system is fully unlinkable for the whole score domain. That is, independently of the score produced by the linkage function, it is equally probable that the two templates stem from the same instance (H_m) or from different instances (H_{nm}). All intermediate values of $\mathrm{D}_{\leftrightarrow}^{sys}$ between 0 and 1 report a decreasing degree of unlinkability (i.e., increasing degree of linkability).

Following the discussion above, we want to measure how likely it is that the linkage function LF produces a score belonging to the *mated instances* scores distribution. This can be achieved by computing the difference $p(H_m \cap s) - p(H_{nm} \cap s)$ and integrating it over the whole score domain:

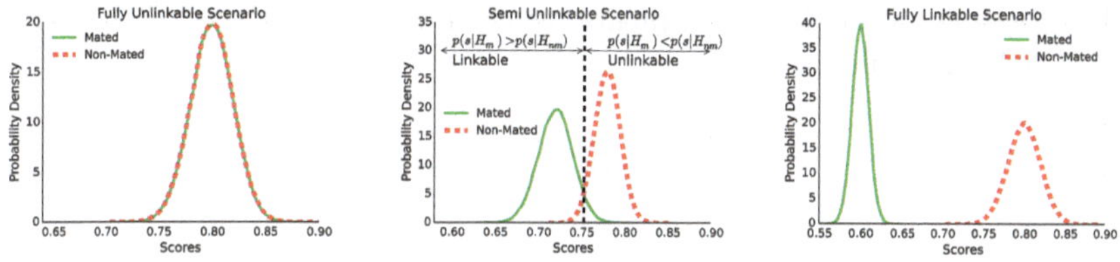

(a) (b) (c)

Fig. 10.2 Examples of *mated instances* (solid green) and *non-mated instances* (dashed red) score distributions yielded by (**a**) fully unlinkable, (**b**) semi-linkable, and (**c**) fully linkable templates. In the middle, (**b**), we can see the linkable score domain, where $p(H_m|s) > p(H_{nm}|s)$, in contrast to the unlinkable domain $p(H_m|s) < p(H_{nm}|s)$, based on computable posteriori probabilities (Source: [11])

$$
\begin{aligned}
&\int p(H_m \cap s) - p(H_{nm} \cap s)\, \mathrm{d}s = \\
&\int p(s) \cdot (p(H_m|s) - p(H_{nm}|s))\, \mathrm{d}s = \\
p(H_m) &\int p(s|H_m) \cdot (p(H_m|s) - p(H_{nm}|s))\, \mathrm{d}s + \\
p(H_{nm}) &\int p(s|H_{nm}) \cdot (p(H_m|s) - p(H_{nm}|s))\, \mathrm{d}s.
\end{aligned}
\tag{10.10}
$$

The second equality holds since $p(s) = p(s|H_m) \cdot p(H_m) + p(s|H_{nm}) \cdot p(H_{nm})$.

Regarding the success of linking two templates, we are only interested in the first addend, that is, in the probabilities stemming from the *mated instances* distribution, since those scores are the ones leading to the successful linkage of two templates. In contrast, the *non-mated instances* distribution reveals information about templates that cannot be linked to a single subject for that particular linkage function, thereby not endangering the privacy of the subjects. Furthermore, as in the definition of the local linkability measure $\mathrm{D}_{\leftrightarrow}(s)$, two templates can be linked only if $p(H_m|s) > p(H_{nm}|s)$. Therefore, we define $\mathrm{D}_{\leftrightarrow}^{sys}$ as

$$
\mathrm{D}_{\leftrightarrow}^{sys} = \int_{\substack{p(H_m|s) > \\ p(H_{nm}|s)}} p(s|H_m) \cdot (p(H_m|s) - p(H_{nm}|s))\, \mathrm{d}s, \tag{10.11}
$$

where the first addend in Eq. 10.10 has been normalized by $p(H_m)$ in order to obtain a measure independent of the prior probability.

Keeping this in mind, we can finally rewrite Eq. 10.11 in terms of $\mathrm{D}_{\leftrightarrow}(s)$ and $p(s|H_m)$, hence defining $\mathrm{D}_{\leftrightarrow}^{sys}$ as

$$\mathrm{D}_{\leftrightarrow}^{sys} = \int p(s|H_m) \cdot \mathrm{D}_{\leftrightarrow}(s)\, \mathrm{d}s. \tag{10.12}$$

This way, the final value of $\mathrm{D}_{\leftrightarrow}^{sys}$ depends on: (i) the range of scores where the system is linkable (determined by $\mathrm{D}_{\leftrightarrow}(s)$); (ii) how linkable the system is in that domain of scores (given by $\mathrm{D}_{\leftrightarrow}(s)$); and (iii) how probable it is that such scores are produced (given by $p(s|H_m)$). As a result, this new global measure assigns different levels of linkability to intermediate scenarios, as opposed to producing only "fully unlinkable" or "fully linkable" verdicts.

The code for this unlinkability framework, including both the local and global measures, is available at: https://github.com/dasec/unlinkability-metric.

3.2 Maximal Information Leakage

Shahreza et al. followed the paradigm described in Sect. 3.1 and proposed a new unlinkability metric in [32] based on the concept of maximal information leakage. Given two jointly distributed random variables X and Y, where X represents some secret information which may be of interest to an adversary, and Y represents the actual observations of an adversary, the maximal leakage, $\mathcal{L}(X \to Y)$, is defined as the multiplicative increase, upon observing Y, of the probability of correctly guessing a randomized function of X, maximized over all such randomized functions [17]. In simpler words, $\mathcal{L}(X \to Y)$ defines the maximal increase of information that Y gives a potential attacker about X, for any possible Y. As it happened before with the probabilities in Eq. 10.3, maximal leakage is not directly computable. However, it is shown in [17] that, for discrete X and Y, maximal leakage can be evaluated via the following simple formula:

$$\mathcal{L}(X \to Y) = \log \sum_{y \in Y} \max_{x \in X : p_X(x) > 0} p_{Y|X}(y|x) \tag{10.13}$$

Which can be extended to continuous variables as:

$$\mathcal{L}(X \to Y) = \log \int_{y \in Y} p_{Y|X}(y|x) \mathrm{d}y. \tag{10.14}$$

In order to use maximal leakage to measure biometric unlinkability, Shahreza et al. then define the following random variables:

- Templates $(\mathbf{T_1}, \mathbf{T_2})$ are random variables taking values in $(\mathcal{T}_1, \mathcal{T}_2)$.
- H is a random variable taking values in $\mathcal{H} = \{H_m, H_{nm}\}$, the two hypotheses defined in Sect. 1.

Then, the maximal leakage metric is defined as

$$\begin{aligned} \mathrm{M}_{\leftrightarrow}^{sys} &= \mathcal{L}\left(H \rightarrow (\mathcal{T}_1, \mathcal{T}_2)\right) \\ &= \log \sum_{\mathbf{T}_1, \mathbf{T}_2 \in \mathcal{T}_1, \mathcal{T}_2} \max\left\{p\left(\mathbf{T}_1, \mathbf{T}_2 | H_m\right), p\left(\mathbf{T}_1, \mathbf{T}_2 | H_{nm}\right)\right\}. \end{aligned} \tag{10.15}$$

To compute $\mathrm{M}_{\leftrightarrow}^{sys}$, it is necessary to know $p\left(\mathbf{T}_1, \mathbf{T}_2 | H_m\right), p\left(\mathbf{T}_1, \mathbf{T}_2 | H_{nm}\right)$ for all possible values of $(\mathbf{T}_1, \mathbf{T}_2) \in (\mathcal{T}_1, \mathcal{T}_2)$, which is prohibitive in a practical setting in terms of computational costs (i.e., it would be comparable to a brute force attack on a large space). Thus, a similar approach to [11] is followed by proposing a linkage function $s = LF(\mathbf{T}_1, \mathbf{T}_2)$, with s taking values in $\mathcal{S}$, and defining:

$$\mathrm{M}_{\leftrightarrow}^{s} = \mathcal{L}\left(H \rightarrow LF\right) = \log \int_{\mathcal{S}} \max\left\{p\left(s | H_m\right), p\left(s | H_{nm}\right)\right\} \mathrm{d}s, \tag{10.16}$$

where $0 \leq \mathrm{M}_{\leftrightarrow}^{s} \leq \mathrm{M}_{\leftrightarrow}^{sys} \leq 1$.

In addition to being a bounded metric, the authors show that the unlinkability metric is also related to verification accuracy as follows:

$$(1 - \mathrm{FMR}) + (1 - \mathrm{FNMR}) \leq 2^{\mathrm{M}_{\leftrightarrow}^{s}}, \tag{10.17}$$

thereby guaranteeing that an adversary cannot decide, based on an observed similarity score s, whether the templates stem from mated or non-mated instances, regardless of what linkage function is used.

This metric is available at https://gitlab.idiap.ch/bob/bob.paper.tifs2023_linkability_ml.

3.3 Likelihood Ratios vs. Maximal Information Leakage

As mentioned in Sects. 3.1 and 3.2, the methods proposed by Gomez-Barrero et al. [11] and Shahreza et al. [32] both build upon the same hypotheses and definitions of the unlinkability criterion, yielding a quantitative and continuous analysis of this key property of BTP schemes. The main difference between the two frameworks lies in how these metrics are defined.

Gomez-Barrero et al. [11] base their computations on the estimation of likelihood ratios between the *mated instances* and the *non-mated instances* score distributions of the linkage function LF, defining two templates as linkable if it is more likely that they belong to the *mated* than to the *non-mated* instances distribution. In contrast, Shahreza et al. [32] build upon the concept of maximal information leakage between the aforementioned distributions, or the amount of information leaked by the linkage function about the underlying protected templates.

In spite of the different conceptual evaluations of these properties, there is a direct correlation between the resulting global metrics. Shahreza et al. show in their work that

$$0 \leq \mathrm{D}_{\leftrightarrow}^{s} \leq \mathrm{M}_{\leftrightarrow}^{s} \leq \mathrm{M}_{\leftrightarrow}^{sys} \leq 1 \tag{10.18}$$

and support this claim with the evaluation of several BTP schemes. In the experiments, it can be observed that $\mathrm{D}_{\leftrightarrow}^{s} \approx \alpha \mathrm{M}_{\leftrightarrow}^{s}$ with a factor of $\alpha = 0.3 \pm 0.05$. Thus, both metrics provide similar global degrees of linkability for a given system, up to a scaling factor of around 0.3, computed from different perspectives: Either probabilities and likelihood ratios, or information leakage from an information-theoretic angle.

Another difference between the two frameworks is the existence of local measures. To provide a full unlinkability analysis, [11] present both a local metric to evaluate the linkability of a given system in a specific range of scores $\mathrm{D}_{\leftrightarrow}(s)$ and a general metric to evaluate the overall linkability of a system in its full score domain $\mathrm{D}_{\leftrightarrow}^{sys}$. This allows for a detailed evaluation of a single system based on $\mathrm{D}_{\leftrightarrow}(s)$, and for a straightforward benchmarking across different systems utilizing $\mathrm{D}_{\leftrightarrow}^{sys}$. In contrast, only a global metric is described in [32]. This could lead to the aforementioned issue that, if a system is on average unlinkable but linkable for a small subset of scores, some templates might not be adequately protected and that would remain hidden within the global measure $\mathrm{M}_{\leftrightarrow}^{s}$. In contrast, $\mathrm{D}_{\leftrightarrow}(s)$ would help us visualize this issue.

4 Why Is It Important to Have Standardized Evaluation Frameworks for Biometric Template Protection Schemes?

As already pointed out, linkability and renewability are two of the key parameters that define the level of privacy and data protection offered by biometric systems by design. As in any other area related to the overall performance of this technology, being able to properly and objectively evaluate such parameters is of paramount importance for the continuous improvement of the technology. We may find a clear parallel to other more advanced areas within the biometrics field, where the development of standardized evaluation frameworks has been key to the progress of biometric recognition, for instance: accuracy evaluation [12], assessment of vulnerability to attacks [14], or estimation of data quality [15]. The existence of clear, well-defined, and theoretically sound metrics and protocols in all these areas is essential for a number of reasons:

- **System improvement and benchmarking**: Specific metrics help identify and quantify limitations of the systems in different areas, allowing for targeted improvements to reduce inaccuracies. Organizations can benchmark their biometric systems against industry standards, enabling them to understand how their systems stack up against others and identify areas for improvement.

- **System performance comparison**: Evaluation frameworks allow for uniform comparison of system performance across different platforms and applications. This consistency ensures that comparisons between systems are meaningful (and as objective and fair as reasonably possible). Furthermore, evaluation metrics and protocols provide the basis for independent competitive evaluations to be organized, which are a reliable source of algorithmic rankings based on data-driven independent evidence, such as the ones generated by NIST.[4,5,6,7,8]
- **State-of-the-art monitoring**: The development of evaluation metrics is essential to keep track of the evolution of a given technology over time. It allows us to determine, in an objective fashion, the real progress made in the state of the art for one specific area (e.g., the increase in data protection due to unlinkability).
- **Innovation**: Metrics and benchmarks provide a foundation for R&D efforts, enabling researchers to systematically explore and enhance various aspects of biometric technology, tracking progress and identifying areas for innovation.
- **Trust and transparency**: Standardized evaluations provide transparency regarding the performance and reliability of biometric systems, as they bring clear explainable independent evidence of their performance (as currently requested by the EU AI Act, for instance). As a result, being able to perform these evaluations helps to increase the trust and acceptance of the end users, as they support the claims made by developers and they increase the understanding of the systems. In consequence, it contributes to the adoption and wider deployment of biometric technology.

Moreover, in addition to having technically sound, solid, and proven evaluation frameworks, another key element that should not be neglected is the importance of standardizing those frameworks. Standard benchmarks promote vendor neutrality by ensuring that products from different vendors can be compared and integrated based on common performance criteria. As such, the standardization process fosters collaboration among all interested parties in the advancement of biometric technology, providing interoperability, and helping to avoid vendor lock-in situations.

To sum up, we can say that the absence of comprehensive testing of biometric technology can lead to vulnerabilities, decreased performance, and a failure to meet user expectations. Testing biometric systems is not optional, but it is a nonnegotiable need. Biometric template protection schemes are no exception to this rule. In this regard, the different approaches reviewed in Sect. 2, and especially the frameworks

---

[4] NIST Fingerprint evaluations: https://www.nist.gov/programs-projects/fingerprint

[5] NIST Face evaluations: https://www.nist.gov/programs-projects/face-projects

[6] NIST Speaker evaluations: https://www.nist.gov/programs-projects/speaker-and-language-recognition

[7] LivDet PAD evaluations for iris, face, and fingerprint: https://www.livdet.org/

[8] ASVspoof evaluation on voice PAD: https://www.asvspoof.org/

presented in Sect. 3 of the present chapter, are of key relevance for the future development of the BTP domain.

5 Conclusion

In this chapter, we have introduced a formal definition of the unlinkability property of BTP schemes, based on the work presented in [11], as a starting point to the subsequent discussion on how to evaluate this key concept. As we can see in Table 10.1, BTP evaluations have considered unlinkability only in the last 15 years. However short, in this time, different approaches have emerged to fill this gap: (i) verbal implications derived from, e.g., cryptographic properties of the system at hand, (ii) theoretical estimations of the adversary's advantage for a particular system, or (iii) more general empirical analysis, mostly based on the evaluation of some kind of linkage function. Although all of these approaches are valuable contributions, these techniques share some common shortcomings, as highlighted in red in Table 10.1. To tackle these issues, Gomez-Barrero et al. proposed in [11] a general framework to evaluate the unlinkability of RBRs based on the estimation of likelihood ratios between the two probabilities described in Sect. 1, i.e., the *mated instances* and the *non-mated instances* score distributions. The authors of [11] propose both a local metric to evaluate the linkability of a given system in a specific range of scores $\mathrm{D}_{\leftrightarrow}(s)$ and a general metric to evaluate the overall linkability of a system in its full score domain $\mathrm{D}_{\leftrightarrow}^{sys}$. This framework, which has demonstrated great potential to compare the linkability level across different systems, has been widely accepted by the biometrics community and is present in the vast majority of empirical evaluations measuring the unlinkability of BTP schemes in the literature. Furthermore, it will be included as an example of metrics that can be used for unlinkability evaluation in the current review cycle of ISO/IEC 30136 on performance testing of BTP schemes [16].

More recently, Shahreza et al. [32] presented an alternative unlinkability metric by moving the basis of the evaluation from probability theory to information theory. They estimate maximal information leakage between the aforementioned distributions in order to provide a global metric $\mathrm{M}_{\leftrightarrow}^{sys}$ for the degree of unlinkability of the system.

Both metrics ultimately rely on the score computation of a given linkage function and estimate the underlying score distributions for a number of different keys or parameters $\mathbf{K}_i$. As in other works, it is assumed that those keys are appropriately selected. Building a comparison with passwords, we should not select two keys whose only difference is a single bit. However, as shown by Kirchgasser et al. in [22], there is still an urgent need to define how to *properly* select those keys in order to truly achieve unlinkability. This is still an open challenge to be addressed in the near future. Another open question is whether it is possible to evaluate the unlinkability criterion based on information other than linkage scores, thereby generalizing the analysis to any possible linkage function.

Another issue, so far not studied in depth in the literature, is the estimation of the number of times that a given protected template can be renewed. It is clear that this number is considerably smaller than the whole key space, since choosing particular keys may lead to very similar templates as shown in [22]. Even if it is hard to calculate this number in a fair manner, we believe that it remains a relevant question, given that it would also serve as an upper and more realistic bound of the unlinkability of a given system: It would provide us with at least an estimation of the number of keys that are "usable" or "adequate" to protect the templates, and in a more optimistic assumption, it would even indicate *which* keys exactly can be used.

Finally, we would like to highlight once again the importance of standardized evaluations of any given system in order to ensure its reliability, accuracy, security, and privacy protection values. For the particular case of biometric recognition, NIST has set an example by evaluating different aspects of face, fingerprint, or voice recognition, not limited to recognition accuracy but also focused on other aspects such as morphing attack detection. Similarly, the LivDet or ASVspoof series have focused on the evaluation of PAD modules. However, there is still no standardized evaluation of BTP schemes, probably due to the absence of standardized metrics in the past. This chapter and book should thus serve as a wake-up call for the biometrics community to start these evaluations for BTP schemes as well.

6 Summary

- Renewability: "*property of a transform or process to create multiple, unlinkable transformed biometric references derived from one or more biometric samples obtained from the same data subject and which can be used to recognize the individual while not revealing information about the original reference*" [13].
- Unlinkability: "*property of two or more biometric references that they cannot be linked to each other or to the subject(s) from whom they were derived*" [13].
- Standardized evaluation of all properties of BTP schemes needs to be carried out, including the unlinkability criterion. There is thus a need for standardized, general, quantitative metrics for each criterion to be evaluated.
- Most theoretical evaluations rely upon assumptions such as bit uniformity, not valid for biometric data, and are not generalizable to further BTP schemes.
- Gomez-Barrero et al. proposed in [11] a general framework to evaluate the unlinkability of RBRs based on the estimation of likelihood ratios between the *mated instances* and the *non-mated instances* score distributions. The framework includes both a local metric to evaluate the linkability of a given system in a specific range of scores and a general metric to evaluate the overall linkability of a system in its full score domain.
- Shahreza et al. proposed in [32] an alternative unlinkability metric by estimating maximal information leakage between the aforementioned distributions in order to provide a global unlinkability metric.

7 Study Questions

1. What is the difference between renewability and unlinkability? Can we use the same metrics to evaluate those criteria?
2. What is the benefit of a continuous instead of a binary unlinkability metric?
3. What properties should a BTP evaluation metric have in order to be useful for standardized evaluations?
4. What is the main difference between the metrics proposed in [11] and [32]?
5. What are the main similarities between the metrics proposed in [11] and [32]?
6. Why is it important to develop standardized evaluation frameworks in the field of biometrics in general, and for BTP in particular?

References

1. Bringer, J., Morel, C., Rathgeb, C.: Security analysis of bloom filter-based iris biometric template protection. In: 2015 International Conference on Biometrics (ICB), pp. 527–534. IEEE, Piscataway (2015)
2. Buhan, I., Breebaart, J., Guajardo, J., et al.: A quantitative analysis of indistinguishability for a continuous domain biometric cryptosystem. In: Proceedings of the International Conference on Data Privacy Management and Autonomous Spontaneous Security, DPM/SETOP, pp. 78–92 (2009)
3. Buhan, I., Merchan, J., Kelkboom, E.: Efficient strategies for playing the indistinguishability game for fuzzy sketches. In: Proceedings of the International Workshop on Information Forensics and Security (WIFS) (2010)
4. Cui, J., Teoh, A.B.J.: Deep index-of-maximum hashing for face template protection. In: 2020 5th International Conference on Computer and Communication Systems (ICCCS), pp. 413–418. IEEE, Piscataway (2020)
5. Dang, T.M., Tran, L., Nguyen, T.D., Choi, D.: Fehash: full entropy hash for face template protection. In: Proceedings of the IEEE/CVF Conference on Computer Vision and Pattern Recognition Workshops (CVPRW), pp. 810–811 (2020)
6. Dong, X., Wong, K., Jin, Z., Dugelay, J.l.: A cancellable face template scheme based on nonlinear multi-dimension spectral hashing. In: IEEE International Workshop on Biometrics and Forensics (IWBF), pp. 1–6 (2019)
7. Drozdowski, P., Buchmann, N., Rathgeb, C., Margraf, M., Busch, C.: On the application of homomorphic encryption to face identification. In: Proceedings of the IEE International Conference of the Biometrics Special Interest Group (BIOSIG), pp. 1–5 (2019)
8. Engelsma, J.J., Jain, A.K., Boddeti, V.N.: HERS: homomorphically encrypted representation search. IEEE Trans. Biomet. Behav. Identity Sci. **4**(3), 349–360 (2022)
9. Ferrara, M., Maltoni, D., Cappelli, R.: A two-factor protection scheme for MCC fingerprint templates. In: Proceedings of the BIOSIG (2014)
10. Gilkalaye, B.P., Rattani, A., Derakhshani, R.: Euclidean-distance based fuzzy commitment scheme for biometric template security. In: Proceedings of the IEEE International Workshop on Biometrics and Forensics (IWBF), pp. 1–6 (2019)
11. Gomez-Barrero, M., Galbally, J., Rathgeb, C., Busch, C.: General framework to evaluate unlinkability in biometric template protection systems. IEEE Trans. Inform. Forensics Secur. **13**(6), 1406–1420 (2017)
12. ISO/IEC JTC1 SC37 Biometrics: ISO/IEC 19795-1:2021. Information Technology – Biometric Performance Testing and Reporting – Part 1: Principles and Framework. International Organi-

zation for Standardization and International Electrotechnical Committee (2021)
13. ISO/IEC JTC1 SC27 Security Techniques: ISO/IEC 24745:2022. Information Technology - Security Techniques - Biometric Information Protection. International Organization for Standardization (2022)
14. ISO/IEC JTC1 SC37 Biometrics: ISO/IEC 30107-1:2022. Information Technology - Biometric Presentation Attack Detection - Part 1: Framework. International Organization for Standardization (2023)
15. ISO/IEC JTC1 SC37 Biometrics: ISO/IEC 29794-4:2024. Information Technology - Biometric Sample Quality - Part 4: Finger Image Data. International Organization for Standardization (2024)
16. ISO/IEC JTC1 SC37 Biometrics: ISO/IEC WD 30136. Information Technology - Performance testing of biometric template protection schemes. International Organization for Standardization (2024)
17. Issa, I., Wagner, A.B., Kamath, S.: An operational approach to information leakage. IEEE Trans. Inform. Theory **66**(3), 1625–1657 (2019)
18. Jindal, A.K., Chalamala, S., Jami, S.K.: Face template protection using deep convolutional neural network. In: 2018 IEEE/CVF Conference on Computer Vision and Pattern Recognition Workshops (CVPRW), pp. 575–5758 (2018). https://doi.org/10.1109/CVPRW.2018.00087
19. Kelkboom, E.J.C., Breebaart, J., Kevenaar, T.A.M., Buhan, I., Veldhuis, R.N.J.: Preventing the decodability attack based cross-matching in a fuzzy commitment scheme. IEEE Trans. Inf. Forensics Secur. **6**(1), 107–121 (2011)
20. Keller, D., Osadchy, M., Dunkelman, O.: Inverting binarizations of facial templates produced by deep learning (and its implications). IEEE Trans. Inf. Forensics Secur. **16**, 4184–4196 (2021)
21. Kholmatov, A., Yanikoglu, B.: Realization of correlation attack against the fuzzy vault scheme. In: Security, Forensics, Steganography, and Watermarking of Multimedia Contents X, vol. 6819. SPIE, Bellingham (2008)
22. Kirchgasser, S., Uhl, A.: Template protection: on the need to adapt the current unlinkability evaluation protocol. In: Porceedings of the IEEE International Conference of the Biometrics Special Interest Group (BIOSIG), pp. 1–5 (2022)
23. Krivokuća Hahn, V., Marcel, S.: Biometric template protection for neural-network-based face recognition systems: a survey of methods and evaluation techniques. IEEE Trans. Inf. Forensics Secur. **18**, 639–666 (2023). https://doi.org/10.1109/TIFS.2022.3228494
24. Lee, H., Low, C.Y., Teoh, A.B.J.: Softmaxout transformation-permutation network for facial template protection. In: 2020 25th International Conference on Pattern Recognition (ICPR), pp. 7558–7565. IEEE, Piscataway (2021)
25. Mai, G., Cao, K., Lan, X., Yuen, P.C.: SecureFace: face template protection. IEEE Trans. Inf. Forensics Secur. **16**, 262–277 (2021). https://doi.org/10.1109/TIFS.2020.3009590
26. Nagar, A., Nandakumar, K., Jain, A.K.: Biometric template transformation: a security analysis. In: Media Forensics and Security II, vol. 7541, pp. 237–251. SPIE, Bellingham (2010)
27. Osorio-Roig, D., Rathgeb, C., Drozdowski, P., Busch, C.: Stable hash generation for efficient privacy-preserving face identification. IEEE Trans. Biomet. Behav. Identity Sci. **4**(3), 333–348 (2021)
28. Pandey, R.K., Zhou, Y., Kota, B.U., Govindaraju, V.: Deep secure encoding for face template protection. In: 2016 IEEE Conference on Computer Vision and Pattern Recognition Workshops (CVPRW), pp. 77–83 (2016). https://doi.org/10.1109/CVPRW.2016.17
29. Piciucco, E., Maiorana, E., Kauba, C., Uhl, A., Campisi, P.: Cancelable biometrics for finger vein recognition. In: 2016 First International Workshop on Sensing, Processing and Learning for Intelligent Machines (SPLINE), pp. 1–5. IEEE, Piscataway (2016)
30. Rathgeb, C., Merkle, J., Scholz, J., Tams, B., Nesterowicz, V.: Deep face fuzzy vault: implementation and performance. Comput. Secur. **113**, 102539 (2022)
31. Rua, E.A., Maiorana, E., Castro, J.L.A., Campisi, P.: Biometric template protection using universal background models: an application to online signature. IEEE Trans. Inf. Forensics Secur. **7**(1), 269–282 (2012)

32. Shahreza, H.O., Shkel, Y.Y., Marcel, S.: Measuring linkability of protected biometric templates using maximal leakage. IEEE Trans. Inf. Forensics Secur. **18**, 2262–2275 (2023)
33. Simoens, K., Tuyls, P., Preneel, B.: Privacy weaknesses in biometric sketches. In: Proceedings of the 30th IEEE Symposium on Security and Privacy, pp. 188–203 (2009)
34. Simoens, K., Bringer, J., Chabanne, H., Seys, S.: A framework for analyzing template security and privacy in biometric authentication systems. IEEE Trans. Inf. Forensics Secur. **7**(2), 833–841 (2012)
35. Singh, A., Srivastva, R., Singh, Y.N.: PlexNet: An ensemble of deep neural networks for biometric template protection. Int. J. Adv. Comput. Sci. Appl. **12**(4), 269–280 (2021)
36. Wang, S., Hu, J.: Design of alignment-free cancelable fingerprint templates via curtailed circular convolution. Pattern Recognit. **47**(3), 1321–1329 (2014)
37. Xu, Z., Hao, D., Wu, Y., Peng, J.: A random binarization scheme for deep face feature protection. In: Proceedings of the International Conference on Computer Science and Application Engineering, pp. 1–5 (2020)

Summary and Conclusions

The *Handbook of Biometric Template Protection: Motivation, Methods, and Metrics* has presented a comprehensive overview of this rich field of research. Part I set the stage by considering the *motivation* for Biometric Template Protection (BTP) research, Part II delved into the technical details behind the wide range of BTP *methods* that have been proposed over the past two decades, and Part III discussed the various *metrics* that have been employed for evaluating BTP solutions. Below we provide a summary of the key takeaways from each part, as well as our concluding remarks.

Part I: Motivation for BTP Research

The motivation behind BTP research was explained from three complementary perspectives: (i) the importance of BTP in light of the various attacks that pose a threat to biometric systems and their users (Chap. 1); (ii) the shortcomings of traditional data protection mechanisms for protecting biometric templates (Chap. 2); and (iii) the need for BTP in order to design biometric systems that are compliant with privacy regulations (Chap. 3).

Chapter 1

Chapter 1 emphasized that the main advantage of biometrics, its immutability, is also its main limitation, since compromised biometrics cannot be replaced or updated. This means that reference biometric templates, which represent the identities of the subjects enrolled in a biometric system, must be protected at all times, including when they are stored in the system's database. Otherwise,

V. Krivokuća Hahn et al. (eds.), *Handbook of Biometric Template Protection*,
https://doi.org/10.1007/978-981-95-0995-9

if stolen (e.g., leaked from the database), they could be misused to impersonate the victims or track them across different systems in which the same biometric templates have been enrolled. This risk is especially serious considering the proven possibility of inverting a biometric template[1] to reconstruct a close approximation of the biometric sample from which that template was originally generated. So, an adversary with access to this information may be able to glean additional information about a person, which is not necessary for verification or identification purposes, but which may be used to marginalize them (e.g., certain medical conditions, or categorical information such as age, sex, and ethnicity). Furthermore, the reconstructed biometric sample could be used to launch a presentation attack, whereby a physical biometric artifact (e.g., a face mask) is used to impersonate an enrolled identity. Such an attack, if successful, would undermine the security of the biometric system. It is thus imperative to put in place strong mechanisms to protect the biometric templates that are employed in biometric recognition systems, to ensure both the privacy of the systems' users and the security of the systems themselves. This is where BTP comes into play.

There are many different types of BTP methods that have been proposed over the past two decades, which are covered in detail in Part II of this book. In general, however, any BTP method should satisfy a number of criteria that are widely agreed upon in the literature and specified in the ISO/IEC 24745 standard on biometric information protection. These criteria, which are discussed explicitly in Part III of this book, most notably include: *recognition accuracy*, which states that the incorporation of a BTP algorithm into a biometric system should not degrade the ability of that system to perform recognition (verification or identification) tasks; *irreversibility*, which means that it should be impossible to recover the original biometric template or underlying sample from a protected template (based on the appropriate threat model); and *renewability* and *unlinkability*, related criteria which ensure that it is possible to replace a compromised biometric template with a new one from the same biometric characteristic, such that the resulting (protected) templates cannot be linked. Evaluation of these criteria is important for understanding the efficacy of a particular BTP method, and it is crucial to keep in mind that BTP evaluations should be performed within the context of a specific threat model. It is clear, therefore, that the development of BTP algorithms is a highly nontrivial, multifaceted task, but one which is necessary to ensure that biometric systems operate in a secure and privacy-preserving manner.

[1] A "template" generally refers to a set of features that represent the underlying biometric characteristic, e.g., an embedding learned by a neural network from a biometric sample (e.g., a face image).

Chapter 2

To further motivate efforts toward BTP algorithm development, Chap. 2 presented a technical discussion on why established data protection methods, which have traditionally been employed for protecting generic (non-biometric) data in computer systems, such as cryptographic hashing and encryption (typically used for protecting passwords and digital traffic), are unsuitable for protecting biometric templates. It was explained that the purpose of cryptographic protection methods, like hashing and encryption, is to destroy patterns in the data to which they are applied. This means that any change in the input to these algorithms, even if it is tiny (e.g., a single bit), would produce a completely different output. For example, two password strings that differ in a single character would, when passed to the same cryptographic hashing function, generate entirely different hashes. While this design is effective for ensuring the integrity (i.e., exactness) of data like passwords, which are easy to reproduce, such methods cannot be applied to inexact or noisy data like biometric templates, which differ to some degree each time they are generated (even if they come from the same biometric characteristic of the same person). For example, cryptographic hashes of templates generated from two different images of the same face would always be completely different; consequently, template matching in the hashed domain would be impossible. The same issue would prevent us from comparing biometric templates that have been secured using an encryption algorithm, additionally because encryption functions are typically designed to generate different outputs (ciphertexts) even for identical inputs (plaintexts), to prevent an adversary from linking two ciphertexts to the same plaintext. A workaround could be to decrypt the encrypted templates when performing the comparison operation (during the verification or identification stage), thereby avoiding template comparison in the encrypted domain; however, this would expose the templates to attacks during each recognition attempt. So, neither encryption nor hashing represents a suitable protection mechanism for biometric templates.

The shortcomings of other, non-cryptographic techniques, such as database decentralization and smart cards, were also discussed in the context of biometric template protection, and it was concluded that these techniques do not provide the necessary data confidentiality guarantees. Furthermore, the chapter also presented a dive into Trusted Execution Environments (TEEs), a promising hardware-based solution for BTP. However, it was noted that TEEs are prone to various attacks and may not yet be sufficiently mature for reliable biometric template protection.

Considering these limitations of existing data protection mechanisms, there is a clear motivation for developing more suitable BTP methods, which explicitly take into consideration the nature of biometric templates.

Chapter 3

BTP research is additionally motivated from a legal perspective, as explained in Chap. 3. In recent years, a number of different privacy regulations have been enforced to deal with growing privacy concerns over the use of our biometric data by various parties across increasingly widespread domains. A prime example is the European Union's General Data Protection Regulation (EU GDPR), which categorizes biometric data as sensitive data and restricts its processing in order to protect the privacy of the individuals represented by this data. As a result, to ensure that biometric data can continue to be used for identity management purposes in a manner that is compliant with the GDPR and other privacy regulations, deployers of biometric systems are under pressure to find a way to protect the utilized biometric data, even when those data take the form of "templates" (compact feature sets) as opposed to raw images or signals. Employing BTP to achieve data protection by design and by default must, therefore, become a priority in the development of biometric systems. This would help ensure that biometric systems, which are indispensable for trustworthy and scalable identity management in our increasingly interconnected society, are developed in line with the appropriate privacy regulations and can be trusted by the public.

From a legal point of view, there is, as of yet, no formal consensus on whether BTP algorithms are entirely sufficient for this purpose. For example, whether or not a BTP algorithm fully protects the privacy of the biometric data to which it is applied, such that the protected templates would *not* qualify as "personal data" under the GDPR (thereby avoiding the restrictions on processing this data), depends on both the algorithm itself and the intended application scenario. Consequently, a thorough evaluation of whether a particular BTP method is able to satisfy the necessary privacy requirements (of the applicable privacy regulation(s)) is likely to require a multidisciplinary effort between system designers and other stakeholders. Nevertheless, an important takeaway from this chapter is that, from a legal perspective, BTP is recognized as a crucial step toward developing biometric systems that are compliant with privacy regulations like the GDPR.

Concluding Remarks on Part I

The development of robust BTP algorithms for protecting our biometric data is necessary to safeguard our privacy in biometric systems, as well as to ensure the security of these systems by preventing various attacks (e.g., template inversion, presentation attacks). Well-established data protection mechanisms, such as cryptographic hashing and encryption, are unsuitable due to the conflict between the properties of these algorithms and the nature of biometric templates. Emerging data protection techniques, such as the hardware-based TEEs, are not yet mature enough to, on their own, reliably protect our irreplaceable biometric data. So, there is a clear motivation to invest efforts toward developing BTP algorithms that are more suited to the characteristics of biometric data. BTP is also considered a crucial component in the design of responsible biometric systems from a legal point of view, to ensure compliance with privacy regulations that restrict the processing of (unprotected) biometric data.

Part II: Types of BTP Methods

The second part of this handbook explored, in detail, the different types of BTP methods that have been proposed in the literature. In the first three chapters, we looked at *handcrafted* approaches, which encompass BTP algorithms explicitly designed by humans. This included feature transformations (Chap. 4), biometric cryptosystems (Chap. 5), and homomorphic encryption (Chap. 6). The last chapter in Part II (Chap. 7) then considered BTP methods that are *learned* by neural networks.

Chapter 4

Chapter 4 discussed one of the oldest BTP method categories, feature transformations, which involves transforming a biometric template from its original space to a new, protected space. The transformation is expressed in terms of a particular algorithm (e.g., a matrix-based projection, a polynomial-based transform), which is usually defined by random and subject-specific parameters or keys (e.g., a projection matrix, the coefficients of a polynomial). Changing the transformation parameters allows for the creation of *renewable* and *unlinkable* protected templates, while the *irreversibility* of these templates depends on the nature of the employed transform. *Salting* transforms, such as the projection-matrix-based BioHashing, generally require the transform parameters or keys (in this case, the seed that defines the projection matrix) to be kept secret; otherwise, an adversary with access to this information could use it to recover (a close approximation of) the original (unprotected) template from its protected counterpart. *Non-invertible transforms*, such as the polynomial-based PolyProtect, on the other hand, employ many-to-one transformations that are mathematically irreversible (non-invertible) even if all the parameters/keys[2] are known. So, the latter type of feature transformation methods usually boasts a higher degree of irreversibility than the former, making them more advantageous in terms of their privacy-preserving properties.

[2] In the case of PolyProtect, this would include the subject-specific coefficients and exponents that define the transformation polynomials.

As for the attainable *recognition accuracy*, non-invertible transforms may generally be expected to incur a trade-off between accuracy and irreversibility, as a result of the information lost in generating the protected template. In other words, the more irreversible the transform (e.g., the more fingerprint minutiae that are mapped to the same cell in a Cartesian transform), the more information about the original template (e.g., original minutiae positions) is lost in the many-to-one mapping used to generate the protected template, thus reducing recognition accuracy. However, the use of subject-specific transformation parameters may help offset this trade-off in some cases, thereby either maintaining the accuracy of the unprotected biometric system or even improving the accuracy in the protected domain. This phenomenon is especially typical of salting methods, which have been shown to be capable of significantly improving the accuracy of the protected system compared to that of the unprotected system. This may generally be attributed to properties such as: (i) the use of distance-preserving transforms (e.g., the use of orthonormal matrices for the projection operation in BioHashing), which helps to maintain the recognition accuracy observed in the unprotected domain as a result of maintaining distances between the templates, and (ii) the use of random subject-specific keys (e.g., a different projection matrix for each enrolled subject), which helps to create more distinct protected templates (since the subject-specific key effectively adds a second authentication factor), resulting in improved recognition accuracy in the protected domain.

Overall, the main takeaway from this chapter is that BTP methods that fall into the feature transformations category are varied, and each one has its own advantages and disadvantages that should be carefully considered when choosing the most appropriate technique for a particular biometric system.

Chapter 5

Chapter 5 considered biometric cryptosystems, which take the form of either *key-binding* or *key-generation* methods. Key-binding techniques involve combining, through some sort of mathematical approach, an external key with the biometric template, such that it should be impossible to recover either the key or the template from the "binding" without access to one or the other. Key-generation methods, on the other hand, involve extracting a key directly from the biometric template itself. Investigations into deep-neural-network-based key-generation methods, such as the generation of stable "hashes" from noisy biometric data, have revived interest in this subfield in recent years. Nevertheless, key-binding techniques remain by far the most widely studied biometric cryptosystems in the literature.

The most well-known key-binding methods are the fuzzy commitment and fuzzy vault schemes, which were the focus of this chapter. One advantage of these schemes is that the "binding" is meant to simultaneously protect both the biometric template and the (secret) key that is bound with the template, assuming that neither is known to an attacker. Since the key is cryptographically hashed, it should be very difficult for an attacker to break this hash to "undo" the binding and recover the biometric template. So, such key-binding schemes technically satisfy the *irreversibility* BTP requirement. However, in practice, the irreversibility of this type of BTP method would be considered broken if an attacker managed to reconstruct the key through another type of attack, such as a false accept attack or a statistical attack, since in such cases the attacker would have gained access to the biometric template.

The main challenge with deploying key-binding methods like fuzzy commitment or fuzzy vault in practice is that they tend to degrade the *recognition accuracy* of the biometric system. There are many reasons for this, including: loss of information as a result of the feature-type transformations that are typically required to put the biometric template into the correct format (e.g., fixed-length binary code) for the binding operation, issues with aligning the reference and probe templates during the comparison stage, reliance on error correction codes (instead of traditional biometric comparators) to deal with inter- and intraclass variance across the reference and probe biometric templates, and so on. Another issue is that key-binding methods typically cannot, on their own, satisfy the *renewability/unlinkability* criterion. In other words, linkage attacks are possible across "bindings" even if different keys were used in their construction, when the underlying biometric template (which is bound with those keys) is the same. A potential solution is to employ a hybrid protection scheme, for example, by randomly transforming the biometric template prior to the key-binding procedure.

Overall, the main takeaway from this chapter is that, although biometric cryptosystems are promising in terms of their (cryptographic) protection properties, they are quite complex to implement properly in practice, which is one of the main reasons for the expected drop in recognition accuracy.

Chapter 6

Chapter 6 presented the final type of handcrafted BTP approach considered in this book: homomorphic encryption. Unlike feature transformations and biometric cryptosystems, which represent traditional (i.e., the oldest) types of BTP approaches, homomorphic encryption has only recently started to be applied to BTP. The main advantage of this method is that it allows us to encrypt both reference and probe biometric templates and then perform template comparison in the encrypted domain. Consequently, biometric templates never need to be decrypted. This is in contrast to conventional encryption,[3] which would require the reference template to be decrypted prior to comparing it with the (also unencrypted) probe template acquired during the recognition attempt. Another notable advantage of homomorphic encryption is that it technically allows us to maintain the *recognition*

[3] Discussed in Part I Chap. 2 of this book.

accuracy of the biometric system into which it has been integrated;[4] in other words, the score obtained when comparing reference and probe templates in the encrypted domain should be approximately the same as the score that would be obtained if the two templates were compared in their original (unencrypted) form. Furthermore, by changing the encryption/decryption keys, we can effectively create different protected versions of the same (unprotected) template, thereby satisfying the *renewability/unlinkability* BTP criterion.

The chief limitation of homomorphic encryption, however, is that the biometric templates remain protected only insofar as the decryption key is kept secret, since an adversary with access to the decryption key could fully reverse the encryption operation to recover the original biometric templates. This means that the *irreversibility* of this type of BTP method relies primarily on keeping the decryption key secret. So, unlike non-invertible feature transformation BTP methods, which remain irreversible even if the transformation parameters/keys are known, homomorphic encryption cannot satisfy the irreversibility criterion under this "full disclosure" (i.e., fully informed attacker) type of threat model. Consequently, for enhanced template protection, it would be advisable to combine homomorphic encryption with a non-invertible transform-based BTP method, such as PolyProtect (which was the example combination mentioned in this chapter).

Another challenge with applying homomorphic encryption for BTP in practice is its high computational complexity, since the number of computations (and amount of memory) required to perform template comparison in the encrypted domain is typically much larger compared to the resources needed in the unprotected domain. As explained in this chapter, however, BTP approaches based on homomorphic encryption can be made more tractable in practice through various techniques, such as by adopting efficient ciphertext packing schemes, decreasing the number of operations (especially multiplications) in the encrypted domain, and reducing template dimensionality where possible.

Chapter 7

The last chapter in Part II of this handbook, Chap. 7, considered the evolution of *learned* BTP methods. Unlike the handcrafted methods addressed in Chaps. 4–6, which are explicitly designed by humans, the BTP approaches discussed in Chap. 7 are learned by neural networks.

The earliest techniques in this category were based on the maximum entropy binary (MEB) codes method, which proposed training a neural network to learn the mapping from a subject's biometric sample (e.g., a face image) to a *predefined* random binary code. This means that, during enrollment into a biometric system,

[4] A small accuracy loss may be encountered depending on how exactly the homomorphic encryption operation is implemented in practice, but this is expected to be negligible.

each subject is assigned their own random code. The codes are then cryptographically hashed and stored in the biometric system's database as representations of the "protected templates" corresponding to the enrolled subjects. During the recognition stage, the trained neural network is responsible for generating the correct binary code for each subject (i.e., the same code that was assigned to this subject during their enrollment). The correctness of this output code is verified by comparing its cryptographic hash to the hash of the reference code stored in the system's database at enrollment. It is thus crucial that the neural network be very well-trained to deal with intraclass variance in the input biometric samples, such that it is able to generate exactly the same code for the same subject during each recognition attempt—otherwise, the probe versus reference hash comparison will fail. Therefore, the ability of this BTP method to satisfy the *recognition accuracy* criterion hinges upon the efficacy of the neural network training. Various techniques have been proposed to help with this; for example, starting the neural network training from biometric features (templates) instead of samples (e.g., images), and using error correction mechanisms for the learned codes. An important advantage of this type of BTP method is its ability to satisfy the *irreversibility* criterion. This is because, since the binary code is randomly generated, it is essentially independent from the template that it represents, and furthermore the code is cryptographically hashed. So, we may assume that it would be extremely difficult for an adversary with access to the hash of a binary code (which represents the protected template of a particular enrolled subject) to recover the biometric template to which this code was assigned during enrollment. Furthermore, the *renewability* and *unlinkability* criteria can technically be satisfied by simply assigning a new code to the compromised subject. However, a critical limitation of this BTP approach is that the neural network must be retrained, either fully or partially, each time a replacement code is generated for any subject, as well as every time a new subject is enrolled into the biometric system. For this reason, the scalability of this method in practice is questionable.

To remove the scalability restriction imposed by the use of predefined codes, the second generation of learned BTP methods focused on training a neural network to learn its *own representation* of a protected template. In other words, instead of preassigning a random code (representing the protected template) to each subject enrolled in the biometric system, the idea is to train a neural network to learn what it "thinks" is a suitable representation of a protected template. So, zero-shot enrollment, where it is possible to enroll new (unseen during training) subjects, should technically be achievable without needing to retrain the neural network each time. The deep neural network decoding for biometric security (DNNDBS) system was presented as an example of a BTP method in this category. In this approach, one component of the underlying neural network is trained to learn binary codes that represent the input biometric samples, by pushing codes from the same subject closer together and those from different subjects further apart, while another component is trained to correct errors in these codes. So, if the neural network is well-trained, the system should be able to handle intraclass variance in the input biometric samples, thereby satisfying the *recognition accuracy* BTP criterion, as well as enroll subjects not seen during the training stage, which would technically make the biometric system scalable in the event of template renewals. However, the main drawback of this BTP approach is that, since the neural network is trained to learn the same (or similar) code for the same subject each time their biometric data is presented to the system, it is not possible to generate more than one (sufficiently different) protected template for a particular subject. In other words, there is no diversity in the generated templates, meaning that template *renewability* is technically not possible.

The only way to achieve template renewability, and thereby satisfy the *renewability* and *unlinkability* BTP criteria, is to incorporate some external, subject-specific information into the template generation process. This is the approach followed in the latest learned BTP methods. For example, the SecureFace method proposed using random, subject-specific keys to change the architecture of the neural network responsible for generating the protected templates, by activating and deactivating different neurons depending on the key. In this way, the neural network would differ for each subject enrolled in the biometric system, and in the event of template compromise, a new network configuration could be allocated to the same subject such that a new protected template could be generated. Other examples of incorporating randomness into the generation of protected templates include: (i) performing certain transformations, such as permutation or shuffling, on either the input biometric template (e.g., Deep IoM Hashing) or the output of a certain layer of the neural network (e.g., SoftmaxOut Transformation Permutation Network), and (ii) concatenating randomly generated keys with biometric templates, then training the neural network to generate unlinkable protected templates by minimizing distances between templates with same keys, and maximizing distances between templates with different keys (e.g., Secure Triplet Loss method).

Although much progress has been made for learned BTP methods, several challenges still remain to be solved. One important consideration is how to approach the evaluation of irreversibility. For example, thus far there has been no in-depth study on how information about a learned protected template could be leaked in different layers of the neural network that has been trained to generate it, especially in the worst-case scenario of a fully formed attacker with full access to the trained network. Furthermore, the scalability of neural-network-based BTP methods remains to be investigated, in terms of how many sufficiently different (unlinkable) templates can be generated for the same biometric template before the neural network must be retrained, as well as the effectiveness of zero-shot enrollment in large-scale biometric systems.

Concluding Remarks on Part II

Having considered both handcrafted and learned types of BTP methods, it is important to emphasize that there is no single "best" approach. Rather, we must carefully consider what type of BTP method is most suitable for the type of biometric system we wish to deploy. If we perform a high-level comparison between handcrafted and learned BTP approaches, we may conclude that: (i) handcrafted techniques tend to be more flexible for integration into existing biometric systems, since they can simply be added on as a module after the feature extractor (for example), while learned methods may be more appropriate for biometric systems that can be trained to incorporate BTP in an end-to-end manner; (ii) handcrafted BTP methods are likely to be easier to evaluate, since they are designed by humans and so we have a better understanding of what exactly is happening during the generation of a protected template, whereas the inner workings of neural-network-learned BTP methods tend to be more difficult to decipher, thereby limiting our ability to properly evaluate them; (iii) learned BTP methods may allow for more complexity and thus potentially the generation of more secure protected templates, since we are not necessarily limited by human knowledge in the design of specific protection algorithms.[5]

Additionally, from our earlier discussion of different types of handcrafted BTP methods, it is clear that each approach has its own particular advantages and disadvantages. Therefore, in some types of biometric systems, it may be wise to consider combining different types of BTP methods to formulate a *hybrid* protection mechanism. This may allow us to build on the benefits afforded by any single BTP method, while simultaneously reducing the effects of certain individual limitations. In reality, hybrid protection mechanisms are most likely going to be the way forward, since no single existing BTP method represents a panacea for the challenging, multifaceted task of biometric template protection.

Part III: Evaluation of BTP Methods

The third and final part of this book presented discussions on the metrics and methodologies used to evaluate the three main criteria that a BTP method is expected to satisfy: recognition accuracy (Chap. 8), irreversibility (Chap. 9), and renewability/unlinkability (Chap. 10).[6]

[5] However, as mentioned earlier, this "mystery" behind neural-network-learned BTP methods may also make them more difficult to understand and evaluate, so we must be cautious in weighing up this trade-off.

[6] General guidelines for evaluating these criteria are furthermore included in the ISO/IEC 30136 standard on performance testing of BTP schemes.

Chapter 8

The *recognition accuracy* criterion, considered in Chap. 8, is usually the simplest BTP criterion to evaluate. This is because we can apply the same techniques for evaluating the accuracy of both unprotected and protected biometric systems. In other words, the metrics that have already been established and are used in practice to evaluate the recognition accuracy of an unprotected verification or identification biometric system (e.g., false match rate (FMR), false non-match rate (FNMR), false positive identification rate (FPIR), false negative identification rate (FNIR)), as well as the various plots that are typically used to report the evaluation results (e.g., detection error trade-off (DET), cumulative match characteristic (CMC), detection and identification rate (DIR)), can equally be applied for evaluating and reporting the recognition accuracy of a BTP-protected system.

The main difference between the two evaluations is that, in a protected system, we often need to consider additional scenarios based on certain assumptions about the employed BTP method and the user (or attacker) of the underlying biometric system. For example, in a BTP method where subject-specific keys are employed for parameterizing the transform (e.g., the projection matrix in BioHashing, or the polynomial coefficients and exponents in PolyProtect), when evaluating the recognition accuracy of the protected system, we should consider at least two scenarios: (i) the "normal" scenario, where each subject dutifully employs their own keys; and (ii) the "stolen-token" scenario, where we assume that an adversary steals an enrolled subject's key and applies it to their own biometric template in an attempt to impersonate that subject.[7] While the recognition accuracy in the former scenario is usually expected to be as good as, or even better than, the accuracy attainable in the unprotected biometric system (as a result of the additional, subject-specific information, which effectively acts as a second authentication factor), in the latter scenario the recognition accuracy of the protected system would often be expected to be worse (e.g., when the BTP method is a non-invertible transform, since this transform necessarily incurs an information loss in the many-to-one mapping from the unprotected to the protected template). Furthermore, within these two scenarios, we should also investigate what happens to the recognition accuracy when the keys or parameters of the BTP method are varied, since this is likely to alter properties such as the dimensionality of the protected template, the amount of information lost in the transformation, and so on.

Therefore, when evaluating the effect of a BTP method on the recognition accuracy of the underlying biometric system, it is important to consider the viable operational scenarios for that system (related to the assumed threat model) and the properties (e.g., parameters) of the BTP method in question.

[7] This is comparable to the case where we use system-specific keys/parameters, such that all enrolled subjects have the same key or set of parameters for the BTP method.

Chapter 9

Evaluations of the *irreversibility* BTP criterion, which were discussed in Chap. 9, are not as straightforward, and there is no widespread consensus on the approach. This is mainly due to the fact that the definition of "irreversibility" is not consistent across the board of different types of BTP methods. More specifically, while in general irreversibility may be understood to refer to the difficulty of recovering (a close approximation of) the unprotected template from the protected template, the way in which this might be achieved differs depending on the BTP method in question. Consequently, an evaluation technique that would make sense for one method may not necessarily be the best approach for evaluating the irreversibility of another method.

In this chapter, two broad types of irreversibility evaluation approaches were considered: theoretical and empirical. It was argued that theoretical guarantees of irreversibility could be achieved for BTP methods based on information-theoretical constructs, such as the fuzzy commitment scheme, where irreversibility could be measured in terms of the number of bits of the unprotected template leaked by the protected template. However, this approach may not present a reliable approximation of the irreversibility of the BTP method in practice, since such theoretical evaluations often rely on ideal (and thus unrealistic) statistical distributions of the underlying biometric features. For BTP methods based on cryptographic constructs, such as homomorphic encryption, theoretical evaluations of irreversibility are often expressed in terms of the strength of the keys used to encrypt the biometric template. In this case, the irreversibility of the BTP scheme depends entirely on keeping the decryption key secret—otherwise, expressing the degree of irreversibility in terms of the difficulty of guessing the decryption key becomes irrelevant.

For other types of BTP methods, such as handcrafted non-invertible feature transformations or neural-network-learned transforms, theoretical evaluations of irreversibility may be difficult to formulate, so it makes more sense to perform empirical irreversibility evaluations instead. This essentially means setting up an experiment where we assume that a motivated attacker, with access to certain information about the BTP method and biometric templates of interest, attempts to invert the BTP transform and thus the protected template(s) of one or more enrolled subjects to recover the unprotected templates from which the protected templates were generated. The success rate of this attack is then used to estimate the irreversibility of this particular BTP method, in the context of a target biometric system. In this case, it is crucial that the irreversibility analysis be based on a reasonable threat model, which describes the capabilities and resources of our assumed attacker as realistically as possible.

Even for BTP methods for which a theoretical irreversibility evaluation is possible, an (additional) empirical evaluation is advisable. This would ensure that certain theoretical assumptions, which may not hold in practice, are accounted for, and that the evaluation results in a more tangible quantification of irreversibility in the context of a specific operational scenario (e.g., attack success rate may be easier to interpret, in terms of what it means practically, than the number of bits of information leaked about the protected template).

Overall, although many avenues for irreversibility evaluation exist in the literature, the BTP research community must attempt to converge toward well-defined evaluation frameworks. This would allow for proper benchmarking of the irreversibility of different BTP methods, which is currently not possible due to the disparate ways in which different BTP methods have been evaluated.

Chapter 10

Chapter 10 explored approaches toward evaluation of the *renewability/unlinkability* criterion in the BTP literature. Although these two criteria are closely related, there is a subtle difference between them: "renewability" refers to the possibility of renewing an enrolled protected template in the time dimension (i.e., template renewals in one specific application at different points in time), while "unlinkability" focuses more on the spatial dimension (i.e., the possibility to enroll different protected templates, representing the same identity, in different applications at the same point in time). Nevertheless, the two criteria essentially consider the same property of a BTP method, which is its ability (or not) to generate sufficiently different (unlinkable) protected templates from the same unprotected template or biometric instance. Consequently, the same metrics can be used to measure both criteria, which were referred to collectively as "unlinkability" in this chapter.

Several different categories of unlinkability evaluation techniques were considered, including: (i) verbal implications, which include statements implying that unlinkability is satisfied by virtue of the ability to change certain parameters of the BTP method in question, but without any formal proof or evaluation of this claim; (ii) theoretical evaluations, whereby relevant properties of the BTP architecture (e.g., the spacing of the codewords in a fuzzy commitment scheme) are analyzed in an attempt to draw conclusions on its ability to satisfy the unlinkability requirement; and (iii) empirical evaluations, which aim to quantify an attacker's chances of success in linking two different templates to the same identity, via some sort of linkage function. Empirical evaluations represent the most common category of unlinkability evaluations in the literature.

The most widely adopted empirical evaluation metrics are based on the likelihood ratios method, which relies on having access to "mated" and "non-mated" score distributions of the biometric system under evaluation. Mated scores come from comparing protected templates that originated from the same biometric instance (e.g., right index finger of a particular subject), but which were generated using different parameters for the BTP method, whereas non-mated scores come from comparing protected templates that originated from different biometric instances (e.g., two different fingers). The idea, then, is to determine, after computing the score between two protected templates, whether it is more likely that those templates originate from the same subject (i.e., mated score distribution) than from different subjects (i.e., non-mated score distribution), in which case we would be able to "link" them to the same identity. The probability of this occurrence is converted into two bounded unlinkability metrics, both lying in the range [0, 1] (where 0 represents full *unlinkability* and 1 represents full *linkability*): One metric gives us the global unlinkability of the biometric system across the entire score range, and the other one provides a score-wise measure of unlinkability.

Another, similar approach toward empirical unlinkability evaluation, based on the concept of maximal information leakage, was also proposed; however, this method gives us only a global unlinkability metric, but not a score-wise one. So, while both approaches can be used for benchmarking the global (across the entire score range) unlinkability of different BTP methods, only the likelihood ratios technique can be used to investigate the unlinkability of a BTP system for specific scores of interest.

Overall, while it is clear from the discussion presented in this chapter that empirical evaluation techniques, especially the one based on likelihood ratios, have become quite common in the BTP literature, there is still room for more in-depth evaluations of the renewability/unlinkability criterion. For example, it is important to consider the possibility of linking protected templates based on information other than comparison scores. Furthermore, evaluations of BTP methods' template renewal capacity (i.e., the number of times that a protected template can be replaced by a new protected template, for the same subject) are currently lacking (and not well-defined).

Concluding Remarks on Part III

If we were to come up with a global conclusion for this part of the handbook, it would lie along the lines of a recommendation that more efforts be invested toward formulating concrete BTP evaluation frameworks. This means converging to a consensus across the BTP research community on what specific metrics and evaluation techniques should be used for evaluating which specific (types of) BTP methods. This would allow for more rigorous and trustworthy benchmarking of different BTP approaches, thereby facilitating the transition of BTP from academic research to practical deployment. In the same vein of thought, it may make sense to focus more on empirical evaluation techniques, which frame the evaluation within the context of specific types of attackers in specific types of biometric systems. Such approaches may be more suitable (compared to theoretical approaches) for performing tangible (i.e., easy to interpret) evaluations of BTP methods in practice. Having said that, to present a complete picture of the efficacy of any BTP method, both theoretical and empirical evaluations should be considered.

Closing Words

The BTP field of research is now at the cross-roads between theory and practice, due in large part to rising privacy concerns and emerging regulations that are forcing deployers of biometric systems to take the protection of our irreplaceable biometric data seriously. As will have become clear to readers of this handbook, BTP research is ripe with ideas for solutions on how to protect biometric templates, as well as techniques that can be used to evaluate the robustness of these protection methods. It is now high time to make use of this considerable body of work, consisting of more than two decades' worth of research, by investigating the applicability of the proposed BTP algorithms for protecting biometric data in real-world biometric systems. Such practically oriented evaluations of BTP methods would provide us with more concrete insights into how we can fully realize the potential of BTP techniques for developing more secure and privacy-preserving biometric recognition systems. This would allow us to continue reaping the numerous benefits of biometric technologies, which are considered indispensable for identity management in today's increasingly interconnected society, without sacrificing our security and privacy in return. The *Handbook of Biometric Template Protection: Motivation, Methods and Metrics* endeavors to serve as a foundational guide toward achieving this objective.

MIX
Papier aus verantwortungsvollen Quellen
Paper from responsible sources
FSC® C105338

If you have any concerns about our products,
you can contact us on
ProductSafety@springernature.com

In case Publisher is established outside the EU,
the EU authorized representative is:
Springer Nature Customer Service Center GmbH
Europaplatz 3, 69115 Heidelberg, Germany

Printed by Libri Plureos GmbH
in Hamburg, Germany